The Uncommon English Teacher
and
The Forgotten Doughboy

*A Memoir About Love, Suffrage, WWI,
Loss, Genetics, and Hope.*

Kathy Rainey Bussmann

Introduction written with Carol Ferring Shepley

The Uncommon English Teacher
and
The Forgotten Doughboy

Copyright @ 2016 by Kathy Rainey LLC

ISBN 978-1-63110-256-1

All Rights Reserved Under
International and Pan-American Copyright Conventions.
No part of this book may be used or reproduced in any manner
whatsoever without written permission except in the case of brief
quotations embodied in critical articles or reviews.

Available online at
www.thedoughboyandmygrandma.com
and
www.mirabooksmart.com

Discount available on orders of 12 or more books –
call Mira Digital Publishing at 1-800-341-9588 for a special discount code!

Cover Illustration by Bryan Haynes, ©2016
Cover Design by Pam Bliss, Bliss Collaborative, LLC, ©2016

Printed in the United States of America by
Mira Digital Publishing
Chesterfield, Missouri 63005

To Lauren and Tyler,

WHO TAUGHT ME TO BE THE STRONGEST MOM POSSIBLE,

To my sister, Alice,

WHO GAVE ME THE GIFT OF LIFE THROUGH HER STEM CELLS,

To my sister, Jean,

WHO MADE ME HER LIFE'S PURPOSE,

To my mom,

WHO WAS MY GUARDIAN ANGEL MY WHOLE LIFE,

To my dad,

WHO GAVE ME A LOVE OF HISTORY,

To my grandmother, Marian,

WHO GAVE ME THE GIFT OF HER WRITTEN WORDS,

To my grandfather, Howard,

WHO SERVED OUR COUNTRY IN WORLD WAR I,

To all my friends and family,

WHO SUPPORTED ME EVERY STEP OF THE WAY DURING MY OWN BATTLE.

CONTENTS

INTRODUCTION
"Genealogy Saved My Life"
vii

1986
"The Letter"
xi

1971
"The Day My Life Changed Forever"
xi

1967
"Mother's Day"
xii

1963
"The Taxi Cab Accident"
xiii

CHAPTER ONE
"Record of Happenings"
1914
1

CHAPTER TWO
"Demon War"
1915
42

CHAPTER THREE
"Pleasant Memories of College"
1915
55

CHAPTER FOUR
"America's Purpose in the War"
1917
85

CHAPTER FIVE
"Go Where No One Else Will Go...."
1918
109

CHAPTER SIX
"The New Woman"
1919
152

CHAPTER SEVEN
"Epilogue"
1920-1993
182

CHAPTER EIGHT
"From Genealogy to Genetics"
2012
216

CAST OF CHARACTERS
225

BIBLIOGRAPHY
227

HOWARD'S PATERNAL FAMILY TREE
232

INTRODUCTION

GENEALOGY SAVED MY LIFE

Before you take a look at my grandmother's diaries and my grandfather's letters, allow me to back up and explain how they fell into my possession. It is a long and sometimes sad story, but I promise you a happy ending.

Although I was unaware of it at the time, I first received the diaries and letters in 1995. Yet, it wasn't until many years later that I even discovered their existence. But the story really starts long before that in 1975 when I was only 17 years old and lost my mom to cancer. I couldn't speak out loud about it for 20 years without choking back tears. I lost so much, but she enriched my life beyond words for that short amount of time we had together. I have been filled with her spirit and optimism my whole life, knowing that she is watching over me every day as my guardian angel.

My mother battled Acute Myeloid Leukemia (AML) for four years. When she took chemotherapy treatments, Mom would spend two weeks in the hospital and two weeks at home. Once, she even went into remission. When she felt better we would cram everything into the good times that we possibly could: movies, shopping, sewing, cooking, and all the things families do together. As difficult as it was living with that specter hanging over us, my mother had a fighting spirit that was wonderful.

My senior year in high school was the worst of times. Christmas 1974 was particularly difficult for me. It was supposed to be a surprise which seniors were picked to be Mary and Joseph in the Christmas Pageant at my high school, so I kept the secret that I was going to play Mary. My mom told me she was going to be able to make it to the pageant but at the last minute couldn't leave the hospital. Before I could get down to the hospital to surprise her, one of her friends had already called her and told her how beautiful it had been. When I brought her the picture on the front page of the school newspaper, she was already crying as I walked in her room. She wanted to share that triumph with me and was heartbroken. She died that spring, the day after Mother's Day, two weeks before I graduated from high school. Mom wanted to be there even if she was in a wheelchair.

My dad told us that life was for the living and that we should live our lives the way we knew our mom would want us to. That is easier said than done.

In 1978, three years after my mom died, my dad remarried, and life changed again for my two sisters and me. His new wife did not believe in sharing our lives together as a family, which I know is not the way my dad wanted it. The dynamics of his new life were set; his new wife made the rules. A few years into his marriage, my father told us that my sisters and I were not allowed into their house anymore. If we wanted to see our father, we could do so at their country club or at one of our houses. Wasn't one loss in our lives enough? But, the rules were made, and we had to abide by them. Obviously, our stepmother did not know how to love the way we did.

In 1995, the moving van pulled up in front of my suburban St. Louis house with the contents of my dad's house. My dad died from lung cancer in 1993; he was a chain smoker. His second wife died in 1995. The contents were going to be divided among his three girls. But, for now, I stored everything in my basement, dining room, and garage. Both of my sisters lived out of town and would come get what they wanted soon. Actually, I really wasn't sure how much there was since I had not been allowed in my dad's house for almost ten years.

A few weeks before the men were moving my dad's furniture into the house, my husband of 15 years had moved his furniture out to a rental house. So, the timing couldn't have been better. My husband took the dining room set, but I replaced it with my dad's dining room set two weeks later. My life was a revolving door at this time. As each piece of furniture came off the truck, I was flooded with the memories of my dad and our family. These old, fond memories were replacing the sad memories of a marriage gone wrong. I was able to fill the void in my life with something positive.

Many years passed, and my sisters had taken their share of the furniture, china, and pictures, but some of the boxes from the moving van delivery sat idle in my basement collecting dust. Life was hectic; I was divorced in 1997 and my two kids were very active. Cleaning and organizing the basement was very low on my priority list. When my daughter headed off to college in 2004, my load grew a little bit lighter. Meanwhile, my longing to connect with my family had grown stronger each year. The more I lost, the more

I wanted to learn. Now that I finally found time, I thought I would continue organizing and identifying some of the pictures. So I started digging through the boxes not knowing all that I would find.

Maybe something in the boxes would fill my need. If I could learn about my family, maybe I would know who I am, where I came from, and why I am the way I am. It would mean so much to me. Pictures of relatives can't talk; I was hoping to learn more.

I unboxed pictures, yearbooks, genealogy books, and then I stumbled upon the most precious treasure of all: my grandmother's, Marian Gertrude Viets, diaries from 1914-1920. The first diary that my grandmother filled was a very plain linen-covered book. The first page says "Record of Happenings beginning Sept. 8, 1914 Marian G. Viets Central High School '15." Her six diaries include one year of high school, three years of college, one filled with poetry relating to her life, and one for the year when she started her career as an English teacher. The diaries were spread out among many boxes. They were difficult to read due to their age, even though she wrote in dark ink. I had some trepidation that I might find out something too secret to share, so I read them before showing them to anyone else. And, I was afraid that my grandparents might be too perfect and that I might not match up to their high expectations. Luckily, I found her charming and inspirational. I figured that if my grandmother saved the diaries all these years, she meant for them to be read by others. Somehow they survived the move from Springfield, Massachusetts, to Mount Holyoke College, to Hudson, New York, and finally to St. Louis, Missouri. I spent many years transcribing the diaries and getting all the details straight.

Several years later, I started investigating the file my dad labeled "Old Papers" that I remembered from my high school years. There I found genealogy charts, land deeds, and another big treasure: my grandpa Howard Eugene Rainey's letters home to his parents from his time in Italy and France during WWI as an ambulance driver corresponding to the same time period as Marian's diaries.

I think it is a miracle that my stepmother saved these precious family papers. I doubt she knew they would mean anything to me.

So, I began my labor of love to put all of the puzzle pieces of my grandparent's lives together. In the end I found exactly what I was looking for, firsthand messages from my grandparents. I really got to know both of their personalities in a way I could only dream about. Now not only did I have many pictures of both of them and their names on the family trees, but I knew them intimately as they put pen to paper. Both grandparents shared a deep love for their family, their country, and their passions. They weren't always perfect either. They went through tough times as everyone does. Through all the transcriptions, the message is loud and clear: if you are lucky enough to have a family that is always there to support you, as both of them did, and love you so much, you can get through tough times. This is in turn why they loved us so much. My mom and dad gave them the greatest gift, their legacy: three granddaughters.

When I uncovered my grandmother's diaries in boxes in my basement, I learned about the impact World War I had on the home front. While my grandfather drove an ambulance in France and Italy, simultaneously my grandma, Marian, was leading an uncommon life as an uncommon woman attending Mount Holyoke during World War I. It was not an ordinary feat for a woman to attend college in 1915-1919, much less an academic institution of the caliber of Mount Holyoke. This college took its responsibilities seriously. "Shortly after the declaration of war, the College was placed at the disposal of the President."(*Into the World of Mount Holyoke*," 1921) In textbooks I had learned about women's efforts during the war serving in the Red Cross, knitting articles for soldiers, cooking with rationed food at home, and participating in fund raising. During the war, the "Red Cross staffed hospitals and ambulance companies and recruited 20,000 registered nurses to serve the military. Additional Red Cross nurses came forward to combat the worldwide influenza epidemic of 1918." (www.redcross.org) Until I read my grandmother's diaries I did not know what role my grandmother and Mount Holyoke played during wartime. My grandmother did not have nursing skills so I knew she did not serve in the military, but I had no idea how much she did accomplish for the war effort. I discovered that during college my grandma tirelessly worked at the war-garden farms that successfully canned thousands of cans of vegetables for rations. On November 6, 1918, Marian attended chapel at Mount Holyoke where she pledged $10.00 (about $170 in today's dollars) towards the war effort. According to *Into the World of Mount Holyoke*," 150 Mount Holyoke women served with war organizations - over 80 overseas. The Alumnae War Relief Fund financed six overseas workers'. Marian received a $200 scholarship that enabled her to attend Mount Holyoke. Since her pledge amount decreased the amount available for her college expenses, it was a huge sacrifice. Marian wrote: "Reverend Edward Lincoln Smith of New York spoke here at chapel. Well, there is nothing left to do but give our utmost. He said it was our last chance to sacrifice, our last chance to help at the end. I have decided to give $10.00. I don't know just where it will come from – spelling pupils, messenger work, a little domestic work, and Skinner farming - quite a nice little sum in all. But, the cause is worth it. Later in the evening a mass meeting was held. The pledges given on the floor raised $16,000 in the college for the War Relief Fund. It is our quota and represents a very large per capita gift. Our slogan is not 'Give until it hurts' but 'Give until it feels good.'" The Mount Holyoke sisterhood nurtured a strong sense of sacrifice and service that became a part of Marian's character for the rest of her life. At home in the summer, Marian volunteered at the Red

Cross. On September 8, 1918 Marian wrote: "It was my last Monday night at the Red Cross and there wasn't a great deal to do. That's all I've done for the war this summer – Monday evenings and knitting two sweaters. It sounds rather insufficient to me. I wish I could give big sums of money to the Red Cross and the Y.M.C.A." Marian was always putting the welfare of others over her needs. Reading her journals, she became my hero.

Even though my dad was for all intents and purposes absent from our lives for at least the last ten years of his life, he did the best he could, given his situation. I knew in my heart that my dad was a good man and that he loved his three girls. My gut tells me that my dad purposely left behind all sorts of little treasures as a sign of his love for our family, for us to find out about his family, including diaries, letters and memorabilia, following his death. Unbelievably, through all of the moves from city to city, my dad carefully preserved boxes and boxes of family treasures, giving his children a legacy and insight into his side of our family tree. He had saved his family's written words for us and these provided my way of connecting to what I knew was true and rediscovering what I had lost. I am grateful to know firsthand that my dad's family bond was as strong as ours was prior to his second marriage. What I had lost, I found again.

Nevertheless, it was out of these losses, the death of my mom, and the estrangement from my dad, that I eagerly began this journey into my dad's family history. Besides how loving and caring his parents were, I learned that they were loyal, patriotic, hard workers, religious, educated, and successful citizens. We are a humble bunch, putting our nose to the grindstone to earn a decent, honest living for our families. Many of the challenges my relatives struggled with are similar to what we struggle with today. My relatives weren't famous or rich, but they made a meaningful life, treating people with kindness along the way. Material goods were not their goal; education, public service, and most of all, loving your family, were our hallmarks.

There was a dark side to their lives too. I learned about it from my father. Once one of my sisters was dating someone my father did not like. When pressed, he explained: "I just don't want her supporting him her whole life the way my mother did my father." Perhaps my grandfather's terrible experiences as an ambulance driver in World War I left him unable to stick to a career. Still my grandparents managed to weather the Great Depression. I loved my Grandpa Rainey. Whenever we went to visit, he was always so kind and patient.

Unfortunately, on September 21, 2012, my life came full circle when I was diagnosed with AML Leukemia, the same blood disease that my mom came down with at 38 years of age in 1971. How could this be a coincidence? My mom fought the cancer for four years and succumbed to it at the age of 42. Her daughters were 11, 17 and 19 years old when we buried her at Oak Grove Cemetery.

When I checked into the hospital, the doctors and nurses told me that my course of treatment would be very different from my mom's treatment forty years ago. Nevertheless I was very afraid of what lay ahead of me because of the four years of pain and suffering I watched my mother endure. Much research and advancement had taken place in the field. In 1971 there was only one type of AML and only one way to treat my mother - chemotherapy. So little was known about leukemia in the 1970's that friends of my mom's would not go near her because they thought leukemia was contagious. She told me how much this hurt her feelings because her doctors assured her she was not contagious. In 1976, a year after my mom died, doctors identified subtypes of AML. That was the beginning of a new arena of discovery about AML leukemia. In my heart, I hope her blood samples helped research discover this breakthrough.

My first course of action was to undergo a bone marrow biopsy so that the doctors could start to take a closer look at my chromosomes through karyotype (the number and visual appearance of my chromosomes in my cell nuclei), cytogenetics (the study of my chromosomes), and molecular testing so that they could determine my treatment. This was quite overwhelming for me. My doctors told me there are four kinds of AML. From the results of my tests, the doctors determined I have a genetic mutation known as FMS-like tyrosine kinase-3 (FLT3-ITD). FLT3 was discovered in 1996 and it is only in the last ten years that it has been used as a predictor for a patient's treatment. My type of AML, FLT3-ITD, is the only type that does not stay in remission and requires a stem cell transplant (SCT). I can only wonder if my mom had the same type of AML as me since she was unable to stay in remission. Research is constantly advancing. My mom used to tell me stories of meeting with doctors and interns who would ask her questions about her disease, lifestyle and family history. I am sure her information helped develop research that benefited me. I doubt that in her worst nightmares she ever imagined that would happen.

So, I was depending on my family to give me the strength, support, and love to get through this serious procedure. Everyone rallied. My daughter, Lauren, kept reassuring me that I was "not alone" in this battle. She told me that over 80 different people delivered meals, wrote cards, sent balloons, and prayer cards. Some friends brought meals many times! My son, Tyler, drove home on the weekends from his teaching job in Nashville to keep me company. He brought me a life size picture of my dog for my room since dogs weren't allowed. That spring before my diagnosis, my son came to cheer me on when I swam competitively in the Senior

Olympics. Tyler kept telling me "you are so strong and in such great shape. You will beat this just like you won your swimming races." I believe entering this grueling process in good shape physically definitely helped with my recovery. My sister Jean and her husband, Jeff, a retired radiologist, were my main caregivers keeping everything organized and under control. And, I depended on my sister Alice to give me the gift of life because she was my stem cell donor, a perfect match genetically. Following an intense series of chemotherapy for thirty days, I went into remission. Once in remission, it was possible for me to get a stem cell transplant from Alice. Alice went through a week long preparation for her apheresis, where her stem cells were filtered out of her blood. Everything had to be timed just right. While Alice was going through her apheresis, I had one more round of intense chemotherapy to prepare me for my SCT. On November 29, 2012, which is also Lauren's birthday, I got Alice's stem cells, which I called my liquid gold, through an intravenous port in just twenty minutes. Now Lauren and I share a celebration every year. I needed to stay in the hospital about thirty days until my counts were high enough to go home. Once home, I could not leave my house for 100 days due to my suppressed immune system. If only this treatment option existed when my mom had AML, if she had FLT3, she might have survived and been able to share more of her life with us.

What beautiful irony. I had spent years studying our family genealogy, and through the genetic analysis of my AML FLT3 gene mutation, and the stem cell transplant from my sister, Alice, my family genes were the only way to save my life. The Rainey genes are strong; both sisters were perfect matches genetically.

I am an ordinary person from an ordinary family trying to help others find hope. I am not trying to deliver a history lesson, nor am I going to quiz any family members on names and dates to make sure they really read my book. But, I do hope that what comes shining through the written words are all of the joys, hardships, and accomplishments that our prior generations experienced, from which we benefited, and which in turn gives our future generations hope. I am here today writing this book because of my family and the donation of their genes. I remained positive and hopeful throughout the entire SCT process knowing that my family went through tough times and that I could survive too.

And I hope that these stories will shed light on that critical period in American history that my grandparents helped to shape. "When it comes to history, what's important? Which facts from the past help us to meet our responsibilities as citizens, cast light on human nature, or entertains us because they seem so unusual?" (*St. Louis – An Illustrated Timeline*), a historian asks today. The answers are very different from when I studied history forty years ago. (Indeed even the question seems different from what historians asked when I was in school.) I was taught wars, treaties, and great men. I dutifully memorized: Civil War, 1861 to 1865, Magna Carta, 1215, and George Washington, 1732-1799, the father of our country. Today, historians also look at the way ordinary people lived, what they read, and thought. Certainly history tells the deeds of extraordinary individuals, but average people made history too.

I take pleasure reading about the way people lived in times past. When she was in high school, my daughter, Lauren, lent me a book she read for history, Gail Collins' "*America's Women, 400 years of Dolls Drudges, Helpmates and Heroines,*" because it was so interesting. For example, one fun fact we learned was that bicycles gave women more independence and also changed the way they dressed. Lauren and I absorb more information while reading real-life historical accounts than we do from textbook memorization. It intrigues us to learn what people went through in times before ours and it helps us appreciate where we are today, especially regarding our family. Unfortunately, I never had the opportunity to share an experience like this with my mother.

What I learned about World War I, I had mostly forgotten even though the German helmet (Pickelhaube) in our family room bookcase served as a constant reminder of our family's participation. My dad told us the story that my grandpa was an ambulance driver in WWI and that he took the helmet off a dead German soldier. Beyond that, I learned in high school about the western front, our Allies, trench warfare, mustard gas, and shellshock (later known as Post Traumatic Stress Syndrome). There were over four million total mobilized forces, 116,516 killed, and 204,002 wounded, 4,500 prisoners and missing, from the United States. This was a 7.1% casualty rate. (www.pbs.org) But, textbooks never provided any additional information about ambulance drivers, information that would have brought the Great War home to me.

Then I discovered my grandfather's letters and the Great War took on a whole new meaning. I read about how difficult it was to drive the crude machines, the lives that were saved by quick response time, the endless nights driving backwards up hills with no lights on, and the part the ambulance drivers played in the Great War.

Until I read the letters of my grandfather and the diaries of my grandmother, I never knew what a difficult decision it was for America to enter the war. Some of Howard's friends went to serve before America officially entered the war. At college, my grandmother heard impassioned speakers argue both sides of the question whether to go to war or not. Aside from numbers and statistics, I had never read about the emotional side of the war as portrayed through a soldier's eye to help me understand the war on a gut level. Howard wrote home September 13, 1918: "The Americans certainly are a wonderful lot. I have seen them with arms and legs shot off and whistling Yankee tunes while waiting to be attended to. One fellow I shall never forget. He was a great big, strong, wonderfully built fellow who had his arm shot off just above the elbow but was happy, and his happiness seemed to inspire the rest. I do not mean that he was happy because he lost an arm but for the simple reason that it was all for a good cause and he had done his bit." Since reading his letters, Howard has become my hero. I cannot imagine the horrors he saw. Without his service, many soldiers would have died on the battlefield.

One late addition to the story I tell through Marian's diaries and Howard's letters are poems. Not only Marian, the English teacher, but also Howard collected favorite poems. It says so much about these people and this time in history that some of their most treasured possessions were poetry. Much of the poetry Marian and Howard treasured are in the public domain now. I think you will find sometimes a poem can say things they could not say in prose. Like music, poetry touches our emotions deeply and instinctively.

The First World War caused an upheaval after which the lives of ordinary men and women would never be the same. My grandparents, Marian and Howard Rainey, lived on the edge of that change. I experienced it too when I read what they wrote. The words of Marian and Howard made history come alive for me. To me, the writings of my grandparents are as important as Georges Clemenceau, David Lloyd George and Woodrow Wilson as far as my understanding of the impact World War I had on the world. Not only diplomacy, but real life also can be significant.

I hope readers of this book will enjoy meeting my family including my grandparents', Marian Gertrude Viets and Howard Eugene Rainey, their son, my mom, and learning about our family leukemia battle. My relatives were extraordinary ordinary Americans who made history.

Written with Carol Ferring Shepley

1986
The Letter

My heart sank into my stomach as I read it. My sisters and I each received a letter from our dad telling us that we were no longer allowed to come into his house. All of the activity of three grandchildren was overwhelming for his wife. It made her so nervous that his wife had to check into the hospital for five days after we visited there the last time, he explained. If we wanted to see our dad, it could be at one of our houses or at a mutually agreed upon restaurant.

After I read the letter, I called my sister Jean who lived three houses away from me at the time and asked her if she got the letter. She was still in a state of confusion and disbelief. Why hadn't Dad called us to talk this over? This is not what our mom would have wanted. Then, Jean and I checked in with Alice to see if she also got the letter. Living in Boston, she seemed to be a bit more removed from the situation.

It was something a child hopes would never happen. We had watched our mom lose contact with her mother, Grammie, at about the same age we are now. Now the same thing was happening to us: we felt like we were losing our dad, what small part was left of our family. We were sure Dad knew he had a problem on his hands with his wife, but the way he was handling it hurt us deeply.

1971
The Day My Life Changed Forever

My mom and dad were sitting in the living room privately enjoying their evening cocktails, just as they did every other evening. My sisters and I waited patiently for dinner, even though we were starving. The phone rang in the kitchen. I ran from the family room to answer it so it would not disturb them. We were not allowed to interrupt them during cocktails.

When I answered the phone, I asked if I could take a message. The man's voice said "please tell your mother this is Dr. Broun." When my mom heard me repeat Dr. Broun's name, she jumped out of her chair, saying she would take the call. I knew it must be very important for her to interrupt her sacred time with dad.

I stood in the hallway outside the kitchen; secretly listening to my mom's half of the conversation. I learned there was something wrong with my mom's blood. The doctor was going to run blood work again. I was so confused. I was only 13 years old and did not know much about blood. My mom didn't seem to act or look sick at all.

After my mom got off the phone, she said, "Don't worry. They think they made a mistake. I will be fine. I am going to have another test tomorrow." The next day I found out she wasn't alright. Mom had a blood disease called leukemia. It was serious. My dad acted very matter of fact about the whole situation, as usual.

Right away my mom checked into Firmin Desloge Hospital in St. Louis for two weeks, the hospital where her adoptive father worked as a radiologist many years ago. Immediately, our lives were turned upside down. My dad worked a full time job, and we were going to school and had lots of activities. Who would cook and clean?

My dad's mom, Grandma Rainey, lived in a nursing home in St. Louis so she couldn't take care of us. I wish she hadn't been in that accident. We really needed her now. Grammie didn't want anything to do with us anymore. We didn't have any aunts, uncles, or cousins. Who would take care of us? If Grandma Rainey would be able to leave the nursing home and come to our house to help, I didn't even know if I would like her cooking. Luckily, our neighbors brought tons of food over.

We didn't know what we had ahead of us. My mom was overly optimistic. I remember washing the dishes with her the first Thanksgiving after her diagnosis when she told me there was nothing to worry about because she was going to be fine. The doctors were going to take good care of her. I wanted to believe her with all my heart but as time went on I wasn't so sure. The chemotherapy started to do awful things to my mom: she lost her hearing for a while; she couldn't stop twitching her eyes; she had constant nausea; and she developed such horrible sores on her feet that we had to cut holes in her shoes for her to walk. Her skinny arms were all black and blue from the needles they stuck in her. She lost all her hair and tons of weight. She was skinny to begin with so she didn't have any extra pounds to lose. Realistically, I wasn't so sure in my gut that everything was going to be fine, as she promised me. I turned to writing in my own diaries because I was so confused. My mom would never give up the fight. I respected her for her optimism. Mom was always hopeful for a miracle. Nevertheless, my sisters and I struggled with what to believe; with what was really going to happen, and how we would be prepared for reality.

1967
Mother's Day

"MOM, MOM a surprise for you." I ran into the house screaming with excitement for my mom. I always got in trouble for screaming! But, I couldn't contain myself. This was a big day! We were getting ready to go to church to celebrate Mother's Day for one of the greatest moms in the world. Someone left a beautiful bouquet of flowers on our front porch. I immediately knew who they were for - my mom. I wondered who sent them. My mom came into the living room and pulled the card out of the flowers. As she read it, her smile suddenly turned sour. "There must be something wrong" she said. I asked her who sent them. And, she said there must be a mistake because she ordered these for her mother, our Grammie. So, she called her mom, our Grammie, to clear this up. Grammie told my mom that she refused the delivery from the florist and told them to return the flowers to my mom. Grammie explained that she had left the Presbyterian faith and joined a new religion, called Hindu. The Hindus told her that she had to get rid of all past relationships in her life and start anew. Therefore, she didn't want any contact with my mom or our family any more. I could see my mom's eyes tear up as she was telling me what happened.

What mother wouldn't want to spend time with her children? I could barely wrap my ten year old brain around this. I never heard of a religion that told you to do something like that. This did not make any sense at all. I didn't want to ask my mom any more questions because it seemed like that would only hurt her more. Because my mom was adopted as an infant, maybe Grammie never felt like a mother to her. Whatever the reason, it was hard to have this happen on this day that should have been one of the happiest days of the year for my mom. I never wanted to see my mom cry like that again.

My mom was the kind of mom that was always there for us growing up. She was very strict but always disciplined us with a loving heart. She was our Girl Scout leader, as well as our Sunday School teacher, worked in the library at our school binding books, typed up the heat sheets at our swim meets, sewed our clothes, and was quite a carpool queen. When she tucked us in bed at night and told us she loved us, sometimes she would tickle our backs to help us fall asleep. She was the kind of Mom my friends wanted to talk to when they couldn't talk to their own Moms. She had a ton of friends and loved her Washington University Pi Beta Phi sorority sisters so much that she helped open up a retail store in St. Louis to benefit Pi Phi charities. She and my dad played bridge and tennis with other couples and travelled with my dad's job.

How could her mom not love her anymore? This is a mystery I will never understand. Thank goodness we still had my dad's mom, our Grandma Rainey. She lived near us in St. Louis now in a nursing home and can't take care of herself anymore. She loved us all a ton. She wasn't going to be mean to us.

Grammie never spoke to or saw my mom again in her life.

1963
The Taxi Cab Accident

The unexpected sudden swerve of the taxi cab on slick ice caused the taxi driver to completely lose control of his car. He crashed into a wrought iron fence. The impact of the crash thrust my grandmother out of the back seat of the cab onto a spoke of the wrought iron fence. My dad said the spoke of the fence impaled grandma's head, crushing her skull. She was rushed to the Hudson Hospital immediately.

In an instant, this lover of the written word would never be the same. From the Bronte sisters, Charles Dickens, and Henrik Ibsen, to Edgar Lee Master, Edgar Allen Poe, Shakespeare, Thackeray, Henry Van Dyke, and H.G. Wells, my grandmother read it all. She shared her love of literature with students and adults alike. Lately, my grandma had been basking in the glory of her well-deserved retirement from teaching. The accident prevented me from ever having the chance to get to know my own grandma as so many other people in her life had.

What a tragedy for such a strong, successful, intelligent woman to lose all that she was in an instant. I wish I could have known her intimately, but our family had visited my grandparents just two times before the accident. I remember going to their house in New York when I must have been about five or six because it was before my sister Alice was born. It was a long drive to New York from St. Louis. I was so excited to see the bed that my dad slept in and was so curious what his house was like growing up. My grandmother was definitely in charge then.

I was only six years old when grandma had her accident. I could not know what part of my grandma I lost. With the part of my grandmother that remained, all I knew what that she loved me and I loved her.

When my dad received the news by phone call in St. Louis, he rushed to Hudson to assess the situation and found it was critical. Grandma had to stay in the hospital for quite a long time recovering from the surgery. After she had had a life filled with so much responsibility, now her son was going to have to start to take responsibility for her even though Grandma Rainey was only 65 years old. The brain surgery would ultimately lead to dementia.

When my dad broke the news to us about grandma's brain surgery, he told us with a very straight face, without shedding a tear. Then again, I realized I had never seen my dad cry or even get agitated enough to raise his voice. He was always even keeled. My mom was the disciplinarian in the family even though we knew my dad was strict too. My dad was kind of an enigma to me. We knew he loved us unconditionally, but, beyond that unstated love, he never was one to show too much emotion. After my mom got sick, he became distant with us. I felt closer to my mom than my dad when I was growing up. My dad seemed to need to always be the strong one. I know he loved his mom and dad, but he did not talk about them very much. I wondered what it was like for my dad growing up. As an adult, he never complained about anything or seemed to want for much. He wore clothes that appeared tattered and worn to me, but he didn't even notice. I did not wonder about my dad's frugality until I was a teenager when I began to understand money and those types of things. My dad never really cared about what other people thought about him. He was who he was, and that was that.

Maybe there was something we didn't know about my dad's childhood that made him the way he was. Did he have the same kind of upbringing we did - living in a four-bedroom house in the suburbs? Maybe he needed to be strong at a young age for some reason. Because we went to private school and were surrounded by children from wealthy families, I thought we were kind of poor even though my dad seemed to have a good job. Money always seemed tight, but it didn't matter to me. I was so happy with my friends and family, attending school, playing sports, and having a full refrigerator. I felt lucky. My dad was like a lot of other dads in our neighborhood; he put on a coat and tie and went to the office every day. Yet, in some ways my dad was unique because he had a very humble and very private nature. He liked to debate serious subjects such as taxes, government, history, elections, investments, or other current events. When we would ask about his personal stories growing up, he would answer with only a few words. It was hard to learn much about our family except that they came over on the Mayflower. He was so proud of that. We didn't have any cousins, aunts or uncles that could tell us stories. My sisters and I wished he would have told us more about our relatives, but we would only hear random snippets of information from my dad. My dad was proud of our heritage; nevertheless, it was as if he wanted us to figure it out for ourselves rather than handing it to us. It made us more curious about what he wasn't telling us.

I wished someday that my grandma could tell me stories about her childhood, about my dad growing up and about what their life was like. After the taxi cab accident, I knew that would never happen because Dad said my grandma was on a downward spiral and wouldn't ever get better. The opportunity to get to know her seemed to have been lost for good.

As time went on, I could only dream of what my grandma had been like growing up, of what her joys in life had been, and of all she had achieved. There was a void in my life that I could not fill. What was her life like before the accident? Was it hard growing up in the olden days? How could I find the answers to so many questions? I would stare at her happy face in all of the old family pictures but could not figure out the story behind the smiles.

"The Indian Serenade"

"I arise from dreams of thee
In the first sweet sleep of night,
When the winds are breathing low,
And the stars are shining bright:
I arise from dreams of thee,
And a spirit in my feet
Hath led me—who knows how?
To thy chamber window, Sweet!"

Percy Bysshe Shelley

CHAPTER ONE

RECORD OF HAPPENINGS

Beginning September 8, 1914
Marian G. Viets
Central High School
Springfield, Massachusetts

"A written word is the choicest of relics. It is something at once more intimate with us and more universal than any other work of art. It is the work of art nearest to life itself. It may be translated into every language, and not only be read but actually breathed from all human lips; -- not be represented on canvas or in marble only, but be carved out of the breath of life itself."
Thoreau

Women weren't supposed to dream about their future, except as a wife and mother. But, this uncommon woman was different. She honored the written word and wanted to have a career.

On September 7, 1914, this precocious sixteen year old took the trolley downtown to purchase her first diary. This treasured purchase marked the beginning of her future dreams. From her cozy second floor bedroom in her quaint New England home, she put pen to paper. She could look out onto her tree-lined street to see the houses of her friends and neighbors with the 735-acre Forest Park as a verdant backdrop. Outside, she could hear the trolley clanging along its path and, downstairs, her mother and father talking in the parlor. She loved them both dearly. Her father worked hard to provide for his family, at times unsuccessfully. Her mother was a homemaker extremely devoted to her only child.

In her diary she was free to write intimately about subjects of interest to her at the time and hone her skills. She wrote about silent movies, plays she attended and participated in, the Debate Club, suffrage meetings, the war in Europe, recipes she prepared, her religious faith, and current issues. She divulged her deepest feelings about her love for her family, friends, and her country. And, often she wrote about her family's unending struggles with money. She recorded her favorite poems by famous or not so famous authors, reflecting the times and giving a picture of her state of mind. After she filled up the first diary, she would go buy another one. Writing was her passion. She liked to describe what she saw through her teenage eyes. Her first diary was titled *Record of Happenings,* and she began to freely write about starting her senior year of high school.

This young woman, full of hope and inspiration, is my grandmother, Marian Gertrude Viets. In my wildest dreams I never thought I would have the chance to meet her posthumously. Her diaries, which were the dearest of relics for me, would survive over 100 years of moving from box to box in city after city. It wasn't until many years after my father, Marian's only child, died in 1993 that I even discovered the existence of her diaries. First, I found one or two diaries in a box among other books. Later, I found several more diaries in different boxes. They were all spread out. Obviously, my father knew of their existence because he purposely saved them all of these years for her granddaughters to unearth. I kept looking for more diaries until I found a total of six.

Marian's diaries would provide an opportunity to record her personal journey on her search for identity and a place in society. Often her jottings reflected the world of any high school girl who was smart, popular, and a leader. Nevertheless, her circumstances presented challenges that forced her to step back and reflect. Marian could have been writing about herself when she said, "I really think troubles are good for people. They just force you to search into your soul for something finer and deeper to take the place of what you have lost."

Marian was no ordinary teenage girl. For one thing, she had dreams that inspired her. First, she wanted to go to college and that alone distinguished her from most of her feminine peers in 1914. Moreover, her family lacked the resources to make her dream easily attainable, and scholarships were rare in her day. Even at this tender age Marian also had an inkling that she wanted to be a writer and have a career. After her high school graduation, she spent an afternoon climbing a mountain in East Granby, Connecticut with her maternal Grandfather Clark, picking black eyed Susan flowers and wild roses. Later she wrote in her diary: "Grandpa is the finest old man. I would like to put him in a book. There are so many people I should like to put in a book." That dream has come real in these diaries.

In her first diary, Marian barely mentions World War I, which officially began on July 28, 1914 in Europe, the summer before she started her senior year of high school. Only her troubles at Christmas caused her to muse: "The Great War rages in Europe, and there is untold suffering. How we in America should rejoice in our safety, although we mourn for those who have died. And, yet, what is it that makes me sad and that makes me feel like crying? Somehow I don't believe there is to be much joy in my vacation." Her family's money problems overshadowed the holiday. Later the sinking of the Lusitania merits only a line or two.

I discovered that my grandmother had a flair for the dramatic; her writings were serious, humorous, and enjoyable. Once I started reading them I couldn't stop. I found her perspective of this time period fascinating. Marian stood at the forefront of the woman's movement, pushing for the right to vote, volunteering for the home front efforts in World War I, and struggling to have a career and a family. She is the woman I would have wanted to be if I had lived in those times.

In 2008, my daughter, Lauren, and I made a pilgrimage to the places that were meaningful to my grandmother. I knew my grandmother's childhood home, 27 Spruceland Avenue, was within walking distance of Forest Park because she had mentioned sledding, watching fireworks, and taking walks there. Within minutes of exiting Highway 91, we approached a quintessential New England neighborhood with Victorian-style, two-story homes. This quaint street turned out to be Spruceland Avenue. We were armed with electronic and printed directions, but we didn't need them. As if I could visualize exactly where the house would be, I drove right up to it. Lauren said, "It felt as if the surrounding city had succumbed to the pressures on modern-day, middle-class America, but this small neighborhood remained untouched." The houses were not only close to the street, but also to each other.

Seeing Marian's neighborhood brought the diaries to life. As Lauren and I stood in front of the charming, yellow frame house with its wrap-around white porch, I could envision my grandmother walking to high school with her neighborhood friends Marjorie Lane, Ruth Woodin, Edna Maxfield and Elizabeth Trask (nicknamed "Joe", "Mit", "Max", and "Bid"), sitting in her room writing in her diary, cooking in the family kitchen, playing the piano, and hosting her many friends and neighbors in the parlor. I could even picture her burying her pet canary in the backyard.

Our next stop in Springfield was the Twin Arbor apartments where the Viets family moved during Marian's senior year in high school since money became too tight to remain in their home. Even though the local economy prospered and Springfield's population grew from 62,000 in 1900 to 129,000 in 1920, Marian's father struggled financially. The town's population growth was the result of a strong industrial economy, including Wason Manufacturing Company (a manufacturer of railroad cars), Smith & Wesson Company (revolvers), Knox Automobiles, Warwick Cycle Manufacturing Company and Indian Motorcycles, Milton Bradley Company, Bosch Company, as well as such financial concerns as Massachusetts Mutual Life Insurance Company where Marian worked in the summers during college. The apartment building has not weathered the changing economic times as well as the Forest Park area. It stood in disrepair. Unfortunately due to the country's loss of industrialization, Springfield has not prospered. Its population peaked at 174,000 in 1964 and has since declined to 149,000, according to a 2007 estimate. Gone are many of the hotels, restaurants, theaters and other attractions that Marian described. Many of the remaining buildings are dilapidated.

Lauren and I also drove further back into Marian's past, to E. Granby, Connecticut, a small town of 600 people about 15 miles southwest of Springfield. My first stop was stop in the Chamber of Commerce in E. Granby where I purchased *East Granby: the evolution of a Connecticut town* by Jane Springman which provided valuable information to help me complete missing pieces of my family genealogy. Both of Marian's parents, Gertrude Mary Clark and Samuel David Viets, were from fifth generation families of E. Granby. Although they died before I was born, they also came alive for me in Marian's diaries. There was a lot of influential history from both sides of Marian's families in this quaint New England town, which shaped Marian's life, and in turn, shaped my life too. It is no wonder that Marian flourished in her nurturing environments, surrounded by her loving family and five generations of proud history. My two sisters and I are Marian's legacies: she passed on to us through her son her strength, determination, belief in the importance of education, family values, and her love for family, friends, and America. I am so proud of Marian.

Our trip even inspired my daughter, the next generation, Lauren to write about the balance she wanted to achieve in her own life. As my daughter and I drove around Springfield, Massachusetts, and E. Granby visiting all of the places that Marian wrote about in her diaries, I felt even closer to my grandmother. In Springfield I could feel the warmth of the neighborhood: the independence of her trolley ride from home to her high school and the days gone by in the downtown area of art, culture, and shopping. In rural E. Granby, the historical significance of our bloodline became meaningful in a way I did not expect. The closeness and personal pride of my family I thought was lost had been found for me.

Marian copied this poem into one of her diaries which expresses changing times from farm living in East Granby to city living in Springfield:

"Young Imagination"

"Where father lived when we was growing up,
They had a barn, a pasture, and a brook,
And cows and calves and chickens and a pup,
And, flowers, till you'd hardly care to look.
And when he sees us children in the street,
With only brick and stone beneath our feet.
And rows of houses walling out the day,
He says: "You need a better place to play."
Where mother dwelt when she was just a child,
The mountains hid their heads among the clouds,
And valleys lay between, with rivers wild,
And giant pine trees growing there in crowds.
Our one lone tree can never grow so high,
Its limbs are lopped to let the wires go by.
"Poor little children! Think of all they miss!"
Says mother often, with her good night kiss.

Poor older folk! They do not know our street.
They work so hard they have no time to play.
They little guess how full of fun, how sweet
And different it is each passing day.
Sometimes it seems an ocean, deep and wide.
And mighty ships go sailing on its tide.
Sometimes a wood, and in the jungle murk
The redskin and the tiger like to lurk.

We fought a splendid battle there last night,
Our cheering lancers charged across the plain.
The bugles called, the banners fluttered bright,
The cannon roared, the foemen all were slain.
And there today, a lusty pirate band.
We cruised with lathy cutlasses in hand:
A prize we seized off Twenty-Fathom Bank,
And made the crew and captain walk the plank.

Our street at times has been a magic road
For Arab troops and Bagdad caravans.
The Yukon River past our door has flowed
(We washed the gold in mother's baking pans),
Across the curb that rims the humble pave
Old Baffin's Bay has dashed an icy wave,
And once, I well remember, 'twas the Nile,
The day we caught the famous crocodile.

Some far off time when all of us are grown
And gone away, our turn will come, perhaps,
To tell the tale to children of our own
Of what we did when we were little chaps.
Then we shall boast of these delightful days
With all their joyful, satisfying plays,
And vow that little lives are incomplete
That never know a brick-paved city street."

L.H. Robbins

Marian's Paternal Family Tree

I learned even more about the deep American roots on Marian's paternal side of the family in one of the books my father saved, *Genealogy of the Viets Family* (F. H. Viets, 1902). Knowing where she came from is reflected in Marian's personality. It is probable the name Viets is from the dialect included under the general term German, or ancient Teutonic, spoken in "former ages in that interesting region which extends from the Alps to the North Seas, a country romantic, and occupied for twenty centuries by a people among the noblest." (Viets) The given name, Viet, corresponds to the word "Guide." Dr. John Veet, a physician, came to New York from Germany in 1700 because he wanted both to see the world and to find a good situation for his practice. He settled in Simsbury, Connecticut in the East Granby area around 1710. Recently discovered copper mines just outside of East Granby drew many people seeking fortune and a better life for their families: "around 1735, the first copper coins made in the English colonies were produced in East Granby." (Springman) Dr. Viets, as the name evolved, was soon deeded eleven acres of rich cropland in what became known as Copper Hill. Future generations of the Viets family worked as landowners, copper miners, cobblers, farmers, selectmen, legislators, traders, shop owners, and innkeepers. Today the Viets Tavern and Inn is listed on the National Historic Register, across the street from the Newgate prison, a National Historic Landmark also once owned by my family.

By the time the shooting started at Lexington and Concord on April 19, 1775, the residents of E. Granby (including Simsbury, Copper Hill, and Turkey Hill) could look back over a succession of colonial wars extending for almost 140 years. The Viets family served in the town militia, defending settlements and bolstering armies. War was no stranger to the men of E. Granby. So, when the call came to serve, Marian's great-great grandfather, Captain James Viets, served in the Revolutionary War in the 18th Regiment of the Connecticut Militia. James Viets was a farmer on the old family homestead. When James served in the war, it took valuable time away from farming. In April of 1775, after the news of the Concord fight, realizing the need for artillery, "a group of Connecticut men organized and financed an expedition to capture British-held Fort Ticonderoga on the western shore of Lake Champlain." (Springman) A Simsbury soldier "gained admission to the fort before the attack and reported back to Ethan Allen that the fortress was in disrepair and the British powder was so poor it had to be dried and sifted before it could be used." (ibid) A small company of British soldiers still manned the Fort. The Connecticut group, including Captain James Viets, left E. Granby for the fort in late April. On May 10, 1775, Ethan Allen and the Green Mountain Boys crossed Lake Champlain from Vermont. Benedict Arnold started out from Boston and joined forces with the group with the same plan. The colonials captured the fort without a single shot. Some of the seized cannons were taken to Boston." (ibid) The French called the fortress, Ticonderoga, "Carillon" meaning "Chime of Bells." The following poem by V. B. Wilson aptly describes the battle Marian's great-great grandfather, Captain John Viets, participated in firsthand.

Ticonderoga "Carillon"

The cold, gray light of the dawning
On old Carillon falls,
And dim in the mist of the morning
Stand the grim old fortress walls.
No sound disturbs the stillness
Save the cataract's mellow roar,
Silent as death is the fortress,
Silent the misty shore.

But up from the wakening waters
Comes the cool, fresh morning breeze,
Lifting the banner of Britain,
And whispering to the trees
Of the swift gliding boats on the waters
That are nearing the fog-shrouded land,
With the old Green Mountain Lion,
And his daring patriot band.

But the sentinel at the postern
Heard not the whisper low;
He is dreaming of the banks of the Shannon
As he walks on his beat to and fro,
Of the starry eyes in Green Erin
That were dim when he marched away,
And a tear down his bronzed cheek courses,
'Tis the first for many a day.

A sound breaks the misty stillness,
And quickly he glances around;
Through the mist, forms like towering giants
Seem rising out of the ground;
A challenge, the firelock flashes,
A sword cleaves the quivering air,
And the sentry lies dead by the postern,
Blood staining his bright yellow hair.

Then, with a shout that awakens
All the echoes of hillside and glen,
Through the low, frowning gate of the fortress,
Sword in hand, rush the Green Mountain men.
The scarce wakened troops of the garrison
Yield up their trust pale with fear;
And down comes the bright British banner,
And out rings a Green Mountain cheer.

Flushed with pride, the whole eastern heavens
With crimson and gold are ablaze;
And up springs the sun in his splendor
And flings down his arrowy rays,
Bathing in sunlight the fortress,
Turning to gold the grim walls,
While louder and clearer and higher
Rings the song of the waterfalls.

Since the taking of Ticonderoga
A century has rolled away;
But with pride the nation remembers
That glorious morning in May.
And the cataract's silvery music
Forever the story tells,
Of the capture of old Carillon,
The chime of the silver bells.

V. B. Wilson

In 1776, General George Washington and the Continental Congress acted to recruit soldiers. Connecticut was to raise eight regiments to serve for one year in a Continental Army. The incomplete records do not show that James participated in this battle; I doubt he did due to the length of time he would have been away from the farm. The call came for more men to join the Continental Line in 1777, but the prevalence of smallpox made the men hesitate. Some soldiers paid for a substitute.

On July 5, 1777, the British occupied Fort Ticonderoga again and sent a detachment to Bennington, Vermont to raid the American supply depot. Under Captain Hezekiah Holcomb, the Connecticut Militia, including Captain James Viets, participated in the Battle of Bennington against the British detachment while they searched for horses, cattle, and grain. It was another American victory and one the men of E. Granby were proud of. Connecticut's farm wives waited for their farmer husbands to rush home from battle to tend their crops.

The farmers of Connecticut played a "major role in winning the war. Connecticut became known as the "Provision State" as her people provided more food for the American army than did any other colony." (Springman) The "shortage of salt was most serious, since people depended on it to preserve meat. New England has no natural salt deposits. For years salt had been brought to Windsor by boat from the Turks Island in the West Indies, but this supply was cut off early in the war by the British naval blockade. Ships were sent under armed convoy to find it wherever they could."(ibid) James Viets served his country in two completely different ways: on the battlefield and on his farmland.

Captain John Viets, James's uncle, had an unusual position during the Revolutionary War serving as the first prison keeper in the first state prison in the new nation. In 1773, the Connecticut General Assembly "decided to convert the main tunnels of the Simsbury Mines on Copper Hill into a prison." (Springman) They chose to name it after the infamous Newgate Prison in London as "a warning to criminals and a deterrent to crime. The English Newgate Prison was a medieval horror with stone chambers of injustice and overcrowding." (ibid) Captain John Viets was to tend to the needs of the prisoners and make sure none escaped. His wife made trousers and knitted socks while "Captain Viets supplied their meals including rum rations. At this time he was charging the colony five shillings a week for each prisoner in his care." (ibid). Sadly, in April of 1777, Captain John Viets died of smallpox at 60 years old.

Following a fire in 1782, Newgate's role in the war came to an end. Not more than 70 prisoners altogether were committed to Newgate during the war. When the Revolutionary War ended on May 12, 1784, the prison was abandoned until 1790 when Connecticut reestablished it. In 1823, the State closed the prison because inmates escaped. Still the prison, now a National Historic Landmark, remained in Marian's family for a period of time until Samuel Viets sold the prison in 1904. According to a book my father saved entitled *Newgate of Connecticut and Other Antiquities of America by S.D. Viets, Proprietor, Copper Hill, Connecticut, 1895,* the prison attracted a growing number of tourists each year, and provided a spot for many family reunions. (S. D. Viets) Marian's father, Samuel Viets, wrote in the introduction: "The famous Newgate Prison of Connecticut, America's only Revolutionary Political Prison, is the most ancient and historical spot in New England."

When my daughter and I visited the prison in 2008, it was closed for renovations. We peeked in the windows, but we could only see the gift shop. The setting high on the hill was beautiful; it looked like a work of sculpture to me. We walked across the street to the Viet's Tavern where John Viets lodged professional miners and other workmen. Seeing this part of our family history was worth the trip, and I hope to go back to see the completed prison renovations. As Lauren and I departed, we shared a laugh over our relatives' private prison proprietorship as a career opportunity.

Many years later, when the call came to serve in the Civil War, participation was not as popular as the Revolutionary War was for the men in E. Granby. A majority of E. Granby's voters in 1861 supported the Democratic Party, which opposed the Civil War. The town never gave a majority of its votes to President Abraham Lincoln or to Connecticut's Governor William Buckingham, both members of the Republican Party, which supported the war. "Many people in Connecticut felt the war was a mistake for economic, political, and even moral reasons." (Springman) The people of E. Granby opposed the war because they had relatives or trading partners in the South; the South also provided a market for local manufactured and agricultural products. Others in E. Granby did believe that the purpose of the war was to "defend and maintain the supremacy of the Constitution and to preserve the Union with all the dignity, equality and right of the several states unimpaired." (ibid) I do not have any record of any of Marian's immediate Viets family members serving in the Civil War.

In Connecticut, the issue of slavery was not as complicated as historians believed it to be. "Through a series of laws beginning in 1774, Connecticut provided for the gradual abolition of the institution within its borders and made it increasingly difficult for people to participate legally in the slave trade. The number of slaves in the state decreased from 2,759 in 1790; to 310 in 1810; to seventeen in 1840. National censuses show five slaves in E. Granby in 1800 and none in 1810 and thereafter. The General Assembly finally outlawed slavery in 1848." (Springman) I am proud that all men that helped the farmers and tradesmen in E. Granby were free men and paid a wage.

Despite the natural beauty of the small town of E. Granby, I can see why Marian's father, Samuel D. Viets, who was well educated, having attended the Academy at Wilbraham, Massachusetts, moved to Springfield, Massachusetts and left the agrarian lifestyle for the city. Perhaps his education inspired him to aspire for more. In 1844, once railroads began running from smaller towns, such as E. Granby, to larger towns, such as Springfield, opportunities opened up for jobs. In 1895, S.D. broke away from his family farm and the small town life of E. Granby to become involved in the grain business in Springfield, Massachusetts that was then a rapidly growing city with a population of over 60,000. In 1900, S.D. and his brother, James, organized a corporation, S.D. Viets Company that sold masons' supplies, seeds, fertilizers, hay and grain. Breaking away from the small town life was a bold move, which unfortunately wasn't always successful due to fluctuations in agricultural markets at the time. James and his wife, Kate, had one daughter, Beula, whom Marian mentioned many times in her diaries. Later, Samuel became an insurance agent, with limited success. While moving the family to Springfield was a difficult business decision, it proved an advantage for young Marian because it gave her the chance to attend better schools and to be exposed to cultural events, an opportunity that enabled her to become the woman she wanted to be.

Marian's Maternal Family Tree

In the small town of S. Hadley Falls, Massachusetts, a very important woman in Marian's life grew up – her maternal grandma - Myra Smith. It is here that Myra lived with her father, who was a Deacon, his third wife, and her brother Charles. In 1862, Myra had dreams of her own. There was a prestigious college within walking distance of their home, named Mount Holyoke Seminary. At sixteen years old, Myra dreamed of going to college the next year but she wondered how the year old Civil War would affect her plans.

Myra's nineteen year old brother, Charlie, was interested in the Civil War discussions swirling around town. An order was issued by the War Department in August of 1862 to draft 300,000 soldiers to serve for nine months to serve in the Civil War. The state of Massachusetts was to fill a quota of 19,019 Union soldiers. Enthusiastic town meetings were held in S. Hadley Falls in hopes of recruiting young men. Charles (nicknamed Charlie), was intrigued by the meetings. The earnest and soul stirring appeals were made to the young men to heed the call of their country. The recruiters appealed to the young men's love of adventure, pride of the North, and their heroic desire to do something for the great cause.

On September 22, 1862, Lincoln issued a preliminary proclamation "warning that he would order the emancipation of all slaves in any state that did not end its rebellion against the Union by January 1, 1863." (Wikipedia) But, the war continued. Later, The Emancipation Proclamation on January 1, 1863, was a presidential proclamation and executive order issued by President Abraham Lincoln which changed the status of more than three million enslaved persons of the south from a slave to a free person.

Much to Myra's chagrin, her brother Charlie became enthralled by the recruiter's enthusiasm and decided it was his heroic duty to join the 52nd Regiment of Massachusetts. On the morning of September 30th, 1862, there was a momentous event in front of the old hotel in South Hadley. The whole village was on hand to bid goodbye and Godspeed. There were huge bouquets of flowers, plenty of food, medicine, and supplies for writing material to mail letters home to their loved ones. Amid the tears and cheers, the soldiers headed off in a big wagon towards Camp Miller. I am sure Myra and her family was there to say their goodbyes. Myra's father was the Deacon of S. Hadley Falls and well known in the community. Charlie would faithfully write home to his family throughout his more than nine month stint using the writing material and stamps they gave him.

The war adventures began for the 52nd Regiment of Massachusetts as they were ordered to New York November, 19, 1862. There they boarded the steamer Illinois bound for New Orleans and Baton Rouge, Louisiana where they were on duty until March, 1863. They attached to the 2nd Brigade, 4th Division, and 19th Army Corps, Department of the Gulf until they returned home to Massachusetts in July of 1863. (www.nps.gov/civilwar)

My father saved the letters that Myra's brother, Charlie Smith, wrote home during the Civil War which documented his variety of war experiences, especially his lack of food and sleep. He also expressed his ambivalence about his participation in the war, and described his homesickness for his family, including his dear sister, Myra. On January 18th, 1863, while stationed in Plaquemine, Louisiana, Charlie wrote: "While sitting by the fire, I cannot help thinking of home. It is the right kind of day to make one homesick. I would like to be with you today, help you do the chores, and sit down with you around the fire this evening. I hope Myra has gotten over the measles. I forgot to say anything about them in my letter to her. I have written very often lately, but cannot help doing it again today. I know you will be glad to hear from me often. I need not ask the question, 'Do they miss me at home?' for I know my name is mentioned constantly and many are the kind wishes and prayers offered for me. Neither does Charlie forget home, but when slowly trenching the sentinels beat, or when at midnight on some lonely outpost watch for the rebels - it is of home and the dear friends that I am thinking my time will soon be over." In February of 1863 he wrote: "There is one thing I became more and more convinced of that they can never make soldiers of Massachusetts farmers. They may make fighting men of them, but never soldiers. I heard last night that preparations had been made by Jefferson Davis [President of the Confederate States of America during the Civil War] for peace on conditions that the slaves should remain as they were. All else would be given up. If the problem can be settled on those terms I wish they would do it for I don't believe they can ever fight it out. And with good due, the proclamation lives, as long as the officers don't reject it. Even here under the command of Lt. Col. Storr of Amherst, slaves are forbidden to come within the lines and when on duty I have turned back many a poor fellow who had come 10, 15, 20 miles to get free. What good does a Proclamation of Emancipation do under such circumstances? I can't tell how many slaves I have let in at the risk of being found out. I know they are free. Why not acknowledge it first?"

In addition to the Civil War letters, I found another unknown treasure: Myra's brother Charlie's Civil War bible. At first when I found the bible I thought it was one of the littlest leather bibles I had ever seen. It had a strap to hold it closed. I really didn't think it was anything special until I opened it and read the inside front cover. Ironically, I discovered this small pocket size bible was a soldier's bible passed from one soldier to another upon capture when each soldier claimed it as their own by writing his name and date on the inside cover. The first soldier to possess the bible was given it as a gift. It says: "To Edmond C Bainbridge from his sister" who must have given this bible with well wishes as her brother set off to serve his country as a Union soldier. Then, below that is written "Captured by F. H. McCollum on the 23rd day of June 1863 at the battle of Brashear City, Louisiana." Brashear City was a Confederate stronghold. So, Mr. McCollum must have been a confederate soldier who captured Mr. Bainbridge and confiscated his bible. On the next page of the bible Myra's brother wrote: "Recaptured by Charles E. Smith a Union Soldier with Company H 52nd Regiment of Massachusetts on Sunday morning June 28th, 1863 at the battle of Fort Butler in Louisiana during the Civil War." Once again, this symbolic and treasured bible changed hands again back to the Union side and Myra's brother. On June 28, 1863, Fort Butler became the scene of a rare night battle that sealed a pivotal Union victory. Fort Butler was designed in a unique star shape by a West Point officer at the junction of Bayou Lafourche and the Mississippi River and constructed in 1862 by freed slaves who lived in the area, in the heart of the sugar parishes. Charlie wrote home "I wish you could have some of the molasses and sugar we get here. There is a sugar house near here with any quantity of it and we help ourselves freely."

Following the Emancipation Proclamation, Charlie mentioned in his letters that he was hospitalized in the Measles Hospital in Baton Rouge where he wrote: "Contrary to the hopes expressed in my list; the measles paid me a visit – completely using me up for a few days" On July 23, 1863, Charlie's nine months of service were over and the 52nd Regiment started home.

On August 3, 1863, Charlie and the other survivors of the 52nd regiment arrived home following their required nine months of service (which was a bit more). The men were haggard, half-starved, sick, ragged, unkempt beyond words, and they looked like walking skeletons. When their train arrived the band started playing "Sweet Home." The sick, including Charlie, were immediately loaded into carriages and taken straight to a hospital. Sadly, Myra's only brother survived for just three days in the hospital. On August 6, 1863 at twenty years of age, before the war ended, Charlie's life ended. His family was able to say their goodbyes. He died in the "rightness of the cause and strong belief in God." (The measles vaccine was not introduced until 1963) Myra cherished her brother's letters and his little pocket sized bible, passed them on to her only daughter, Gertrude, who in turn gave them to my grandmother Marian, as a remembrance of the short yet heroic life of the beloved Union soldier Charles Smith. Ironically, the pain of war was now a part of their family, symbolized by the little bible. As I read about my relatives and all that they sacrificed throughout their lives, I am grateful for all that they did for us to be able to live in freedom in America. I am overwhelmed with a sense of pride.

In the fall of 1863, Myra Smith reluctantly left for Mount Holyoke Female Seminary in South Hadley, Massachusetts several weeks after her brother's passing (In 1858 Mount Holyoke obtained collegiate status but the name Seminary was not dropped from the name until 1893) It was required that she board at the Seminary and she was "expected to furnish her own towels, napkins, and napkin ring, one pair of sheets and pillow cases, and one blanket, also a table or dessert spoon and a tea spoon" according to the 1863-64 Annual Catalogue. She attended college for only one year, at the age of seventeen years old, during the middle of the Civil War. I wonder if Myra quit college following the tragic loss of her only brother because it was too much for her to bear boarding at college away from her family. I experienced a similar incident when I left for college three months after my mom's passing. I thought I was ready to be on my own, but I soon discovered it wasn't as seamless a transition as I thought it would be. I missed my little sister the most. The first year following my loss was the most unbearable. I wonder if Marian's grandmother influenced her only granddaughter to fulfill the college dreams she was unable to finish.

The Civil War ended on May 9, 1865, with over 600,000 soldiers lost in the line of duty and over 200,000 died from diseases. Charlie Smith was sorely missed by his family and friends at such a young age and wouldn't be forgotten. I love his picture below signed "Very respectfully, Chas. E. Smith." He looked so healthy and vibrant which is a wonderful way to remember him.

Charlie Smith, Myra's brother

Through all of her loss, Marian's grandmother, Myra, found happiness when she married farmer Benjamin Pinkley (B.P.) Clark of E. Granby in 1870, several years after the end of the Civil War. They had three children, Gertrude (Marian's mother), Charles, and Dan (nicknamed Umpa by Marian). The love and warmth in the Clark family home comes shining through in Marian's writings in her diaries. The town of E. Granby held a special place in Marian's heart, especially on the holidays at the family farm on South Main Street. Their influence in her life is reflected in Marian's diaries.

Marian's maternal grandfather, Benjamin Pinkley Clark (born in 1840), decided not to fight in the Civil War, although he was only three years older than Myra's brother, Charlie Smith. B.P. Clark might have hired a substitute so that he could remain on the family farm and not go to war. Hiring a substitute helped to fill the state's quota. The Clarks were originally attracted to the E. Granby area because of available land with rich soil for farming. By 1840, many farmers discovered that their land was particularly favorable to the cultivation of tobacco. "Men were able to develop Connecticut Valley Broadleaf, a tobacco with a large fine-textured, aromatic leaf. It was particularly suitable for cigar wrappers. By the time Horace Clark's sons (including B.P.'s father) inherited his land, they were probably planting this improved tobacco." (Springman) There was a large amount of tedious handwork involved with tobacco while constantly battling worms and weeds. The Clarks prepared and seeded their tobacco beds in early spring. Then, they fertilized the tobacco beds with manure they "dragged" in. In the late summer they cut the plants off at the base of the stalk; "stuck" them or speared their ends onto a wooden lathe in the kitchen and hung them upside down to cure in their barns and cider mill. During the winter months, the Clarks took the plants down, stripped the stalks and bundled the leaves for hauling to market. They built a tobacco warehouse in front of the cider mill where they stored tobacco before reselling it or making it into cigars. Horace Clark employed as many as seventeen people. "One year they produced 800,000 cigars, valued at $32,000." (ibid) (In today's dollars that would be over $800,000.) Clark sold his tobacco as far away as Baltimore, but usually he "sold to cigar makers and tobacconists in Suffield, which was at one time the marketing center of business." (ibid) I find it sadly ironic that the livelihood for my dad's maternal great-grandparents, farming tobacco, ultimately caused my dad's addiction to smoking and his death from single cell carcinoma lung cancer in 1993. Farmers were unaware of the side effects of smoking tobacco.

Just as in the Revolutionary War, farmers in E. Granby provided produce and tobacco for the soldiers in the Civil War. There was no mention of any members of the immediate Clark family fighting in the Civil War. Their passion was farming and they served a purpose providing the fruits of their labor during war time. "Tobacco prices increased as Southern tobacco disappeared. The market for the wool of their sheep "increased when cotton was no longer available from the South." (Springman) The military needed cloth for their uniforms and blankets. The women at the Soldiers' Aid Society at the Congregational Church "rolled bandages, sewed and knitted clothes, and collected food for the soldiers."(ibid) Following the end of the Civil War on May 9, 1865, "E. Granby became solidly established as an agricultural town in a state that was becoming more and more industrialized. The population of the town declined from 853 in 1870 to 661 in 1890 as families continued to move to the cities." (ibid)

In the boxes in my basement, I discovered a gorgeous marbleized ink covered ledger book B.P. Clark used to keep a daily log or diary of his farming and activities. Inside the front cover he wrote: "Commenced Jan. 1st 1871 until August 17th 1896." Marian was probably inspired by her grandfather's journaling to start her own diaries about her life's journey. B.P. Clark's entries into his ledger book were usually only one line, although Marian would go into greater detail about personal matters in her diaries. Each day he described the weather, how he felt, or what he did, such as: "butchered a hog", "went after coal", "had my clothes on for the first time since sick", "sold heifer", "sore throat", "was up long enough to have bed made", "took down tobacco", "drew wood", "filled the ice house", "stripped tobacco", "sold cattle", "thrashed rye", "baby Gertie born", "Father Smith gave Myra a cow", "visited a relative", "went to church", etc. I think it is funny that the birth of his daughter, Gertrude (nicknamed Gertie), merited only a line item among many others in his journal.

Diaries were also important to other farmers in Marian's family at this time, especially to record weather which was a constant concern for farmers, because of their dependency on their crops for food. Many farmers also "read the forecasts in their almanacs as faithfully as they had one read their Bibles. Each growing season brought the threat of crop damage from hail, wind, frost, drought, and excessive rain. Floods damaged more than crops. Elmore Clark (B.P.'s brother) recorded in his diary that on April 17, 1854, there was a severe snowstorm and the brooks rose to new heights. Oats not sown, fences not mended, feed cattle as in winter, and now we are drowned out. I have 1 ½ feet of water in my cellar. The Connecticut River is higher than it was in 1800, what was called the Jefferson Flood. Scotland and Tariffville bridges are gone, and I hear that nearly every bridge on Salmon Brook is gone. Covered bridge at Windsor is gone." (Springman) "Lightning storms took their toll of animals, trees, and buildings and there was only a bucket brigade to fight the fires it caused" (ibid) But, Horace Clark (B.P.'s grandfather) seemed to write about the joyful gifts of nature that I imagine Marian would have done. "Each year he recorded the arrival of the individual species of birds, the greening of different trees, and the blossoming of the various flowers." (ibid) He wrote eloquently about the total eclipse of the sun on June 16, 1806, in "the time of the greatest observation, the dew fell, hens went to roost, the whippoorwill sang his morning song, the cock crowed as for day, and finally everything wore the appearance of a new day." Horace died in 1842, but it sounds like he and Marian were kindred spirits.

In the close knit community of E. Granby, farms were usually passed down through the family or sold to relatives. Therefore, most of the neighbors were close family or friends who helped each other out. Marian's mother, Gertrude, had two brothers, Charles and Daniel, who farmed nearby on Clark property. Daniel was also a tobacco farmer, a member of the Connecticut legislature, and an Amherst College graduate, class of 1904. I have the lap desk Daniel carried with him to classes at Amherst. I cannot imagine having to carry your desk from class to class. Marian affectionately called her mother's brother, Daniel Clark, "Umpa" throughout her diaries. And, she called his wife Theodora "Theo". Gertrude's brother, Charles, married Fern but did not have a nickname. Neither Charles nor Daniel had any children of their own. Marian was the only grandchild on the Clark side, and the family doted on her.

After visiting E. Granby, our last stop was the 19th century native quarried stone Congregation church built in 1830 which remains near the old town center and was an important part of the Clark family in times past. As religious as the Clark family was, I was sad I could not see the inside of the almost 200 year old church.

I did not know until I set foot on the ground where my ancestors lived, worked, worshiped, and fought, that I would feel the emotions that I did. I had spent so much time reading old papers and looking at pictures, that it all seemed purely informational. But, when I saw the church and the prison in person, I felt like I had taken a time travel trip into the past. I sensed that I belonged to my relatives and I was a part of something greater than I was aware even existed. I learned so many personal things that I am proud of, and I am sure there are some things I do not know that I might not be so proud of. But, it was especially meaningful for me to make this connection at a time in my life when I felt detached and broken from my family. I am so proud of what my dad's maternal family accomplished in their lives. Along the way, I had no idea I would learn so much about the Revolutionary War and the Civil War, from my own family member's perspectives. I realize that none of my relatives are famous, but they made a difference in history. I certainly did not learn the emotional side of the wars from textbooks in school. No wonder my dad saved all of this paperwork. I was the lucky one to be able to put our family history puzzle pieces together.

It is no surprise that Marian's small and happy world revolved around New England towns all within an hour train ride of each other: E. Granby, Springfield, and S. Hadley. Her love for her family and country is expressed in her diaries through her own writings and also through the poetry of some of her favorite authors. This particular poem written in 1909 by Henry Van Dyke, a Presbyterian minister, expresses his love for America:

"America For Me"

TIS fine to see the Old World, and travel up and down
Among the famous palaces and cities of renown,
To admire the crumbly castles and the statues of the kings,—
But now I think I've had enough of antiquated things.

So it's home again, and home again, America for me!
My heart is turning home again, and there I long to be,
In the land of youth and freedom beyond the ocean bars,
Where the air is full of sunlight and the flag is full of stars!

Oh, London is a man's town, there's power in the air;
And Paris is a woman's town, with flowers in her hair;
And it's sweet to dream in Venice, and it's great to study Rome;
But when it comes to living there is no place like home.

I like the German fir-woods, in green battalions drilled;
I like the gardens of Versailles with flashing fountains filled;
But, oh, to take your hand, my dear, and ramble for a day
In the friendly western woodland where Nature has her way!

I know that Europe's wonderful, yet something seems to lack:
The Past is too much with her, and the people looking back.
But the glory of the Present is to make the Future free,—
We love our land for what she is and what she is to be.

Oh, it's home again, and home again, America for me!
I want a ship that's westward bound to plough the rolling sea,
To the bléssed Land of Room Enough beyond the ocean bars,
Where the air is full of sunlight and the flag is full of stars

Henry Van Dyke

Henry Van Dyke impressed Marian with his themes of religion, and his views about American life. Perhaps Marian felt his poems described her love for her 200 year family legacy in New England. Henry Van Dyke graduated from Princeton University in 1873 and Princeton Theological Seminary in 1877. After serving as a Presbyterian minister, he became a professor of English at Princeton University 1899 to 1923. In 1913, Mr. Van Dyke was appointed by President Wilson, a friend and former classmate, to become the minister to the Netherlands and Luxembourg. Shortly after his appointment, war broke out. Eventually he "returned to the United States and was elected to the American Academy of Arts and Letters." (Wikipedia)

Marian's diaries start at the beginning of her senior year of high school. At first Marian began her writings describing typical high school activities. But, with time, the depth of her dreams as a woman who wanted more in her life became clearer.

Tuesday, September 8, 1914 • Springfield, Massachusetts

Well, back to school again after a good old summer, especially the time from August 27th to September 5th at Provincetown, Massachusetts — quaint, dear, old Provincetown. It doesn't seem possible, dear memory book, that I am a high school senior. It has always been the ambition of my life to be one, but until the last few years, I had never dared to look beyond to college.

"Cape Cod" (Verses IV, V, and VI)

Serene, the wildernesses stretch away
With woodland glories gay,
Blue-berried, fragrant, thick with stunted growth,
Moorland and forest, both.
Deep in their solitudes the hermit lake
Is fringed with birch and brake.
And through the stillness, far from all abodes,
Wind dim and silent roads.
The cranberry, in level fruited fields,
A spicy harvest yields,
And all the springtime glades are odorous
With virgin arbutus.
Above the tangled reach of brier and brush
Hymns loud the holy thrush,
While to a hidden pool, umbrageous, clear,
Plunges the thirsty deer.
From these romantic realms how faint and far
The modern turmoils are!
What quietness the meadowy uplands hold,
Bequeathed from days of old!
And how, in these hushed woods so seldom stirred,
One tranquil voice is heard --
From these quaint ways the Pilgrim feet have trod:
"Be still, and know your God!"

Amos Wells

It seemed so good to walk home again with Marjorie Lane, Ruth Woodin, Edna Maxfield, and Elizabeth Trask, nicknamed "Joe," "Mit," "Max," and "Bid." And, what joy of joys to get inside dear old C. H. S. again and see all the dear old bunch: "Pris" Spaulding, Marjorie Sawhill, Margaret Kemater, and Marjorie "Spot" Lyman.

But there was a delightful surprise awaiting me. Last June, I had been ruled out of senior room on account of my name being at the end of the alphabet. But I had gotten in — such joy — and I sit way up high in the very next to the back seat. Isn't that joyous? Dr. Law (Director, Department of History) gave us all such a dear talk, the kind I've always heard she gives to every senior class. She said that we were the very best senior class yet. Of course, 1915 is the best year there ever was and ever will be. I saw Mr. Hill (Principal, C.H.S.) for a few minutes in the hall. He looks well. He is just the best principal ever. Well, I did have some homework at the end of the day, but cheer up. School is a joy anyway.

Friday, September 11, 1914 • Springfield, Massachusetts

Senior class elections today after school. Very exciting as elections always are. Poor Alex was knocked down from the presidency, which he has held ever since the Class of 1915 was organized; but Dick Burdett got it, which was perfectly fine, I think. Dick B. is so brilliant and all around nice. And now, dear memory book, I am going to let you guess who vice president is. No, you never could guess who it is — just insignificant little me. Isn't that queer? But, really, I was never so happy in my life. All the congratulations didn't amount to anything compared with that glad, glad feeling inside. I just couldn't wait to get home and tell mother. News like that just makes her face shine. And dear mother needs lots of good news, for these are hard days.

> America was the richest country in the nation during the Progressive Era (1890-1920) which saw economic, political, and cultural changes that affected every aspect of Marian's life. By 1900, many homes in the cities had indoor plumbing, electricity, telephones, kitchen appliances, and automobiles. While Marian's mother benefited from the new technologies as a homemaker, she still felt the stress of tough economic times for her family. In the Viets' home money was tight. Technology created a shift for women, away from the time-consuming household chores to the freedom to participate in a public life through working or volunteering. Marian's mother volunteered at the YWCA but she lacked a college degree or skills for employment to ease the family burdens. Marian was determined to take a different path in life than her mother.

Tuesday, September 15, 1914 • Springfield, Massachusetts

Well, I've been to school a week now, and it's glorious. Everything is just fine, and I adore every subject except MATH. That subject is stupid at best, but when you have 15 theorems and 31 exercises in one night, it's time to strike. But, I consider myself most fortunate to only dislike one subject when so many of the girls hate them all. American History with Dr. Law is full of interest. She is a wonderful teacher and can fire interesting information at you in such a way that you don't realize that you're learning.

Friday, October 2, 1914 • Springfield, Massachusetts

We had a sad surprise awaiting us this morning. Jimmy, my canary bird, was found dead in his cage. We simply can't imagine how it happened, for he was chipper as anything the night before and had plenty of seed and water. He lay just as if he were asleep. Dear little bird. We shall miss him. He was always so cheerful with his merry song. I guess he just lived long enough to give the world his song and then left us. I just cried and cried but went to school nonetheless.

In the evening, we had our senior social in the girl's gym. Just our class! I went down in the auto with Edna and Ruth. We had a jolly time although there were very, very few boys. There are 56 girls and 28 boys in our class, and only a few of the 28 boys came and half of them didn't dance. Dick B., our class president, managed the social, and I can't say enough in admiration of him that night. He danced with nearly all the girls but mostly with those who otherwise would have had no dances at all. He just gave up his own time to be agreeable to others. Lots of the girls spoke to me about him and said they thought he was just the best president a class could have. His dance committee was composed of rather queer fellows in the class. He's just trying to give everyone a finger in the class pie and, although he's a fraternity man, Alpha Delta Sigma (ADS), he's no snob. I'm sure of that. At intermission, Dick B. sat with the faculty and made himself generally agreeable. Jimmy Doherty brought a bunch of us home in his car. He stalled his engine on High Street but got it started again.

Saturday, October 3, 1914 • Springfield, Massachusetts

I had a horrid poky day and was just longing for some Saturday night excitement when the telephone rang, and it was Dick B. He said that they were having an ADS initiation and would like to bring the "goat" over to call on me. I said sure thing. There was my excitement!! And it sure was.

I didn't have to wait long before the doorbell rang, and Dick B. was at the front door. A whole mob of ADS fellows were on the sidewalk, and the poor "goat" was down on the corner. The whole bunch came in. But you should have seen the goat. He had on an old pair of trousers; a coat turned wrong-side out and hind-side forward with the pockets pulled wrong-side out; and a potato sack over his head. They yanked him in the house, and I went out in the kitchen and fixed up the worst mess ever — a glass of water flavored with paprika, cayenne, and mustard and a hard crust of bread just covered with mustard. Then, I sat out in Mother's big chair, and the goat, which was kneeling, was forced to propose to me. I don't know who the fellow was, but he made quite a decent proposal. The fellows kept yelling to him to put a little action in, but thank goodness he didn't. Then, I went to the piano, and they tried to make him sing "Smother Me with Kisses," (Harry Carroll) but they couldn't get a word out of him. He ate the mustard sandwich and drank the mess like a Spartan. Poor fellow. After that the boys all left. (Dick B. sure is a peach).

Sunday, October 4, 1914 • Springfield, Massachusetts

We buried Jimmy Jim, my canary, this morning out in the back yard. Father had fixed him so dear in a little tin box with tissue paper lining. And, he made a little tissue paper pillow for his head. I took a class of boys in Sunday school this morning. They are about nine years old and regular little terrors but awfully dear never the less.

Monday, October 12, 1914 • Springfield, Massachusetts

In the evening, father, mother, and I went to see "Cabiria," the great drama in moving pictures. It was wonderful. It pictured the eruption of Vesuvius, the sieges in the Punic War, and other spectacular features.

> The successful movie, *Cabiria*, was written and directed by Giovanni Patrone in 1914. It takes place during the third century B.C. when a girl, *Cabiria*, is separated from her parents during the Punic Wars. Moving pictures did not have soundtracks yet, but there were titles in the film accompanied by a piano score. The Italian movie industry produced many historical epic movies before the beginning of World War I. In 1914, *Cabiria* was shown on the White House lawn. (IMDB)
>
> Following the invention of the movie camera by Thomas Edison, movies became one of the most powerful new art mediums for Americans around 1911. The silent film era is commonly referred to as the "Age of the Silver Screen." Hollywood was born, stars emerged, companies were formed, and movie theatres were built.
>
> In 1912, Mack Sennett founded the Keystone Studios in California. Many actors started their careers with Sennett, including Charlie Chaplin, Roscoe Arbuckle, Gloria Swanson, The Keystone Cops, and W.C. Fields. By 1914, some 25 million people a day spent anywhere from a nickel to a quarter to laugh at the slapstick of Mack Sennett's Keystone Kops or shiver at overacted melodramas with custard pie warfare and wild car chases. The Keystone Cops (1912-1917) were fictional incompetent policemen who served as supporting players. The nickelodeon (Odeon is Greek for roofed theatre) was a multipurpose theater that was popular from 1900-1914. Synchronized dialogue did not appear until the late 1920s, with "talkies" becoming more and more commonplace after 1927. (Wikipedia.org)
>
> Marian loved going to the movies to see places she had never seen before, dream of romance, and identify with celebrities. With the absence of any media in homes at the time, the movies were a novel experience that captured her attention and interest.

Tuesday, October 13, 1914 Springfield, Massachusetts

We had Phi Gamma Chi finals at the house today. Got in some perfect peaches. We had given them a pretty stiff initiation.

> At the time, high school sororities and fraternities, modeled after their college counterparts, were very active, despite opposition from teachers and administrators. By the 1920s, they became almost obsolete. In 1914 at Central High School, Marian and her tight-knit circle of girlfriends were members of their sorority, Phi Gamma Chi. Marian was president of the sorority, which actively rushed and initiated girls into membership, hosted dances, and held social activities.

Saturday, October 17, 1914 • Springfield, Massachusetts

Such news! We have rented our house on Spruceland Avenue and have got to get out by November 10th. I hate to leave so badly. The thought of moving into an apartment haunts me, but we can make it easy, I'm sure. I just hate to leave the street with all the dear girls. We haven't an idea where we're going, but we have to decide soon. I certainly have had some good times in the dear old house. But it's goodbye now — forever, probably.

Tuesday, October 20, 1914 • Springfield, Massachusetts

This was a busy day. Had a math exam that I've dreaded for weeks. But, like most things, the realization was not as bad as the expectation. About a half an hour after the close of school, we had a Pierides Debate Team meeting, and I argued for the resolution "that the minimum wage law should be applied to the factories, industries, and sweatshop of the U.S." After the meeting, I had to rush home to try on my dress. It's a dear new school dress, brown broad cloth trimmed with a dark green mixture. And, now it's evening, and I'm so sleepy that I can hardly write.

Thursday, October 22, 1914 • Springfield, Massachusetts

At three o'clock I met Barbara White and we went to the moving pictures at the Bijou Theatre. They were wildly exciting. Afterwards, we went into Jensen's Ice Cream Shop and had chocolate marshmallows. Barbara also bought some chocolates. She's a dandy girl, not because she bought me the chocolate either.

Friday, October 23, 1914 • Springfield, Massachusetts

"Mit" Woodin and I went down to Spare's Restaurant for lunch after school. Then, we got a college ice at Jensen's Ice Cream Shoppe. Honestly, those college ices at Jensen's are the most yummy, peachy, absolutely wonderful things; chocolate ice cream, then marshmallow cream, then sweet chocolate grated over the whole thing. That's a chocolate shot. There was some time left after Jensen's, so we went up in Forbes and Wallace's Department Store restroom and listened to the Victrola. It's certainly adorable up there.

At ten minutes of three, Ruth and I met at the corner of State and Main to go up to the Phi Gamma Chi meeting. The meeting was at Margaret Kemater's house. The girls talked mostly about the dance, which is to be a week from tomorrow night — October 31st — Halloween. We are giving the dance with Kappa Phi at the Women's Club House. But, I am not going. I can't afford the $1.50 nor have I a dress, evening coat, or all the things needed. I just told the girls the reason, and really it took more courage. I do care a whole pile about missing it, but mother mustn't know. I have told her that it didn't matter at all. I'm going to our Easter dance, though, if I die in the attempt.

"I Wish I Were Rich"

"When I worked in an office from early till late,
And my pocket was empty of cash,
I looked at the glittering autos go by
With brasses and crystal a flash;
The varnish and leather and luxury used
My envious eyes to bewitch,
I yearned for a car and I sighed to myself;
"I wish I were rich!"

I gazed in a jeweler's window at rings
And watches in gorgeous array,
I lingered to stare at a beautiful coat
In a furrier's over the way,
I peeped in a hall with a velvety rug
And statues and palms in a niche,
I passed by a mansion of marble, and cried:
"I wish I were rich!"

> *One morning Dame Fortune appeared at my door,*
> *Behold! I was rolling in wealth.*
> *But the care of my millions took all of my time,*
> *And soon I was broken in health.*
> *My mail was a bundle of plaintive appeals,*
> *And copies of newspapers which*
> *Assailed me in merciless skits and cartoons*
> *Because I was rich.*
>
> *I wistfully peered from my new limousine*
> *At a workingman walking along*
> *In holiday garb, with his pretty young wife,*
> *And little ones rosy and strong,*
> *And I said: "If I only could be in his place,*
> *Oh! Never again would I itch*
> *For the brummagem baubles that money can buy,*
> *Nor wish to be rich."*
>
> *If you sleep like a top, if your conscience is clear,*
> *If your steak and potatoes taste good,*
> *If you get your envelope on Saturday night,*
> *And keep Sunday the way that you should.*
> *Though you sit on a stool with a ledger all day,*
> *Or labor away in a ditch,*
> *Give thanks to the Lord for his blessings you have,*
> *Don't wish to be rich."*
>
> *Minna Irving*

I stayed overnight with "Mit." She and I walked around by the Bemis's house on Spruceland to see the wedding excitement. Mrs. Bemis is giving a dinner dance for the bridal party for Marian Bemis and Frank Schlesinger. They are to be married tomorrow night. They danced between courses, which is, of course, the latest thing. How I loved all the wonderful, many colored gowns, the men in evening clothes, and the gay music. It was a beautiful sight.

"Mit" and I went home after our peeping. We had a fit of looking at old things long forgotten paper dolls we used to play with, old letters, and many reminders of old times when we were really "kids." I don't call myself a kid now for I'm seventeen next week.

> As Marian was exploring her future dreams for college, a career, marriage, and a family, being an active spectator of her neighbor's wedding was important to her. She hadn't had a boyfriend yet and was anxious to meet someone special.

Saturday, October 24, 1914 • The Bemis Wedding

All day I have watched the preparations at the house across the way on Spruceland Avenue. There is a long awning canopy from the door to the street, and the piazza doorway is hung with autumn leaves. The florists have been there at work all day, and all day I have been looking forward to the wedding.

Mother and I went about 6:30 pm to the church. Mr. and Mrs. Pease took Ruth Kenyon, mother, and I over. Father didn't feel like going. We were awfully early, but we got what we wanted, the first row in the balcony where we could see everything. The ushers were all good-looking fellows. We could watch all the people come in, in their stunning gowns. Some of the older girls were certainly dressed in the latest, with very low necks, and some of the gowns were the most brilliant colors imaginable.

A wedding never has meant so much to me, I supposed because I'm older, but my heart just beat like a trip hammer during the whole performance. It sounds silly to say that, but it's true. Marian looked so graceful and dear, all in white with a long train. She wore a dear little cap from which came her veil. You should have seen Frank watch her come up the aisle. And his smile, when he took his place beside her, was wonderful. It was all over in such a short time.

When Marian and Frank came down the church together, they smiled and bowed at everyone. Then, off to the reception at the house directly across the street from ours. Mother and I didn't go to the reception because we had no suitable clothes, but that didn't prevent us from sitting in the window and watching the people come and go in the beautiful big limousines and private open cars. We couldn't see the house, of course, because of the canopy. About half-past nine there was loud cheering and excitement, and Frank and Marian climbed into a big lighted limousine. They waved all the way down the street until they were out of sight. And now I'm writing it all down before I crawl into bed and think about it till midnight.

Marian was on the cusp of feeling "older" with grown up dreams, yet fondly remembering her dear father with this poem.

"The Baby Who Romped With Dad"

OH, little girl, with the braids grown long,
And the laughing lips and heart of song,
And the slim cool hands, each night you wait
As you once did by the arbored gate,
But when your daddy turns in the street
No more you scamper on dancing feet,
With wind-blown curls, and your arms out so-
As you did ever so long ago!

Now you stand waiting him, tall and and straight
And self-possessed; and you swing the gate
To let him through, and you tippytoe
For his kiss, and arm in arm you go
Up the long walk where the red rose bends,
Each rose on its stalk and you are friends,
You smile at the world, and it looks glad;
But where is the baby who romped with Dad?

Oh, where is the babe with her rush and shout,
Her hair blown wild, and her arms held out;
With the wee hurt where she slipped and fell,
Which only the kiss of her dad made well?
She stands wide-eyed with her lips apart,
Her hands clasped over her fluttered heart;
With fluffy curls in a shining strand,
And gazes into the Grown-up Land.

And just last evening a tall youth stood
By the gate with her; and the distant wood
Shone green and gold in the setting sun;
A bird in its shady depths - just one -
Trilled a low note to departing day;
She stood and watched when he turned away -
Then ran, arms wide, where her father smiled,
And clung to him like a little child.

> *And he knew - and, knowing, his eyes grew dim -*
> *How much of that loving was meant for him;*
> *And he stood that night by her snowy bed.*
> *As she slept, one arm 'neath her little head,*
> *And he thought long thoughts, and his heart was sad*
> *For the wee girl who had run to Dad*
> *With a happy shout on those far off nights,*
> *For kiss-healed bruises and pillow-fights.*
>
> Judd Mortimer Lewis

Thursday, October 29, 1914 • Springfield, Massachusetts

Seventeen years old today! And now I wish that I was back to sweet sixteen again. I never had such a quiet birthday, no fuss of any kind but just an ordinary day of school. And, a quiet evening at home with mother; father was out.

Grandmother Clark gave me $5 and a white lace collar for my birthday. With the $5 I bought a hat. Mother gave me a dear dark green bag lined with gray silk, and fitted out with a mirror. Mary gave me a crepe-de-chine tie of Roman stripes, and Ruth two dear handkerchiefs. Gertrude, Grandpa and Grandma Viets sent me cards. No school tomorrow on account of teachers' conventions. Hurrah!

The purchasing power of Grandmother Clark's 1914 gift of $5 would be $120 in today's dollars, a generous sum that was very gracious and appreciated. As Marian had another birthday, life seemed to become ordinary.

"The World Gone By"

> "Sun-rise and moon-rise
> And lure of earth and sky;
> Sun-rise and moon-rise
> And echoes that reply;
> With hours between to sigh in,
> To laugh in and to cry in-
> To dream in-and to die in
> And so the world goes by!
>
> Sun-set and moon-set
> And bird and butterfly:
> Sun-set and moon-set
> And shadows dim which lie:
> And happy days and drear days.
> And bitter days and dear days.
> And cloudy days and clear days-
> And so the world goes by!
>
> Sun-shine and star shine
> And hopes unborn that cry:
> Sun-shine and star shine.
> And dreams that will not die
> With flight of rook and swallow,
> And songs we fain would follow
> Loud-flung from hill and hollow-
> And so the world goes by!

> *Day-light and gray-light*
> *And wonder in the sky:*
> *Day-light and gray-light*
> *And wings wherewith to fly:*
> *And loss and death to grieve us*
> *And frowning Fates to weave us*
> *A shroud when breath shall leave us.-*
> *And so the world goes by!*
>
> *Oak leaf and ivy leaf.*
> *And laurel leaf and all:*
> *And hero wreath and angel wreath*
> *And something waxing small.*
> *And base thoughts and holy thoughts*
> *And silence-after all!*
>
> *Green leaf and red leaf*
> *And rainbow banded sky:*
> *Spring home leaf and autumn leaf*
> *And flowers that droop and die:*
> *And birthday and bridal days*
> *And none to tell us why!"*
>
> Arthur Goodenough

Friday, October 30, 1914 • Springfield, Massachusetts

I'm going to try to begin to write better.

This afternoon I went down to school with about ten boxes of candy in my arms. About six of the 1915 girls were down there, and we put the candy we had solicited in bags. They are ten cents each with ten pieces of candy for tonight's performance. We did up 100 bags in all and decorated the candy tables in the assembly hall. Florence Fisk, chairman of the committee, had bought red and gold crepe paper, the class colors, and had made the letters 15 out of cardboard to put on the front of the tables. The performance for tonight is an affair given by the class of 1915. Professor Crosby of Brown is to read from the play "If I Were a King." He charges $50, and we have to pay his expenses. Well, the reading went off well. We had about 300 in the audience and sold lots of candy. We had big baskets tied around our necks with red and gold ribbons. Mother and Ruth Kenyon went down together. We covered expenses and a little over.

Saturday, October 31, 1914 • Halloween

In the morning, I helped mother pack for our move on Thursday. In the afternoon, the Kematers called for me in the auto and I went up there for supper and all night. Before supper, Mr. Kemater, Elizabeth, and I played pool. It was my first experience. Margaret dressed for the Phi Gamma Chi dance. Elizabeth is not going since she is too young (only 15), and I am not going for reasons already stated.

Arthur came after Margaret for the dance about 7.30 p.m. The rest of us went to the Polis Theatre. The show was very good. After the Polis, we had a college ice. Elizabeth and I didn't go to sleep until Margaret got home about 12.30 am because we wanted to hear about the dance. Margaret told us that the Phi Gamma Chi girls sang better than the Kappa Phi girls. I was so glad. They're peachy girls all right, and I'm happy to be their president.

Sunday, November 1, 1914 Springfield, Massachusetts

I taught Sunday school today. The boys were good today. After dinner I wrote in my good times book which really is the best part of a good time – the living over of it again in memory.

Thursday, November 5, 1914 • Springfield, Massachusetts

We moved into the "Twin Arbor" apartments today. I went to school as usual, but the men moved the furniture while I was gone. I came home after school, not to the house at 27 Spruceland Avenue, but to the fourth floor of the Twin Arbor apartments. Everything was mixed up, but we managed to get supper and make up beds for the night. It is really very pretty and cozy, but a bit strange. There's only one thing I mind, and that's the fear of fire up so high. But, I'll get over that.

Friday, November 6, 1914 • Springfield, Massachusetts

Before going over to the church supper, I went over to the Ellis's house at 23 Spruceland Ave. to get the darning. I do the Ellis's darning now every week for 25 cents. There are usually about seven pairs of stockings. Our old home at 27 Spruceland Ave. looked so lonely, all shut up and empty. But, there was a tiny light down in the cellar where father was shoveling rubbish into the furnace. While Mrs. Ellis was upstairs getting the stockings together, I talked with Sherman about college. I saw his fraternity pin, which is very clever looking. I'm not sure whether it is Psi or Chi Phi. I think the latter.

After supper, Jack took "Bid" Trask and me to the show. It was a Zobo [kazoo] band. Then, all the girls had our fortunes told. I am to become "more self-confident, have a happy future, and be greatly puzzled between the choice of two men." How exciting!

Wednesday, November 11, 1914 • Springfield, Massachusetts

I went to Louise, "Squeeze's", for an overnight. Louise and I studied a little and then went to bed. I told her about my crush, but she wouldn't tell me hers. Who is mine? Why, dear memory book, it's Dick B., of course — our class president. He is my crush, but alas, he doesn't even acknowledge my existence. Well, such is life! Lucky day! Mrs. Bemis has given me the most wonderful evening dress — pale blue with shadow lace and crystal opalescent trimming. The blue part is satin. It is low in back and front, and fits me perfectly. I'm the happiest girl ever!

Friday, November 13, 1914 • Springfield, Massachusetts

I went to Aunt Mame's house on Spruceland and made her a cake - it came out well, I'm happy to say.

Monday, November 17, 1914 • Springfield, Massachusetts

Aunt Mame and I went to the Broadway Theatre. The pictures were very good; "Ready Money" (Apfel) was a detective play, and wildly exciting. One of the men actors was a wonder. He had the most wonderful smile. He's the cutest movie man ever. When we arrived at Aunt Mame's house after the theatre we had a feed in the kitchen. I stayed all night at her house. It seemed funny to be going to school from Spruceland Avenue again.

Tuesday, November 18, 1914 • Springfield, Massachusetts

A bunch of us read two perfectly killing farces by W. D. Howells: The Mouse Trap and other Farces (1889) and The Register (1911) during commercial period. Beatrice Putney and Priscilla Spaulding did the love scene to perfection. In The Mouse Trap, we all had to stand on our chairs because of the "mouse." Of course, the period changed just then, and all the boys crowded around the door and laughed at us.

> The second decade of the twentieth century was termed the "Little Renaissance" because it was a period of artistic awakening for artists, including writers. Writers wanted to try new styles and ideas that reflected the realities of life in America. W. D. Howells was the editor of the important Atlantic Monthly magazine, and known as the "champion of realism, and his novels carefully interweave social circumstances with the emotions of ordinary middle-class Americans." (IIPDigital.usembassy.gov) Howells was quoted as saying, "I hope the time is coming when not only the artist, but the common, average man, who always "has the standard of the arts in his power,' will have also the courage to apply it." "Love, ambition, idealism, and temptation motivated his characters;" (ibid) all of which are subjects Marian relished.

Friday, November 20, 1914 • Springfield, Massachusetts

We have a dressmaker at the house to make me a yellow evening dress. There's quite a little story about the cloth. Mrs. Ellis gave it to me, and it had been given to her daughter, Elizabeth, the year she died five years ago. Mrs. Ellis said that the whole family agreed to give it to me. I certainly appreciate it and feel honored.

Marian and her family had some of their clothes made for them by a dressmaker, which was common during this time period. The ready-to-wear market was beginning to gain popularity in the mass market. Many women sewed their own clothes at home as an alternative. As women became more active, such as riding bicycles, participating in sports, and working, fashion began to change. Many of the corsets and petticoats were gone, and dresses were becoming shorter.

It seems very poignant that Mrs. Ellis gave Marian the cloth given to her daughter who died. Perhaps she knew how Marian had to miss the sorority dance because she did not have appropriate clothing.

Saturday, November 21, 1914 • Springfield, Massachusetts

I went to the Broadway Theatre with a bunch of the girls as "Spot" Lyman's guest. The picture was fine. It was The Man from Home (1914, Cecil B. DeMille, Director).

After supper, Dick B. was over calling on Gertrude across the street from "Spot's" house. We called Gertrude up and fooled with her, and then Dick B. called us up. He talked with all of us in turn, and it took about half an hour in all. Yes, memory book; I still have a crush on him, and I can't shake it off. And, he's worth it, too. I wish you weren't a book so that you could see him and sympathize with me.

Cecil B. DeMille directed dozens of silent films from 1914 to 1923 until "talkies", films with recorded sound, became more prominent in the late 1920's. DeMille's prolific career included his production of "The Ten Commandments" in 1923 and again in 1956, which were very different films with the same title. DeMille won an Academy Award for best picture and a nomination for best director for his production of "The Greatest Show on Earth" in 1952. To this day, the Hollywood Foreign Press Association presents the Cecil B. DeMille Award at the Golden Globe Ceremonies for outstanding contributions to the world of entertainment. Mr. DeMille won the award in 1952, Walt Disney in 1953 and in 1962 the first woman – Judy Garland. In 2005, Robin Williams took the award, as did Woody Allen in 2013.

As part of the Clark family Thanksgiving tradition Marian read the second verse of the poem "Persons" from the book "Bittersweet" by the American novelist and poet Dr. Josiah Gilbert Holland before their feast. In 1850, he was the Editor of the Springfield, Massachusetts Republican newspaper. Later, he helped found the Scribner's Monthly. It is appropriate that Marian honored a local poet on this special New England holiday.

Thursday, November 26, 1914 • Thanksgiving in East Granby, Connecticut

"It is the Puritan's Thanksgiving Eve,
And gathered home from fresher homes' around
The old man's children keep the holiday,
In dear New England since our fathers slept,
The sweetest holiday of all the year."

J. G. Holland

A beautiful Thanksgiving Day in a dear New England town at Grandfather Clark's house, an ideal place to have this holiday. Uncle Charlie Clark was not able to be present on account of his operation, which was performed just yesterday in the hospital at Hartford. He had the third finger of his left hand amputated. Consequently, Aunt Fern didn't come either. But Uncle Dan "Umpa" Clark and his wife, Aunt Theo, were here. I never knew Uncle Dan to be so adorable. He was just as funny as he could be the whole time. We had the most wonderful, wonderful Thanksgiving dinner with a big fat turkey, which weighed 10 ½ pounds. And, of course, there were oysters, potatoes, turnips, giblet gravy, cranberry sauce, squash, pie, mince pie, and chilled grapefruit. Also, there was fudge at the end. I enumerated the courses in rather mixed-up order.

Grandma Clark's Oysters Supreme

1 pint oysters, chopped or thru meat grinder
1 ½ cup cracker crumbs (1 ½ crumbs equals 24 saltines)
1 pint milk
1/4 cup butter
1 egg
1 teaspoon salt

Melt butter and mix with crumbs.
Pour milk on oysters and season with salt and pepper.
Mix together.
Put in buttered baking dish.
Bake in hot oven [350 degrees] ½ hour in round dish

After dinner, we all helped clean up (Grandmother's woman was sick). In the afternoon, Father and Theo played "500" against mother and Umpa. Umpa had to name the sides something crazy, of course. Theo and father were the "Northern Lights," while he and mother were the "Archipelago." Father and Theo won.

I read Queed, a novel by Henry Sydnor Harrison (Harrison), which is a splendid story. Theo and Umpa didn't leave until late in the evening. We had a wonderful Thanksgiving day.

I discovered Marian's hand written cook books in the boxes in my basement beside some of her diaries. Most of the recipes did not mention specific cooking times or temperatures or exact measurements. In 1896, Fannie Farmer published her well-known cookbook, *The Boston Cooking-School Cook Book*, (Farmer) which introduced standardized measurements. The appearance of gas stoves in most homes provided more accurate cooking times and temperatures. A "hot" oven in Marian's recipes is approximately 375 degrees, while a "slow" oven is about 325 degrees, using today's precise ovens (an oven thermostat was invented in 1915).

Technological advances changed the way women cooked and did housework. Electricity simplified many household tasks, including cooking. Between 1910 and 1920, E. Granby "residents had their houses wired in anticipation of the coming of the lines, often boarding the electricians while they worked. When power was turned on, many of the houses along the main street lit up together." (Springman) I imagine that Marian's grandparents had electricity at their Thanksgiving feast in 1914. "Right behind the electric lines, came electrical appliances. In 1919 the proprietor of the Viets store advertised a demonstration of an electric range; in 1920 the Congregational parsonage acquired an electric vacuum cleaner." (ibid) Most households relied on an icebox (melting ice) to keep food cold. Refrigerators appeared on the market in 1917, but they were too costly for most Americans. The first refrigerator to see widespread use was in 1927. "The first furnace on record was installed in the home of Charles P. Viets at 81 North Main Street in 1907. The Congregational church used its furnace for the first time during the 1914 Christmas service." (ibid)

It is interesting that Marian calls a ten-and-a-half pound bird "a big fat turkey." A good-sized Thanksgiving turkey today would weigh twenty pounds at least.

I tested Marian's recipes for accuracy and added necessary information to produce a successful result using today's equipment. Many of her recipes were from friends and family members hand written into her tattered book.

At this time, a popular form of entertainment following a meal was playing cards. 500 is a trick-taking card game. Players play in pairs similar to bridge, opposite each other. One round of bidding takes place with the option to either bid or pass. The player who wins the bidding starts the tricks.

Friday, November 27, 1914 • East Granby, Connecticut

A quiet day following the holiday. I didn't get up until eleven o'clock a.m. I finished reading Queed. Now, as I write, Grandmother Clark is getting supper, and it has grown dark outside. I can hear the November wind howl around the farmhouse. When I look out of the window I see a cozy light in each of the neighboring houses. There is something dear about the country, which the city never can have. Last night, before I got into bed, I looked out of the window, and the moon and stars looked so wonderful across the broad expanse of heaven. On the moonlit snow the dark pines and gnarled apple trees made shadows in the yard, while the old colonial house stood in all its somber shadows of forgotten times. Perhaps the brave George Washington came to that old house when it was a tavern. Perhaps not. It is the story anyway. But, I know that there were many evenings long ago when couples danced the merriment to the scrape of some rustic fiddler. There is an old ballroom on the top floor, where, Grandfather says; he can just dimly remember these balls were held. I can see him as a little fellow watching the dancers who now are mostly all dead. But, the old house stands.

> Time spent at the family farm was filled with love and support which nourished Marian's soul and dreams for the future. The following is another one of Marian's favorite poems by Henry Van Dyke. It reminded her of the Clark family home and farm which she called an "ideal place to have this holiday"

"The Ancestral Dwellings"

Dear to my heart are the ancestral dwellings of America,
Dearer than if they were haunted by ghosts of royal splendour;
They are simple enough to be great in their friendly dignity,--
Homes that were built by the brave beginners of a nation.

I love the old white farmhouses nestled in New England valleys,
Ample and long and low, with elm-trees feathering over them:
Borders of box in the yard, and lilacs, and old-fashioned roses,
A fan-light above the door, and little square panes in the windows,
The wood-shed piled with maple and birch and hickory ready for winter,
The gambrel-roof with its garret crowded with household relics,--
All the tokens of prudent thrift and the spirit of self-reliance.

I love the weather-beaten, shingled houses that front the ocean;
They seem to grow out of the rocks, there is something indomitable
about them:
Their backs are bowed, and their sides are covered with lichens;
Soft in their colour as gray pearls, they are full of a patient courage.
Facing the briny wind on a lonely shore they stand undaunted,
While the thin blue pennant of smoke from the square-built chimney
Tells of a haven for man, with room for a hearth and a cradle.

I love the stately southern mansions with their tall white columns,
They look through avenues of trees, over fields where the cotton is growing;
I can see the flutter of white frocks along their shady porches,
Music and laughter float from the windows, the yards are full of hounds and horses.
Long since the riders have ridden away, yet the houses have not forgotten,
They are proud of their name and place, and their doors are always open,
For the thing they remember best is the pride of their ancient hospitality.

> In the towns I love the discreet and tranquil Quaker dwellings,
> With their demure brick faces and immaculate marble doorsteps;
> And the gabled houses of the Dutch, with their high stoops and iron railings,
> (I can see their little brass knobs shining in the morning sunlight);
> And the solid self-contained houses of the descendants of the Puritans,
> Frowning on the street with their narrow doors and dormer-windows;
> And the triple-galleried, many-pillared mansions of Charleston,
> Standing open sideways in their gardens of roses and magnolias.
>
> Yes, they are all dear to my heart, and in my eyes they are beautiful;
> For under their roofs were nourished the thoughts that have made the nation;
> The glory and strength of America come from her ancestral dwellings.
>
> Henry Van Dyke

Monday, December 21, 1914 • Springfield, Massachusetts

Another meeting of the Senior Play Committee. We decided upon The American Citizen, a comedy by Madeline Lucette Ryley (1897). The tryouts are to be held January 5, 1915, and the play will be given about the first of March. Why do I record the Senior Play Committee meetings? Simply because Dick B. is there, and I am just silly, silly, silly. But I like him very much.

It is fitting that a woman, Madeline Lucette Ryley (Ryley) wrote the play chosen for Marian's senior class to perform. Ryley was a pioneering playwright at a time when the stage was a male-dominated profession and she introduced more female parts. Marian played the part of Georgia Chapin, one of the smaller female characters. Ryley began her career as an actress and singer. Then, she became a well-known author of light comedies, musicals, and farces in America's Progressive Era theatre. In 1897, *The American Citizen* began a long engagement at the Knickerbocker Theatre, "in presence of an uncommonly fine and highly appreciative audience last evening." (October 19, 1897 nytimes.com) Two of Ryley's plays, including "*Mice and Men*" in 1903, were eventually made into films.

Wednesday, December 23, 1914 • Springfield, Massachusetts

School let out today for dear old Christmas vacation. We had shortened periods and much fun. Our annual Christmas concert came at the end. I sang in the French chorus, and we sang the dear old carol "Noel." The German chorus boys' glee club, the mandolin club, and the orchestra all made the program good. After the concert, we all wished everybody a Merry Christmas and hung around school for a while. Lots of the alumnae were back, and we really had an audience for the concert. In the afternoon, I sewed and made Christmas candy. In the evening, father and I went out and mailed our cards and parcels. It is such fun at Christmas, for there is surely a spirit in the air. I love to see all the red and white bundles, the gay Christmas magazines, and the wonderful stores. It is, in truth, a season of joy.

Thursday, December 24, 1914 • Christmas Eve

The day before Christmas and a very busy one, too. I made Christmas candy and helped mother with Christmas baking.

In the afternoon, I went up to the McKinnions with a big box of candy for them. And, then I went down to the bank to cash my check for $5 from Grandfather. The bank was filled with people, and my crisp new bill was given to me in a holiday envelope. They put the five-dollar gold pieces up in gay little red boxes. I went shopping with the $5. I bought a book of Songs of the Eastern Colleges and tried to find a skating cap and muffler, but the stores were all out of them. When I got home, Sherman Ellis was here. We fooled around a little and then went out with Christmas bundles. The snow was falling, and it looked so adorable and Christmassy.

And now it is Christmas Eve. I am sitting here in the living room with just Father and Mother. Everything is different and a little sad this Christmas. It is the first year away from the old home on Spruceland, for I don't remember Christmases at 248 Pine Street. Then, there is very little money — so little, in fact, that mother had to give up giving presents this year, and I gave a very few. Dear Father does not give up. How I admire him! Never once does he complain of the hard work and little returns. And mother is tired, so tired and pale; but I cannot write of all this.

The Great War rages in Europe, and there is untold suffering. How we in America should rejoice in our safety, although we mourn for those who have died. And, yet, what is it that makes me sad and that makes me feel like crying? Somehow, I don't believe there is to be much joy in my vacation. But, I get my pleasure in a very peculiar way. I plan out and live through the Christmas vacations of girls whom I know are to have a wonderful time. Who are they? Oh, there are a host of them. Yet, my best friend is having her first Christmas without a father, a father who was her companion so much of the time. Oh, Jesus, whose birth we now celebrate, bless equally those who are rejoicing and those whose hearts are sad.

"The Christmas Ship"

To the land where saddened children
With wistful faces pale,
Peer out 'neath the dark war cloud,
With its sting of angry hail;
Where lonely hearths are waiting
For the loved who do not come,
And the sobs of burdened mothers
Break the stillness of the home!

Where laughter, fun and frolic
Were banished long ago.
With father's awful summons
To meet the dreaded foe!
To this land of desolation, -
Of woe and want and wail,
On its ministry of comfort
A Christmas ship will sail.

"Fair upon the far horizon, -
Watched by wondering children's eyes, -
Like the swift-winged carrier pigeon –
Some day its sails will rise;
And as those who've wept in darkness,
Know the joy the day-star brings,
So the vision of this vessel,
Bearing healing in its wings.

Like the mission of the Master
Aching hearts to soothe and cheer.
Let his birthday ship go laden
On this sad, eventful year!
From the land of peace and plenty,
From the land where kind hearts glow,
On its ministry of mercy,
Help the Christmas Ship to go!"

Elizabeth F. Bingham

Friday, December 25, 1914 • Christmas Day

A beautiful, sun-shiny day with the sun shining on the white snow. There was the spirit of Merry Christmas in the air. How could I have said that this day was to be sad? It was so happy. My presents were wonderful: a lovely, pink crepe de chine wrap from Mrs. Bemis, a pair of skates from Father, a pair of rhinestone silver buckles for evening slippers, a box of correspondence cards, hat pins from Aunt Jo, a picture of Helen Francis, a handkerchief, $5 from Grandfather, $2 from Uncle Dan, silk stockings, silver underwear clasps, sachets, a pin cushion, a letter holder, and many, many cards.

Mother gave none and consequently received few gifts; her unselfishness and bravery are wonderful. All morning we made ready for the Christmas dinner. Grandpa and Grandma got here at noon. Our dinner was perfect.

Menu:

Soup
Turkey
Potato & Onions
Cranberry Sauce
Ice Cream Cake
Nuts & Candy

Just as I was starting to think I was really getting to know the "serious" Marian and all of her deep thoughts and feelings, she surprised me with a sarcastic poem amidst all of her sadness about lack of money and the impending war. I truly believe she expressed herself through poetry and I was glad she had a sense of humor and enjoyed life. Marian carefully chose a wide variety of poems: some contemporary and some many centuries old, some about the war and some about love, some famous and some not well known. But, instinctively I could tell which poem related to what was going on in her life and the world at that particular time.

"A Christmas Prayer"

"Maker of Christmas, You intended that day to be both sacred and joyous – oh, forgive us for setting aside Your ideal! Forgive me for feeling pretty mean because I received the same old bunch of white ties from my little kids, the same slippers from their mother, the same cheap edition of Longfellow's poems from Brother Will, the same everything else from the relatives who thought they had to remember me. Forgive my little kids for bragging of their toys before the neighbor children. Forgive their mother for crying because I couldn't find just the thing she wanted – oh, Lord how was I to know what it was? Forgive us if we gave only the gifts we thought we had to or be disgraced among our friends and folks. Bless the poor – we didn't have time to. The grand scramble is all over. Help us to see just how little it paid. And, finally, prosper us in our new duties – for we are all broke!' Amen."

1912, "The Judge" Volume 63

Saturday, December 26, 1914 • Springfield, Massachusetts

Great excitement! Our apartment caught on fire; not our apartment, but a part of the apartment block. We knew nothing of it until the fire engine drove up in front of the block. The front corridor had smoke in it. Mother got together her jewelry, silver, and furs and made for the back stairs. Grandma and I followed. We went into the apartment on the second floor, and smoke was coming up from the cracks in the floor. We shouted out the front window of that apartment and found that the fire was out. The woman on the first floor had had the fat on her stove catch on fire.

Sunday, December 27, 1914 • Springfield, Massachusetts

A busy day. Church and Sunday school in the morning. The sermon was appropriate for the New Year. I had dinner with Ruth Woodin. Her sister, "Dot", is engaged to Paul and all we heard was Paul, Paul, Paul.

Monday, December 28, 1914 • Springfield, Massachusetts

Another busy day! I went downtown in the morning to get presents for my Sunday school class to hang on the tree at the pantry in the afternoon. I made a cake, and mother made a lot of sandwiches before going over in the afternoon. The party was a great success. There was so much cake, candy, and ice cream left after the children had eaten that the teachers had a feast. It made me feel very ancient when I recalled that I used to come to those parties as a kid and get a present from the Christmas tree.

Mother's Chocolate Cake

Very large Tablespoon of butter, beaten
1 ½ cups sugar
1 egg
1 teaspoon vanilla
Sift:
½ cup cocoa
2 cups flour
1 teaspoon baking powder
1 teaspoon baking soda
Add:
1 cup milk

Stir together. Put in 9 inch round buttered and floured pan. Put hot oven [375 degrees] 25 minutes and bake quickly until it comes up, then turn low [325 degrees] for 15-20 minutes until toothpick comes out clean.

Friday, January 1, 1915 • Springfield, Massachusetts

The first day of the New Year. In the evening, Sherman Ellis brought over two Wesleyan fellows to call. Marjorie "Joe" Lane was here, also. I saw Sherman alone for a little while. He's the best friend I've got among the boys and a regular brother to me. I'm thankful for some good advice … really not advice but approval that he gave me. I thought college had changed him when he tried a little "fussing," but he told me afterward that he was just trying me out. I'll never forget the way he said, "Little girl, you're all right. A fellow thinks no less of a girl when she says no. I have heard them talk, and I know." He is truly my "frater ex officio," as he signs his letters.

Monday, January 18, 1915 • Springfield, Massachusetts

Wild excitement! I am in the senior play cast. We have had tryouts and have been on pins and needles to know the cast. My part is Georgia, and the play is An American Citizen. I'm so happy!

Tuesday, January 26, 1915 • Springfield, Massachusetts

I was elected President of the Pierides Debate Team today. No more Chairman of Program Committee, thank goodness!

Wednesday, January 27, 1915 • Springfield, Massachusetts

I went to high school mid-year graduation in the auditorium. Mother and I had tickets in entirely different places. "Spot" sat up in the balcony with me. And who else do you suppose, dear memory book? Dick B.! He sat beside me during all the exercises. Oh, I was thrilled, thrilled, thrilled. The exercises were fine, and the president of Amherst who spoke, was wonderful. He spoke on "Work and Play." After the exercises I had the opportunity to introduce Dick B. to mother. She liked him very, very much. I can scarcely realize that the next graduation in the auditorium will be my own, or rather my class's.

Thursday, January 28, 1915 • Springfield, Massachusetts

This is the last day of the half-year at school. We got report cards and made out programs. I was on the honor roll and had four A's and one B (in math.) I've certainly worked for that B. I made out my program for the last time in high school, for next June is graduation. My order of classes has changed a good deal, but everything is perfectly satisfactory. Mother went to East Granby. She will be gone for two days, and I am to keep house for father.

Friday, January 29, 1915 • Springfield, Massachusetts

In the evening after supper, father and I played a very exciting match of "Rum." I won by only 3 points, the score being 178-175. Mother comes home tomorrow, and I'm very thankful. I miss her, just lots, although I'm glad she's having a little change.

Saturday, January 30, 1915 • Springfield, Massachusetts

I made a cake this morning and cleaned the big pieces of silver to surprise mother. She got home about half past twelve, and I had a nice cheese soufflé baking in the oven. I was so glad to see her! A quiet evening at home, as usual.

Cheese Soufflé

2 Tablespoons butter
3 Tablespoons flour
½ cup milk
½ teaspoon salt
½ cup grated cheese
Dash of cayenne pepper
Yolks of 3 eggs
Whites of 3 eggs

Melt butter, add flour.
When well mixed add milk gradually. Then, add salt, cayenne and cheese.
Remove from fire.
Add yolks of eggs beaten well.
Cool mixture and cut and fold in whites of eggs beaten until stiff and dry.
Pour into a buttered baking dish and bake 20 minutes in slow oven [325 degrees]

Wednesday, February 4, 1915 • Springfield, Massachusetts

The first rehearsal for the senior play was scheduled for this afternoon. We all got there, but our coach never showed up. We thought that we might as well go through the first act alone. Talk about fun! I never laughed so much in my life. Malcolm Law was a perfect scream. In the evening, Sherman Ellis and one of his college friends came over. Rather dull, as calls usually are.

While Marian peacefully enjoyed her family and friends in America, times were changing in Europe, which Marian wrote about in her diaries. Overseas, in 1915, British soldiers were training for and fighting in battles on land and sea. Two famous English poet-soldiers, Rupert Brooke and Wilfred Owen, wrote poems about their first hand experiences. Marian carefully copied the poems *The Soldier* and *The Dead* by an English poet soldier Rupert Brooke (1887-1915) into her diary. She was curious about the war "over there" and poems, newspapers, and movies gave her a glimpse into the lives of soldiers. His five most famous poems were published in the autumn of 1914 after the outbreak of the First World War. The collection included: I: *Peace, II: Safety, III: The Dead, IV: The Dead, and V: The Soldier*. Brooke's poem *The Soldier* was about the death and accomplishments of a World War I soldier in England. Shortly after his poems were published, Brooke enlisted in the Royal Naval Division Antwerp expedition in October 1914. He returned that winter for training camp in Dorset, England. Then he sailed with the British Mediterranean Expeditionary Force in February of 1915 in the Dardanelle campaign. He never reached his destination. The following are two of Marian's favorite poems by Rupert Brooke that she transcribed into her diaries:

"The Soldier"

"If I should die, think only this of me.
That there's some corner of a foreign field
That is forever England.
Where shall be in that rich earth a richer dust concealed,
A dust whose England bore, shaped, made aware,
Gave, once, her flowers to love, her way to roam,
A body of England's, breathing England's air,
Washed by the rivers, blest by suns of home.
And think, this heart, all evil shed away
A pulse in the eternal mind, no less
Give somewhere back the thought by England given;
Her sights and sounds, dreams happy as her days
And laughter, learnt of friends, and gentleness
In hearts at peace, under an English heaven."

Rupert Brooke

The first three lines of Rupert Brooke's poem, *The Dead*, are engraved on the Memorial Arch at the entrance to the Royal Military College of Canada in Kingston, Canada. Upon arrival at the College, it is a tradition for the new cadets to march through the arch in the Arch Parade.

"The Dead"

"Blow out, you bugles, over the rich Dead!
There's none of these so lonely and poor of old,
But, dying has made us rarer gifts than gold.
These laid the world away; gave up the years to be
Of work and joy, and that unhoped serene,
That men call age; and those who would have been.
Their sons, they gave, their immortality.
Blow bugles, blow! They brought us, for our dearth.
Holiness, lacked so long, and Love and Pain.
Honour has come back, as a king to earth,
And paid his subjects with a royal wage;
And Nobleness walks in our ways again;
And we have come into our heritage."

Rupert Brooke

Ironically, Brooke's poems foreshadowed his demise. On February 18, 1915 he developed sepsis from an infected mosquito bite and died on April 23, 1915 in a French Hospital ship moored in a bay off the island of Skyros, Greece in the Aegean Sea, where he is buried. He was only twenty seven years old when he passed away. His poems live on today in popular culture.

A touching tribute to the poet Rupert Brooke was written by Joyce Kilmer, in his book, *Main Street*. Kilmer, an American from New Brunswick, New Jersey, wrote his poetry before he joined the National Guard and transferred to France in October of 1917. As a Catholic convert, Kilmer exhibited humility and a deep respect for God and nature in his poetry.

"In Memory of Rupert Brooke"

In alien earth, across a troubled sea,
His body lies that was so fair and young.
His mouth is stopped, with half his songs unsung;
His arm is still, that struck to make men free.
But let no cloud of lamentation be
Where, on a warrior's grave, a lyre is hung.
We keep the echoes of his golden tongue,
We keep the vision of his chivalry.
So Israel's joy, the loveliest of kings,
Smote now his harp, and now the hostile horde.
To-day the starry roof of Heaven rings
With psalms a soldier made to praise his Lord;
And David rests beneath Eternal wings,
Song on his lips, and in his hand a sword.

Joyce Kilmer

In contrast, the English author and poet Wilfred Owen wrote an antiwar poem, *Dulce et Decorum*, during the same time period. Owen joined the "Artists" Rifles O.T.C. in 1915, was sent to the Manchester Regiment, and served with the 2nd Battalion in France from December 1916 to June 1917. His preface to his book, *Poems by Wilfred Owen*, was found, in an unfinished condition, among Wilfred Owen's papers:

"Preface"

"This book is not about heroes. English Poetry is not yet fit to speak of them.
Nor is it about deeds or land, or anything about glory, honour, dominion or power, except War.
Above all, this book is not concerned with Poetry.
The subject of it is War, and the pity of War.
The Poetry is in the pity.
Yet these elegies are not to this generation,
This is in no sense consolatory.
They may be to the next.
All the poet can do today is to warn.
That is why the true Poets must be truthful.
If I thought the letter of this book would last,
I might have used proper names; but if the spirit of it survives Prussia, -
My ambition and those names will be content;
For they will have achieved themselves fresher fields than Flanders."

Owen's poem, *Dulce et Decorum est*, describes the horror of a gas attack, the death of a wounded man, and a waking nightmare. The title is a Latin saying (taken from an ode by Horace) and was widely understood and often quoted at the start of the First World War. It can be translated as "It is sweet and right" and in the last sentence "pro patria mori" means "to die for your country."

"Dulce et Decorum est"

"Bent double, like old beggars under sacks,
Knock-kneed, coughing like hags, we cursed through sludge,
Till on the haunting flares we turned our backs,
And towards our distant rest began to trudge.
Men marched asleep. Many had lost their boots,
But limped on, blood-shod. All went lame, all blind;
Drunk with fatigue; deaf even to the hoots
Of gas-shells dropping softly behind.
Gas! GAS! Quick, boys!—An ecstasy of fumbling
Fitting the clumsy helmets just in time,
But someone still was yelling out and stumbling
And flound'ring like a man in fire or lime.—
Dim through the misty panes and thick green light,
As under a green sea, I saw him drowning.
In all my dreams before my helpless sight
He plunges at me, guttering, choking, drowning.
If in some smothering dreams, you too could pace
Behind the wagon that we flung him in,
And watch the white eyes writhing in his face,
His hanging face, like a devil's sick of sin,
If you could hear, at every jolt, the blood
Come gargling from the froth-corrupted lungs
Bitter as the cud
Of vile, incurable sores on innocent tongues,—
My friend, you would not tell with such high zest
To children ardent for some desperate glory,
The old Lie: Dulce et decorum est
Pro patria mori."

Wilfred Owen

(Later, in October of 1918, Owen returned to the Western Front as a commander of a company, taking part in some heavy fighting. He was killed on November 4, 1918 while trying to get his men across the Sambre Canal (the river Sambre is in the Meuse basin) at Landrecies and the Oise (Seine basin) is at Tergnier. This was one of the last battles before the Armistice.)

Monday, March 1, 1915 • Springfield, Massachusetts

It is vacation this week. Mother and I went up this afternoon to see cousin Buela's baby. He is awfully dear and walks all by himself. I took him up a little rag picture book.

Tuesday, March 2, 1915 • East Granby, Connecticut

I went down to Grandpa Clark's on the afternoon train. Grandpa met me at the station. East Granby looked so little, dear, and cozy.

Wednesday, March 3, 1914 • E. Granby, Connecticut

Got up late this morning. In the afternoon made fudge and popped corn with Umpa. He was loads of fun and just cut up all the time.

Friday, March 5, 1915 • Springfield, Massachusetts

Came home from East Granby yesterday. This afternoon a crowd of us girls went on a hike. We walked to Agawan Center, got a feed at a store, and walked back. We all did a very undignified thing going back, we caught a ride on a poky old team for about half a mile.

Saturday, March 13, 1915 • Springfield, Massachusetts

Play rehearsal in the morning. It didn't go very well; everyone was so full of the dickens. In the afternoon, we had a Phi Gamma Delta sorority meeting. We've decided on the dance for the 26th of this month and a rush party in the near future

Tuesday, March 16, 1915 • Springfield, Massachusetts

Mother's birthday. Grandma Clark was here for it. They went down to the theatre in the afternoon, and I stayed home to get ready for the evening's fun. I finished the tea apron I was making for her and decorated the table with St. Patrick's fancy paper. I had a lovely big white birthday cake with green and white candles. Mother was so surprised! We had a lovely time.

Friday, March 19, 1915 • Springfield, Massachusetts

Play rehearsal, as usual, was loads of fun. Dick B. and I played "matching pennies." [A two strategy game similar to rock paper scissors] I won so that I have quite a lot owed to me now. The rehearsal was comical; everyone made so many silly mistakes. Three weeks from tonight is the play. Mother and I went to the dressmakers in the evening. When I got home, I wrote some verses for father to read at the Insurance Banquet tomorrow. There is going to be a contest in the company, which is to last until May 31st. There are two sides, the Reds and the Blues. Father is leader of the Reds. I wrote verses in praise of his side. I hope he'll win. Rah-rah! Rah!

Monday, March 21, 1915 • Springfield, Massachusetts

I asked Dick B. to the Phi Gamma dance this coming Friday, the 26th. It took piles of courage because he has never taken me anywhere, and I feel as if it was pure and simple nervy. But he's coming. After school at three o'clock, I went to Miss Roger's house on Temple Street. She asked to see me about the College Club Scholarship, which I have applied for. She is seeing all the applicants. I'm just hoping that I can get it, although I don't consider that there is a great deal of chance. It will mean $200 towards next year's expenses at Mt. Holyoke College.

I met mother downtown after that call, and we did some spring shopping. She bought a new spring hat and coat for which I am truly glad. I bought a coat, too, which I like very, very much. It is cut in the new loose short style. It is a mixture and has handsome bright steel buttons. The collar is a lovely soft shade of green and the buttons are piped with green. I love it really. I wonder if I'll have a good time Friday night. It'll be here soon, and then I'll know.

Tuesday, March 22, 1915 • Springfield, Massachusetts

Miss Lockwood came here to the house to call. She is a member of the Springfield Scholarship Committee. I perfectly loved her.

Friday, March 26, 1915 • Springfield, Massachusetts

The Phi Gamma dance was wonderful. I wore my yellow dress. We had it in the Worthy Ballroom instead of the Country Club as planned, since repairs are going on at the club. Howard took Dick B. and me down in his car and also brought us back. I got home about 1.45 A.M.

March 27 to April 4, 1915 • Springfield, Massachusetts

A week of tonsillitis. I missed five rehearsals and worried most of the time about it. However, I was only in bed three days which I consider quite lucky.

Thursday, April 8, 1915 • Springfield, Massachusetts

Dress rehearsal and loads of fun. We all had to be down there at seven o'clock but the scene shifters couldn't get the first act scenery up till about eight o'clock. Then, the whole cast had their pictures taken by flash light. So, at about 8.30 pm, the rehearsal began. We left the building at 12.15 am. All our costumes had to be packed away in the supply room before leaving. Florence Fisk missed her last trolley car, so she came home and stayed all night with me. Harry took the whole crowd home in his auto — that is the whole crowd that lived up our way — about 10 of us. Malcolm Law asked to go home with me, which I thought was very nice of him since he would surely have had to walk home afterwards. Florence and I had a midnight spread in the kitchen and retired. The play is tomorrow night!!!!!

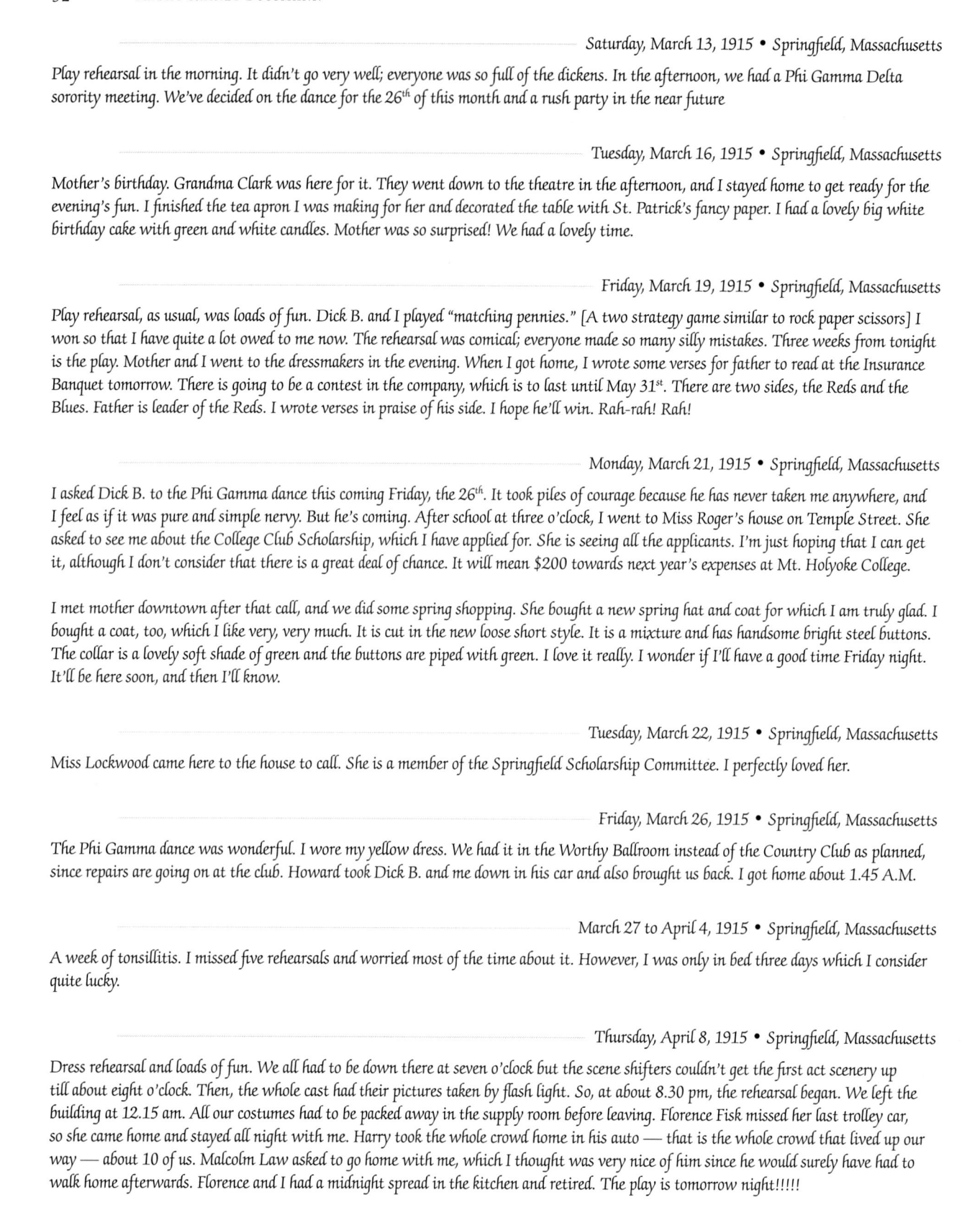

Friday, April 9, 1915 • The Play

The American Citizen was presented by the Senior Class of 1915 of C.H.S., April 9th and 10th. Our whole cast had to get down to school at 6.30 pm to be made up. Oh, such fun and excitement. After the boys had been made up, they played cards behind the scenes to keep up their nerve. At last, 8.15 pm arrived and the curtain went up. We had a huge audience, larger than any that has attended a senior play — over 700. Malcolm was the first on the stage. Just before the curtain went up he shook hands all around, and we wished him the best of luck. Then, the excitement began, and it was real excitement.

My costume in the first act was an adorable white suit of Mrs. H. R. Bemis's, white shoes and stockings, my own new spring hat, and a loose veil. My hat is light sand-colored straw with a stitch up of rose balls. I was crazy about the idea of wearing a veil too. My make-up was good. The other girl's costumes were adorable, too, and you wouldn't know some of the boys. My second-act costume was a pale blue taffeta silk with shadow lace, and my hat a white straw with blue velvet and pink roses. The dress was Mrs. Bemis's, and the hat from Forbes and Wallace. My third-act costume was a blue mescaline evening dress with opalescent trimming and crystal fringe. Oh, it was one dream, really. My fourth-act costume was a navy blue silk suit with black fur, and Edna's white satin hat with black fur and a pink rose. The Phi Gamma crowd sent the girls a big bunch of violets with pink roses. Sherman suddenly appeared to take me home when I thought he was at college. I shall never forget that night of the play. It was just wonderful, and such a fine crowd of fellows and girls too.

> I found it quite humorous that Marian only mentions her costumes and nothing about the meaning of the play.

Saturday, April 10, 1915 • Springfield, Massachusetts

The play again to as fine an audience as last night. It poured rain but luckily father and I were picked up by a taxi. It went off just as well tonight. I'm so thankful that I didn't have to be prompted.

Wednesday, April 14, 1915 • Springfield, Massachusetts

Report cards! And I got A's in everything but math in which I drew a B. I was really surprised. At three o'clock, I had my graduation pictures taken at Colliers Photo Studio. Sherman Ellis was at the house when I got home. We popped corn and fooled around generally. In the evening, I went to the theatre with friends. We had a college ice afterwards at Thompson's Restaurant, and a ride in an auto. We got home about twelve o'clock on a school night!!!

Friday, April 16, 1915 • Springfield, Massachusetts

In the evening, there was a dance at James "Jimmy" Doherty's and more fun than ever. The Doherty house is as large as a country club with the enormous big living house and a piazza running all around the house. There was a wonderful crowd there — 15 couples of high school people from Kappa Phi and Phi Gamma girls, ADS, and Gamma fellows. We had stunning programs with all the names of the dances and the music to be played printed inside. And, the eats! Punch all the time and the dining room table just loaded with every kind of candy, nuts, and fancy cakes imaginable. At intermission, we had coffee mousse with marshmallow whip and cherries, and fancy cakes. I had a circus dancing. The dance ended at one o'clock. Then, I came home in the auto. Some time!!!!

I have received the College Club Scholarship for $200. It really seems too good to be true. $200 is a fine big start toward college at Mt. Holyoke. Mother and Father are as glad as I am.

> It was not an easy task for a woman to go to college 100 years ago and one that Marian could only dream about. Since it was presumed that women would become homemakers, a college education was perceived as unnecessary. Women worked until they got married, and then they never worked again. For motivated, intelligent young women, timing was everything. Opportunities to attend college were finally beginning to open up. Though neither of Marian's parents had gone to college, they supported her quest for higher education when many families did not.
>
> The numbers tell the story. In 1900, when the population of the United States was 76 million, only 5,237 women in America graduated from college. By 1920, that number had increased more than threefold, still only 16,642 women graduated from college. In contrast, in 2010, 943,264 women in America graduated from college, 180 times more than those who did in 1900. (Department of Education National Center for Educational Statistics) Over the corresponding period, the population of the United States increased to 290 million, almost four times what it was in 1900.

Thus, Marian had the confidence and support to tackle uncharted territory. She was the epitome of the "New Woman," striving to become independent, educated, and equal to men. Her close, loving relationship with her parents would provide a strong foundation in the years to come.

Moreover, Marian's family did not have the financial means to pay for her college education. Receiving this scholarship was life altering for my grandmother. Without the generosity of the College Club Scholarship, Marian would not have been unable to attend Mount Holyoke College. The College Club scholarship was the first stepping-stone on her journey to get an education and become an English teacher.

May 3 to May 6, 1915 • E. Granby, Connecticut

I spent the first part of my vacation at Grandma Clark's. Mother went down, too. I had the funniest experience Wednesday night. We all went to the church to hear an illustrated lecture on the Canadian Rockies. The man who was to give the lecture was the former minister of the town and the preacher who married mother and father. I love the audiences in a country church, and I love the funny little kerosene lamps. When the time came for the man to begin, the janitor creaked down the center aisle and blew out the kerosene lamps. All went well for about three views until the lantern absolutely refused to work, and the pictures thrown on the screen were dim and hazy. No repeated efforts could make the lantern work, so the audience departed for their homes to convene a week later when a new lantern was to be supplied.

Friday, May 7, 1915 • Springfield, Massachusetts

We received news tonight in the paper of the sinking of the Lusitania by German submarine's torpedoes. Over 1,000 persons drowned. The ship sank in about 20 minutes. Will war result for us? No one knows, but everyone has implicit confidence in our splendid president, Woodrow Wilson, the greatest, many believe, since Lincoln.

Marian, along with most Americans, was concerned about the Lusitania incident and whether it would be the catalyst to draw America into the war. Woodrow Wilson, the twenty-eighth president of the United States from 1913-1921, was elected on a campaign to stay out of the war. Wilson continually tried mediation and protested strongly against the Germans. (Wilson's Secretary of State, William Jennings Bryan, a pacifist, resigned when America decided to enter the war.)

Unbeknownst to most Americans, the Lusitania was secretly subsidized by the British Admiralty with the understanding that at the outbreak of war the ship would be appropriated for service. In 1913, as war loomed on the horizon, the Lusitania was fitted for war service with ammunition magazines and gun mounts. On May 1, 1915, the ship departed from New York City bound for Liverpool, England, with a hidden cargo of munitions and contraband to aid the British war effort. On May 7th, at 2:10 p.m., off the coast of Ireland, a German U 20 submarine hit the Lusitania. Within 18 minutes, the giant ship slipped beneath the sea. The sinking of the Lusitania killed more than 1,000 passengers, including 124 Americans.

Many Americans believed Woodrow Wilson was one of the greatest presidents since Lincoln. Marian and her family had confidence that he would do the right thing for America and they placed their trust in his decisions. Wilson proved himself to be a leader, scholar, educator, and a man of peace. Prior to becoming President of the U.S. he was the Governor of New Jersey (1911-1913) and the 13th President of Princeton University (1902-1910). He initiated progressive legislation, including the Federal Reserve Act (1913) which created a centralized banking system that issued notes, paving the way for the Liberty Loans in the future. As an enthusiastic orator, he was the first president to "personally deliver what is known today as the "State of the Union Address" (www.woodrowwilson.org) and he held regular news conferences.

But, Wilson's greatest challenges would lie ahead in the years to come in his role as an international peace negotiator. Out of necessity, President Wilson would be the first President to "cross the Atlantic Ocean while in office." (ibid)

Tuesday, May 11, 1915 • Mount Holyoke

The Springfield Club at Mt. Holyoke College invited all the girls from Springfield who are coming up next year to spend the afternoon of the eleventh at the college as the club's guests. Five of us went up on the 20-minutes-of-three trolley car from Court Square. We had a lovely ride up, and a big crowd of the girls met us at the gate. I knew most of the girls. They took us all over the grounds and buildings. Late in the afternoon, we had a feed in a freshman's room — strawberry ice cream and cookies. The girls sang songs of welcome to the class of 1919. We left for home about six o'clock. I simply love Mt. Holyoke and can't wait to get there.

> Thanks to the scholarship, Marian was on the way to fulfilling one of her lifelong dreams: attending college. Most important, she was going to a highly selective, nondenominational, liberal arts college for women in the Ivy League. Mount Holyoke College is located in South Hadley, Massachusetts about 15 miles from Marian's home, not too far away from her parents.

Saturday, May 15, 1915 • Springfield, Massachusetts

Cousins Martha and Mabel were here to lunch. Cousin Martha has always had such a hard life and yet is so brave and sweet, not a bit embittered. I really think troubles are good for people. They just force you to search into your soul for something finer and deeper to take the place of what you have lost.

Monday, May 17, 1915 • Springfield, Massachusetts

Asked to Class Day! Such excitement after class this morning! Dick B. asked me to our Class Day upon Mt. Tom State Reservation in Holyoke, MASS. Think what fun. I'm simply so happy that I'm walking on air. In the afternoon, the Pierides Debate Club held their annual prize debate in the Woman's Club House. The subject was "Resolved that there should be a legal wage for women in the U.S." Alice won Prize No. 1, and Priscilla Prize No. 2. They were $20 and $10. Last year I got the $20 prize. This year, I presided as president.

Tuesday, May 18, 1915 • Springfield, Massachusetts

I'm very, very, very, happy today. In morning assembly Mr. Hill announced the Honor Pupils for the four years. I was one, and I am so pleased. There were four girls and ten boys on the list. The girls were Priscilla Spaulding, Beatrice Putney, Ruth S., and myself. Father and mother are so happy!!

Wednesday, May 26, 1915 • Springfield, Massachusetts

Most of the Pierides Club ushered at the auditorium at the big meeting of the Equal Suffrage League. We all wore yellow daffodils and dressed in white. Dr. Anna Howard Shaw spoke. She was well worth hearing and very winning.

> At the time she attended the meeting of the Equal Suffrage League, Marian was an honor student preparing go to Mount Holyoke College. Yet, in an era when woman were entering the workforce and attending college in greater numbers, there was still one thing that they could not do: VOTE. As more women began to serve their country during World War I, they felt that they deserved more rights at home. While it seems self-evident to us today that women deserve the right to vote, Marian and her friends were taking a courageous stand. By the standards of her day, she was considered what we call today a feminist because she believed in equal rights for women.

> I doubt that my grandmother would have ever used the word "feminist" to describe herself in 1915. But, according to the definition — "an advocate of women's rights on the grounds of political, social, and economic equality to men" — Marian was on the cusp of embracing feminism. Until I read her diaries, I never knew how much she struggled internally during her formative years to find her place as a "New Woman" in her society. I never imagined that my grandmother was uncomfortable with the traditional female roles because I never saw her drive a car, wear anything but a dress, or speak much about her teaching career. Rather, I saw her in the more traditional role of mother and grandmother, cooking and taking care of their house, her husband and my dad, her only child. I had no idea how important it had been to her to be able to combine her roles as a mother, wife, and professional teacher. By the time I knew my grandmother, her goals had been achieved.

Dr. Shaw who spoke that night devoted her life to working for women's suffrage after meeting Susan B. Anthony in 1888. Dr. Shaw was an ordained minister, physician, temperance lecturer, women's suffrage orator, and peace advocate. She was president of the National American Woman Suffrage Association from 1904-1915. When she spoke at the meeting of the Equal Suffrage League in Springfield, the suffrage movement had picked up momentum by bringing working women into the fold. Marian proudly wore the official suffrage colors to the meeting, carrying yellow daffodils and dressing in white, in support of the cause.

In order to give women the right to vote, the United States Constitution had to be amended and each state had to ratify the amendment. Thus, the campaigns in the states were crucial to the overall success of the national Constitutional Amendment. The Northeast, where Marian lived, was the most resistant region to the suffrage movement due to the opposition of the liquor industry and the urban machine. The Temperance Movement often went hand in glove with the Women's Anti-Suffrage Movement.

Much of the anti-suffrage movement was supported by the liquor industry, as opposition to liquor emerged as a woman's issue. The liquor industry felt that women wanted the right to vote in order to ban the sale of alcohol. The urban machine politicians distrusted women whom they associated with reform movements. Ultimately, prohibition became law in 1919 about the same time as women gained the vote.

The efforts of suffragette leaders, such as the Reverend Dr. Anna Howard Shaw, contributed to the eventual passing in 1920 of the 19th Amendment, nicknamed the Anthony Amendment, which stated: "The rights of citizens of the United States to vote shall not be denied or abridged by the United States or by any state on account of sex."

The following poem is from an earlier, lesser known feminist, Katie Field (1838-1896). She was one of the first female reporters at the New York Tribune and the New York Herald and an unorthodox crusader of social causes.

"Woman's Sphere"

"They talk about a woman's sphere
As though it had a limit:
There's not a place in earth or heaven,
There's not a task to mankind given,
There's not a blessing or a woe,
There's not a whispered yes or no,
There's not a life, or death, or birth,
That has a feather's weight of worth,
Without a woman in it."

Katie Field

Thank you, Grandma, for doing your part to help us earn the right to vote. I am so proud of you for taking a stand for women.

Thursday, May 27, 1915 • Springfield, Massachusetts

The most insulting piece came out in the paper this morning against high school frats and sororities. They called the girls snobs and said that they went on joy rides late at night with frat fellows. They said that the boys' meetings were regular "booze parties." The School Committee threatens to kill all frats and sororities. We were forced to sign a paper in school saying whether or not we belonged to a sorority or fraternity.

Friday, June 4, 1915 • Springfield, Massachusetts

Before Phi Gamma final initiation, I gave a tutoring lesson. I'm so pleased that I have a tutoring job. I tutor Raymond in Latin and Caesar for 50 cents an hour. It is a three-week job. Programs for Class Day were given out at school today. Class Day is tomorrow. I can't wait. "Dot" composed the song, which is printed on the program; it's really clever. Rah! Rah! Rah 1915.

Saturday, June 5, 1915 • Class Day

I've been looking forward to Class Day for so many weeks that it didn't seem possible when it really arrived. Dick B. came up after me about 12.30 pm. We rode down to Court Square in the autobus. There wasn't much of a crowd when we got down there, as it was a bit early. Soon, however, people began to gather, and at one o'clock, our special car left Court Square for Mt. Tom. Our crowd got the seats that faced each other up front.

At the foot of the mountain, we took the cable car. Some of us rode on the platform in front. It's somewhat terrifying to look up the track and see how steep it is. When we got up to the top, we checked our lunch and other belongings at the mountain house and just fooled around until time for exercises.

At 3.30 pm, we all assembled in the auditorium of the mountain house. Dick B. opened the program with the president's address. Then we had the class oration, which really was splendid, followed with the class poem, which was so good that I can't wait to see it in print to read it again. Then, there was the prophecy. I helped write that prophecy, so I was a bit anxious to see how it would go over. It really took better than I had hoped. Beatrice Putney's class history was splendid. Then the junior class presented a gift, which Dick B. accepted. The gift was a painting. We, in turn, give it to the school. Our class song at the end, which everyone sang, was very well received.

Isn't 1915 wonderful, dear memory book?

From the end of exercises until suppertime, we just wandered around. The boys took piles of pictures on the rock. I'm just crazy to see them. About six o'clock we took our supper down into the woods below the Mountain House. After supper, we sat out on the rocks and watched the wonderful, wonderful sunset. Then it began to grow dark on the mountain, and the lights began to twinkle down below. At seven o'clock, the musicians arrived, the Society Six Banjo Orchestra. We danced until nine pm, 10 dances. I had a fine program and danced with Malcolm, Jimmy, and Dick B.

It was over all too soon, and we were descending the mountain to catch the last car down to Mountain Park. Oh, we had such fun going home, singing, eating, and cheering. We sang, "I've Been Working on the Railroad," "Dear Eveline," "Goodbye Girls," again and again. And, not least of all, we sang our (class) song.

When we stopped in Holyoke we cheered different people: Dr. Saw, Mr. Hill (Principal), Mrs. Hill, and all the teachers. Donald and Beatrice had stuck together so persistently all day that we could not refrain from cheering the combination. And since this is just between you and me, dear memory book, I will say that they cheered Dick B. and me. It simply thrilled me through and through. I don't mean that they coupled the names together. No indeed, that wouldn't be in the least appropriate.

When we got into the city, Dick B. and I got off to get something more to eat. Wasn't that the limit? I had chocolate ice cream soda with strawberries in it and whipped cream. We got home about 11.30 pm.

It was a wonderful Class Day.

> In 2008, as I toured the Mt. Tom State Reservation, I envisioned Marian and her classmates enjoying their Class Day celebration. The natural beauty of the park remains intact with views of the Connecticut Valley, the Berkshire Mountains to the west, and the rock formations.
>
> In 1897, the Mt. Tom Railroad was constructed to connect with the streetcars of the cities, such as Holyoke and Springfield. An electric cable-trolley train would take passengers from the Lower Station to the Upper Station on the top of Mt. Tom where there was an observation deck with telescopes, a pavilion, and the Summit House. The Summit House was built in 1901 by the Holyoke Street Railway and stood four stories tall with a large observation room. The ivy-covered-ceiling dining hall seated 300 people. Unfortunately, in 1929, the Summit House was destroyed by fire.

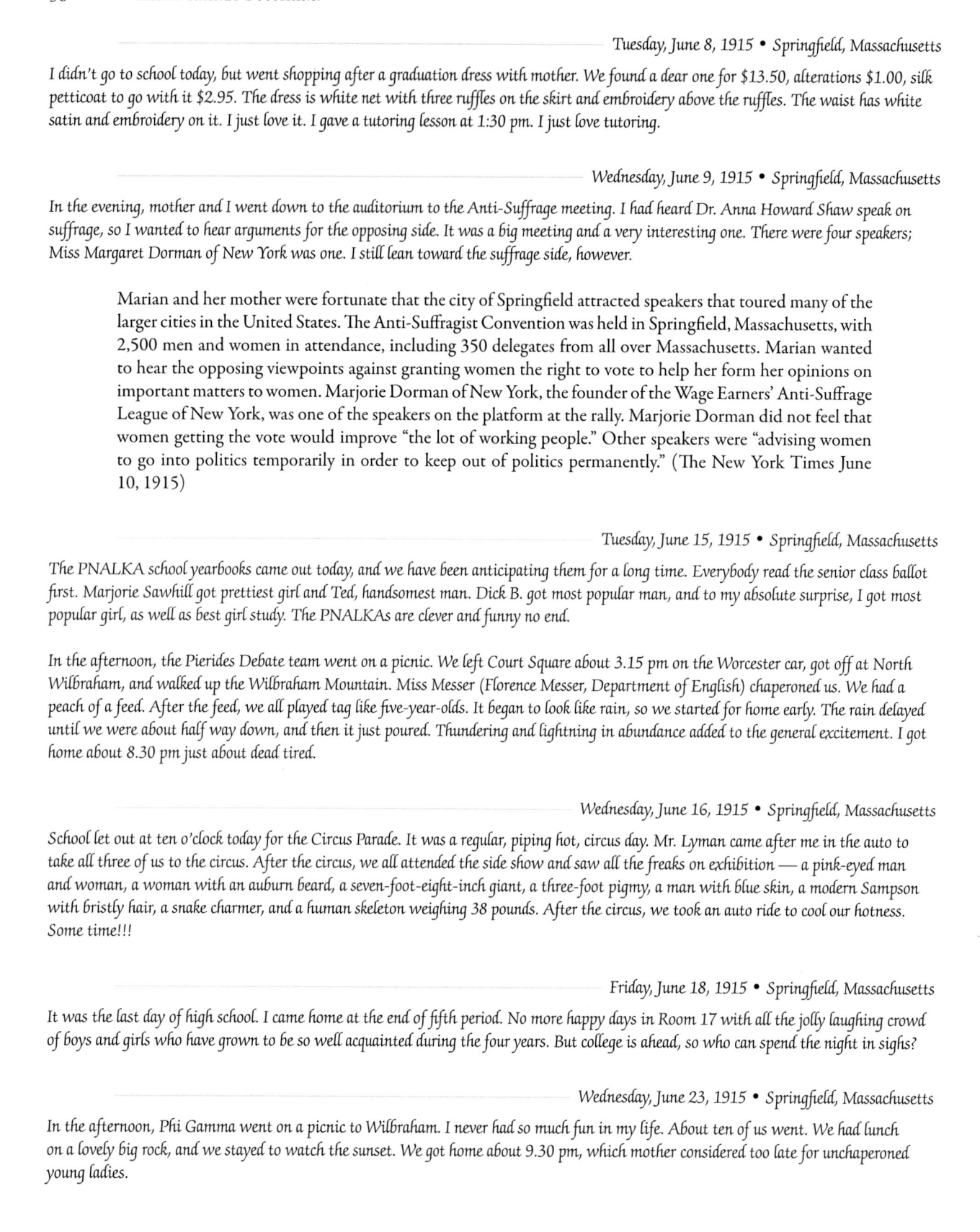

Tuesday, June 8, 1915 • Springfield, Massachusetts

I didn't go to school today, but went shopping after a graduation dress with mother. We found a dear one for $13.50, alterations $1.00, silk petticoat to go with it $2.95. The dress is white net with three ruffles on the skirt and embroidery above the ruffles. The waist has white satin and embroidery on it. I just love it. I gave a tutoring lesson at 1:30 pm. I just love tutoring.

Wednesday, June 9, 1915 • Springfield, Massachusetts

In the evening, mother and I went down to the auditorium to the Anti-Suffrage meeting. I had heard Dr. Anna Howard Shaw speak on suffrage, so I wanted to hear arguments for the opposing side. It was a big meeting and a very interesting one. There were four speakers; Miss Margaret Dorman of New York was one. I still lean toward the suffrage side, however.

> Marian and her mother were fortunate that the city of Springfield attracted speakers that toured many of the larger cities in the United States. The Anti-Suffragist Convention was held in Springfield, Massachusetts, with 2,500 men and women in attendance, including 350 delegates from all over Massachusetts. Marian wanted to hear the opposing viewpoints against granting women the right to vote to help her form her opinions on important matters to women. Marjorie Dorman of New York, the founder of the Wage Earners' Anti-Suffrage League of New York, was one of the speakers on the platform at the rally. Marjorie Dorman did not feel that women getting the vote would improve "the lot of working people." Other speakers were "advising women to go into politics temporarily in order to keep out of politics permanently." (The New York Times June 10, 1915)

Tuesday, June 15, 1915 • Springfield, Massachusetts

The PNALKA school yearbooks came out today, and we have been anticipating them for a long time. Everybody read the senior class ballot first. Marjorie Sawhill got prettiest girl and Ted, handsomest man. Dick B. got most popular man, and to my absolute surprise, I got most popular girl, as well as best girl study. The PNALKAs are clever and funny no end.

In the afternoon, the Pierides Debate team went on a picnic. We left Court Square about 3.15 pm on the Worcester car, got off at North Wilbraham, and walked up the Wilbraham Mountain. Miss Messer (Florence Messer, Department of English) chaperoned us. We had a peach of a feed. After the feed, we all played tag like five-year-olds. It began to look like rain, so we started for home early. The rain delayed until we were about half way down, and then it just poured. Thundering and lightning in abundance added to the general excitement. I got home about 8.30 pm just about dead tired.

Wednesday, June 16, 1915 • Springfield, Massachusetts

School let out at ten o'clock today for the Circus Parade. It was a regular, piping hot, circus day. Mr. Lyman came after me in the auto to take all three of us to the circus. After the circus, we all attended the side show and saw all the freaks on exhibition — a pink-eyed man and woman, a woman with an auburn beard, a seven-foot-eight-inch giant, a three-foot pigmy, a man with blue skin, a modern Sampson with bristly hair, a snake charmer, and a human skeleton weighing 38 pounds. After the circus, we took an auto ride to cool our hotness. Some time!!!

Friday, June 18, 1915 • Springfield, Massachusetts

It was the last day of high school. I came home at the end of fifth period. No more happy days in Room 17 with all the jolly laughing crowd of boys and girls who have grown to be so well acquainted during the four years. But college is ahead, so who can spend the night in sighs?

Wednesday, June 23, 1915 • Springfield, Massachusetts

In the afternoon, Phi Gamma went on a picnic to Wilbraham. I never had so much fun in my life. About ten of us went. We had lunch on a lovely big rock, and we stayed to watch the sunset. We got home about 9.30 pm, which mother considered too late for unchaperoned young ladies.

Thursday, June 24, 1915 • Springfield, Massachusetts

My graduation day! We had a rehearsal in the morning at the auditorium and practiced marching and receiving diplomas. Central High School marches first; then, Commercial High School; then, Tech High School. Grandma Clark and Theo came on the noon train. Right after lunch, I got dressed. My dress is very dainty; it is white embroidered net and white satin. Mrs. Bemis took us down in her lovely big car.

We began our march from down in the basement at 2.30 pm. The auditorium was crowded with people. It really was very solemn marching down that aisle to the slow beat of the music. The exercises were lovely. Miss Woolley (Mary Emma Woolley, Mt. Holyoke President) spoke. The C.H.S. chorus sang, the orchestra played, and our diplomas were presented to us. That took a long time. Dr. Seelye, President Emeritus of Smith, performed the religious part of the service. Then, we marched out while the audience remained seated.

Mrs. Bemis took us home in her car. I had not been home long before some flowers came in a great big box. I was so excited! I opened them. They were beautiful white sweet peas, and in the center a wonderful big pale lavender orchid. And the card, which was enclosed, said "Best wishes and Congratulations from Jack (Sawhill)." You can imagine how completely surprised I was. We had a kind of birthday graduation supper and strawberry ice cream. It is very near Grandma's (Myra Smith Clark born 6.26.1846) 69th birthday, and it is my graduation day.

Mrs. Bemis (Driving), **Gertrude Viets** (Rear Right)

This was the first of many speeches by Miss Woolley that Marian would hear the years to come. At Mount Holyoke, Marian would devour every word that Miss Woolley preached at vespers on alternating Sunday evenings. Her dynamic personality and the depth of her messages touched Marian's heart. Marian grew to idolize and respect Miss Woolley over the next four years.

Friday, June 25, 1915 • E. Granby, Connecticut

In the afternoon, mother and I went to East Granby with Grandma Clark and Aunt Theo.

Sunday, June 27, 1915 • E. Granby, Connecticut

Such a quiet day in the country. In the morning, everyone went to church except Grandpa Clark and me. He rested while I read some of Quincy Adams Sawyer. (Pidgin)

In the late afternoon, I went down to be with Grandpa. We went up onto the mountain after the cows. We picked black eyed Susan's and wild roses while we were up there. The view was wonderful. Grandpa is the finest old man. I would like to put him in a book. There are so many fine people I should like to put in a book, but I know that I never can. No! That sounds discouraged. I would rather say I fear that I never can. And, yet perhaps, how I should love to write, just write down things as I see them. But, I am only seventeen now. It is a queer thing, but I don't feel seventeen. I feel older than that. I couldn't say a definite age, just older. I'm glad that I'm going to college in the fall. I know that something will be there that was never at high school – something that I have always found lacking at high school, something bigger, broader, more vast. Yes, I'm glad that I'm through high school. I wouldn't be back even a month, and surely not a year. Although this last year has been full of many, many things that have been splendid. I do not even hate to leave the girls, for I will meet new girls – I really can't wait to meet those new girls. I know that there will be many at Mt. Holyoke who will measure up to my ideal of what a girl should be. I have not found my ideal yet. How I would love to measure up to my ideal self. I am not there yet by any means. It is the little thoughtless things I do that disgust me so. I feel that my intentions are always good but what of intentions, if the power to carry them out is not present.

How I have rambled on. There is not a place for this sort of thing in a Memory Book, and yet what I have said is a memory of my thoughts at this time. Probably in the future, such ideas as these may seem very foolish indeed. I must stop now for I could wonder on over the pages that remain in the book and even beyond, perhaps.

Even at the very early age of 17, Marian was already dreaming about writing a book about all the fine people she knew in her life. Her family motivated her to follow her passion. She wrote this quote by Thoreau into her diary as a reminder of the amount of devotion it would take to accomplish her goal:

"To read well, that is, to read true books in a true spirit, is a noble exercise, and one that will tax the reader more than any exercise which the customs of the day esteem. It requires a training such as the athletes underwent, the steady intention almost of the whole life to this object. Books must be read as deliberately and reservedly as they were written."

Thoreau

July 2 to July 16, 1915 • Springfield, Massachusetts

I took care of Richard, an adorable little three-year-old. I went over every morning at 8.30 am and stayed until about six o'clock. Two nights, I stayed all night when his parents were gone in the evening. I got $3 per week and was very happy with my $10, which will go for clothes at college.

Sunday, July 10, 1915 • Mount Holyoke

Father, Mother, and I went up to Mt. Holyoke College today and took our lunch. We ate lunch up on Prospect Hill and afterwards walked around the campus. How I love it there!!!

July 22 to August 1, 1915 • E. Granby, Connecticut

I spent a little over a week down at Grandmother Clark's farm. Mother was there with me the last part of the time. One day we went up to Aunt Theo's for the afternoon and supper. The rest of the time at Grandma's I spent mostly reading, eating, and sleeping!

Thursday, August 12, 1915 • Nantasket Beach

Such a glorious time as we had today! At seven o'clock in the morning, we started for Boston by auto with the Coe's and Miss Piper. We had a lovely surprise when down at State and Main we also added Mrs. Woodin to our party. We didn't make a single stop with the exception of a few minutes at Worcester, MASS. We had a lovely luncheon at Nantasket Beach in Hull, MASS. It seemed so good to see the dear old ocean again, the rocks and lighthouses, etc. We didn't leave the beach until about four o'clock in the afternoon. Then, we left Miss Piper with some friends in South Weymouth, MASS. Coming home was the exciting part.

All was well until after we reached Worcester where we had supper. After leaving Worcester and heading for Palmer, we became hopelessly lost. We landed in the small towns of Ware and Thorndike, and other places not supposed to be included in the route. Finally, we got into a seemingly endless woodsy road. We didn't meet a soul of whom to inquire the direction. In the midst of all our bewilderment, our lights went out on the front of the car. We were able to revive them only to flickers. Finally, we stopped at a farmhouse. Mr. Coe got out and knocked on the door. A man appeared at the door in his "robe de nuit." "We're lost," announced Mr. Coe. After many inquiries, it was found that we must go back over the same road in order to strike the right one. We reached home finally about midnight in the midst of a pouring rain.

Tuesday, August 31, 1915 • Springfield, Massachusetts

Mr. Coe came up to dinner. After dinner in the evening, we all went down to Riverside Park along the Connecticut River, in his car. There was dancing as usual in the huge open pavilion. Mr. Coe and I danced eight times together. He is a wonderful dancer and taught me all the new steps. We got home after eleven. Such fun.

This was the last entry Marian recorded in her first diary. Her writing improved as senior year progressed. Even as I read this first diary, I was struck by the changes going on in her young life, as she experienced her first crush, considered both sides of the suffrage debate, dealt with difficult economic times at home, and instinctively sensed that "something was missing in high school." If ever a person could make lemonade out of lemons, it was my grandmother. She found "joy of joys" in the smallest things, firmly turned her back on disappointments, and saw beauty everywhere she looked. Her sense of curiosity and desire to absorb knowledge were already well established. As she moved toward the next stage of her education, she could not know what awaited her, but she was prepared for what would surely be a great adventure.

CHAPTER TWO

DEMON WAR

"Under the Harvest Moon"

"Last year the harvest moon looked down
On bounteous fields of grain
A peaceful scene where lovers strolled
Along the shady lane.

In happy homes the mothers sang
Their evening lullaby,
And little children had no fear
Of danger lurking nigh.

But now the demon war is loosed
And terrors fill the night,
The dangers of the burning home,
The dangers of the flight.

Mothers and children hide and wait,
They listen, fear, and pray,
While shells are bursting all around
And armies pass their way.

Tonight upon the harvest field
The moon is shining bright.
Where soldier forms lie mute and still,
With faces ghastly white.

O what a reaping. O what loss!
The flowers of earth cut down, -
The voice of mourning in the field
And by the ruined town!"

Alma Pendexter Hayden

Far away from the bursting shells, terrors, and dangers during "the war to end all wars" in Europe, Marian and her family learned about the effects of the war through poetry, newspapers, films, posters, word of mouth, lectures at Mount Holyoke College, and books from the safety and tranquility of their home. In America, discussions about the "Great War" were taking place on front porches, dinner tables, and anywhere neighbors and friends gathered. Without television or radio, information was confusing; making the decision to serve even more difficult for some.

While Marian was concentrating on her studies in college, many young American men felt the call to serve in an unofficial capacity. My grandfather, Howard Rainey, and his generation, would bear the responsibility to provide soldiers, if America officially entered the war in the future. Howard was born in 1895 in the small river town of Hudson, New York to adoring parents, Ida and Samuel Mitchell Rainey. Howard was one of many conscientious young men wanting to do the right thing for both his family and his country. The allure of an adventure "across the pond" was tempting. But, the decision to serve in a war America had not officially entered yet could wreak havoc in his family.

Howard and Mother, Ida

In the summer of 1915, Howard and his mother, Ida, sat in their hammock relaxing on the front porch of their beautiful two-story Victorian house at 426 Allen St. in the quaint river town of Hudson, New York, struggling with the confusing and overwhelming decision about the war that resurfaced more and more those days. In the photo albums I found in the treasure boxes in my basement, there is a particular photograph of the Rainey's peaceful life in Hudson, New York, worlds away from the war that had been going on overseas. Howard was looking intently at the camera that his father, Samuel Mitchell Rainey, was holding, while Ida was staring at her son, the apple of her eye. Howard wanted to enlist but he was not sure in what capacity. He knew the worries and pain war would bring upon his mother made it overwhelming for Howard to consider signing up at this time. He loved his family with all of his heart. Howard knew the time was not right yet.

Howard's mother was not alone in her time of sorrow lamenting the thought of sending her only son off to war. The President of the National American Woman Suffrage Association, Dr. Anna Howard Shaw (1904 to 1915), gave a particular speech at the Proceedings of the American Arbitration and Peace Congress convention in 1907 where she said that women need to vote to have arbitration at the ballot box. And if they can vote, "women will think twice before they vote their sons to death."

As more of Howard's friends unofficially enlisted, he considered his responsibilities more often. Should Howard enlist in the army and go to Europe as a soldier on the front or return to school at Pawling Prep and graduate? There were more questions than answers. Each time Howard brought the subject up; he knew it would stir up very difficult emotions for his parents, especially his mother. Howard was not only their only son, but also their only child; his parents lost twin sons, Robert Mitchell and Samuel Miles, born on August 4, 1898, in infancy when Howard was only three years old. His brother, Samuel Miles Rainey, died on October 28, 1898 at two and half months old. Three days after Ida's first son died, her family received word from the Army that her brother, Eugene Miles, died on October 31, 1898, in the Spanish American War from Typhoid Fever in Puerto Rico. Then, Ida's other twin son, Robert Mitchell, died on November 9, 1898 at only three months old. Ida lost three people she loved within a time span of fourteen days. I cannot imagine the pain Ida went through. She must have been so brave. The thought of her only son, Howard, going off to war probably seemed unfathomable at this time. Ida knew that it wasn't only the war that was worrisome but the diseases soldiers caught, as her brother did, in poor living conditions. It was risky on several fronts.

The memories of her deceased twin sons and the tragedies of the loss of her brother in a past war were ever present in Ida's mind. Seventeen years ago might seem like a long time but for Ida the pain lingered. When her only brother, Eugene M. Miles, left his job in Hudson to enlist in the Spanish-American War in 1898 as a volunteer engineer, Ida and her family did not think it would lead to his demise. Ida's brother felt the call to serve his country. But, this position required skills that enabled the men to lay streets, erect tents, drain marshes, and construct roads, sinks, waterworks, lighting, and telephone systems and not engage in battle. Eugene was stationed near Coamo, Puerto Rico (American usage: Porto Rico until 1938). His family was sure an engineering position would be less risky than infantry. Puerto Rico was an island they knew little about that seemed like worlds away to them. The Spanish American War was a war between the United States and Spain that resulted from the U.S. intervention in the Cuban War of Independence. The war was fought in both the Caribbean and the Pacific. The war began on April 25, 1898 and ended on August 12, 1898 – lasting only 3 months 2 weeks and 4 days. On August 13th President William McKinley signed an armistice, known as the Treaty of Paris. Spain relinquished sovereignty over Cuba, and ceded Puerto Rico, Guam and the Philippines to the United States for 20 million dollars. (Wikipedia.org) Following the Armistice, Eugene continued to finish engineering projects in Coamo. Unfortunately, Eugene's health took a turn for the worse due to the swampy conditions, and hot and humid weather most Americans from New England were not familiar with. On October 29th, a letter from Eugene's Captain Wm. G. Hauesay to Eugene's father, A. Eugene Miles, arrived at the family home at 454 Allen Street in Hudson, New York which notified his parents that their son "was taken sick with Typhoid Fever in Camp and at first his indisposition appeared to be slight - but as it got worse it was deemed best to send him to the Division Hospital near Coamo on the north. Since being there he has had every attention and care possible in a field hospital including the best nursing by trained nurses. Today his condition has assumed a serious nature." The next fateful letter written two days later announced the sad and painful news that Eugene died at 2 pm on October 31st, 1898. Ida lost her only brother and his parents lost their only son at the young age of 23 years. On March 7th, 1899, Ida's father received word from the Quartermaster General of the U.S. Army that the remains of Corporal Eugene M. Miles, late Co. A. 1st Volunteer Engineers, would arrive in Hudson at the end of the month. Shortly after, in 1900, the U.S. Army scientists discovered that "a common domestic mosquito spread the disease." (www.pbs.org) This discovery was too late for Ida's family. Fewer than 400 soldiers were killed in combat in the Spanish American War while more than 2,000 contracted yellow fever, and 1,500 died from typhoid. Thankfully, today we have vaccines for these diseases.

Eugene M. Miles Spanish American War

Realizing the depths of his mother's grief, Howard made the decision to continue his studies at the private, all-boys Pawling Preparatory School (Pawling, New York) in the Fifth and Sixth Forms, an English term for junior and senior, from 1915 to 1916, until America officially entered the war. The school motto was the "Fighting Gentlemen" which seemed appropriate for my grandfather. He made many great friends and excelled in sports as a "cracking good third baseman, basketball star, and good golfer." The yearbook wrote about Howard in jest: "He has always been noted for his peculiar dislike for anything that looks like work, and he is a charter member of the Sons of Rest. In spite of this morbid propensity to sloth and procrastination, he is one of the best athletes in the school." He was the Leader of the Glee Club, and a member of the Dramatic Club Quartet, while enjoying his passion for music. He was one of the "best singers in the school" according to the yearbook. His nickname was "Lefty." The yearbook accurately described him as I knew him, a man of "inexhaustible good nature." And it was his easy going, good nature that would help him through the tough times ahead, yet could also have a negative side in his life.

The following American anti-war song written by Lyricist Alfred Bryon was a hit in 1915 and its success helped solidify the anti-war movement on the national stage. The irony of war was between different mothers' sons killing each other and that victory was not enough to console any mother for the loss of her son. This song became known in other countries that were already at war, especially Britain and Australia. The Australian Women's Peace Army sang the anti-war song at their demonstrations until it was banned by the Australian government under the Australian War Precautions Act of 1915.

"I Didn't Raise My Boy to be a Soldier"

Ten million soldiers to the war have gone,
Who may never return again.
Ten million mother's hearts must break
For the ones who died in vain.
Head bowed down in sorrow
In her lonely years,
I heard a mother murmur thru' her tears:
I didn't raise my boy to be a soldier,
I brought him up to be my pride and joy.
Who dares to place a musket on his shoulder,
To shoot some other mother's darling boy?
Let nations arbitrate their future troubles,
It's time to lay the sword and gun away.
There'd be no war today,
If mothers all would say,
"I didn't raise my boy to be a soldier."
What victory can cheer a mother's heart,
When she looks at her blighted home?
What victory can bring her back
All she cared to call her own?
Let each mother answer
In the years to be,
Remember that my boy belongs to me!

Byron

In contrast, the following song is one of many parodies of "I Didn't Raise My Boy to Be a Soldier." I was surprised to find a parody included in with my grandmother's paper because she usually seemed so serious about supporting the soldiers.

"I Didn't Raise my Ford to be a Jitney"

Hiram Lord from Wellsboro,
He bought a Ford a week ago,
And he paid for it in reg'lar dough,
Then took a trip to town;
While goin' up the big main street
A man whose nerve could not be beat
Jumped right up into Hi's back seat,
But Hi he slowed right down.
The man said as he held five cents,
"The jitney bus is sure immense."
But Hi his anger was intense
As he turned to him and said,
"Get out! Get out!
I know you hate to walk.
No doubt! No doubt!
But 'tain't no use to talk."

I didn't raise my Ford to be a jitney bus,
So don't humiliate my poor machine;
Henry Ford made walking a pleasure,
But don't take my little treasure
Or I'll run you out of gasoline.
You'd better take the street car right away, sir,
You're the meanest man I've ever seen;
You're in an awful pickle,
Take back your goll darned nickle,
I didn't raise my Ford to be a jitney.

Hiram said, "I'd like to know
Why ev'rybody snickers so
When down the boulevard I go;
They're jealous! I don't care.
A very weary life I've led;
The other day a fellow said,
'Fords go where angels fear to tread,'
That means most anywhere.
One day I cranked to beat the band,
The darn thing slipped out of my hand,
I thought that it would never land,
For it nearly touched the sky.
I'm sad! I'm sad!
I've got a car and so I'm mad! I'm mad!
I want the world to know."

Jack Frost

The war raging in Europe was constantly on Howard's mind. Despite his desire to put his mother's mind at peace, Howard considered enrolling in the preparedness training camps funded by pro-Allied Americans during the summer of 1916. The month-long camps trained Army officers in various cities, including nearby Plattsburg, New York. There Howard would have learned basic training such as how to shoot and march. Still, he knew there would be too much danger for an officer on the front line. Howard decided not to attend preparedness training; this was a welcome relief for his mother. In 1916, Howard graduated in the Sixth Form from Pawling Prep at 20 years old and continued his studies at Union College in Schenectady, New York.

Howard kept in contact with his Pawling classmates; however, it would be on the Western Front. Two of his friends decided to join the unofficial war effort, driving ambulances for the American Field Service (AFS) prior to America officially entering the war: Jack (John) Lummis (1913 Pawling Fifth Form) and Phil Carter (1915 Pawling Fourth Form). Phil was the captain of the Pawling golf team, which Howard played on, and a successful amateur golfer. Phil took time off from golf tournaments to voluntarily enlist in the AFS.

Pawling Preparatory School Golf Team 1915

Thousands of American men volunteered to support Allies in Europe in a variety of capacities before America declared war in 1917. The American Red Cross and the AFS both established ambulance units. Red Cross ambulance units worked in France and Italy under the command of the French or Italian armies. By "the spring of 1917, it had forty-six ambulance units supporting the Allies." (history.amedd.army.mil) One particular Red Cross ambulance driver in France, named Ernest Hemingway, volunteered to serve before the official American war effort. Later, he was transferred to the Italian front and was the first American wounded in Italy. Hemingway later wrote about his adventures in his book *Farewell to Arms* (Hemingway). The largest volunteer ambulance group belonged to the AFS. By May of 1915, the AFS was operating "60 ambulances organized in 3 sections; by late 1917 it had 1,220 ambulances in 31 sections supporting 66 French divisions" (ibid) "These volunteer ambulance units "refined motorized evacuation techniques that were later adopted by the U. S. Army when it entered the war." (ibid)

Howard cut this poem by Alan Seeger out of the newspaper and stuck it in with his World War I letters. I doubt he shared this poem with his mother because of its solemn nature. Seeger graduated from Harvard in 1910 and lived a bohemian lifestyle in New York where he wrote his poetry. In 1914, he volunteered with the French Foreign Legion for two years; "as an American citizen he could not join the French military, so he did the next best thing and joined the Legion, since the United States had not yet entered the war against the Central Powers." (www.english.emory.edu) Alan Seeger was the uncle of American folk singer Pete Seeger (1919-2014), and a classmate of T. S. Eliot at Harvard. (Wikipedia.org)

"I Have a Rendezvous with Death"

I have a rendezvous with Death
At some disputed barricade,
When Spring comes back with rustling shade
And apple-blossoms fill the air-
I have a rendezvous with Death
When Spring brings back blue days and fair.
It may be he shall take my hand
And lead me into his dark land
And close my eyes and quench my breath-
It may be I shall pass him still.
I have a rendezvous with Death
On some scarred slope of battered hill,
When Spring comes round again this year
And the first meadow flowers appear.
God knows 'twere better to be deep
Pillowed in silk and scented down,
Where love throbs out in blissful sleep,
Pulse night to pulse, and breath to breath,
Where hushed awakenings are dear…
But I've a rendezvous with Death
At midnight in some flaming town,
When Spring trips north again this year,
And I to my pledged word am true,
I shall not fail that rendezvous.

Alan Seeger

Unfortunately, on July 4, 1916, Seeger's premonition in his poem became a reality and he had a rendezvous with death at Belloy-en-Santerre, France. His poems were not published until 1917, a year after his death. A statute modeled after Seeger is found on the monument honoring fallen Americans who volunteered for France during the war, located at the Place des Etats-Unis, Paris. Seeger is sometimes called the "American Rupert Brooke" (Wikipedia.org) I sure hope Howard wasn't content with a possible rendezvous with death if America entered the Great War.

Howard's Paternal Family Tree

A very deep family legacy rested on Howard's shoulders to honor his paternal grandmother, Helen Mitchell Rainey, and all that her family had done in many different ways to make America a better place for their families. It is a complicated yet very interesting family tree. I followed the paper trail for over 300 years back to Howard's nine times grandfathers, John Howland and John Tilley, who firmly and proudly planted the roots of the beginning of our family tree on Plymouth Hill in Plymouth, Massachusetts at the site of the Pilgrim's first watch tower in 1620. It is here that the early settlers rest that were heroes of the Revolution and other wars. It is here that our family tree would grow rapidly and broadly, expanding in many different directions, adding new branches. From this trunk another branch on the family tree grew, Howard's eight times grandfathers, Thomas Macy and Tristam Coffin, who were among the original proprietors of a magical Faraway Island, known as Nantucket Island, off the south coast of Cape Cod. The next generation, Howard's seven times grandparents, the Mitchells, formed another branch on this growing and expanding, and somewhat confusing, yet important and strong family tree.

From the meticulous family records and papers my father left behind, I sensed how important it was to our family to know where we came from and all that our ancestors fought for in their country. My grandfather, Howard's life was defined by his past. Our family members were survivors. From the Pilgrims John Howland and John Tilley on the Mayflower in 1620 who sons fought in King Philip's War, to the whalers on a Faraway Island called Nantucket Island, and to Howard's great uncles who fought in the Civil War hailing from Hudson, New York in 1861, Howard honored his relatives and knew the details of the depths of their struggles and accomplishments, and they influenced his opinions about fighting in World War I in his own future.

As I began my journey searching through the extensive documents of our family tree, I was struck by many differences between my life and theirs. First of all, my relatives had many children in their families. Sometimes there were as many as 13 children in a family, usually at least ten or eleven. Not all of the children would survive due to diseases and lack of vaccines and medicine. Some children died within the first year, others when they were in their teens. Luckily, I never experienced the personal loss of a child or sibling. But, in such large families, it seemed that at least one or two children passed away before they were old enough to start their own families. I noticed sometimes when one daughter or son would die; a subsequent child would be given the same name of the deceased child in the same family. It seemed strange to me, but maybe it was done to honor the deceased child. Also, many mothers died in childbirth or several years after giving birth. Oftentimes there were two or three mothers on a family tree. When my mother died in 1975 it was an anomaly for the time period. In an odd way, reading the details on paper about all of my relative's losses helped me deal with my own losses and realize that I was not alone. Despite all the years that separated me from these relatives, we had something in common: the will to carry on.

The first generation of Helen Mitchell Rainey's family tree traced back to a young man, John Howland, from the farming community of Fenstanton, Huntingdonshire, England. He wanted to take the adventure of a lifetime to a land across the ocean called North America that not many people knew much about. He signed on as the manservant for Governor Carver. Although John Howland did not seem to be motivated by his religion to make the trip, most others on the Mayflower were. The "Separatists" on the Mayflower were an off shoot of the Puritans. They considered the Church of England beyond reform. Puritans were a group of Protestants that opposed many of the customs of the Church of England in the 16th and 17th centuries.

All of John Howland and Elizabeth Tilley Howland's children had very large families, so the Howland family tree branch expanded quickly. Today there are millions of Americans, famous and not so famous, that descended from this marriage. Among the notables on the Howland side are poets including: Henry Wadsworth Longfellow and Ralph Waldo Emerson, and politicians including Nathanial Gorham, the Bush family, and Franklin Delano Roosevelt and the Baldwin family of actors, according to the John Howland Society. There are many books written about the family lineage but for the purposes of my story, I am only following my family tree, which is confusing enough on its own.

My relatives were very proud to be Mayflower descendants and my father loved to tell us of John Howland's treacherous trip across the ocean in deplorable conditions. A copy of the family membership in the Society of Mayflower Descendants was framed and hung in our family room growing up. The story goes that Howland fell off the Mayflower during a storm and grabbed onto the topsail halyard rope and pulled himself to safety. He should have perished. My father claims that Howland fell overboard because he had too much beer. I wasn't sure when I was young if this was a proud moment in our family history for me or not. I didn't think I wanted to tell the story to my friends that my relative on the Mayflower fell overboard. I later discovered there is actually truth to that story. As the water supply diminished on the boat, beer was safer to drink because its alcohol content killed germs. Howland's physical strength saved his life when he fell overboard and also got him through the first brutal winter in Plymouth in 1620. Due to disease, lack of shelter, and general conditions, 45 immigrants of the original 102 Pilgrims died during the Pilgrim's first horrific winter, including both of Elizabeth Tilley's parents. John Howland was the 13th man to sign the Mayflower Compact "which is considered the first written constitution for a representative government of the people, by the people and for the people." (Wikipedia.org). He was a fur trader, and assisted in making a treaty with the great Indian Sachem Massasoit. In 1624, John Howland married Elizabeth Tilley, an orphan at this time. In the years to come, the couple had ten children and 88 grandchildren.

The Howland sons, part of the second generation, served as officers in the Plymouth Colony Militia which was a requirement for all able bodied men between the ages of 16 and 60, under the direction of Captain Miles Standish. From the beginning of the colonization, Captain Standish set up a small fort with cannons and placed the first houses with maximum defensibility. Captain Standish provided mental strength and training with muskets. The militia befriended the Indian sachem (tribal leader) Massasoit. Howard's relatives were defending their settlement serving in the militia.

During the time period from 1630-1640 approximately 20,000 colonists came to New England in what was termed The Great Migration or the Puritan Migration. In 1629, King Charles I of England dissolved Parliament with no intention of summoning a new one. "With the religious and political climate so hostile and threatening, many Puritans decided to leave the country. (Wikipedia.org) Two of John Howland's brothers, Henry and Arthur, came to New England within the next few years, which I am sure was a welcome sight to see family again.

John and Elizabeth Howland's daughter, Desire Howland Gorham (one of the ten children) married John Gorham. In 1652, they settled on land that John Howland bought or exchanged in Barnstable, Massachusetts on Cape Cod about 30 miles south of Plymouth. John Gorham owned a grist mill and tannery in town. They had 13 children with quite creative names: Desire, Temperance, Elizabeth, James, Lt. Col. John Gorham IV, Joseph Gorham Sr. Ensign (a commissioned officer in the US Navy), Lydia, Hannah, Shubael, Thankful, Isaac, Jabez, and Mercy. Desire's father, John Howland, passed away in 1672/3, the last of the original Pilgrims, leaving his younger wife, Elizabeth, behind before King Philip's War began. After the beginning of the war in 1675, many Plymouth colonials, including Elizabeth, went to safer places, such as Barnstable to stay with family. Elizabeth was fortunate to live with her daughter, two of her other children and some of her grandchildren in Barnstable during this tumultuous time period. Elizabeth's grandchildren included: three Lydias, three Hannahs, three Mercys, two Isaacs and two Shubaels among others. Sadly, John Gorham, a Captain in the Militia during the King Philip's War, died in 1676 from his war wounds.

The King Philip's War, sometimes called the First Indian War, or Metacom's War, arose from a land dispute between the Wampanoag chief, Metacom, the second son of the Wampanoag chief Massasoit, and the settlers in New England. Metacom believed the settlers were encroaching on Wampanoag lands. Up until this time the Pilgrims had peacefully coexisted with his father, Chief Massasoit. The war was considered to be the deadliest war in the history of European settlements in North America in proportion to the population. "In the space of a little more than a year, twelve of the region's towns were destroyed and many more damaged, the colony's economy was all but ruined, and its population was decimated, losing one-tenth of all men available for military service." (Wikipedia.org) The war ended in 1678 with the signing of a treaty called the Treaty of Casco Bay in April 1678.

To honor the early settlers of the colony of Plymouth, the heroes of the Revolution and of later wars, and the men who went down to the sea in ships, the Burial Hill sits "165 feet above the sea level, and rises abruptly just back of the town's busiest thoroughfare. It is irregular in form and contains about eight acres." (Perkins) From this elevation the visitor "has the splendid panorama of ocean and country. Nestling at his feet, between the hill and the sea, are the thickly clustering roofs of the old town. Turning his eyes northward, he sees in the far distance the villages of Kingston and Duxbury and the monument on Captain's Hill, erected in memory of Myles Standish, the doughty Pilgrim commander. To the west stretches a rolling swell of hills, ending in an almost unbroken forest, through whose shade Massasoit led his warriors to meet the Plymouth colonists. On the south shrouded in purple mist, are the "Pine Hills" of Manomet. Looking eastward, across the bay he spies the green dot known as Clark's Island where the Pilgrims spent their first Sabbath; and far beyond the shining strand of Plymouth Beach, if the day be clear and his vision keen, he can just discern Provincetown, at the point of Cape Cod – the "tip end of Yankee-land." (ibid)

Farther south, thirty miles off the southern coast of Cape Cod, is Nantucket Island or the Faraway Island, named by the 3,000 natives of the Wampanoag tribe that inhabited the 47 square mile island full of ponds, sand dunes, and fish. The Indians lived here peacefully undisturbed until England deeded the island to Thomas Mayhew in 1641. In 1659, Thomas Mayhew sold Nantucket to the nine original proprietors for "30 pounds and two beaver hats", which included two of Helen's relatives: Tristam Coffin from Simsbury, Massachusetts (formerly of Plymouth, England) and Thomas Macy from Newbury, Massachusetts (formerly of Chilmark, England and a cousin of Thomas Mayhew.) The English settlers lived peacefully among the native Wampanoag Indians as a community of small farmers and sheep herders selling wool. The new settlers learned to fish from the natives, including drift whales that washed ashore. Word spread about the island and its opportunities for religious freedom and job opportunities. Settlers started coming from near and far. When I studied the genealogy chart that my great grandfather so carefully organized, it is easy to see how tightly knit the island community was. I also began to realize that almost everyone on the island was related to each other, the names started to all sound familiar. It is here that another branch of the complicated family tree of Helen Mitchell Rainey's Cape Cod relatives merged by marriage with Nantucket families when the grandson of Desire and John Gorham, Stephen, left Barnstable and settled on Nantucket Island and married Elizabeth Gardner in 1704. Elizabeth was from an old Nantucket family – her grandfather was a seaman and Chief Magistrate of the island.

Around 1715, America, and Europe were forever changed by the discovery of deep-sea whale fishing and the sperm oil that was the "head matter" of gigantic sperm whales on Nantucket. The oil provided light for homes and street lights for business. Spermaceti candles were the finest household illuminants because they kept the houses clean when burning. The Nantucket economy grew as supporting businesses needed ropes, blacksmiths, boat builders, ship chandleries, boarding houses, and shops of all kinds. At the height of the whaling industry, many of our relatives prospered on the island. Nantucket was the whaling capital of the world. Whale fishermen would have to go out deep into the water to find sperm whales and would be gone for months or as long as five years. Women waited anxiously for their family members to return; with no communication during that time. Many women lost their husbands, and children lost their fathers. It was a dangerous yet prosperous lifestyle. There are many books written about the island of Nantucket and the whaling industry. An 1820 incident with a sperm whale sinking a ship was made famous by Herman Melville's novel, *Moby Dick*."

Growing up, our dad told us that we had relatives that founded the island of Nantucket but he didn't give us any details beyond that. Of course, my first question was "do we still own any land there?" Unfortunately, the answer was no. We never knew anything else about why our relatives lived there or why they left. So, in the summer of 1992, my sisters and I decided to take our annual "sister trip" to Nantucket and do our own research. We took the ferry over to the quaint island of Nantucket to find out the facts about our relatives we had heard so much about. Upon docking, the island was a tourists' paradise. From its cobblestone streets to its beautiful historical brick buildings, the town of Nantucket was a dream come true for us with quaint buildings on every corner. Even the street signs had familiar family names we recognized, especially Macy and Coffin. All sorts of tourist shops begged us to come in to purchase scrimshaws (items made with whale bone) and memorabilia. At the time, we did not know that many of our ancestors where successful whalers on the island. We stayed in a restored bed and breakfast in town to get a real feel for life on the island. All three of us were curious about our ancestry and we scheduled a visit with the town librarian for assistance to answer some of our questions. It was important enough to us to forfeit a beautiful day on the beach to sit inside a library. The librarian pieced together what little we knew with the vast amount of information in the library. While we were visiting the library, we saw a poster about one of our relatives, Tristam Coffin, for sale. We were so excited to find this that we bought the poster for our dad for his upcoming birthday and had it beautifully framed. On his birthday in August, I had everyone over to my house for an August birthday celebration. (We weren't allowed in my dad's house at this time). After my dad unwrapped the present he thanked us very much and then said "I have all that information in boxes in my basement." We were shocked. Why didn't we know anything about these papers? And, it was impossible for us to go through the boxes on our own since we weren't allowed into their house. What a disappointment! There was valuable information in dad's house unavailable to us.

Many years after that experience, following my dad's death in 1993, we were able to rummage through the "old papers." I discovered more information about our relatives that were risk takers and adventurers. This side of the family tree also included Barnards, Bunkers, Coffins, Gardners, Gorhams, Macys, Mitchells, and Starbucks; many of these relatives took risks in their search for religious freedom and a better life. We enjoyed our trip to Nantucket Island but it left us confused again about how little our dad shared with us about our ancestors. As we got back on the ferry, we realized our trip gave us a greater sense of where we came from and we appreciated our time on this beautiful island which is now a popular tourist adventure.

By 1783, many of the islanders on Nantucket sought a safe, deeper, harbor where they could rebuild their trading empire, primarily whaling and shipping, which they had lost by the end of the Revolutionary War. During the Revolutionary War, Nantucket was in the unique position of remaining neutral and did not pay taxes to England, although it was a Province of New York. Following the war the island became part of the Commonwealth of Massachusetts. So, a group of Proprietors including two of Howard's relatives, Reuben Macy and Alexander Coffin, travelled up the Hudson River in 1783 with hopes to build a modern city, eponymously named Hudson, New York. This "bustling town could claim to be the first city to be chartered under the flag of the new United States of America (in 1785) and the first city in the new nation to be built as a planned community." (Fone) The Nantucket islanders that decided to leave the island for other places seemed to travel in groups. In Hudson, they brought with them the frames of simple New-England style homes and Nantucket style salt box houses. Many of the same familiar names from Nantucket reappeared in Hudson, New York and formed a tight knit community.

From this bustling seaport, 120 miles from the Atlantic Ocean, "ships sailed from Hudson on whaling and sealing voyages to the south Atlantic and Pacific Oceans, and traded with ports of call in Europe and the Caribbean, returning to Hudson with exotic goods, barrels of whale oil, and tons of "whale bones" and harrowing tales of encounters with pirates corsairs, slave traders, cannibals, enraged whales, and the navies of unfriendly nations. Shipyards, candle factories, rope walks and warehouses clustered near the port, while stately mansions and glittering storefronts were raised on the hills above." (Schram)

Cornelia Helen Macy married Alexander Coffin Mitchell, who came to Hudson from Nantucket. Their third child, Helen Cornelia Mitchell, born in 1838, married Samuel Rossman Rainey in 1868 and bore four children, including Howard's father, Samuel Mitchell Rainey, in 1871. This is where the simple Rainey family tree and the extensive Mitchell family tree merged. Two of the Helen's brothers felt a strong sense of loyalty to their country and were compelled to fight as Union soldiers in the Civil War. Howard's great uncle, Frederick William Mitchell, boarded at Phillips Academy in Andover before attending Williams College. He left college to enlist as a private on April 23, 1861; eleven days after President Lincoln issued his first call for volunteers for the Civil War. Frederick was the first man to leave Williams College for the war, and the class escorted him to the station. He served with the 13th New York Regiment and then re-enlisted in the 12th Illinois Cavalry, known as the McClellan Dragoons, in which he reached the grade of captain. He served with the army of the Potomac and during the last year of the war fought against bushwhackers in Louisiana. Following the war, Captain Frederick Mitchell served in the medical division of the pension bureau for over forty years with the U.S. Government.

Helen's younger brother, Howard Elliot Mitchell voluntarily enlisted in August of 1862 when he was only eighteen years of age. He was a Captain of Company "K" 128th Regiment of the New York Infantry in the Civil War at his discharge in July of 1865. Fortunately, both brothers survived the Civil War in good health and lead successful lives.

Appropriately tucked inside the family papers was a "broadside ballad" or hymn: "I Want to Be a Soldier" about a young man pleading to his mother to be a Union soldier. During this time period, "broadside ballads" (usually a song or poem printed on a single sheet of paper) were sold in the streets by itinerant vendors. The ballads were a sub-genre of street literature which commented on current events and topical issues of the time, such as war. They served as a mirror of popular contemporary attitudes to historical events. "Broadside ballads" were meant to be ephemeral, similar to newspapers, which were printed on cheap, thin paper. This particular hymn (without music) was important enough for Howard to save it all these years. Both of his great uncles were Captains in the Civil War. Maybe that is why Howard saved the hymn to plead his own case to be a soldier.

"I Want To Be a Soldier"

"I want to be a soldier
And like a soldier stand,
A knapsack on my shoulder, And a musket in my hand;
And with my bayonet gleaming,
So glorious and so bright,
I'll join our gallant army,
And for the Union fight.

I Know I'll oft be wounded
But I will not shed a tear;
And in the midst of danger,
I will not feel a fear;
But, brave and patriotic,
Like our brave Sires I'd fight
And with ten thousand soldiers,
Put Rebels all to flight.

I know I'm young and tender;
But, mother, dry your tears,
For, many young, as I am,
Have joined our Volunteers,
And, mother, should I perish,
And for my Country die;
I'll think of you and sister,
And meet you in the sky.

So, let me be a soldier,
And like a soldier stand;
A knapsack on my shoulder,
And a musket in my hand;
And, with my bayonet gleaming,
So glorious and so bright,
I'll join our Union army,
And for the Union fight!"

J. Wrigley, Publisher of Songs, Ballad's and Toy Books, New York

The Rainey Family

"May the road rise to meet you.
May the wind be always at your back.
May the sun shine warm upon your face."

Irish Blessing

This favorite Irish blessing served as a reminder that we are held safe in God's loving hands, as we travel on our life's journey. Robert Rainey, my three times great-grandfather, crossed the pond in the 1820's, on his long and brutal journey to America leaving his loving ones behind.

My Irish relatives lived in the breathtaking countryside of Derry County Ireland amongst the rugged rocky coast, with lush valleys flowing from the Sawel Mountains in the south, and the natural beauty of the northwest shore of the only freshwater lake in Northern Ireland, Lough Neagh or LochNeagh. The Giant's Causeway (the result of an ancient volcanic eruption) in County Antrim is an area of 40,000 basalt columns, the result of an ancient volcanic eruption. In Irish mythology the pagan gods of Ireland grew smaller and smaller in the popular imagination until they turned into fairies while the pagan heroes grew bigger and bigger until they turned into the giants.

This picturesque setting provided the perfect climate for farming flax in County Derry. The moist air, abundant rainfall, and lack of extremes lured farmers to the land. Flax particularly favors well-drained, sandy soil in temperate climates which County Derry provided. The mild winters on the island are warmed by the North Atlantic current all year. To process the flax the farmers needed to scutch (separate the woody fiber from flax by beating), spin, bleach, and weave the flax on a loom into linen. Mill towns sprung up to meet the demand.

In 1796, the Board of Trustees of the Linen and Hempen Manufacturers of Ireland encouraged the growth of flax seed by awarding spinning wheels or looms for planting between one and five acres. Individuals who planted one acre were awarded four spinning wheels, while those planting five acres were awarded a loom. What a humble lifestyle the Irish lead. During this same period, Marian's grandfather was planting up to 800 acres of land with a variety of crops. I can see why America seemed like the land of plenty.

My four times great-grandfather, David Rainey, was a cloth merchants in County Derry, Ireland and his brother Samuel was a flax dealer in Dublin, Ireland. David's son, Robert, born in 1795, sought out a more stable life in America in the 1820's arriving in Hudson, New York.

I am pleased that I really do have the luck of the Irish in me. My dad never talked about the Irish Rainey bloodline and he never mentioned anything special on St. Patrick's Day about our family tree. There weren't any "Old Papers" in my dad's files about the Rainey family in Ireland.

Once again, I was amazed that another one of my relatives took the chance to leave their loved ones behind for a chance to start a better life in America. Robert Rainey decided to endure the grueling 12 week trip on a ship in steerage in deplorable conditions. He brought with him his families expertise with farming, spinning, and selling flax cloth. The allure of prosperity in America and the freedom of religion were powerful enough to take a huge risk. "Emigrants during the 1700s were mostly Presbyterians from the north of Ireland, the so-called "Scotch-Irish." "By 1776, nearly 250,000 Irish Protestants had immigrated to North America."(www.historyplace.com) The Rainey family's life in Northern Ireland was clouded by religious tensions. As very strong Presbyterians, who were not willing to convert, the Rainey family was subjected to the rules of the Anglican Church. The Penal Laws in Ireland at the time were an attempt to force Irish Roman Catholics and Presbyterians to accept the reformed denomination of the English State established Anglican Church. Presbyterians had to pay tithes, were banned from interfaith marriages, banned from membership in Parliament, and other restrictive laws. Robert Rainey made the difficult decision to board a ship bound for New York where he would be free to make religious choices and get out from under control of the restrictive Penal Laws. What a huge choice for such a young man to make.

The word spread afar about this successful city, Hudson, New York and Robert Rainey must have been intrigued by the possibilities of starting a new life in this river town. By 1784, Hudson was the second most active port in the state of New York, behind New York City. Shortly after his arrival in Hudson, Robert Rainey married a Hudson woman, Mary Perse. The first of their three sons arrived in 1831. Their third child, Samuel Rossman Rainey, Howard's paternal grandfather, was born in 1838. Hudson was very good to the Rainey family. Robert's occupation was listed in the census documents as a "carman," the driver of a horse drawn vehicle for transporting goods. A "carman" was often employed by railway companies for local deliveries and collections of goods and parcels. Robert and Mary Rainey were hard working and devoted parents who educated their sons at the private Hudson Academy to be successful business men employed in sperm oil and candle manufacturing, bookkeeping and management at the Hudson Iron Works, and as tellers and managers at the Hudson City Savings Institution. These opportunities for Robert's family wouldn't have been available to them in Ireland. As an important part of their new freedom to choose in America, the Rainey family joined the First Presbyterian Church of Hudson which was built in 1837 at the corner of 4th and Warren Street. They were very devoted and involved members all of their lives.

Robert Rainey truly had the luck of the Irish in his bloodline. Unbeknownst to him, about twenty years after he left Ireland the Great Famine also known as the Irish Potato Famine struck. It resulted in the deaths of approximately one million people. The famine lasted from 1845 to 1852 with mass starvation, disease, and emigration. What amazing timing!

Howard's grandfather, Samuel Rossman Rainey, chose a business career and community service over war. Many immigrants from countries such as Ireland moved to America to get away from that brutal aspect of European life and did not want to get involved in war again. As immigrants, the Rainey side of the family did not feel the call to serve in wars in the United States once they were settled in their new life. In 1862, a year after the start of the Civil War, Samuel was granted a business license to operate a ship chandlery and hardware store at the corner of Warren and Ferry Street (at the river) named Benedict & Rainey, when he was 25 years old. In an advertisement I found in the "Old Papers" file for the store said "Those wishing anything in our line would do well to examine our goods and prices. Our motto is: Quick Sales and Small Profits." I can see why the store didn't stay in business long! After the war ended in 1865, Samuel Rossman Rainey married Helen Cornelia Mitchell in 1868 and had four children, including my great grandfather S. Mitchell in 1871. Samuel R. went on to manage a clothing business, a steam fire engine company and the Hudson Iron works. In 1882, he was elected Secretary and Treasurer and a Trustee of the Hudson City Savings Institution until his death. Not only was he known in financial circles, but he devoted his energies to serve as the first Board of Water Commissioners and as the Secretary of the Board of Managers of the Hudson House of Refuge for Women. The Rainey family embraced their life in America and the opportunities they were afforded. They were highly respected for their financial opinions, judgement, knowledge, and experience. They took a risk to have a better life in America and they lead successful and purposeful lives. It is doubtful that the Rainey family could have accomplished so much and made such a difference in so many lives in Ireland. America truly was the land of opportunity for my relatives.

Howard's father, S. Mitchell, was equally as successful and respected in the city of Hudson for his financial acumen and service to his community as his father, In fact, S. Mitchell took over his father's position at the Hudson City Savings Institution upon his father's death in 1900. S. Mitchell married Ida Miles in 1884 and raised their only son, my grandfather, Howard, in Hudson.

Howard knew his grandfather, a second generation Irish American, was not deeply committed to the American Civil War, as his grandmother's brothers were. But, Howard was different. He took after the maternal Mitchell side of his family and he knew he wanted to serve his country. He wasn't sure when or where yet.

Given all of this family history, proud moments, awards won, battles fought, and pride in being an American, it is easy to understand why my grandfather wanted to serve in the war, if America officially entered. In 1916, Woodrow Wilson successfully ran for re-election on the promise of neutrality with the slogan: "He kept us out of the war." (Willmott) Would he be able to keep his promise to his voters?

CHAPTER THREE

PLEASANT MEMORIES OF COLLEGE

"The founders of this institution expect (and have a right to expect) that it will be a fountain of good in the world."
Mary Lyon, founder of Mount Holyoke Seminary • November 7, 1837

In 1969, my family took my grandmother, Marian, to her fiftieth reunion at Mount Holyoke College. I was not at all pleased because it meant I had to miss on my own milestone: my sixth-grade graduation and parties with all of my friends in St. Louis. However, my father, Marian's only child, insisted that we go with Grandma to Massachusetts because she was physically unable to make the trip on her own following her accident. This return to her alma mater was incredibly important to her.

Despite Grandma's enthusiasm manifested in the stories she often told us about her days at college, we children found it difficult to see the appeal of such a place. Often, in conversation, she said she would pay for any of her grandchildren to go to college at Mount Holyoke, if we chose to go there. I am sure my father was ready to take her up on the offer, but my sisters and I secretly cringed at the thought of going to an "all-girls'" school.

As soon as we arrived at the campus, my grandmother ran into old friends and classmates and began to introduce us. We checked her into her dorm room where she would stay with her best friends while they attended the festivities. I had to admit that South Hadley was charming, the quintessential New England college town with its ivy-covered buildings and quaint town square, all surrounded by beautiful mountains. As we were leaving her for the night, I looked back and witnessed my grandmother with the biggest smile on her face I had ever seen. I knew Mount Holyoke had been a prominent part of her life, but until that moment I had never understood how important it was to her. What was so special about this college? How did it change her life?

Fortunately, my grandmother left us her diaries of her personal journey through her college years. In them, she described how much Mount Holyoke meant to her, the bonds she formed, the mentors and teachers who held her hand and guided her along the way, the incredibly high academic standards, and how she became a leader for her generation. Her college experience was quite different from mine; it seemed more serious and steeped in tradition. But, my grandmother was accomplishing something that was very uncommon for women at this time. And, I think Marian took it seriously that she was one of the few women privileged to go to college. I cannot imagine the pressure Marian felt to honor the scholarship she received from the Springfield Club that gave her this opportunity. I am so proud of her and all of her accomplishments. I know now that Mount Holyoke was instrumental in helping her become the person she wanted to be — her "best self."

Reading her diaries, I am blessed to be able to look into my grandmother's mind and see how Mount Holyoke changed her. She talks about Mount Holyoke traditions such as Freshman Mountain Day when the college president declares a school holiday on a perfect day; the faculty skit, an elaborate, original performance that takes place once every four years; dancing with girls which seemed a bit odd to me; and listening to a wealth of provocative speakers including Robert Frost. Marian also reveals preoccupations of her life outside of school, especially with regards to men. She eagerly drinks in the details of a friend's wedding and wonders if she will ever care about a man that deeply. She delights in the close love of her family and mentions without self-pity that money is scarce. As for the world beyond western Massachusetts, the distant conflict begins to rumble across these pages quietly at first and then with a crash as America enters the Great War.

When I was a child, I had no idea what an accomplishment it was for Marian to go to college. Every girl I knew planned to get a higher education. But in my grandmother's day, it was an anomaly. In this time period, Mount Holyoke and the other colleges for women provided the friendliest environments for them to pursue an education while escaping discrimination.

To give an idea of what Marian was up against, people considered it unhealthy for young women like my grandmother to strive for a higher education, even physicians. In 1870, Dr. Edward Clarke, a medical doctor and professor of medicine at Harvard University, published a book that stated a woman could indeed study and master the same college subjects that a man studied. But in doing so, "she could not do all this and retain uninjured health and a future secure from neuralgia, uterine disease, hysteria, and other derangements of the nervous system." (Clarke) No wonder an all-female college was the most likely place for a young woman to get an education in those days. Forty-five years after that report, Marian Viets was determined to get a college education at Mount Holyoke.

Fast forward another 41 years to the summer of 2008, when my daughter, Lauren, and I visited the college. As we approached South Hadley from the south, we could see the tall, ivy-covered, brick college campus and buildings on the right and the charming college town on the left. The impressive campus is nestled between the Holyoke and Tom Mountain ranges and has two lakes, upper and lower, that are used for canoeing, ice-skating, and reflective thinking. Marian and her friends were constantly taking walks around campus on Prospect Hill and Morgan Road, sledding down the hills, a "bat" (picnic) on Button Field, looking for trailing arbutus and ivy, and spending time outdoors, no matter what the weather.

Lauren and I decided to walk around the Mount Holyoke campus to really experience the college. It was a gorgeous day and we could not believe how beautiful the campus was. We sensed the tradition of academic excellence everywhere. In the distance we heard laughing, yelling, and music in the outdoor amphitheater. After visiting the library and purchasing the book, *"A Memory Book, Mount Holyoke College 1837-1987"*, I told the librarian about my project transcribing my grandmother's diaries. She strongly suggested my daughter and I walk over to the Convocation ceremony. The librarian told us it would be worth our time to catch a glimpse of the activities. As we arrived, we noticed that each class seemed to be dressed in different colors. The seniors wore traditional caps and gowns adorned with boas, hats, wigs, and colorful accessories. It really gave me a sense of my grandmother's life at Mount Holyoke. While frivolity marked the occasion, it was obvious that the seriousness of academics was just around the corner for the Mount Holyoke students. Convocation marks the beginning of the academic year. During Marian's years at Mount Holyoke, the students gathered in Abbey Chapel for Convocation. Following her opening ceremonies, the robed faculty lined the path to college founder Mary Lyon's grave, while the seniors walked through the throng to place a wreath at her grave which resides in the center of campus with a decorative fence around it. As the seniors passed, the faculty members applauded, thereby acknowledging them for the first time as scholars and colleagues. While some things changed; much remains the same at Mount Holyoke.

Steeped in a rich history, Mount Holyoke was founded in 1837 by chemist and educator Mary Lyon, nearly a century before women won the right to vote. Her famous charge - "Go where no one else will go; do what no one else will do" - continues to inspire students to this day. Many of the traditions in her honor are still practiced, such as Founders Day and the wreath-laying ceremony on Mary Lyon's grave.

Throughout her life, Marian was fortunate to be mentored by women of intellect and leadership. Perhaps most of all, Marian adored and admired the dynamic personality of Mary Emma Woolley, the President of Mount Holyoke and a seminal figure in the college's history. Miss Woolley's early years were strongly influenced by Mary Lyon, as a student and teacher at Wheaton Seminary. It is clear Marian relished Miss Woolley's speeches to the new students and Sunday Vespers in the Chapel because her diary entries describe in detail the message and content of these sermons. Fortunately, Mary Emma Woolley remained as President of Mount Holyoke College for 37 dynamic years, from 1900-1937. She was a leader and mentor to students and faculty and an advocate for the educational equality for women, as well as for world peace and feminist causes. During her tenure, she improved Mount Holyoke's resources, status and standards to make it the great institution it is today. "During the decade prior to the First World War, the academic and administrative structures of the college and those activities pertaining to student life became formalized, developing into the pattern which essentially persists to the present day." (Edmonds)

Miss Woolley's heritage includes many accomplishments: In 1894, she was the first woman to receive both an A.B. and an M.A. from Brown University. Subsequently, she was appointed to the faculty of Wellesley College where she was professor and head of the Department of Biblical History and Literature from 1895-1900, at which time she assumed the presidency of Mount Holyoke. "Wellesley, founded by a Mount Holyoke trustee inspired by Mary Lyon's ideals, and presided over during its first years by a Mount Holyoke graduate, was steeped in the traditions of her new charge and conversant with the more recent developments in the growth of higher education for women." (Edmonds) In Marian's writings, it is apparent the strong influence Miss Woolley had on Marian at her chapel talks, "her keen memory for names and faces, her succession of prize Scotch collies, and the students' pride in the Mount Holyoke she portrayed to the world." (ibid)

Since 1915, Mount Holyoke has belonged to The Seven Sisters, a consortium of prestigious East Coast liberal arts colleges for women. The consortium meets to discuss issues of common concern, such as fund raising, institutional goals, and curriculum matters. Originally, the consortium included Mount Holyoke, Vassar, Smith, Wellesley, Bryn Mawr, Barnard, and Radcliffe colleges. Today, only five of the Seven Sisters remain women's colleges because Vassar has gone coeducational and Radcliffe has merged with Harvard.

The 1921 publication *Into the World of Mount Holyoke* describes the college as follows: "Here more than 800 American girls pass four formative and critical years. Here they meet, in most cases, their first real tests, realize for the first time their full capabilities. Here they make use of instruments, which have been perfected during nearly a century, for strengthening will power, developing mentality, securing bodily health. From the contact of the historic college with the youth and vigor of its students springs a life that is each year more vital, confident, and full of promise to the country. Mount Holyoke is still able to give to the homemakers, teachers, social workers, missionaries, businesswomen, and leaders of the future what they need to be their best selves."

A whole new world of higher education for women was opening up for my grandmother when she began her inaugural fifteen-mile train ride to spend her first night in her dorm room with her Springfield friend Helen Francis in Mead Hall Dormitory. She was a trailblazer. After reading Marian's diaries, however, I discovered that she was on the cusp of a feminist movement. It wasn't outward appearances but internal struggles to pursue voting, careers, equality, and service to others that made Marian a feminist.

I owe Mount Holyoke College a debt of gratitude for the college's contributions toward the formation of such a strong woman, my grandmother. Mount Holyoke was a pioneer on behalf of women's education but also helped Marian search for her identity as a woman and figure out her place in society. It is that sense of purpose that she left as her legacy for her grandchildren and beyond.

What follows are Marian's diary entries from freshmen year on campus, her summers spent at home in Springfield, Massachusetts, and holidays with her grandparents in E. Granby, Connecticut. The world as seen through Marian's eyes, are reflected in the books, magazines, newspapers, and poems she read, plays and movies she watched, and her private thoughts where she wrote about her hopes, dreams and goals for her future.

Tuesday, September 21, 1915 • Mount Holyoke

I came to college today in the pouring rain. Some very cordial upperclassmen met the Springfield freshman at the trolley station. I came with Doris Gidley, Helen Francis, Helen Gidley, and "Dot" Williams (Central High School graduates). Helen Francis and I room together in 77 Mead Hall Dormitory. Mead Hall is on campus in a very desirable location, overlooking Prospect Hill and the lake. Our room is on the fourth floor, but I am used to living on the fourth floor. College is wonderful, even though I did arrive in a rather dismal amalgamation of the elements.

Wednesday, September 22, 1915 • Mount Holyoke

The girls continued to arrive all day today. I kept meeting new girls who came in just to get acquainted. Our room was full of visitors. Everyone is so cordial and dear here. My trunk had come so I unpacked a little.

Helen Francis and Marian Viets (right)

Friday, September 24, 1915 • Mount Holyoke

Chapel this morning. A junior girl from Chicago took me, as my Big Sister. The service was beautiful. Miss Woolley is so altogether splendid.

Many of Mount Holyoke's traditions are still observed. The Big/Little Sister custom helped Marian adjust to her new life at college by pairing juniors and firsties (first-year students). Those who are paired up take part in organized, and unorganized, events together, all coordinated by the Junior Class Board. Marian loved all of the Mount Holyoke traditions, especially when she was able to spend time with upper classmen. As an only child, Marian craved the closeness of all of her "sisters."

Saturday, September 25, 1915 • Mount Holyoke

Classes today for the first time. In the afternoon, the YMCA reception for entering students took place in the gym. Almost the whole college was there. Margaret, a sophomore, took me.

*In the evening, Ruth Gorman, came to call on me. I haven't seen Ruth for two years, when we were at Falmouth Heights on Cape Cod, Massachusetts. She is a senior and a **dream**. She is really very beautiful with big dark eyes and black hair. But, the girl she brought with her – a perfect beauty – tall and regal looking with light brown wavy hair and eyes like violets. After they left I found out that the tall, beautiful girl is Senior Class President. Just think! In my room the class president - a Senior!*

Marian participated in the Young Women's Christian Association (YWCA), which sought to deepen the spiritual life at Mount Holyoke. The YWCA "welcomed new students, kept in touch with alumnae, and furthered the work of missionaries abroad. Mary Woolley could proudly announce that thirty-one Mount Holyoke women had gone overseas during the first decade of the century." (Edmonds) Back at home, Marian's mother volunteered for the YWCA, also.

Friday, October 1, 1915 • Mount Holyoke

Miss Woolley spoke to the freshmen class this afternoon at 4.45 o'clock. She was truly wonderful. She talked of college as an obstacle race. The obstacles are 1) our own inertia, 2) the charm of people, 3) lack of system, and 4) lack of concentration. I sat in the front row of the assembly hall because, when Helen, "Pris", and I came in Miss Woolley asked us to come down front. Thus, when she spoke she was very near to me. Oh, she seemed so beautiful in the sense of the spirit. Her presence and the greatness of her soul could be felt. At the end of her talk, she asked two girls to stand by the door and collect slips. "Pris" and I volunteered. Of course, we had to hand her all the slips we collected at the end. We were so thrilled. Then, joy of joys most complete, we walked down the stairs with her. It was too grand for words!

Tuesday, October 5, 1915 • Mount Holyoke

There was a Belgian concert here this afternoon for the benefit of the war sufferers. Belgians took part entirely. Then, a collection was taken up. Helen Francis, Helen Gidley, Doris Gidley, and I sat together. We all felt silly and as a result giggled during the entire performance. It was really awful! In the first place, we got up and changed our seats after all the Belgians had come out, bowed, and then retired. We sat down right in back of the piano on which a light-haired Belgian lady executed difficult tunes. All was well until the fair-haired lady turned around and asked Helen Gidley to turn the pages for her. Of course, poor Helen was FRANTIC. The lady rushed out behind the scenes and brought back with her another pale, friendly-looking Belgian gentleman. Helen and I sat down on a chair and turned the pages. The eagle eyes of several of the faculty were upon us. That only made things worse, of course. We were heartily glad when the last Belgian had performed.

This is the first mention of Marian's involvement in war activities at college, including fundraising. The war had been raging in Europe for over a year. While most Americans wished to remain neutral, many supported the countries that would become their Allies. On August 3, 1914 Germany declared war on France, and presented Belgium with an ultimatum "demanding rights of transit through that country. The next day, after learning that its demand that Belgian neutrality be respected had been answered by invasion, Britain declared war on Germany. The violation of Belgian neutrality made the Germans ogres in the eyes of the world's press." (Willmott) The occupation of Belgium's capital, Brussels, on August 20, 1914, by the Germans was unopposed because the "Belgian army had retreated north to Antwerp, allowing the Germans to pass unimpeded through central Belgium." (ibid)

Americans' support for Belgium was growing. There were well-documented incidents of atrocities against civilians by the Germans: burning their homes and libraries, and executing civilians, including women and children. In sympathy for the overrun Belgians "millions of women back home, organized committees to roll bandages, raised relief funds," and more. (Willmott) Marian and her fellow classmates felt the need to do their bit to support the Belgians, even though Marian did not seem to take her attendance at this event seriously. She did take the time to copy a poem about King Albert I of Belgium (1875-1934) who was the King "throughout the war, organizing resistance to German occupation of Belgium." (Wikipedia.com) Albert I moved the Belgian government to LeHavre, France where he continued to govern his nation. The following poem was tucked into Marian's diary:

"Albert of Belgium"

"His pomp is a part of the past
And his court but a memory
And his bloom by an east-born blast
Was seared and swept to sea.

The subjects he ruled are slaves
Of the union of Hunger and Hun.
Or molder at peace in the graves
They received from the sword and the gun.

Yet still as a king he reigns
And still his sword he wields
And the blood will leave his veins
Ere the King of the Belgians yields

They have driven him from his land.
They have stolen his palace and crown.
They have left him a battered band
Of heroes they could not down.

He scorns the excuse of a King.
He scorns the safety of flight.
Till the last foe's steel shall ring
Will the King of the Belgians fight.

He shares the fate of his men
Of peril and pain and cold.
Trenches and forest and fen –
The peer of the heroes of old.

When the world to hate was moved
Of all the kingly clan
A king of the Belgians proved

That a king could be a man.
To the glistering roll of fame
That the poets of mankind sing
Must mankind add the name
Of the Belgian hero King."

Sidney S. Rittenberg

The Prime Minister of the British Empire Herbert Henry Asquith declared war on the German Empire on August 4, 1914, in response to the German demands for military passage that were forced upon Belgium. (Wikipedia) The United Kingdom – England, Scotland, Wales and Ireland – joined forces as one of the Allied Powers during the First World War fighting against the Central Powers (The German Empire, the Austro-Hungarian Empire, the Ottoman Empire and the Kingdom of Bulgaria.)

Friday, October 8, 1915 • Mount Holyoke

In the evening, there was a Student's League meeting. The president is very dignified. The meeting was long, and there was much business transacted.

The Students' League, the student governing organization, was first introduced at Mount Holyoke in 1898. "The purpose of the Students' League is to "enact and enforce rules and regulations, according to the grant of powers given by the faculty; to maintain the highest ideals of honor and integrity in all matters of personal conduct; to encourage active co-operation in the work of self-government; and to form an official body to give expression to the opinion of the students on matters of general college interest." "In 1905 it was given a formal grant of power and, in addition to taking responsibility for monitoring church and chapel attendance, quiet hours, and "the ten o'clock rule," it now also administered the rules for absence from college and the registration for those absences, and regulated the number of organizational offices that any student could hold." (Edmonds)

Saturday, October 9, 1915 • Springfield, Massachusetts

I went home to Springfield with the Francis's in their auto. Father and mother were glad to see me. We spent a quiet evening at home.

Wednesday, October 13, 1915 • Mountain Day

Mountain Day! We put up our lunch and started at 8.30 o'clock. Helen and I went with a crowd of sophomores. We walked the Holyoke Range, which is about 10 miles. There are seven peaks, and each is steep and rugged. We ate our lunch when we were half way over. We were hungry as bears. We didn't reach the Notch (a pass on Route 116) until about 5 o'clock. I really was tired out, but nevertheless felt repaid, for all along the range there are beautiful outlooks, especially on Bare Peak.

Directly after dinner, I received a telephone call from Ingham Baker (CHS) saying that he was coming over with another freshman from Amherst College. He got over here about 8 o'clock. There was a junior prayer meeting in the parlor. In consequence, I had to walk around with him. The freshmen friend, Mr. Moore, was very peculiar, rather meek, and silent. Suddenly, Mr. Moore asked me to the Theta Delta Chi frat dance at Amherst. Taken completely by surprise, I accepted and was immediately sorry that I had.

Marian awoke to her first Mountain Day at Mount Holyoke to the ringing of the bells from Abbey Chapel, another favorite tradition. It was a beautiful New England autumn day secretly chosen by the president of the college. All classes were cancelled for the day. In 1939, Mount Holyoke Trustee (1905-1931) Joseph Skinner donated the Summit House Hotel, and the Holyoke Range property to the Commonwealth of Massachusetts as a State Park, renaming it Joseph Skinner Park.

Thursday, October 14, 1915 • Mount Holyoke

Helen and I went rowing in the afternoon on Prospect Lake. We took separate boats! After we had been out about ten minutes, some little boys about ten years old called to us from the shore and asked us for a ride. Helen took one, and I took another. They were so cunning and reminded me of the dear little Sunday school boys. "Dick" Gidley came over in the evening, and we fooled and laughed the whole time. It really did us good to be silly.

Friday, October 15, 1915 • Senior-Freshman Reception

Dr. Underhill [Resident Physician] gave a very stupid hygiene lecture. It is impossible to follow her drift of thought.

In the evening, I went to the Senior-Freshmen Reception with a senior, Ruth Gorman. Ruth was beautiful in taffeta. I had dances with wonderful seniors. In intermission the seniors gave a moving picture play entitled "Mary Pickford at Holyoke." Mary Pickford and Charlie Chaplin were cleverly imitated by the girls. I had a wonderful time! The senior president was beautiful in lavender. There was a long receiving line of faculty and class officers. When we freshmen got home, we found our beds turned down and dear little notes from the juniors on our pillows. "Sisters" are dear to the little freshmen.

P.S. Earlier in the evening I had a telephone from Mr. Moore at Amherst College saying that he would be after me the next day at 1.30 o'clock. I was too surprised to refuse, but, of course, I can't go to an afternoon affair without a nice hat and an afternoon gown. What shall I do? I'm wild!!

Thursday, October 21, 1916 • Mount Holyoke

Today was the class meeting for the nomination of temporary officers. They put me up for chairman, but I felt that I must decline. Studies for me come first this year, and an attempt not to get overtired.

Saturday, October 23, 1915 • First Set of Interclass Hockey Games

We had a field hockey game this afternoon. Our freshman team did wonderfully well against the Junior Championship team. Dorothy "Dot" Williams played splendidly. After the game, we had a supper party in our room. We had wonderful eats and a glorious time.

> The Athletic Association at Mount Holyoke was organized in 1903 in order to further the athletic interests of college through interclass games in basketball, field hockey, tennis, track, volleyball, and baseball. "The concept of vigorous outdoor sport as part of the students' exercise regimes was advocated by Mary Woolley" (Edmonds) Marian did not seem as interested in sports as her son or grandchildren. But, she supported the teams enthusiastically!!

Tuesday, October 26, 1915 • Freshmen Serenade to the Junior Class of 1917

The freshman class had a practice sing in the Assembly Hall. Our cheerleader is enthusiastic and very good. We have some good songs, some original songs, and other Mount Holyoke sister class songs. In the evening, our whole class went in back of Dwight Hall — the darkest place on campus. From there, at 9 o'clock pm, we adjourned to all the halls and serenaded the juniors. Oh, it was so thrilling! And all those darling juniors sang back so adorably. They clapped and thanked us a whole bit. We surely had great fun.

Friday, October 29, 1915 • Marian's 18th Birthday

18 years old today, long looked forward to as the ideal age. It didn't feel so different, after all. There was lots of mail in the box and a sweet present from Helen — a little face chamois in a dear little case. Mother and Grandmother Clark arrived at 11 o'clock am. I showed them around and then took them to luncheon. Grandmother gave me such a lovely warm, pink and grey bathrobe and some money. Oh, the eats that they brought: apples, nuts, cookies, candy, and nut bread. Father came at 4 o'clock pm. We walked around again, and they left at 5.30 o'clock pm. "Dot" Williams and "Dick" Gidley came over in the evening and brought chocolates, a three-layer box. It's just great to have friends who love you.

I never appreciated anything so much in my life as the dear little things mother did for me. She would do anything for me, and so would father. Mother sacrifices so much and never thinks of herself. Love as strong as ours is the strongest thing on earth. Love for me brought dear little Grandmother Clark from East Granby just to see me on my birthday. What a happy, happy day I had.

Saturday, October 30, 1915 • Holyoke, Massachusetts

"Dick" and I went to Holyoke, Massachusetts, to the movies at the Globe Theatre, the one on Dean Purington's approved list. It's a very cheap-looking affair with 5-cent admission. We couldn't believe that it could be the right place. We were dying for a *very* flippant picture, but alas, it was a tale of old Roman life, full of historical allusions. There is no rest for the weary. In the evening, I went to Le Giocese Dance and had great fun dancing. We had cider and doughnuts.

> Le Giocese was founded in 1905 for the purpose of promoting the social life of the college. It was open to all members of the college. Once a month, there was a dance in Chapin Auditorium, Mary E. Woolley Hall. "The membership for the year 1917-1918 is five hundred twenty, a little less than in previous years, due probably, to

war conditions." (Llamarada) Most dances were all-girl affairs with full dance cards. Marian was in a sorority in high school but they were banned by Miss Woolley in 1910 because they were "secret, exclusive and self-perpetuating." (Edmonds)

Saturday, November 6, 1915 • Mount Holyoke

This afternoon I went to the field hockey game. It was a great game, with the juniors and freshmen winning. We were simply hilarious with joy. In the evening, we celebrated, of course. Freshmen and juniors met on the green. We had tin pans, spoons, trays, dinner bells, and horns. The lanterns and torches gave the light. We went around to all the big dorms and yelled "freshmen '19 this way and '17 this way." Then, toting and waving lights, we marched to the hockey field to wait for the team. We built a big bonfire and stood dangerously near because it was so cold. Someone passed around lollypops. We sang and cheered. And, when the team came! There was wild excitement. We marched home at last. Ye good village folk of South Hadley popped their heads out of their windows to watch the excitement.

Sunday, November 7, 1915 • Mount Holyoke

Mother, Aunt Mame, and Mr. and Mrs. McCord came up to spend the afternoon and go to vespers. I showed them around campus. Miss Woolley led vespers. We were glad that she led because Mr. and Mrs. McCord had never seen her before. They all left after the service.

Monday, November 8, 1915 • Mount Holyoke

Priscilla "Pris" Spaulding, "Dick" Gidley, Helen Francis, and I went for a lovely walk after classes. We got to arguing about Tech and Central (High Schools in Springfield, Massachusetts) and from that to gossiping most horribly about things at home. Such flippant things for college girls! And *trig* waiting to be done. Sad but true! How I loathe the stuff! It's abominable. I must learn to love it; it's the only way to get through.

Tuesday, November 9, 1915 • Founder's Day

Founders Day! Helen and I rose late. We went to the service. It was very impressive. The faculty and trustees marched in, in cap and gown. The colors, signifying various degrees, were lovely. Then, the seniors, and lastly the choir.

President Thwing, of Western Reserve University, gave the address. He spoke on "The Scholar." The scholar, he said, should be an apostle and a priest. Scholarship should be for service. In the recessional, the choir formed a long line through which seniors and faculty marched. Helen and I waited on tables at the grand event at noon. Miss Woolley, trustees, and all guests ate at Mead Hall. The dinner lasted from 1 pm until 3 pm. It was a great dinner for great people.

> Founder's Day at Mount Holyoke, honoring Mary Lyon, is traditionally held on the Sunday closest to November 8th, the date of the opening of Mount Holyoke in 1837. Elizabeth Storrs Mead, President 1890-1900, began the tradition in 1891. Mary Lyon's grave proudly stands in the middle of campus. Marian relished traditions in her life, especially with her "sisters."

Wednesday, November 10, 1915 • Mount Holyoke

We had a lovely Thanksgiving party here at Mead Hall. Each attraction was 5 cents for the benefit of South Hadley's poor. There was "Senior Show" and "Junior Lunch." "Senior Show" was very clever. First, there was a shadow play presenting *The Seven Ages of Men*. Then, there was a shadow dance. The second part was a cute pantomime play including the cast: college fellow, pretty girl, and aged couple. The last act was a display of magic by Yatsi, the Chinese senior. There was dancing to Victrola music after the show. Mead Hall furnishes good times, all right!! College is perfect!

Thursday, November 11, 1915 • Mount Holyoke

Mother and the Woodins came up today. In the evening, I went to hear Dr. Calkins of Cambridge preach on "Is Faith in God Reasonable?" It was truly wonderful and most inspiring. He said that people raised three objections most of all: first, you can't see God; second, you can't prove that there is a God; third, how could a God exist in a world so full of sin? In answer to the first, he said that many of the most wonderful things cannot be seen. In answer to the second, he said that you could prove that there is a God, but not of course by the same standard of reasoning as $2 + 2 = 4$. The truth of God may be proved, but in a different way. Third, God, he believes, cannot prevent all terrible things from happening. He must maintain the universe, which he created in an orderly manner. Elements must conflict. God restrains his hand from interfering. Then, God does not remove sin, because in so doing he would rob man of his birthright, the freedom of choice. Character must be molded by the execution of the will.

Friday, November 12, 1915 • Mount Holyoke

Grinding [studying] today for the most part. In the evening, I did trig. I'm getting positively desperate on the subject of trig. I'm so afraid of a flunk. Wouldn't that be dreadful? I can't conceive of how terrible it would be. Alas! Such are the freshman's woes.

Sunday, November 14, 1915 • Mount Holyoke

Sundays at college are wonderful days. I lay in bed until 9:30 am. The church service was conducted by Reverend Raymond Calkins of Cambridge. His subject was "Our Need for God." He spoke about a man who said that if he could have $10,000 a year income and health for all in his family he would have nothing against religion, nor indeed anything particular for it. Dr. Calkins said that the greatest trouble with this statement was that this man could never be sure of his income or his health. Nothing is sure but God.

Tuesday, November 16, 1915 • Mount Holyoke

Priscilla "Pris" Spaulding and I went for a beautiful walk up Morgan Road way over the hill. It was freezing cold and very windy, but we had a perfectly wonderful walk. I received a sweet little note from that unquenchable Mr. Moore asking me to the Pratt Dance at Amherst College. I answered right back, "No!"

Thursday, November 18, 1915 • Mount Holyoke

Trig quiz of monstrous dimensions. I almost perished. If I haven't passed it, I don't know what will happen. Needless to say, I'm horribly frightened. I visited the post office and found a box of eats from Grandmother Clark. Unable to contain my curiosity, I opened the package in class meeting and found applesauce cake and chocolate frosted cupcakes! Heavenly!! After class meeting, three of us ate under a tree in the moonlight. The moon is up now by 6 o'clock. Quite weird, was it not?

Friday, November 19, 1915 • Mount Holyoke

A rainy, damp, cold, and clammy day, but not so my spirits. In the evening, there was a required French lecture in the chapel on "The Salon of Madame de Rembouillet and the Court of Louis XIV." The woman who spoke was attired in gorgeous garb of 16th century art — yellow and blue satin — and a train of great length born by a little page, "sous petit fils." She had three long ostrich feathers sticking up at all angles in her curly hair. She spoke excellent French I was deeeeeeeeeeelighted to be able to understand. It got a bit boring along the end. She showed lantern slides at the end. The poor man at the lantern was almost asleep. He got about every other picture bottom side up. He turned off a picture and flashed on another at irregular intervals. The page tapped on the floor when a picture was to be turned off. Between the mistakes of the pages and the lantern man, Madam was scowling most of the time. Quite a thrilling evening.

Saturday, November 20, 1915 • Mount Holyoke

The Trig quizzes were not returned. The suspense is awful. I tremble inwardly most of the time. In the afternoon "Pris", Helen and I walked to Granby, Massachusetts - four miles. We called on Bodeine Smith. She was entertaining a club. We felt horribly ill at ease in our hike rigs. Conversation lagged a bit, and all our wild tales of college produced not even a smile. The Smith's house is very beautiful. We reached home from Granby at 5.30 pm. Lie in bed tomorrow, I hope! Me weary bones need rest.

College is perfect!!!!

Sunday, November, 21, 1915 Mount Holyoke

Late rising and church going. Mr. Tweedy of Yale Divinity School preached a fine sermon. His text was "I will give you a thousand horses if you can put riders upon them." He said that we must have riders for our circumstances, doubts, etc. We can overcome the constraints of ill health and poverty.

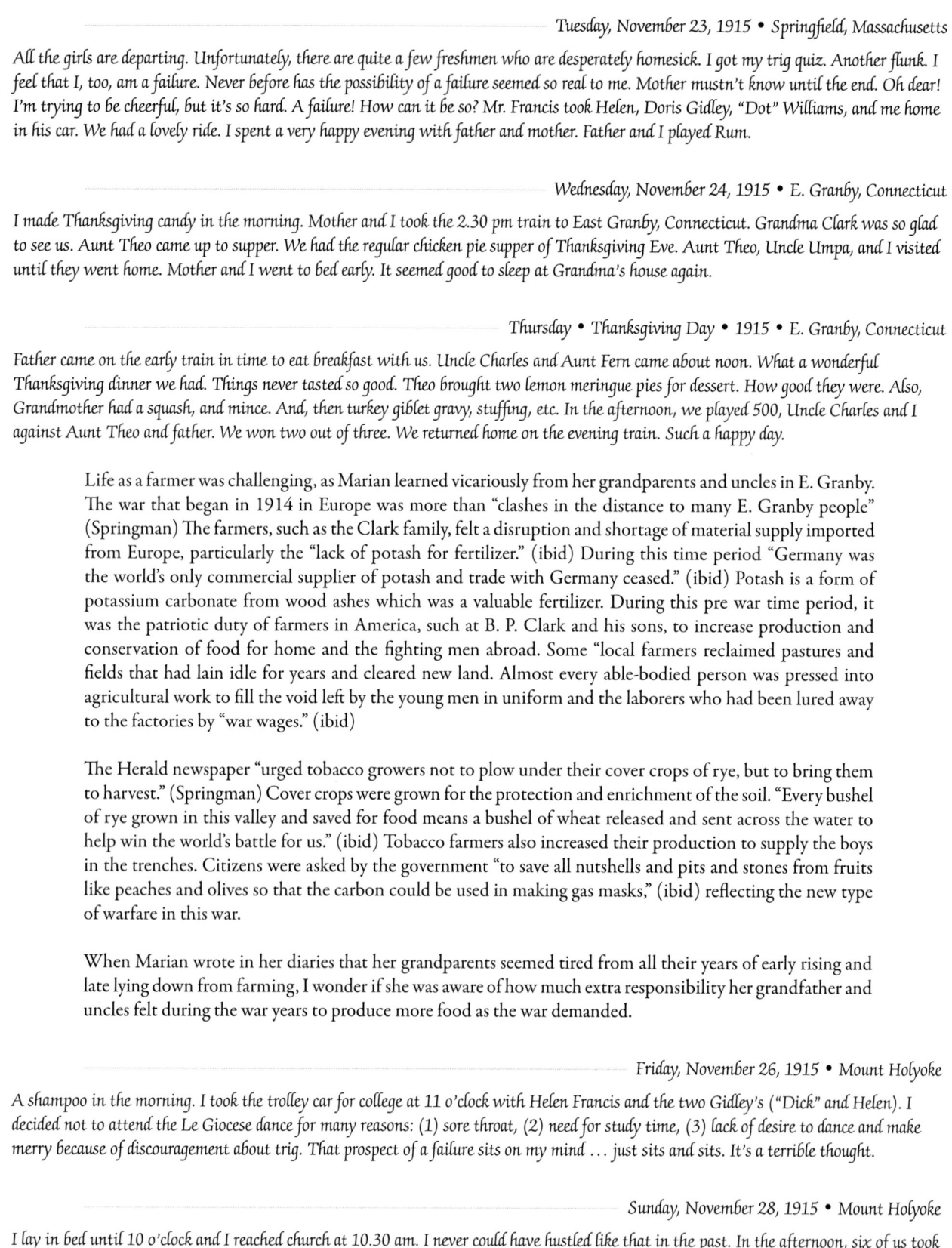

Tuesday, November 23, 1915 • Springfield, Massachusetts

All the girls are departing. Unfortunately, there are quite a few freshmen who are desperately homesick. I got my trig quiz. Another flunk. I feel that I, too, am a failure. Never before has the possibility of a failure seemed so real to me. Mother mustn't know until the end. Oh dear! I'm trying to be cheerful, but it's so hard. A failure! How can it be so? Mr. Francis took Helen, Doris Gidley, "Dot" Williams, and me home in his car. We had a lovely ride. I spent a very happy evening with father and mother. Father and I played Rum.

Wednesday, November 24, 1915 • E. Granby, Connecticut

I made Thanksgiving candy in the morning. Mother and I took the 2.30 pm train to East Granby, Connecticut. Grandma Clark was so glad to see us. Aunt Theo came up to supper. We had the regular chicken pie supper of Thanksgiving Eve. Aunt Theo, Uncle Umpa, and I visited until they went home. Mother and I went to bed early. It seemed good to sleep at Grandma's house again.

Thursday • Thanksgiving Day • 1915 • E. Granby, Connecticut

Father came on the early train in time to eat breakfast with us. Uncle Charles and Aunt Fern came about noon. What a wonderful Thanksgiving dinner we had. Things never tasted so good. Theo brought two lemon meringue pies for dessert. How good they were. Also, Grandmother had a squash, and mince. And, then turkey giblet gravy, stuffing, etc. In the afternoon, we played 500, Uncle Charles and I against Aunt Theo and father. We won two out of three. We returned home on the evening train. Such a happy day.

> Life as a farmer was challenging, as Marian learned vicariously from her grandparents and uncles in E. Granby. The war that began in 1914 in Europe was more than "clashes in the distance to many E. Granby people" (Springman) The farmers, such as the Clark family, felt a disruption and shortage of material supply imported from Europe, particularly the "lack of potash for fertilizer." (ibid) During this time period "Germany was the world's only commercial supplier of potash and trade with Germany ceased." (ibid) Potash is a form of potassium carbonate from wood ashes which was a valuable fertilizer. During this pre war time period, it was the patriotic duty of farmers in America, such at B. P. Clark and his sons, to increase production and conservation of food for home and the fighting men abroad. Some "local farmers reclaimed pastures and fields that had lain idle for years and cleared new land. Almost every able-bodied person was pressed into agricultural work to fill the void left by the young men in uniform and the laborers who had been lured away to the factories by "war wages." (ibid)
>
> The Herald newspaper "urged tobacco growers not to plow under their cover crops of rye, but to bring them to harvest." (Springman) Cover crops were grown for the protection and enrichment of the soil. "Every bushel of rye grown in this valley and saved for food means a bushel of wheat released and sent across the water to help win the world's battle for us." (ibid) Tobacco farmers also increased their production to supply the boys in the trenches. Citizens were asked by the government "to save all nutshells and pits and stones from fruits like peaches and olives so that the carbon could be used in making gas masks," (ibid) reflecting the new type of warfare in this war.
>
> When Marian wrote in her diaries that her grandparents seemed tired from all their years of early rising and late lying down from farming, I wonder if she was aware of how much extra responsibility her grandfather and uncles felt during the war years to produce more food as the war demanded.

Friday, November 26, 1915 • Mount Holyoke

A shampoo in the morning. I took the trolley car for college at 11 o'clock with Helen Francis and the two Gidley's ("Dick" and Helen). I decided not to attend the Le Giocese dance for many reasons: (1) sore throat, (2) need for study time, (3) lack of desire to dance and make merry because of discouragement about trig. That prospect of a failure sits on my mind … just sits and sits. It's a terrible thought.

Sunday, November 28, 1915 • Mount Holyoke

I lay in bed until 10 o'clock and I reached church at 10.30 am. I never could have hustled like that in the past. In the afternoon, six of us took a lovely walk up Morgan Road. "Dick" and I walked together quite far behind the others. I love that girl a whole heap. I took some camera pictures of the crowd.

Thursday, December 2, 1915 • Mount Holyoke

It snowed today when we came out of chapel. Miss Woolley made a speech on her western trip. Her talk was very humorous and of course wholly splendid, as usual. The snow fell all day in big soft flakes that made me think of Christmas. All this week I've had the hardest time studying since college opened. I love the work, so I don't mind the grind.

Friday, December 3, 1915 • Junior-Freshman Reception

A truly delightful surprise in the form of an "A" on the Latin quiz. I don't know when I have been so happy. If only I can do well on the trig tomorrow. I have no confidence in that. In the evening, I went to the Junior/Freshman Reception with a junior, Dorothy. I had a wonderful time. First, I was taken through the receiving line. We danced 10 dances and 2 extras. Every girl I danced with was a wonderful dancer. It was such fun. The play, "What If?" that the juniors gave was clever. It was about the dream of a freshman at a college where there were *no lessons*. Just think not even *trig*. It was a wonderful evening.

Saturday, December 4, 1915 • Mount Holyoke

The trig quiz was abominable. I feel like a limp rag after it. Despair has me in its clutches all right. I'm afraid there is no hope now.

Sunday, December 5, 1915 • Mount Holyoke

In the afternoon, Mother, Father, Uncle Dan, and Aunt Theo came up to vespers. I walked around campus with them before the service. The minister was very peculiar with his gestures and funny voice. We could hardly hear a word he said. After the service, Mr. Hammond (Professor, Department of Music) gave an organ recital of Christmas music. The folks went home afterwards. They brought me magazines and candy.

Tuesday, December 7, 1915 • Mount Holyoke

I got back my trig quiz. I didn't dare look at it until I was safely shut up in my gym locker. Then, an A+. I never was so happy in my life. It was unbelievable. In the afternoon, Helen and I walked up to the Croysdale Inn in The Village Commons, where there was a display of Christmas gifts. I bought a fine, little, white collar for mother. How I should love to buy everything for mother.

Wednesday, December 8, 1915 • Mount Holyoke

It snowed hard all day today, big soft flakes. How I love it! In the evening, I went to hear the famous Norman Angell, author of the *Illusion*, speak on "American's Future Foreign Policy in Relation to the War." He emphasized the fact that American must have a definite foreign policy in order to be an agent for peace. With America's present wavering policy, she is only contributing to prolonging the war. He declared firmly that this country would inevitably be involved in war. His talk was very interesting and showed the workings of a great and thoughtful mind.

As Marian continued her interest in war issues, she was forming opinions about what America's role should be in the future. Since Marian never had the opportunity to go to Europe, she visited vicariously through pamphlets and lectures such as this. Sir Ralph Norman Angell (1872-1967) was an English writer, lecturer, and a Member of Parliament for the Labour Party. Even though he was an executive for the World Committee against War and Fascism, he felt that it was inevitable that America would become involved. In 1909 Mr. Angell wrote his pamphlet, Europe's Optical Illusion, which was published the following year as the best-selling book of the era, *The Great Illusion: A Study of the Relation of Military Power in Nations to their Economic and Social Advantage*. (Angell) Angell wrote that adding territories to increase a nation's wealth was an optical illusion. "The thesis of the book was that the integration of the economies of European countries had grown to such a degree that war between them would be entirely futile, while making militarism obsolete." The anti-war film *The Grand Illusion* took its title from his pamphlet. (Wikipedia)

Five years after Angell wrote his book, England declared war on Germany. During the prior decade there had been a series of crises in Europe, which resulted in an unstable system of alliances. There was also a paradigm shift in Europe where people took pride in their nationalism and cultural differences that were not based solely on monarchies anymore. The final catalyst for the war was the assignation of Archduke Franz Ferdinand, heir to the Habsburg Empire, in Sarajevo, Bosnia-Herzegovina on June 28, 1914.

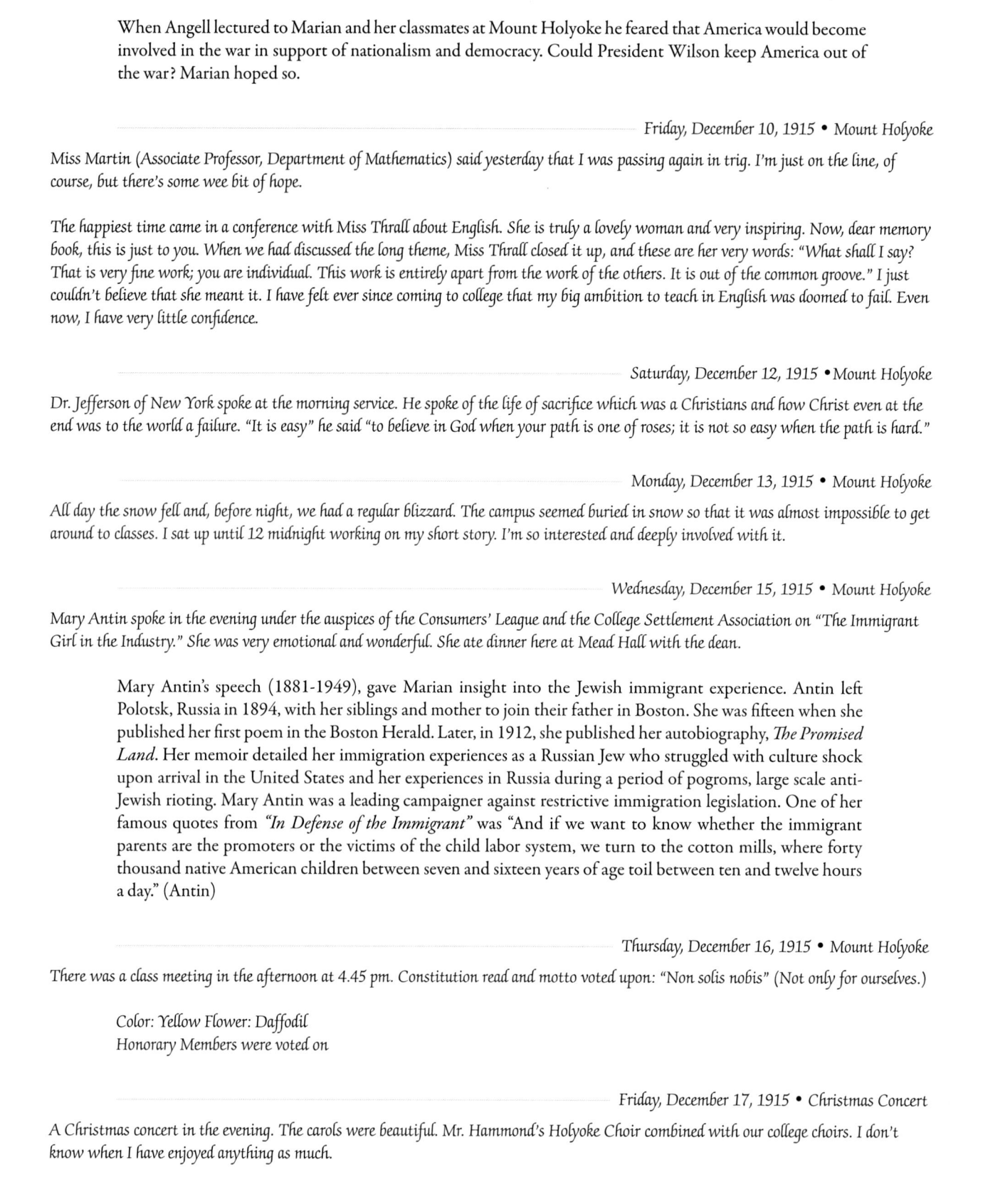

When Angell lectured to Marian and her classmates at Mount Holyoke he feared that America would become involved in the war in support of nationalism and democracy. Could President Wilson keep America out of the war? Marian hoped so.

Friday, December 10, 1915 • Mount Holyoke

Miss Martin (Associate Professor, Department of Mathematics) said yesterday that I was passing again in trig. I'm just on the line, of course, but there's some wee bit of hope.

The happiest time came in a conference with Miss Thrall about English. She is truly a lovely woman and very inspiring. Now, dear memory book, this is just to you. When we had discussed the long theme, Miss Thrall closed it up, and these are her very words: "What shall I say? That is very fine work; you are individual. This work is entirely apart from the work of the others. It is out of the common groove." I just couldn't believe that she meant it. I have felt ever since coming to college that my big ambition to teach in English was doomed to fail. Even now, I have very little confidence.

Saturday, December 12, 1915 • Mount Holyoke

Dr. Jefferson of New York spoke at the morning service. He spoke of the life of sacrifice which was a Christians and how Christ even at the end was to the world a failure. "It is easy" he said "to believe in God when your path is one of roses; it is not so easy when the path is hard."

Monday, December 13, 1915 • Mount Holyoke

All day the snow fell and, before night, we had a regular blizzard. The campus seemed buried in snow so that it was almost impossible to get around to classes. I sat up until 12 midnight working on my short story. I'm so interested and deeply involved with it.

Wednesday, December 15, 1915 • Mount Holyoke

Mary Antin spoke in the evening under the auspices of the Consumers' League and the College Settlement Association on "The Immigrant Girl in the Industry." She was very emotional and wonderful. She ate dinner here at Mead Hall with the dean.

> Mary Antin's speech (1881-1949), gave Marian insight into the Jewish immigrant experience. Antin left Polotsk, Russia in 1894, with her siblings and mother to join their father in Boston. She was fifteen when she published her first poem in the Boston Herald. Later, in 1912, she published her autobiography, *The Promised Land*. Her memoir detailed her immigration experiences as a Russian Jew who struggled with culture shock upon arrival in the United States and her experiences in Russia during a period of pogroms, large scale anti-Jewish rioting. Mary Antin was a leading campaigner against restrictive immigration legislation. One of her famous quotes from *"In Defense of the Immigrant"* was "And if we want to know whether the immigrant parents are the promoters or the victims of the child labor system, we turn to the cotton mills, where forty thousand native American children between seven and sixteen years of age toil between ten and twelve hours a day." (Antin)

Thursday, December 16, 1915 • Mount Holyoke

There was a class meeting in the afternoon at 4.45 pm. Constitution read and motto voted upon: "Non solis nobis" (Not only for ourselves.)

Color: Yellow Flower: Daffodil
Honorary Members were voted on

Friday, December 17, 1915 • Christmas Concert

A Christmas concert in the evening. The carols were beautiful. Mr. Hammond's Holyoke Choir combined with our college choirs. I don't know when I have enjoyed anything as much.

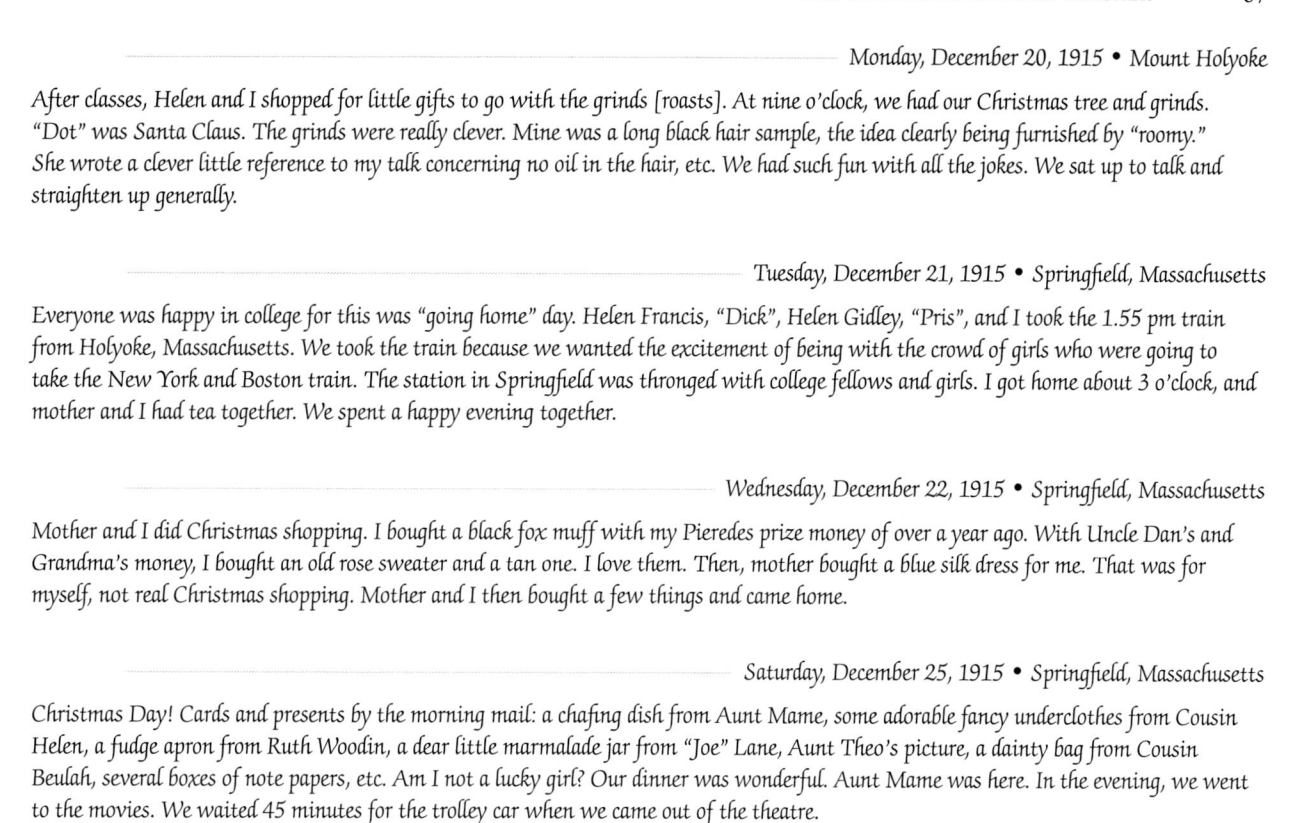

Monday, December 20, 1915 • Mount Holyoke

After classes, Helen and I shopped for little gifts to go with the grinds [roasts]. At nine o'clock, we had our Christmas tree and grinds. "Dot" was Santa Claus. The grinds were really clever. Mine was a long black hair sample, the idea clearly being furnished by "roomy." She wrote a clever little reference to my talk concerning no oil in the hair, etc. We had such fun with all the jokes. We sat up to talk and straighten up generally.

Tuesday, December 21, 1915 • Springfield, Massachusetts

Everyone was happy in college for this was "going home" day. Helen Francis, "Dick", Helen Gidley, "Pris", and I took the 1.55 pm train from Holyoke, Massachusetts. We took the train because we wanted the excitement of being with the crowd of girls who were going to take the New York and Boston train. The station in Springfield was thronged with college fellows and girls. I got home about 3 o'clock, and mother and I had tea together. We spent a happy evening together.

Wednesday, December 22, 1915 • Springfield, Massachusetts

Mother and I did Christmas shopping. I bought a black fox muff with my Pieredes prize money of over a year ago. With Uncle Dan's and Grandma's money, I bought an old rose sweater and a tan one. I love them. Then, mother bought a blue silk dress for me. That was for myself, not real Christmas shopping. Mother and I then bought a few things and came home.

Saturday, December 25, 1915 • Springfield, Massachusetts

Christmas Day! Cards and presents by the morning mail: a chafing dish from Aunt Mame, some adorable fancy underclothes from Cousin Helen, a fudge apron from Ruth Woodin, a dear little marmalade jar from "Joe" Lane, Aunt Theo's picture, a dainty bag from Cousin Beulah, several boxes of note papers, etc. Am I not a lucky girl? Our dinner was wonderful. Aunt Mame was here. In the evening, we went to the movies. We waited 45 minutes for the trolley car when we came out of the theatre.

> While Marian enjoyed her peaceful Christmas with her family in New England, she was aware that many other families in Europe were not. This inspirational war poem was written by Alma Pendexter Hayden. She won a Carnegie Medal, the British Literary award for outstanding literature for children and young adults. Marian copied this into her diary, knowing her own father was close at her side.

"The Little Refugee"

"Last year, her father's arms so strong
Lifted her high to see,
The lights and all the precious toys
Upon the Christmas tree.
"But now there is no home." she said,
"Nor any where to go.-
The big guns battered down the church-
And every place I know.

"We came away so quick — and yet,
How plainly I can see-
My little table set with cups-
Where I was playing tea."

"We came so far I never hear,
From papa any more,-
The bugles called — he said good-by-
And kissed me at the door.

"I dreamed last night he stood by me,-
His hand upon my head.
"God bless and keep my little girl."
The words he softly said."

"His head was bowed, he looked so sad-
The room grew strangely light-
And as I woke he said 'good-by'
And faded from my sight!"

Alma Pendexter Hayden

Sunday, December 26, 1915 • Springfield, Massachusetts

A stormy day without and a quiet one within. I read *The Turmoil* by Booth Tarkington. We had a late dinner of Christmas leavings. (Tarkington)

The bestseller list, a trade barometer dreamed up in 1895 by the editor of the literary review *The Bookman*, was a reliable guide to popular American culture. As an avid reader, Marian read many of the top sellers. In 1915, the top seller was *The Turmoil* by Booth Tarkington. It was a "tale of coming of age in small-town America" (Tarkington) during the Progressive Era 1901-1914. It was set in a small city - never named but resembling the author's hometown of Indianapolis. "The spokesman for adolescent America turned from light-hearted fare to produce a deeply-felt indictment of a ruthless businessman and "any city, every city that makes Bigness its god." (www.wikipedia.org)

Monday, December 27, 1915 • Springfield, Massachusetts

Shopping with mother in the morning, then a movie with "Pris" in the afternoon. We saw Fanny Ward in "The Cheat." (Ward)

Fannie Ward, born in St. Louis in 1872, had a successful career as a stage star from 1890 until 1914 in America and London. In 1915, Cecil B. DeMille convinced her to star in his new sexploitation silent movie, *The Cheat*, which co-starred Sessue Hayakawa. (The Cheat) Hayakawa played an ivory merchant who had an affair with Fannie Ward. This was the beginning of a thriving film career for her for several years.

Sessue Hayakawa was the first Asian-American screen star of the 1910's. He rivaled the popularity of Caucasian male movie stars and became one of the highest paid actors in Hollywood. "Hayakawa made his career in melodrama playing romantic heroes and charismatic heavies." (www.imdb.com)

Wednesday, December 29, 1915 • Springfield, Massachusetts

In the afternoon, went to the College Club Reception. There was dancing. I went through the various formalities of hand shaking and tea drinking. It seemed so good to see the girls again.

Friday, December 31, 1915 • Springfield, Massachusetts

I went coasting [sledding] in the afternoon in Forest Park. It was great. There were some rather fresh fellows on a ripper.

I sat up to watch dear 1915 out and 1916 in all alone. Mother and Father had retired. I had my Trig book and Pickwick Papers for company.

Marian's extensive reading included English, as well as American, authors and poets. *Pickwick Papers* was the first novel by the British Victorian novelist, Charles Dickens. It was published as a series of chapter-by-chapter monthly installments in magazines starting in 1836. Dickens's procedure of serial publications was summed up in the formula, "Make them laugh; make them cry; make them wait." (www.answers.com) *Pickwick Papers* was published in book form in 1837. Charles Dickens is best known as the author of *A Christmas Carol* published in 1843. (Dickens)

Wednesday, January 5, 1916 • Springfield, Massachusetts

Mother and I packed my little steamer trunk. I took the 3:30 pm train for college. It seemed nice to be back again with the girls. It was such fun to greet the new arrivals.

Friday, January 7, 1916 • Mount Holyoke

Miss Woolley announced in chapel that we would have outdoor chapel for a week; that is, no service but outdoor exercises instead. In the afternoon, Helen and I went for a walk. Marian C. joined us. She informed us that she would like most of all to be a professional dancer. Helen and I almost collapsed. Freda Harris and I went coasting this afternoon. We had Helen's sled and went down Morgan Road, one on top of the other. We went like the wind. Then, we decided to sled down the slope of Prospect Hill. On the crest, the runner became stuck when we were halfway down, and the sled turned a somersault. Freda and I were thrown off and began rolling down the hill so fast that we couldn't stop. Oh, it was funny, though Freda was all scratched up. We came home and bought some chocolate éclairs on the way.

Saturday, January 16, 1916 • Mount Holyoke

Aunt Theo sent me a dozen sugared raised doughnuts, in a corset box.

Monday, February 7, 1916 • Mount Holyoke

I haven't written for ages and ages, but there's a reason. To begin with, I went home Friday, Jan. 21st with a light attack of tonsillitis, which I had been having at college for two or three days — just barely dragging around. Exams are over with and passed, even trig. We haven't our report cards, so I don't know the marks, but I consider myself the luckiest, happiest girl alive to have passed. I couldn't have afforded to have tutoring, and it was just wonderful that I got through.

I believe that there is a God, who is all powerful, kind, and true who watches over us all and me. I believe that I shall get through the four years of college even though the money is very scarce. Oh, it's wonderful to be alive when you're so happy. I'm going to write often now and just let this be a big fat record of a wonderful year in college.

Tuesday, February 8, 1916 • Senior Faculty Play

Such fun we had tonight. Florence, Alice, Helen, and I went to watch the Senior Faculty Play. Some of the faculty looked so perfectly unnatural in their glad rags. Miss Griffith (Instructor, Department of English) was a scream. As we were turning the field glasses upon her, she looked up, saw us, and bowed. Oh dear, it was funny! We just giggled and couldn't bow at all. Then, the dancing, which was rare. The senior girls looked lovely in big picture hats and beautiful gowns.

> The Faculty Show takes place once every four years which enables each student to see it once during their four years at Mount Holyoke. Faculty members create a show that parodies themselves and their students.

Saturday, February 12, 1916 • Graduate Council Luncheon

The Graduate Council had a luncheon at Mead Hall at 1.30 o'clock. Miss Macomb chose six of the table waiting girls to officiate. Ruth and I were at Miss Woolley's table. It was a very grand luncheon with flowers on the tables and the best silver. The council is made up of alumnae who are either well known or quite prosperous. Of course, the grandest "councilors" sat at Miss Woolley's table. The luncheon was in four courses and very dainty. They didn't finish until 3 o'clock when we partook of the repast. It was really fun. The funniest part of it all came beforehand when Miss Macomb kept changing her mind about the one to whom the second bouillon cup with the gold rim should go. Of course, one went to Miss Woolley.

Sunday, February 13, 1916 • Mount Holyoke

A blizzardy day. I didn't go to church at all but read and wrote four letters. Helen and I learned a lot about the poem Il Penseroso (first verse) or "The Pensive Man."

"Il Penseroso"

"Hence, vain deluding joys,
The brood of folly without father bred,
How little you bested,
Or fill the fixed mind with all your toys!
Dwell in some idle brain,
And fancies fond with gaudy shapes possess,
As thick and numberless
As the gate motes that people the sunbeams,
Or likest hovering dreams,
The fickle pensioners of Morpheus' train."

Milton

John Milton was an English poet and author born in 1608. Morpheus is the minister of Som-nus or Sleep, and a pensioner is a train attendant. Milton wrote *Il Penseroso* in 1632. Milton was writing at a time of political and religious flux in England, and his poetry reflected his deep convictions. His religious views were described broadly as Protestant.

Monday, February 21, 1916 • Junior Prom

Prom dinner! The freshmen waited on the juniors and their men. It was a dandy dinner. I ushered at the Glee Club concert afterward. It was held in the new Student Alumnae Hall. The auditorium and stage are beautiful. The concert was good throughout. Ruth Gorman, all in white with a great bunch of deep red roses, was a dream! After the concert, there was dancing in the big ballroom below. Seniors also brought men.

"Woven into the fabric of a student's four years at the college were a series of rituals associated with her progression through the classes, such as Junior Prom, Senior Mountain Day, and the graduation traditions, which in the early 1900s, featured the Step Exercises, Rope Skipping, Ivy Planting, the May Day pageant, the crowning of the May Queen, and a dramatic presentation." (Edmonds)

The "successful completion of the seventy-fifth anniversary campaign's Half Million Dollar Fund made possible the building of the Student-Alumnae Hall and redeemed the promise made by the Skinner Family of Holyoke and South Hadley to provide a classroom building for English, history, mathematics, Latin, and other non-laboratory fields" (ibid) The Student Alumnae Hall (S.A.H.) building was renamed the Mary E. Woolley Hall in 1945 to honor Miss Woolley. "During Mary Woolley's administration, sixteen major buildings were added to the college plant." (ibid)

Thursday, February 24, 1916 • Mount Holyoke

Today in history, Miss Putnam called me to the desk and asked me to come to her room at 1.30 pm. Helen also had been summoned. Well, she accused Helen of having copied my map because of the similarity of spelling. We explained how I had done my map before going home sick, and Helen bravely confessed that she had copied the spelling because of the poor map in the history book. "Well, forget this," said Miss Putnam; "but Miss Francis you may do another map." Helen said, after we have left, "I'm a culprit."

Saturday, March 4, 1916 • Mount Holyoke

The basketball game and the 1919 girls were in yellow sunbonnets and waving big yellow balloons. We had our banner and mascot. I took Miss Ely (Mary Redington Ely, Holder of the 1886 Fellowship), a class honorary member, a dear and like my own mother. The mascots were the chief part of the program. Our team played splendidly and put up a good fight against the juniors, the victors.

Thursday, March 8, 1916 • Mount Holyoke

I am required by a note to appear at Dean Purington's office at 2 o'clock today. I waited one hour and finally secured admission. Dean Purington had such a startling thing to say, namely that a man in New York has given a sum of money to be given to college girls who want to be economied just for fooled things. She gave me $5 and the man's address: Mr. Scott of Broadway! I spent the afternoon in the library reading George Curtis' Prue and I for my essay. (Curtis) In the evening, Helen and I went to a talk on "Literary Work." It was interesting but the speaker said that there were not many fields for college women in it.

> George Curtis was an American writer and public speaker born in New England in 1824. He spoke in favor of civil rights and African-American equality. Curtis wrote a number of essays for *Putnam's Magazine* and *Harper's Monthly*, including *Prue and I* in 1856. It was a sentimental, tender, and humorous story of life. Alas, more discouragement from a respected male writer about careers for women in the literary world.

Friday, March 10, 1916 • Senior Show

In the evening, it was the Senior Show, and it was a wonderful surprise for everyone. The name was The Tempestuous Tale, and it was an unusual comedy composed entirely by the girls of 1916. After the show, 1918 went down in front and sang to their senior sisters. I shall never forget the Senior Show.

Wednesday, March 15, 1916 • Mount Holyoke

Frost, the poet, spoke in the evening in S.A.H. Miss Marks [Lecturer, Department of English Literature] gave a long, introductory speech titled "We do not recognize our poets." Frost read from "North of Boston" (Frost) and several newer poems. Then, he spoke of tone in poetry and tone in sentences. At the end, we were free to ask questions. One girl asked him why he always wrote in blank verse. He said, "Why, it's just the way I happen to feel." Then, he told us how he wrote in answer to the call and only then when he was young, he said, the call came, but he could not find adequate expression. Miss Woolley's request was for another poem. He read a humorous verse that was really funny. I don't know when I have enjoyed an evening more.

> Marian was fortunate to experience first-hand the readings by famous authors and poets, such as Robert Frost (1872-1963). Frost taught at Amherst College from 1916-1938. In 1916, Frost was elected a member of the National Institute of Arts and Letters. "Often Frost used the rhythms and vocabulary of ordinary speech or even the looser free verse of dialogue." (famouspoetsandpoems.com) Frost seemed to have a humorous view of the world, and made remarks such as "I never take my side in a quarrel." (ibid) Marian really seemed to enjoy his sense of humor. In 1920 Frost purchased a farm in South Shaftsbury, Vermont, near Middlebury, Vermont where he cofounded Bread Loaf School and Conference of English. (Marian later attended his school to get her Master's Degree.) Mr. Frost taught at Amherst College on and off for forty years. He was appointed a Simpson Lecturer for Life in 1949 at Amherst. In 1958 he was made poetry consultant for the Library of Congress. In 1961, Frost participated in the inauguration of President John Kennedy. Two years later at the time of his death, Frost was remembered for "observing the details of rural life, which hide universal meaning." (ibid)
>
> The following poem, *Mending Wall*, was one of the most popular poems from *North of Boston* (1914), which deals with tensions and distance between men and the complex nature of fellowship:

"Mending Wall"

SOMETHING there is that doesn't love a wall,
That sends the frozen-ground-swell under it,
And spills the upper boulders in the sun;
And makes gaps even two can pass abreast.
The work of hunters is another thing:
I have come after them and made repair
Where they have left not one stone on a stone,
But they would have the rabbit out of hiding,
To please the yelping dogs. The gaps I mean,
No one has seen them made or heard them made,

But at spring mending-time we find them there.
I let my neighbour know beyond the hill;
And on a day we meet to walk the line
And set the wall between us once again.
We keep the wall between us as we go.
To each the boulders that have fallen to each.
And some are loaves and some so nearly balls
We have to use a spell to make them balance:
"Stay where you are until our backs are turned!"
We wear our fingers rough with handling them.
Oh, just another kind of out-door game,
One on a side. It comes to little more:
There where it is we do not need the wall:
He is all pine and I am apple orchard.
My apple trees will never get across
And eat the cones under his pines, I tell him.
He only says, "Good fences make good neighbours."
Spring is the mischief in me, and I wonder
If I could put a notion in his head:
"Why do they make good neighbours? Isn't it
Where there are cows? But here there are no cows.
Before I built a wall I'd ask to know
What I was walling in or walling out,
And to whom I was like to give offence.
Something there is that doesn't love a wall,
That wants it down." I could say "Elves" to him,
But it's not elves exactly, and I'd rather
He said it for himself. I see him there
Bringing a stone grasped firmly by the top
In each hand, like an old-stone savage armed.
He moves in darkness as it seems to me,
Not of woods only and the shade of trees.
He will not go behind his father's saying,
And he likes having thought of it so well
He says again, "Good fences make good neighbours."

Robert Frost

Thursday, March 16, 1916 • Mount Holyoke

Dear mother's birthday! I met her at the two o'clock trolley, and she came directly to my room. Then, I took her down to meet Freda. We had a cozy feast at the tearoom. We were so happy together, and she is so very beautiful. My dear mother! When I returned to Mead Hall after seeing mother off, the girls said that I had been elected vice-president at the afternoon's class meeting. I was pleased because I knew that mother and father would be.

Saturday, March 18, 1916 • Mount Holyoke

In the evening, I met Mr. Ellis on the 7.30 pm trolley car. He was to be judge at the debate. The debate was splendid — Wellesley and Mt. Holyoke — and I must tell it quickly that we won! Each judge cast an individual ballot, so Mr. Ellis said. Such singing then! The Wellesley girls took defeat splendidly. We had a huge bonfire outside and sang the junior goodnight song around it. One more item - I omitted the subject of the debate — "Resolved that the federal government should own and operate the railroads"

> Marian was involved in her high school debate team and continued her involvement at Mount Holyoke. The Debating Society at Mount Holyoke "is one of the stern factors in our extra-curriculum life — an organized effort to crystallize thought, to make the expression of that thought clear and effective, and to induce the debaters to have a complete and thorough grasp of the subject. Toward this aim, the Society is working through its monthly meeting and through the hexagonal league, which is a kind of measure to Vassar, Wellesley, Smith, Barnard, and Radcliffe of the caliber of work which Mount Holyoke can show on an annual occasion." (Llamarada)

Thursday, March 23, 1916 • Springfield, Massachusetts

Home! Grandma and mother were there to welcome me. We had a supremely happy time together.

I saw Grandma off on the train and went to the movies with "Pris"; Dustin Farnum was great in Ben Blair!

> Dustin Farnum was an American, actor in silent movies, usually westerns. *Ben Blair* was released in 1916 as a traditional western and romantic drama with the themes of righting the wronged. (Farnum)

Wednesday, March 29, 1916 • Springfield, Massachusetts

I received a postal from Freda Harris saying she would arrive by the 4.38 P.M. train today. In the evening, "Joe" Lane came over to meet Freda.

Thursday, March 30, 1916 • Springfield, Massachusetts

"Joe" gave a 500 party this afternoon. Freda had never played, but mother and I coached her so that she did OK. "Joe" had about 25 girls all of whom I wanted to meet Freda. It was a lovely party with ice cream in molds, cake, nuts, and many prizes.

Friday, March 31, 1916 • Springfield, Massachusetts

About 3 o'clock, Freda and I started for the Mt. Holyoke Alumnae tea in the Women's Club House. There was an unusual program and some alumnae dressed as kids who sang Mother Goose rhymes. Good eats and college songs by the undergrads completed the program.

Saturday, April 1, 1916 • Springfield, Massachusetts

Freda and I had the wildest time this morning. We went to have our palms read. I had my palm read first, and what a tale: "I should have been born a man." I am to be married twice, have five children, travel, etc. We are to leave the city in about six months. I am to marry a man who is my inferior mentally. I am to be a public speaker." Oh dear, such a lot of things she seems to think I must do. Then, Freda's fortune: she is soon to marry and move into many parts of the country. She has literary talents and should go into newspaper work. Well, we missed the train; it was just pulling out of the station. Such a time! Freda took the 1.57 pm train to Hartford. She is a darling, and we had a lovely time together.

Wednesday, April 5, 1916 • Mount Holyoke

Back to college again. Florence and Freda descended upon us in the night because they had a rat in the room hanging by a claw from the screen.

Wednesday, April 19, 1916 • Mount Holyoke

Helen and I took a short walk on Prospect Hill before our 2 o'clock classes. I told Helen that I was to room alone next year. Poor child; she wept until late in the evening. I'm so sorry, but it can't be helped. I love her to death but do not care to room with her another year.

Sunday, April 23, 1916 • Mount Holyoke

Easter Sunday dawned cold and stormy. I ushered in church. All the afternoon, we talked and wrote letters in Freda's room. They are such dear girls.

Wednesday, April 26, 1916 • Mount Holyoke

The freshman drew numbers for rooms. Florence Sheppard asked Helen Francis to room with her. I'm glad that Helen is happy. She needs someone to love her.

Friday, April 28, 1916 • Mount Holyoke

I received notice that I have a scholarship for $150 from the College Club of Springfield. God is indeed good to me. Another year at college is assured. In the evening, we went to the Student League meeting. There was a procession with lovely girls and an automobile for the honored ones.

Saturday, April 29, 1916 • Mount Holyoke

A perfect day! Ruth Woodin and Marjorie Lyman came up from Springfield, Massachusetts in the afternoon until 5 o'clock. We walked around campus, had popcorn and ice cream, and had a good time generally. I wish those girls could be at college.

Sunday, April 30, 1916 • Mount Holyoke

Mr. Black preached at morning service. He spoke on the high call of duty and the necessity of mixing responsibility with pure pleasure. Mother, Father, and "Joe" Lane came up in the afternoon. We walked around Upper Lake and had a happy time together.

Monday, May 1, 1916 • Senior Rope Jumping

Senior Rope Jumping at 5 o'clock! It was an impressive sight to see them all in caps and gowns. They formed a long procession and advanced, singing to Williston steps. We formed a long line by the sidewalk while they jumped down the center, and then everyone dispersed over to campus to have a good time in general. Room choosing tomorrow!

> Another Mount Holyoke tradition was the senior rope jumping. "The seniors appear in a long line of black figures, two by two, coming down one of the winding paths through the grove. The entire undergraduate body is assembled to witness their maneuvers and applaud their efforts, for it requires ingenuity to manage the long skirts and flowing sleeves. It isn't quite fair to pin back the sleeves" (Edmonds) On May 1st, the seniors bring out their ropes, and for one day in the year, abandon their dignity. This tradition, and the junior top spinning, discontinued in 1935.

Thursday, May 4, 1916 • Mount Holyoke

The "Llamy's" yearbooks came out tonight in a novel manner - 1917 asked us to a dance in S.A.H., and, at that dance, the yearbooks came out. Lauren, editor in chief, told a little story to preface it. It was surely wildly exciting to push through the jam and grab your book. They are splendid, too.

Saturday, May 6, 1916 • Springfield, Massachusetts

I took Florence home with me on the 1.53 pm train from Holyoke. We shopped with Mother, and I bought a dress — blue with crocheted buttons. Mother took us to Jensen's. In the evening, Father took us to the Broadway Theatre.

Sunday, May 7, 1916 • Springfield, Massachusetts

In the afternoon, Florence and I went over to "Joe's". "Joe" bought us candy and ice cream at the drug store. With her silk dress and white fur and big dark purple hat, she looks quite stylish. "Joe" is a businesswoman now and can afford to dress well. In the evening, we had a happy, quiet time at home singing old songs and talking. Oh, the love that lives in our home with dear father and mother, all unselfishness and sacrifice.

Monday, May 8, 1916 • Mount Holyoke Junior Top Spinning

The juniors spun their tops today, and it was a lovely sight. They had dresses and bonnets of green and yellow crepe paper and dear little frilled pantalets around their legs. They also had big hoops. They sang adorably. I took Mrs. Hammond (wife of William Hammond, Professor of Music) and her little boy, Lansing, at the request of Ruth Williams. Mrs. Hammond asked me for dinner Friday.

> Marian made quite an impression at the Junior Top Spinning celebration with her guests, Mrs. Hammond and her son. It was enough for her to receive an invitation to the Hammond's home for dinner. By extending such a cordial dinner invitation, Mrs. Hammond included Marian in a select group for an impressive evening with one of Mount Holyoke's largest benefactors, the Skinners, touring the Skinner's chapel and home prior to dinner. It didn't matter that Marian wasn't talented musically; she still wanted to experience Mr. Hammonds beautiful programs. He knew that Marian would appreciate every second of the evening.
>
> Marian had such a zest for life - meeting new people, devouring literature, listening to music, and being grateful for new experiences. Mostly it was Marian's warm personality and deep caring for friends, family and teachers that attracted her to so many people, and they in turn to her. These skills would be a gift for a teacher to be successful.

Friday, May 12, 1916 • Holyoke, Massachusetts

A truly interesting day!

Joy of joys — I took the 4.30 pm trolley car for Holyoke, Massachusetts, with about six other girls. We met Mr. Hammond at the Second Congregational church. He took us into Skinner Chapel, which is a gem of art, with carved ceilings and beautiful windows. We then adjourned to Mr. Skinner's home. Mrs. Skinner received us at the door, which was held open by a very solemn butler. Their home is beautiful, very old fashioned. The rooms have high ceilings and great pictures, cut-glass chandeliers, and polished floors. We went through the conservatory where many queer foreign birds were hung in great cages.

Then, we went to the music room, the object of our visit. It is a long white room with high, curved ceilings, stained with blue, and scattered with cherub's heads. I cannot begin to tell of the rare and choice instruments that fill that room. There are four organs, one of the 16th century, pianos, and harpsichords. There is one harpsichord that cost $15,000 from the 17th century in Paris. Mrs. Skinner considers it one of her best specimens. The case is painted by a master whose name I can't recall. There's also a harp owned by Gregory XIII (can it be true!! Dear Gregory of history and fame whom Putty loves to tell of) Mr. Hammond played on all the instruments. The harpsichord sounded wonderfully sweet in "Drink to me only with Thine Eyes."

About 6.45 pm, we went to the Hammond's house for dinner taking leave of the richly gowned, most polished in manner, Mrs. Skinner. At the Hammond's, it was all homelike and cozy. The dinner was very attractive. There were three small tables in the dining room. Mr. Allen, a composer, sat at mine, or rather, I sat at his. Dear little Lansing Hammond, said grace in German. Such a meal! Strawberries on ice cream, creamed chicken, little round potatoes with much warm butter and parsley.

After dinner, we sat in the living room on a big deep couch before an open fire. Mrs. Hammond talked of the war and her friends abroad. Lansing told many jollies and submitted puzzles. We took the 9.30 pm trolley back to college.

It was an honor for Mr. Hammond to take Marian to visit Joseph and Martha Skinner, important benefactors of Mount Holyoke. In addition to Skinner Hall that they donated along with Joseph's brother William, the Skinners gave the college The Orchards golf course and the Skinner Museum. The Skinner brothers operated William Skinner and Sons and the Skinner Manufacturing Company in Holyoke, Massachusetts.

When I was in the town of Holyoke in 2008 (it is confusing: Mount Holyoke is in South Hadley), I saw a sign for Skinner Chapel and tried to get into the church but it was locked. The town was so sad and run down with its industry gone. It reminded me of Springfield. And, north of Mount Holyoke on the way to Amherst is the Skinner Museum. It was closed also so I peeked in the windows.

Friday, May 19, 1916 • Mount Holyoke

In the evening, Granville Barker spoke on the "Staging of Shakespeare." He was intensely interesting, and his readings from Macbeth were fine. As usual, Florence, Helen, and I sat in the front, in back of Miss Woolley. He spoke for simplicity in the dramatization of Shakespeare, and not cutting out what seem to be unimportant scenes.

Harley Granville-Barker (1877-1946) was an English actor, director, playwright, and critic. He revolutionized the way Shakespeare's productions were performed with naturally spoken dialogue.

Saturday, May 20, 1916 • May Day

May Day dawned clear and bright! Mother and Mrs. Lane came up on the 1.30 pm trolley. The revels on the pageant grounds were beautiful: May pole dance, natural dancing by a professional, and the crowning of the sweet May Queen, Elizabeth. Eight girls drew her chariot and she sat on an improvised toad stool around which were grouped three little Brownies. Helen, Florence, and I served a lunch to Mrs. Lane and Mother. They left on the 5:30 pm trolley. I think Mother had a happy time.

One of the annual traditions introduced by Mary Woolley was the May Day Pageant. Miss Woolley's concern for the proliferation and secret societies and social clubs was emphasized by her comments in 1902:

"The woman's college has seen a marked change in the direction both of greater freedom and of increased attention to the social life: organizations have multiplied; and receptions, dramatic and other forms of social gathering, unknown to the earlier college, have become a recognized feature of life. The change is a healthful one, but a note of warning may not be out of place. The social life should be distinctly a means to an end and not an end in itself, a recreation relieving the strain, rather than adding to it, an amusement, not a business." (Edmonds) All secret societies at Mount Holyoke were abolished in 1910. Moving forward, social clubs that were formed were open to all members of the college. "A limit was placed on the number of social events that could occur." (ibid)

Monday, May 22, 1916 • Freshman-Senior Picnic

Freshman-Senior picnic! I took Miss Ely, Holder of the 1886 Fellowship, and Margaret took Dr. Morgan. We had five special cars to the farm. It was only a short walk from the car to a lovely pasture! A friendly (?) cow greeted us, but our members, 400 strong, appalled him. We had our lunch accompanied by soft drinks. The "circus" came at 6.30 o'clock. Margaret had managed it, and that was a great success with tightrope walker, elephants (raincoats with girls underneath), a brass band, and senior crush chorus. Peanuts were passed out during the performance. Then, we started down the hill. We sang all the way home in the cars!! Much fun! Dr. Morgan is a wonder, not less Miss Ely.

Tuesday, May 23, 1916 • Mount Holyoke

Florence and I spent the afternoon lazily discussing subjects of intimate interest.

Friday • May 26, 1916 • Mount Holyoke

After classes in the afternoon, Helen and I rowed on the lake. We drew our boat up close to a lovely bank and talked. We do have happy times together. In the evening, we didn't go over to Le Giocese to dance but got plates of ice cream at intermission and took them home to eat on the piazza. The night was glorious.

Saturday, May 27, 1916 • Freshman Mountain Day!

After lunch a bunch of us started to walk up the Mt. Tom Mountains. The walk was glorious, and we made it in one hour 30 minutes. The girls who rode up in the barges got up later. Wasn't that queer? Some girls took the cable car up to the mountain house. I climbed the stairs; there were 520 of them. Once up in the mountain house, we had the stunts. Hilda Jones was the caller with a big megaphone. Every Hall had a stunt. There were about 15 in all. Florence, our Mead Hall wit, made up our stunt. It was a poem of much length in which all of us Meadites were ground [satirized]. Freda was the judge in a senior gown, and Florence did the initiations. Other halls had clever things: Byron Smith Hall did a Memory Book of the year, Porter Hall was a pipe organ upon which Elizabeth McNary played, and Wilder Hall had a faculty meeting. I rode home in a barge. There were about 25 of us, and we did have a right jolly old time. We sang all the way and ate the remains of our repast. The wagon ahead sang to us, and we to them. I was happy and tired at night.

Monday, May 29, 1916 • Mount Holyoke

The last classes of the year were today. Then, ten days of exams, commencement, and home! Helen and I took the 6.01 pm transfer home for the holiday. Father met us at the Springfield train station. In the evening, father, mother, and I just talked and were, as always, supremely happy together.

Friday, June 2, 1916 • Mount Holyoke

The math exam came today. Well, it wasn't up to Trig at midyear anyhow.

Sunday, June 4, 1916 • Mount Holyoke

Such a beautiful day! Reverend Lyman Abbott from New York spoke at church in the morning. He spoke of the woman, and most of all her place in the home. He regards the family as one of the greatest of all institutions. It is the greatest thing in the world to bring children up to good living. In the afternoon, Helen and I took pillows and walked beyond the cemetery and read. It was sweet there, and we were happy together.

> Lyman Abbott was an ordained minister of the Congregational Church in 1860. He resigned his pastorate in 1869 to devote himself to literature. First, he worked in the publishing profession as an associate editor of the Harper's magazine. Then, Abbott was the editor in chief of *The Outlook* in 1893 which advocated social reform. Abbott was a constant supporter of Theodore Roosevelt's progressivism for almost 20 years. In 1913, Abbott was expelled from the American Peace Society because *The Outlook* advocated military preparedness while under his direction. During World War I, Abbott was a strong supporter of the government's war policies.

Wednesday, June 7, 1916 • Mount Holyoke

In the evening, Miss Woolley spoke at our class prayer meeting in Rocky (Rockefeller) Hall parlor. The parlors were crowded and overflowing. She spoke on the text, "Let the beauty of the Lord, our God, be upon us, and establish throu the work of our hands upon us." She spoke of the cheerful worker the "beauty of the Lord our God" may grace the most menial task. She told us that we must be careful not to be discontented if this summer we were not to be all that we most wished. Her talk was beautiful. That I believe, is the secret of life, to be happy and cheerful, there is no place for the discontented one.

Helen received the "round robin" with joy, especially one part. Shall I ever care for a fellow like that?

> A "round-robin" was a circulated letter by an author which is copied and send to multiple recipients. In Helen's case it involved a male author. Marian was so envious of Helen's "round-robin" letter that following graduation her close group of friends, "Pop", "Pris", Doris, "Dot", "Shep", "Canary", and "Hild" nicknamed themselves the "Robin's Gang" and circulated "round-robin" letters to each other to stay in touch their entire lives. Marian would write a letter to "Pris." Then, "Pris" would write her own letter and attach it to Marian's letter and send both to the next recipient, Doris. And so on and so on. When the letter would make its way back to Marian she would start it over with a new letter. This is a variation of the chain letters that I used to receive growing up but the "Robin's Gang" was much more personal.

Saturday, June 9, 1916 • Mount Holyoke

We wound the laurel rope [chain] for the Laurel Parade at graduation on Monday. The laurel rope was done by 5.30 pm. At dinner, Dean Purington entertained her class of 1886. There were five courses, and we girls had some of the ice cream afterwards.

In the evening was the alumna fete in S.A.H. (Student Alumni Hall). Ten classes were back. 1891 got the silver cup for the largest percent back. All had some costumes, which identified their class from the rest. One class had green sunbonnets; another had blue berets; and 1906 had middies with their class numerals stamped on the collar and belt. There was a grand march and then dancing. The Senior Serenade took place at 9.30 pm in the big open space of south campus. The seniors were all in academic garb and carried big Japanese lanterns. The campus was crowded with the fond parents, mothers, sisters, etc. who have begun to arrive in great numbers.

> By 1900, the Laurel Chain originated as one of the most beloved traditions at Mount Holyoke. The "seniors dressed in white and linked by the chain, carry it up to Mary Lyon's grave, where the chain is solemnly and slowly wrapped around the fence enclosing the grave. The chain is made out of mountain laurel chosen to represent the bay laurel used by the Romans in wreaths and crowns of honor. Originally, the chain was made of laurel handpicked by freshman, but when mountain laurel became scarce the chain was made out of daisies or ribbon, and was eventually obtained from a florist at the expense of the freshman class. In 1932, the Laurel Chain became the crowning glory of the Alumnae Parade, which it remains to this day." The Laurel Chain tradition "marks the transition from the student community of Mount Holyoke to the life of a proud alumna." (www.mtholyoke.edu)
>
> Another tradition during commencement ceremonies was the Ivy Planting. "As seniors head out into the world, they look back and hope that they won't soon be forgotten." (ibid) Ivy Planting offered a way to leave a bit of remembrance behind. The senior class "processed in an orderly line, the president and vice president at the head, bearing small plants of ivy. They lead their classmates to a designated spot against a wall. The building varied, from academic to residential. The class year was carved into a stone of one such building. The class president and vice-president used a silver trowel to plant their bit of ivy as their class watched, quiet and solemn. The Ivy "would grow and spread over the building, enhancing the old brickwork, creating a lasting, living legacy" (ibid) However, the tradition of ivy planting ended with the class of 1963.

Sunday, June 10, 1916 • Baccalaureate Sunday

I was forbidden to go to church this morning, seeing how it was Baccalaureate Sunday and only senior guests or choir could go. I rested and wrote letters. I set tables for dinner, a new job. At dinner, there were lots of parents, and the seniors seemed so happy. Vespers in the evening was a beautiful service. Miss Woolley spoke on the text, which included "from strength to strength." She spoke of the need of a strong woman in the world. There was special music afterwards with the organ, violins, cello, and a harp. The chapel was packed.

Monday, June 11, 1916 • Ivy Day

A heavenly morning! Some of the freshmen went over to the gym and dragged the laurel chair between Brigham Hall and Safford Hall for the seniors to carry. About 10 o'clock, we gathered near Mary Lyon's grave to watch the line of seniors who were to march with the laurel chair to Mary Lyon's grave. When the seniors came, the sophomores sang the song "Real and Low" ["Bread and Roses" today] very softly. The seniors were all in white. Evelyn and Dorothy, in the lead, carried beautiful bouquets of forget-me-nots. It was most impressive.

Later in the day, there was the Ivy Oration at S.A.H. and least of all the surrendering of Willeston steps by the seniors to the juniors, and the giving of the cap and gown. It was a bit sad. Frances H. read the last will and testament of the senior class. After lunch, Helen and I went for forget-me-nots over by Morgan Road. Wet! Wet! Wet! It started to rain. We were without coats, and the wind in the swamp oozed into and over our rubbers. But, the flowers were exquisite, and we gathered an armful each. In the evening, some of us went over to watch the senior dance in S.A.H. It was a lovely sight and the men were great dancers. They had it all over the prom men of the juniors.

"Bread and Roses"

As we come marching, marching in the beauty of the day,
A million darkened kitchens, a thousand mill lofts gray,
Are touched with all the radiance that a sudden sun discloses,
For the people hear us singing: "Bread and roses! Bread and roses!"
As we come marching, marching, we battle too for men,
For they are women's children, and we mother them again.
Our lives shall not be sweated from birth until life closes;
Hearts starve as well as bodies; give us bread, but give us roses!
As we come marching, marching, unnumbered women dead
Go crying through our singing their ancient cry for bread.
Small art and love and beauty their drudging spirits knew.
Yes, it is bread we fight for—but we fight for roses, too!
As we come marching, marching, we bring the greater days.
The rising of the women means the rising of the race.
No more the drudge and idler—ten that toil where one reposes,
But a sharing of life's glories: Bread and roses! Bread and roses!

James Oppenheim

The seniors wear white because that is what the suffragettes wore when campaigning for women's right to vote. The song "Bread and Roses' is about the suffering of women and mill workers at that time and is symbolic of the support of women that Mount Holyoke represents." (www.mtholyoke.edu/commencement) At the laurel parade wearing white is a sign of women's solidarity.

The speech by Rose Schneiderman on April 2, 1911 published in the Jewish Women's Archives (www.jwa.org) following a fire at the Triangle Shirtwaist Factory inspired the poem by James Oppenheim, first published in The American Magazine in December of 1911. (Oppenheim)

Tuesday, June 13, 1916 • Mount Holyoke

We got up early this morning to serenade the class of 1891 and to gather buttercups and daisies to decorate the hall. We also serenaded dear Mary Ely who is to leave us next year. The last chapel of the year was this morning. I took a lesson in putting out mail, set tables for dinner, and packed all day. Ruth Williams rescued me and took me out for a college ice about 4 o'clock. My trunks went before six, and my packing box was also mailed up.

Although Marian received a generous partial scholarship for tuition from the Springfield Club, it didn't cover room and board which was $275.00 in 1916-17. Marian earned money on campus by doing work-study such as putting out mail, setting and waiting on tables, and polishing silver to reduce her living expenses.

Wednesday, June 14, 1916 • Mount Holyoke

Graduation Day! Cornelia, Ruth, and I went over by "Rocky" (Rockefeller Hall) to watch the processions of seniors and faculty in gowns and hoods. Then, we were fortunate to have tickets presented to us for the exercises. We sat in the gallery. Dr. Jefferson of New York spoke very clearly and forcibly on "America and the War." He made clear that military preparedness was wrong; that Germany was not coming; that we must rather be prepared to meet God, our judge, morally, politically, and industrially prepared.

I left to set tables in the middle, but I went back in time to see the presentation of diplomas to the seniors and the M.A. degree to two elderly women. The people didn't get to lunch until 1.30 pm, and lunch wasn't through until about 2.15 pm. Then, there was a hustle for the three o'clock trolley. Mr. Francis met Helen and me at the Springfield station and took us home in the car. Oh, such a happy Viets' family.

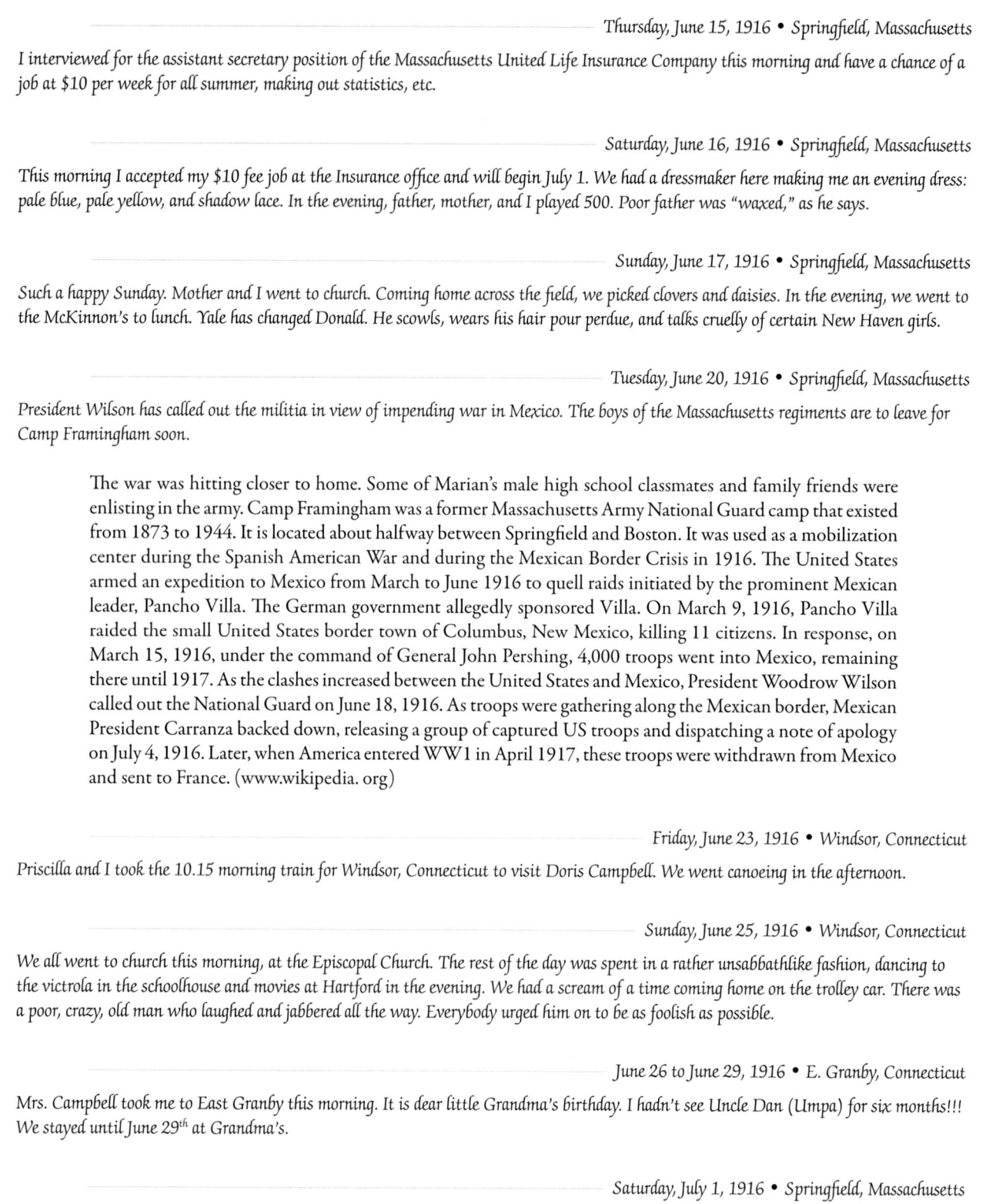

Thursday, June 15, 1916 • Springfield, Massachusetts

I interviewed for the assistant secretary position of the Massachusetts United Life Insurance Company this morning and have a chance of a job at $10 per week for all summer, making out statistics, etc.

Saturday, June 16, 1916 • Springfield, Massachusetts

This morning I accepted my $10 fee job at the Insurance office and will begin July 1. We had a dressmaker here making me an evening dress: pale blue, pale yellow, and shadow lace. In the evening, father, mother, and I played 500. Poor father was "waxed," as he says.

Sunday, June 17, 1916 • Springfield, Massachusetts

Such a happy Sunday. Mother and I went to church. Coming home across the field, we picked clovers and daisies. In the evening, we went to the McKinnon's to lunch. Yale has changed Donald. He scowls, wears his hair pour perdue, and talks cruelly of certain New Haven girls.

Tuesday, June 20, 1916 • Springfield, Massachusetts

President Wilson has called out the militia in view of impending war in Mexico. The boys of the Massachusetts regiments are to leave for Camp Framingham soon.

> The war was hitting closer to home. Some of Marian's male high school classmates and family friends were enlisting in the army. Camp Framingham was a former Massachusetts Army National Guard camp that existed from 1873 to 1944. It is located about halfway between Springfield and Boston. It was used as a mobilization center during the Spanish American War and during the Mexican Border Crisis in 1916. The United States armed an expedition to Mexico from March to June 1916 to quell raids initiated by the prominent Mexican leader, Pancho Villa. The German government allegedly sponsored Villa. On March 9, 1916, Pancho Villa raided the small United States border town of Columbus, New Mexico, killing 11 citizens. In response, on March 15, 1916, under the command of General John Pershing, 4,000 troops went into Mexico, remaining there until 1917. As the clashes increased between the United States and Mexico, President Woodrow Wilson called out the National Guard on June 18, 1916. As troops were gathering along the Mexican border, Mexican President Carranza backed down, releasing a group of captured US troops and dispatching a note of apology on July 4, 1916. Later, when America entered WW1 in April 1917, these troops were withdrawn from Mexico and sent to France. (www.wikipedia.org)

Friday, June 23, 1916 • Windsor, Connecticut

Priscilla and I took the 10.15 morning train for Windsor, Connecticut to visit Doris Campbell. We went canoeing in the afternoon.

Sunday, June 25, 1916 • Windsor, Connecticut

We all went to church this morning, at the Episcopal Church. The rest of the day was spent in a rather unsabbathlike fashion, dancing to the victrola in the schoolhouse and movies at Hartford in the evening. We had a scream of a time coming home on the trolley car. There was a poor, crazy, old man who laughed and jabbered all the way. Everybody urged him on to be as foolish as possible.

June 26 to June 29, 1916 • E. Granby, Connecticut

Mrs. Campbell took me to East Granby this morning. It is dear little Grandma's birthday. I hadn't see Uncle Dan (Umpa) for six months!!! We stayed until June 29th at Grandma's.

Saturday, July 1, 1916 • Springfield, Massachusetts

I started on my job this morning at the Massachusetts Mutual. It is detail work but entirely mechanical. I hope I can do well with it. In the late afternoon, I went to the Woodin's for a picnic supper in the grove. There were five couples there: "Dot" Woodin and Paul, Louise Talbot and her fiancé Larrie, Jimmy and Ruth Woodin, Marshall and Gia, Hawley and myself. Jimmy took Gia, Hawley and me home in his runabout about 9.30 pm, after we had danced on the piazza and had a heap of fun. Poor Jimmy got a flat tire, so we had to wait in the garage for repairs. Hawley is interesting because he's so old and has had so many experiences. He is a graduate form the Boston Law School, as well as college, and he has now been admitted to the bar.

I received my college report card today: one A, two B+, one B, one B-, and one C.

Tuesday, July 3, 1916 • Springfield, Massachusetts

Hawley took me to the Chocolate Soldier at Court Square. "Dot" and Paul were also there, much to our surprise. It was a good show. After the theatre, Hawley suggested a supper party, so we all went to the Worthy Hotel, had crab salad and water, and watched the dancing. We stayed until midnight and watched the Fourth of July in. Hawley kidded me about my youthfulness and, of course, I had to call him an old man. He is about ten years older than I, which is considerable.

> The *Chocolate Soldier* is an operetta by Oscar Strauss based on George Bernard Shaw's 1894 play *Arms and the Man*. The humorous anti-romantic play takes place during the 1885 Serbo-Bulgarian War and shows the futility of war. The heroine discovers that the Serbian Captain that searched her home does not carry pistol cartridges but chocolate. How ironic to perform this operetta where weapons were made of chocolate with the horrors of trench warfare going on in Europe in a conflict that started off in Serbia. (Shaw)

Wednesday, July 4, 1916 • Springfield, Massachusetts

Although the skies seemed threatening, mother, father, and I took our lunch in the Forest Park. We had to eat it in a little pavilion after all, but we didn't mind. Then, we wandered around the beautiful gardens. The fireworks at 8.30 pm were splendid — big, noisy, brilliant skyrockets one after another. We spread newspapers over a wet settee and then managed to have a fine seat during the show. The park was beautifully decorated with literally thousands of Japanese lanterns from the entrance to the ball grounds. Their candlelight was soft and glowing through the big dark trees. It was a real fairyland.

Thursday, July 12 1916 • Springfield, Massachusetts

Mother and I went to the movies together and had the best time. Mary Pickford was her own adorable self in Dawn of Tomorrow. (Pickford)

> Marian identified with the heroines on the screen, especially the perky Pickford. Women "spent much more time reading, thinking and talking about movie stars. Gossip, for all its destructive potential, had always been an important way for women to bond with one another, affirm their social values, express insights about human character, and experiment with new ideas about what was and was not permissible behavior." (Collins) Mary Pickford, "the girl with the curls," was a favorite of girls Marian's age for her "spunky child-heroine" Mary Pickford "received 500 fan letters a day by 1915. A professional actress since her actual childhood, Pickford had always be her family's meal ticket, and she was a tough contract negotiator who managed to become one of the very few women to get a foothold in the production end of the business, as a founding partner of United Artists. But on-screen the public demanded that she remain a golden-haired girl, and she played children's roles into her thirties." (ibid)

Saturday, July 14, 1916 • Springfield, Massachusetts

Mother and I spent a happy afternoon in Forest Park reading. Then, we did errands. Sherman Ellis came over in the evening. We were drinking ginger ale in the kitchen and looking over my photograph book when in one fell swoop I tipped over about half a bottle all over poor Sherman. He was awfully decent about it. We had great fun talking over what people we know are doing and are likely to do.

Sunday, July 15, 1916 • Springfield, Massachusetts

The quiet days are best. Mother and I went to church this morning. We all got dinner together. Father and I took a walk in the late afternoon and brought home raspberry ice cream and chocolate peppermints. We had a regular feast. We are the happiest family I believe that ever lived.

> Although Marian was quite a social butterfly, she treasured her quiet time, especially reading and writing in her diary. The following poem "Silence" was appropriately tucked into her diary:

"Silence"

I have known the silence of the stars and of the sea,
And the silence of the city when it pauses,
And the silence of a man and a maid,
And the silence of the sick
When their eyes roam about the room.
And I ask: For the depths,
Of what use is language?
A beast of the field moans a few times
When death takes its young.
And we are voiceless in the presence of realities --
We cannot speak.

A curious boy asks an old soldier
Sitting in front of the grocery store,
"How did you lose your leg?"
And the old soldier is struck with silence,
Or his mind flies away
Because he cannot concentrate it on Gettysburg.
It comes back jocosely
And he says, "A bear bit it off."
And the boy wonders, while the old soldier
Dumbly, feebly lives over
The flashes of guns, the thunder of cannon,
The shrieks of the slain,
And himself lying on the ground,
And the hospital surgeons, the knives,
And the long days in bed.

But if he could describe it all
He would be an artist.
But if he were an artist there would be deeper wounds
Which he could not describe.

There is the silence of a great hatred,
And the silence of a great love,
And the silence of an embittered friendship.
There is the silence of a spiritual crisis,
Through which your soul, exquisitely tortured,
Comes with visions not to be uttered
Into a realm of higher life.
There is the silence of defeat.
There is the silence of those unjustly punished;
And the silence of the dying whose hand
Suddenly grips yours.
There is the silence between father and son,
When the father cannot explain his life,
Even though he be misunderstood for it.

There is the silence that comes between husband and wife.
There is the silence of those who have failed;
And the vast silence that covers
Broken nations and vanquished leaders.
There is the silence of Lincoln,
Thinking of the poverty of his youth.
And the silence of Napoleon
After Waterloo.
And the silence of Jeanne d'Arc
Saying amid the flames, "Blessed Jesus" --
Revealing in two words all sorrows, all hope.
And there is the silence of age,
Too full of wisdom for the tongue to utter it
In words intelligible to those who have not lived
The great range of life.

And there is the silence of the dead.
If we who are in life cannot speak
Of profound experiences,
Why do you marvel that the dead
Do not tell you of death?
Their silence shall be interpreted
As we approach them.

Edgar Lee Masters

Edgar Lee Masters (1868-1950) was born and raised in the Midwest. After practicing law for years in Chicago, he honed his writing craft and submitted his poems to the *Reedy's Mirror* in St. Louis, Missouri. The result, *Spoon River Anthology*, was a "collection of monologues from the dead in an Illinois graveyard. The Spoon River of the title is the name of an actual river in Illinois, but the town combines Lewistown, where Masters grew up, and Petersburg where his grandparents lived. These poems were serialized in *Reedy's Mirror* from 1914-5." (www.poets.org) The "aim of the poems was to demystify the rural, small town life of America." (www.wikipedia.com) Spoon River Anthology includes two hundred and twelve separate characters. The Anthology was Masters greatest success and it became one of the most popular books of poetry in the history of American literature.

Thursday, August 17, 1916 • Springfield, Massachusetts

Father, Mother, "Dot" Williams, and I went out to Loon Pond after work today. It seems so good every afternoon to leave the office and the adding machine and the rows and rows of figures. I am now completing the premiums. Later, "Dot" showed me her trousseau, all but her wedding dress. She asked me to be "aisle girl" at the wedding in October.

Saturday, August 26, 1916 • Springfield, Massachusetts

I quit the job today, after eight weeks and $80. Our boss bid me a stunning farewell. The assistant secretary said I could probably come in next summer.

Saturday, September 16, 1916 • West Springfield, Massachusetts

Mother and I had lunch at the Woodin's house in West Springfield. Ruth has started in at Bay Path Institute and she told us all about this work. "Dot's" wedding invitations came in the afternoon. She is to be married to Paul October 11th, and I am to be one of the bridesmaids or aisle girls. In the evening, mother and I read Booth Tarkington's Penrod aloud. (Tarkington, Penrod) It is screamingly funny.

Penrod is a series of children's books by Pulitzer Prize-winning author Booth Tarkington. Through a collection of comic sketches, the book tells the trials and tribulations of eleven-year-old Penrod Schofield.

Before America entered the war, Marian was especially interested in the poetry of the English poets, including Alfred Noyes (born in 1880 in Wolverhampton, England), which gave insight into the realities of war on the western front that were already affecting lives in Europe.

"On the Western Front" (Verse I)

"I found a dreadful acre of the dead,
Marked with the only sign on earth that saves.
The wings of death were hurrying overhead,
The loose earth shook on those unquiet graves;

For the deep gun-pits with quick stabs of flame,
Made their own thunders of the sunlit air;
Yet, as I read the crosses, name by name,
Mort pour la France (Died for France), it seemed that peace was there;
Sunlight and peace, a peace too deep for thought,
The peace of tides that underlie our strife,
The peace with which the moving heavens are fraught,
The peace that is our everlasting life.

The loose earth shook. The very hills were stirred
The silence of the dead was all I heard."

Alfred Noyes

Marian did not write in her diaries during her sophomore year which began in the fall of 1916, as the world entered the eye of the tornado. The Mount Holyoke students continued their studies while chaos and death swirled around them. Junior year at Mount Holyoke was a different place when Marian was there, as reflected in the changes in the coveted traditions. In the Class Book of 1919 the editor's wrote:

-We DIDN'T Have: Prom, Junior Lunch, Boxes from home, Sings, Warm weather, much time to play, or College Crackers.

-But, we DID HAVE: Little sisters, Better complexions, Fish, A surgical dressings record, Sleigh rides, One sit-up a week, Our Llammie, Four Phi Betes, Top spinning, Shower-baths, The farm, The News, The "Marseillaise" and "Rule Britannia", Championship in the Intercollegiate, Emergency courses, Junior-Freshman houses, and To get up an hour early."

Marian knew any sacrifice on her part was for a just cause. How would their lives change in the years to come?

CHAPTER FOUR

AMERICA'S PURPOSE IN THE WAR

In May of 1915, Marian had a premonition that the sinking of the Lusitania by Germany would result in America's involvement in the war in Europe. Marian wrote: "everyone has implicit confidence in our splendid President, Woodrow Wilson, the greatest, many believe, since Lincoln." Almost two years later, Marian's premonition became a reality.

A series of events pushed America to the brink of war. On January 19, 1917, British naval intelligence intercepted and decrypted a telegram sent by the German Foreign Minister Arthur Zimmermann to the German Ambassador in Mexico City. This is famously known as the "Zimmerman Telegram." On February 24, 1917, Britain disclosed the telegram to America. On February 1, 1917 Germany resumed unrestricted submarine warfare in the North Atlantic and the Mediterranean. Following the Zimmerman telegram interception and the resumption of submarine warfare, President Wilson deliberated for several months whether or not to declare war on Germany. (US Department of State, Office of the Historian) President Wilson was ready to present his case to Congress and the nation.

On April 2, 1917 Woodrow Wilson petitioned Congress for a declaration of war against Germany saying: "The world must be made safe for democracy." Wilson spoke before Congress asking for a declaration of war on Germany:

"America's Purpose in the War"

"It is a fearful thing to lead this great peaceful people into war, into the most terrible and disastrous of all wars, civilization itself seeming to be in the balance. But the right is more precious than peace, and we shall fight for the things which we have always carried nearest to our hearts-for democracy, for the right of those who submit to authority to have a voice in their own governments, for the rights and liberties of small nations, for a universal dominion of right by such a concert of free people as shall bring peace and safety to all nations and make the word itself at last free.

The world must be made safe for democracy. Its peace must be planted upon the tested foundations of political liberty.

To such a task we dedicate our lives and our fortunes, everything that we are and everything that we have, with the pride of those who know that the day has come when America is privileged to spend her blood and her might for the principles that gave her birth and happiness and the peace which she has treasured.

God helping her she can do no other."

FROM PRESIDENT WILSON'S WAR MESSAGE TO CONGRESS, APRIL 2, 1917

Four days later on April 6, 1917, President Wilson received an overwhelming vote of support for the war: "373 to 50 in the House of Representatives and 82 to 6 in the Senate." (Willmott) Following the vote, President Wilson declared war against Germany. On June 25, 1917 the first contingent of US troops landed in France. America would officially join our Allies – France, Russia, Great Britain, and Italy – at the front.

At college, according to Marian's copy of *A Memory Book: Mount Holyoke 1837-1987,* " the faculty and students needed little more than President Woodrow Wilson's call to the country to propel the college's already sympathetic support for the Allies into a patriotic fervor of activity." (Edmonds) The college converted twenty-nine campus acres to farming to combat a projected food shortage, and all students participated in tending crops. "Although initially regarded with skepticism, the young women proved industrious and indefatigable and were soon in great demand." (ibid) – even though they wore skirts as they labored in the fields. In addition, Mount Holyoke women made surgical dressings, knit garments, and even worked in factories for the Women's Branch of the Industrial Service Section of the Ordinance Department. Selling War Savings Stamps and Liberty Loans and sponsoring other fund-raising for war-relief efforts, the college raised $168,113.72, far exceeding their goal.

On May 18, 1917, due to the small size of the American army, Congress passed the Selective Service Act. And, on June 5, 1917, the first Selective Service Act draft registration was enacted for all men between the ages of 21 and 31 (United States Draft Record.) Just three weeks later, on June 25, 1917, the first contingent of U.S. troops landed in France. It was clear, my grandfather and his generation would bear the responsibility to provide soldiers for the war.

In Hudson, New York in the summer of 1917, Howard learned from another Pawling Prep friend, Hubert Grabau, that the army was recruiting an elite group of men, among them Ivy League students and bankers' sons, to join the United States Army Ambulance Service (USAAS) Station in Allentown, Pennsylvania at Camp Crane. Over 40 colleges and universities were forming sections. The USAAS had been created by the "War Department General Orders No. 75" (history.amedd.army.mil) on June 23, 1917. (Three months after Howard's prep school friend Phil Carter joined the AFS, this ambulance corps would become part of the USAAS.) After finishing one year at Williams College, Hubert Grabau (1916 Pawling Sixth Form graduate) decided to take time off from college to train at Camp Crane in the Williams College Ambulance Service unit.

This new opportunity deserved Howard's serious consideration. While driving an ambulance was a dangerous endeavor, Howard believed that it was relatively safer than serving as an officer on the front line. Of course, Howard's mother knew because of her brother's death, that there was risk going to war no matter what area soldiers served in because of war conditions which festered diseases. If Howard wanted to serve his country, the ambulance corps offered this small consolation for his mother. The pressure Howard felt to be present in his loving parents' lives as the only son was immense. Still Howard felt confident that enlisting as an ambulance driver was the right decision for both him and his family.

On October 12, 1917, at the age of 22, after a few semesters at Union College in Schenectady, New York, and a fledgling career as a stock broker, my grandfather made the life-altering decision to voluntarily enlist in the USAAS as a Private First Class. He left the comforts of home for Camp Crane in Allentown, Pennsylvania, a mere three hours away, to enlist in Section #521. As Howard's parents took him to the station to board the train bound for Camp Crane, Howard had to contain his enthusiasm for the adventures ahead for him. It would be his first experience across the pond. Yet the tears in his mother's eyes brought the seriousness of his decision to mind. She could think of nothing except that this might be the last time she would ever see her only child. She did not yet know that she would be fortunate to get word from her son frequently in the mail.

Samuel, Howard, and Ida Rainey 1899

The recruits at Camp Crane had been carefully selected based on their ability to drive and repair an automobile, to get a job done, and to find their way to and from hospitals and the battlefront. Only since 1908 had the Ford Model T maneuvered American roads, so driving a car would be a new skill for some. Most likely Howard already knew how. On October 31, 1917, Howard's Section #521 left Allentown for 19 days of encampment at Guth Station, a field training site in Pennsylvania complete with trenches and mud. Drivers returned to Camp Crane for additional training on evacuating casualties. My grandfather grew anxious to leave for Europe.

The USAAS incorporated the American volunteer ambulance units of the American Red Cross and AFS into the Army as enlisted men to provide uninterrupted ambulance service in France. Most of these volunteers had joined the Army during the buildup of U.S. involvement in the war. Because of the need to first train and then transport troops, creating the U.S. troop presence in France took many months. By May 1918, there were over 500,000 American troops in France. By mid-July 1918, there was double that amount; two million Americans fought in Europe by the end of the war. (Willmott) And, Howard was a part of it.

In May 1918, an estimated 1.4 million deployed troops, also known as "Doughboys," wrote letters home specifically to their mothers. The letters "were put on the fastest ships and sent to New York. All had 'Mother's Letter' written in place of a stamp." (www.commandposts.com) Although President Wilson officially proclaimed Mother's Day to be the second Sunday in May beginning in 1914, the national day of celebration hadn't gained much recognition outside of Protestant churches and Sunday schools up until this time. The Mother's Day campaign was promoted on the front page of the Stars and Stripes Newspaper, "which brought American moms to the forefront of everybody's mind." (ibid) According to a report in the *New York Times*, the men wrote their letters on May 12, and "white flowers (were) pinned on the khaki uniforms of more than 500,000 American service men in France," (ibid) in honor of their mothers. Receiving the letter was a small consolation and ray of hope for many American mothers. For some, this may have been the last communication with their sons. During this Mother's Day campaign; Howard was in training at Camp Crane, still on American soil.

Marian's diaries resumed on June 8, 1918 at the end of her junior year. It is a mystery why there is such a large gap. Perhaps she was too busy to keep diaries during her sophomore and junior years due to the war activities and farming in particular. Maybe she threw them away. Perhaps they were lost. My sisters and I have been unable to find them, if they existed. Marian did return to writing in her diary more regularly during her senior year, even though it seemed that every free minute she had she was farming for the war effort.

Saturday, June 8, 1918 • Springfield, Massachusetts

I left college about 10.30 am for home, after farming about an hour. Helen Francis and I are weeding the garden, and it's a mess. I met the girls in Winchester Square to go to Margaret Kemater's "shower" out at "Spot" Lyman's in Wilbraham, Massachusetts. We had an adorable luncheon. There were corsage bouquets of Ophelia roses, sweet peas at each place, and dear little bride place cards. Such a lunch after college fare: sour bread because of lack of wheat flour to make it keep, fruit cocktail, chicken in patties, salad, ice cream with fresh strawberries, macaroons, ladyfingers, and nuts.

After the luncheon, we had the shower. The packages were done up in a mighty new and attractive way — all in white tissue paper like a bouquet of white roses with green around. Mother purchased my gift — a little straw envelope basket with beads and silk cord on it for trimmings. I love it.

I reached home about 6 o'clock. I don't know when I have enjoyed an afternoon more. It seemed so good to see all the girls. Louise "Squeezie" is as beautiful as ever and engaged, of course, to Larrie. Ruth C. is also engaged and expects to be a farmer's wife. I can't quite imagine it with her cars, her trips south, and her money.

Sunday, June 9, 1918 • Mount Holyoke

Back to college in the morning. It is Baccalaureate Sunday, a solemn day for the seniors. I came back in order to wait on tables for the big dance at Pearson's Hall where all the parents ate, that is of the seniors who are there. Some of the families surprise you as not being equal to their college daughters; with others, I wondered why the daughters didn't live up to them. I guess that's what they'll wonder about *me* when they see father and mother. The campus is alive with company and stunning machines. I love commencement time.

Monday, June 10, 1918 • Mount Holyoke

We juniors "took" the Williston steps this morning from the returning seniors. We marched solemnly up singing, "Senior steps that we have honored, since we entered Holyoke's gates." Poor Sonny fainted just before the seniors gave up the steps. She's such an adorable, beautiful girl. All the seniors are dog-tired, with their exercises and functions galore. And, things are simpler this year, too, because of the war. All the afternoon I farmed. I cut hay and helped cut the lawn. Helen was there, too, so we had a lark. I received $1.00 in pay.

> Marian's friend, Sonny, was a year older than Marian and a member of the graduating class of 1918. Sonny accepted a teaching position in the city of Hudson, New York, a small river town about an hour and half west of Mount Holyoke. Dean Purington served as a placement service matching graduating seniors with available positions. In one more year Marian would begin her job search with Dean Purington's assistance. If Sonny was happy in Hudson maybe it would be worth looking into if a position was available next year for Marian.

Tuesday, June 11, 1918 • Commencement Day • Mount Holyoke

Commencement Day. I ushered at the exercises in the morning. They were very impressive, as usual. The music was magnificent — a big orchestra and the choir in the second balcony. The academic procession was as awe inspiring as it was intended to be. I left for home on the 1.30 pm trolley. Such a rush! Mother met me in Springfield, and we purchased a bathing outfit. I went to Jensen's where a 10-cent college ice is perfectly glorious. I suppose it's a sacrilege to describe ice cream as glorious.

Wednesday, June 12, 1918 • Windsor, Connecticut

At 10:11 am Pris, "Shep", "Pop", and I boarded the NY, NH and Hartford train for Doris' house party. It poured when we reached Windsor so we went down to the shack later. It's a love of a spot – down by the river – high on a bank above in a little cleared spot above with white birches and lovely pines.

We went to bed early after a meal prepared by all of us. "Shep" is the chief cook, dear old "Shep" who can do everything so well. We slept on army cots on the piazza – eight of us in a row. Somehow the bedding is terribly inefficient.

> Marian would return home to spend the summer with her family in Springfield before the start of her senior year at Mount Holyoke. She could only hope for an end to the war soon, as all of our Allies did. Marian and most of her classmates at Mount Holyoke made the conscious decision to work quietly on the completion of their college degrees despite the fact that the world was on fire with battle and intrigue. At Mount Holyoke, she relished the spirit of patriotism, the love of service, and the strong conviction that America and her allies fought in pursuit of a right and just cause.

On the Deep Blue

After almost eight months of training, on June 13, 1918, Howard joined the combined Section #521 that was placed in the Italian Contingency to set sail on the Giuseppe Verdi, the second largest and fastest passenger steamer belonging to the Italian Government. Section #521 of the USAAS still belonged to the American Expeditionary Forces "in matters affecting organization, discipline, and supply." (history.amedd.army.mil) Under Colonel Persons' leadership, "thirty units comprised of 76 officers and 1,641 enlisted personnel" (ibid) arrived in Genoa, Italy where they were greeted with a short parade. Howard was able to write home, albeit censored versions of his experiences, courtesy of the YMCA.

Howard Eugene Rainey, 1918

To ease the strain of war, the YMCA played a crucial role in the social welfare for the troops overseas. The YMCA stationary had the following heading: "Army and Navy, Young Men's Christian Association With the Colors." On the left of each page the American flag is depicted; on the right is the YMCA logo, a red triangle. The bottom of the stationery reads: "To the writer, Save by writing on BOTH sides of this paper. To the Folks at Home: Save Food, Buy Liberty Bonds and War Savings Stamps." Howard told his parents that the YMCA limited soldiers to writing two letters per week. All letters were censored before they were mailed. The YMCA provided moral support, entertainment, food, and services for the soldiers as well as bringing speakers and lecturers to the front. The YMCA also provided R&R, canteens, and overseas exchanges. According to William Howard Taft, the YMCA was:

...one of the greatest achievements of peace in all the history of human warfare. The American Young Men's Christian Association in its welfare work served between four and five millions of American soldiers and sailors, at home and overseas. As General Pershing has said, it conducted nine-tenths of the welfare work among the American forces in Europe. Moreover, alone among American welfare societies, this organization, first and last, ministered to not less than nineteen millions of the soldiers of the Allied Armies and extended its helpful activities to over five million prisoners of war.

Service With Fighting Men: An Account of the Work of the American Young Men's Christian Associations in the World War (Taft)

The letters that arrived at the Rainey household on Allen Street in Hudson, New York were such a welcome sight, as this was the only method of communication between Howard and his parents. Most of Howard's letters were addressed to "Dearest Mother," "Dear little Mother," or "Dear Mother." How could Ida bear to lose a child in the war, especially when it was a war that Ida had conflicted feelings about? Howard recognized this, so he repeatedly wrote not to worry; "I am perfectly happy, which fact may be some consolation to you."

The following are Howard's letters home, interspersed with chronological diary entries written by my grandmother, Marian. The contrast is stark. Howard's first censored letter was written on board the Giuseppe Verdi passenger steamer.

Dearest Mother,   *On the deep blue, June 13, 1918*

This is my first chance to write you, and even now I feel I can not write much for the censor rules are many. I dare say you were somewhat surprised when you learned that I had gone from the old U.S. I had begun to be a little discouraged for, as you know, we were being told every few days that we were leaving soon and then did not leave. But, at last, we are sailing and if all goes well will arrive at some unknown-to-us place where at last I may be of some service.

I wish I could tell you what vessel we are on but of course I cannot. All that I can say is that it is a fairly good one although I can not appreciate its full advantages for I am traveling steerage which fortunately you know nothing about.

Now, for what we do each day. We arise at 6:00 am and breakfast at about 7:30am. At 9:00 am we have boat drills and at 9:30 am exercises, at 10:40 am Italian class, and luncheon at 12:30 pm. We then have the entire afternoon to ourselves. It really is fun having not much to do and we have been most fortunate in being allowed Wednesday on deck at practically all times. No smoking on deck after dusk but that is about our only restriction.

How is Aunt Mary Rainey enjoying her vacation? Well! I did beat her across (the pond) on that.

The water has been beautiful and the sunsets gorgeous. I have never seen the water so blue. This certainly is a wonderful experience. I would not miss it for anything. This is my first and probably my last steerage trip and it is most interesting.

Will close now and go to breakfast. You never knew me to do anything before breakfast but sleep, did you? The army is getting me into bad habits. No more sleeping until 10:00 or 11:00 o'clock and having breakfast in bed while reading the morning paper.

How is American Sumatra Tobacco Co. stock selling now? It must be around $125/share. Why did I not hang on and give Dad power of attorney?

Love to all and my best to any that you may see in town. (In addressing the envelope, do not abbreviate anything. We had a most mild trip.)

I must write Aunt Alice Rainey next and then the remainder of the family after that.

With lots of love, You'sr son

> It is difficult for me to imagine Marian "sleeping until 10:00 or 11:00 o'clock." My grandfather was definitely a very good natured and easy going person. Despite the sacrifices Howard chose to make, Marian continued to enjoy her summer vacation traveling with friends to Doris Campbell's cabin and the Silver Bay Conference, working at Massachusetts Mutual, and volunteering at the Red Cross before heading back to Mount Holyoke for her senior year. Marian's diary entries are interspersed with Howard's war news.
>
> The following poem about sorrow during wartime was clipped out of the Westminster Gazette, an influential Liberal newspaper based in London, by Marian and entered into her diary. The words "Ochone" and "Wirra" are Irish or Scottish terms used as an exclamation of grief, concern, or sorrow.

"Sorrow"

"OCHONE, it's the sorrow that's upon me!
(Childer, quit yer playin' at the door!)
The sun was shinin', but I knew it wouldn't last,
The signs were bad, an' I saw it comin' fast;
Did ye hear last night the wailin' in the blast?—
An' sorrow came down upon the wind.

> Wirra, it's the grief that's come upon me!
> (Childer, quit yer talkin' at the door!)
> The farm dog barked, an' the red cock crew,
> An' the fire went out when the cold wind blew;
> I've heard bad news, an' I know it's true,
> For sorrow came down upon the wind.
>
> Ochone, it's the grief that's come upon me!
> (Childer, quit yer shoutin' at the door!)
> Him that was young, an' beautiful, an' tall!
> When he waved good-bye I niver thought he'd fall;
> It's meself doesn't know what til do, at all, at all,
> For sorrow's come down upon the wind.
>
> Ochone, it's the fear that's come upon me!
> (Childer, quit yer laughin' at the door!)
> Himself worked hard for til gain our daily bread,
> An' now it's the childer that be til go unfed,
> For far on the battlefield he's stretched out dead,
> An' sorrow's come down upon the wind.
>
> Dear God, it's the sorrow that's upon me!
> (Childer, quit yer cryin' at the door!)
> There's naught til do but to kneel an' humbly pray
> To Christ in Heaven to be our help this day,
> An' to care for the soul in him that's gone away—
> For sorrow's come down upon the wind."
>
> *E. Margaret Du P. Archer*

Thursday, June 13 to Saturday, June 15, 1918 • Windsor, Connecticut

Heavenly days at the little shack. It's the dearest place. It has one big room of all wood with a "vic" [Victrola] and a fireplace, besides regular chairs and table, a kitchenette, and, best of all, the big screened-in piazza. We spent most of our time these dream days canoeing, swimming, eating, preparing eats, and reading out loud (usually done by "Pop"). We surely have indulged in eats. Mrs. Spaulding sent some "surprise" cookies, sugared doughnuts, etc. We blew ourselves to a steak one day, and, in the end, all the eats only amounted to $3.00 apiece.

"Dot" and "Hild" came Thursday full of tales of West Point commencement and wearing their brass buttons proudly. They are easily the most stunning girls in the crowd.

In America, Flag Day is celebrated on June 14th. "It commemorates the adoption of the flag of the United States in 1777." (www.wikipedia.org) Henry Van Dyke wrote the poem *"Who Follow the Flag"* and these are the first two verses:

"Who Follow The Flag" (Verses I and II)

> "All day long in the city's canyon-street,
> With its populous cliffs alive on either side,
> I saw a river of marching men like a tide
> Flowing after the flag: and the rhythmic beat
> Of the drums, and the bugles' resonant blare
> Metered the tramp, tramp, tramp of a myriad feet,
> While the red-white-and-blue was fluttering everywhere,
> And the heart of the crowd kept time to a martial air.

"O brave flag, O bright flag, O flag to lead the free!
The glory of thy silver stars,
Engrailed in blue above the bars,
Of red for courage, white for truth,
Have brought the world a second youth
And draw a hundred million hearts to follow after thee.
Old Cambridge saw thee first unfurled,
By Washington's far-reaching hand,
To greet, in Seventy-six, the wintry morn
Of a new year, and herald to the world
Glad tidings from a Western land,--
A people and a hope new-born!
The double cross then filled thine azure field,
In token of a spirit loath to yield
The breaking ties that bound thee to a throne.
But not for long thine oriflamme could bear
That symbol of an outworn trust in kings.
The wind that bore thee out on widening wings
Called for a greater sign and all thine own,--
A new device to speak of heavenly laws
And lights that surely guide the people's cause.
Oh, greatly did they hope, and greatly dare,
Who bade the stars in heaven fight for them,
And set upon their battle-flag a fair
New constellation as a diadem!
Along the blood-stained banks of Brandywine
The ragged troops were rallied to this sign;
Through Saratoga's woods it fluttered bright
Amid the perils of the hard-won fight;
O'er Yorktown's meadows broad and green
It hailed the glory of the final scene;
And when at length Manhattan saw
The last invaders' line of scarlet coats
Pass Bowling Green, and fill the waiting boats
And sullenly withdraw,
The flag that proudly flew
Above the battered line of buff and blue,
Marching, with rattling drums and shrilling pipes,
Along the Bowery and down Broadway,
Was this that leads the great parade to-day,--
The glorious banner of the stars and stripes.
First of the flags of earth to dare

Heraldry so high;
First of the flags of earth to bear
The blazons of the sky;
Long may thy constellation glow,
Foretelling happy fate;
Wider thy starry circle grow,
And every star a State!"

Henry Van Dyke

Saturday, June 15, 1918 • Springfield, Massachusetts

"Dot" and I went to Margaret Kemater's Wedding. Carolyn took me in the car. The Kemater's house looked lovely all banked with flowers and pervaded with the wedding atmosphere. "Kennie" made such a sweet bride. The bridesmaids were rainbow girls, each as one soft color — pink, lavender, yellow, and pale green. I like Roger Laurence a lot. He adores Margaret and thereby shows his sense.

Early in the evening, "Larrie" came for Louise Talbot in his car. She invited us to fill up the back of the car and "chase" when the bride and groom went away. They left in the Cadillac "8," and we trailed in a Dodge, tearing down the road almost to Palmer, Massachusetts, at 40 miles per hour. It was heaven! We haven't any idea where they went.

Sunday, June 16, 1918 • Windsor, Connecticut

Back to Windsor. Doris and "Hild" met us at the station in the machine. The shack looked like home again. We had a marvelous dinner, two quarts of ice cream for seven people, with piles of ripe red strawberries picked wild out in the sunny field. Oh, it was great! Late in the afternoon, Doris took me over to Grandma's at E. Granby, Connecticut. All of us went. The machine acted terribly; the engine balked on all the hills. "Dot" got quite raving mad.

It was so good to see the farm and Grandma and Grandpa and Umpa again. Umpa came out to the car and talked with the girls. He was so dear. We had a lovely quiet evening all together. Theo came up, so we had a regular family party.

Monday, June 17, 1918 • E. Granby, Connecticut

Grandma and I visited all day and I took the evening train home. Father met me at the station. Two more days before the Silver Bay YWCA Conference in Lake George, New York! I'm so excited. It is to be my big time all right. It's great to be young and looking forward to things.

> Marian was a member of the Silver Bay Club at Mount Holyoke, which comprised those who have attended any of the Silver Bay Conferences at the YMCA Silver Bay campus on Lake George. "At the meetings there are informal discussions of religious problems in college. A constant effort is made to bring back to college some of the impressions received at Silver Bay." (Llamadra Yearbook) "The mission of Silver Bay of the Adirondacks is to offer all people opportunities to renew, refresh, and nurture their spirit, mind and body." (www.silverbay.org)

Tuesday, June 18, 1918 • Springfield, Massachusetts

Miss Clarke refused to move from Spencer Street to sew for us, so I went to her. She saw fit to lecture me on extravagance, neatness, and utter lack of intelligence in the line of sewing. I was *boiling*, but managed to hold it in until I got home. I wish I could have kept from blurting it all out to mother.

Wednesday, June 19, 1918 • Springfield, Massachusetts

The little steamer trunk is all packed for Silver Bay and all the clothes in it are clean and whole, thanks to mother who, while I have run errands, has done just everything.

Thursday, June 20, 1918 • Silver Bay Conference • Lake George, New York

On the 12.40 pm B &A Railroad (Baltimore & Annapolis), I started on my journey. Father insisted that I have a chair. I insisted the other way with a view to War Savings Stamps, but it didn't do any good. And, of course, it was heavenly and luxurious. The people in the car are so exciting looking with that air of having seen it all, which I don't share. There was a baby and her mother and her nurse. And more fuss over that two year old! They carried a special suitcase for her toys and waited on her hand and foot. Mostly, she screamed and cried. Also, there was a refrigerator with her ice water in it. The porter had to carry everything out when they reached Pittsfield. I had almost an hour's wait in Albany. The station is fascinating. I reached Glens Falls, NY about 7.15 pm after a three hour, halting ride on an "every-hitching-post" local. Florence W. met me at the station, and we had dinner at 7.30 pm in her house. I was surely starved ... not a bite since 11.30 a.m.

Friday, June 21, 1918 • Silver Bay YWCA • Lake George, New York

I got on a train this morning from Glen Falls to Lake George that the entire Silver Bay crowd inhabited. Such a grand crowd of college girls from all over. The boat ride, for two hours across Lake George to Silver Bay, was great. The Mt. Holyoke delegation sat together and sang. We reached Silver Bay about 2.00 o'clock and didn't get lunch at the hotel until 3.00 pm because of a delay. Eleanor and I are in an adorable cottage, "The Birch," back of the hotel and high over the lake. It is a two-room affair, and Abigail and Ingrid have the other room. They are Holyoke class of 1920. A mass meeting in the evening opened the conference.

Saturday, June 22, 1918 • Silver Bay Conference • Lake George, New York

The classes began today with a big enrollment in the chapel. I am in a class on "Eternal Life and Life Today" and a class on "The Path of Labor." I like them both. Then, at 11 o'clock, I had student government council. There was a tea at 4 p.m. at which I had to speak on "War Work at Mt. Holyoke." Five of us from different colleges spoke. We were glad when it was over. In the afternoon, we had a swim in the lake. The water was terribly cold, but awfully good. You can wade out for ages to the safety line. It seemed so good to be "in the swim" again. In the evening after "second" supper, we had a sing by colleges. Mt. Holyoke's delegation is just all right. The weather continues very cold and rainy. We can't see the mountains half the time for mist. I know what a gorgeous place it will be when the sun does shine out. The evening meeting was splendid.

Sunday, June 23, 1918 • Silver Bay Conference • Lake George, New York

Cold and rainy still. There was a denominational meeting in the afternoon. Congregationalists are planning the conquest program for next year with the idea of "conquering the world by love." The sad old world needs love, and if we Congregationalists can help, we must. If a conquest by love had begun before, there would have been no war.

Monday, June 24, 1918 • Silver Bay Conference • Lake George, New York

My class continues to be marvelous. The minister believes so thoroughly in the eternal life. He says that the men in France *believe* too; it is the foundation of their faith. He traced this belief historically for us and showed us that always men have longed for this belief and sought to express it. He does not believe in Hell fire. Our punishment after death will lie in separation from God. And that is the great and terrible punishment. He showed us that God is everywhere – in all beauty of nature and in the beauty of womanhood. It is only when sinful man destroys the beauty that God is not there. The weather is beautiful at last. The mountain, trees, and water – all is beautiful. Instinctively we all worship the creator.

Tuesday, June 25, 1918 • Fort Ticonderoga • Ticonderoga, New York

After an early lunch, we went to Fort Ticonderoga on the little boat launch from Oneita Bay. We went up to the northern end of Lake George, so I have seen the extent of it. Then a buckboard wagon ride through the town, Ticonderoga, and finally landing at the fort on the top of Lake Champlain. Our guide instructed us in history and geography. It is a picturesque old ruin. Coming back, we sang all the way and feasted on ice cream cones.

> The star shaped Fort Ticonderoga, originally Fort Carillon, was built by the French Military between 1755 and 1759 to control Lake Champlain. The fort was successfully defended by a French army of 3,500 by an attack of the British army of 16,000. "This was France's greatest victory in the Seven Years' War." (fort-ticonderoga.org/history) The following year, the British defeated the French taking the fort back.
>
> Marian's ancestors were involved in the successful retaking of the fort and artillery during the Revolutionary War at Fort Ticonderoga. She probably did not mention it because she was so involved with her Silver Lake experience but I know she was proud of her ancestor's bravery, loyalty and patriotism. I think Marian drew strength from her ancestry to fight her own battles in life.
>
> Today the fort, grounds, and museum are preserved by the Fort Ticonderoga Association on 2,000 acres situated in the six million acre Adirondack Park. Fort Ticonderoga was named a National Historic Landmark in 1960.

Friday, June 29, 1918 • Silver Bay Conference • Lake George, New York

This morning at 4 a.m., a crowd of us climbed Sunrise Mountain and found a gorgeous view of the whole lake and the mountains round about. It was a steep short climb, and with no breakfast to stay me, I made poor work of it.

In the afternoon was the ballgame between the recreation leaders and the ministers. The ministers were killing in middy blouses and shirts. Some of them wore high white shoes. It was a farce of a game and screamingly funny.

In the evening was the competitive sing at which Mt. Holyoke owes thanks to the stiff training given to us. We won the silver cup lined with gold. The song was really fine. The chorus ran this way: "Thru Silver Bay thy spirit give and teach us how to nobly live."

Saturday, June 30, 1918 • Silver Bay Conference • Lake George, New York

Our last day of classes. I had to give part of a debate in Miss Laughlin's class on what women in general can do for other women. In the evening, there was a big rally and a summary of YW work, past and to come. I packed my trunk after the delegation meeting. Just a word about my roommate, Eleanor. She's a dear. We've had the best times together. She is a wealthy girl but doesn't let her money poke in and spoil the sincerity of friendship.

Sunday, June 31, 1918 • Silver Bay Conference • Lake George, New York

The last day! I went to four meetings in all. The minister has just returned from France. Her message to us was brief and to the point. She said that her experiences there had led her to despise all insincerity. It was only the *real* qualities that counted in a great crisis. She spoke of the effect of the uniform – how it was such a great leveler and how those whom the frivolity of fancy clothes had formerly made attractive were unattractive in the plainness of the uniform. She was, of course, speaking of women. We had a sing on the wharf at sunset. The water was so still and the great mountains. We sang "Fairest Lord Jesus" last of all. We hated to break up- even to hear Miss Conde speak. None of us talked much as we strolled up to the assembly hall from the quiet wharf.

In the evening, Miss Bertha Conde, spoke to us in her sweet, thoughtful way. She speaks like Miss Woolley in many ways. She pleaded for our acceptance of the "abundant life." Her life, we all know, is an example of one who for years has sought to follow Christ.

> Bertha Conde was an author and prominent in YWCA work. She wrote a paper entitled "Glimpses into the Student Movement of Other Lands." It seems ironic that the minister spoke of women in uniform when she had just returned from France where all the young military men were dressed alike.

Monday, July 1, 1918 • Springfield, Massachusetts

The boat left at 8.30 am this morning in the driving rain. I looked a long time back at Silver Bay. I don't believe that I shall ever see it again. We had a nice boat trip singing all kinds of college and war songs on the deck until the rain drove us inside. We made the train all right at Lake George station. Father met me at the Springfield, Massachusetts station, and I reached the house about 7 o'clock. It was so good to see mother. It's *always* so good to be home, no matter how delicious the place you have left behind, and Silver Bay *was* delicious.

Tuesday, July 2, 1918 • Springfield, Massachusetts

Back to the Massachusetts Mutual with so many familiar faces, and in fact everything about it is familiar after two summers there. My boss accompanied me to the tax department – also gave me a real talk on past lack of earnestness, etc. I guess I really haven't made good there. I can't endure the dull old round of office work. Well, I'm trying to excuse myself and there's no use. The first day ended well. It was good to see "Mit", "Joe", "Pris" and Helen, all down there and to chatter to the folks in the evening all about Silver Bay. Will I ever have such a heavenly June again?

> While Marian was singing war songs on the shores of beautiful Lake George at the Silver Bay Conference, and debating whether love could have prevented the conflict, Howard was sightseeing in Italy, perched on the precipice about to plunge into the fighting.

Italy

Howard arrived safely in Genoa, Italy with the USAAS Section #521 in July of 1918, despite the threat of German submarines. He spent two months working at the motor assembly parc of the Ford ambulances, performing guard duty in Genoa, and enjoying the beaches near the camp at the Lido (south of Venice). He saw the magnificence of Composanto, a monumental cemetery in Pisa; the Righi Fortress in Genoa; the grandeur of the palaces of Garibaldi near Parma; and the contrasting squalor of the birthplace of Columbus. He wrote that "we saw no active warfare" in Italy.

At the Italian motor assembly plants, Ford Model T ambulances arrived in parts and the soldiers would put them together. While frames, wheels, transmissions and motors came intact, they used wooden crates to construct the ambulance body. The Model T four-cylinder engine had to be started by hand with a crank. The ambulance cars became a 'symbol of American spunk' because of how quickly they could get wounded soldiers from the battlefield to the hospitals.

The American Field Service Bulletin published the parody of Rudyard Kipling's 1892 rhyming narrative "Gunga Din" about the Model T. Kipling's poem was written from the viewpoint of an English soldier in India and his poor treatment of his water-bearer (a bhishti). Kipling wrote about his regrets of the abuse he dealt to Din and admits that Din was the better man of the two. This parody was about the abuse of the Model T by the soldiers.

"Yes, Tin, Tin, Tin,

You exasperating puzzle, Hunka Tin,
I've abused you and I've flayed you,
But by Henry Ford who made you,
You are better than a Packard, Hunka Tin."

Before World War I, Rudyard Kipling had already endeared himself to the American public for his magical children stories and poems, including *The Jungle Book*, in 1894. Kipling was born in India and educated in England. He married an American woman and moved to her hometown in Vermont in 1892 where he wrote some of his best and well known work. Many of his magical stories drew from his own childhood experiences in India. In 1907 he won a Nobel Prize in Literature. He died in 1936 and his ashes are buried at Westminster Abbey in Poet's Corner next to the grave of Charles Dickens. (Wikipedia.com)

July 4th, 1918

Dear Mother,

This is my first letter from Italy. This country certainly lives up to its description as sunny and a darn hot sun it is. The trip across was exceptionally calm. I wish that I might tell you all about it but I am afraid that I cannot at present. We had quite a heavy convoy coming into post and it certainly was a wonderful sight. We arrived at about sun up and believe me, I was on deck to see us stream into the old post. I cannot now tell you what post but can soon, I guess.

The first two nights on dry land, we spent in an old fort. The second night we were allowed down town and, of course, some of the lads had to abuse their privileges and ruin it for the rest of us. Now we are allowed only one day and evening down town and then only when accompanied by a non-commissioned officer. It certainly is mean to have no freedom just because of a few who did not know how to behave. The second day I had luncheon and dinner in town and certainly did enjoy them. Between meals we visited several most interesting places and on the whole had a fine time. I found that with only very limited knowledge of French that I could at least make myself understood.

We are allowed to drink light wines and beer. The wine, as usual, is I guess, even more plentiful than water. It is very cheap for we buy a liter for 3 or 4 liras.

I changed some of my American money at a very good rate, getting 8.7 at the American Express Co. We have a representative of the National City Bank of N.Y. in camp for the transaction of money affairs. I may as well open an account with them but have not fully decided to do so.

There is no telling how soon we will get to the front but I guess as soon as our cars are assembled. On our arrival, we had a short parade and then went to our barracks. We received a most cordial and demonstrative welcome. Flowers were literally showered upon us as we walked through the streets. Today being the 4th, we had another parade with some sort of demonstrations.

We are allowed but two letters a week but you may count on a regular correspondence when possible. I neglected to say in my past letters that I had my hair cut off entirely. I surely did look funny with my peculiarly shaped head but the hair is beginning to come in again.

We have a cracking good Y.M.C.A. with us. Our food has been splendid. As I am limited to four pages, I must close.

My love to all and loads for yourself.
Your son, Howard

Friday, July 5, 1918 • Springfield, Massachusetts

I spent the night with "Mit". We went to the Polis - hot as a pepper in there - hardly possible to breathe until you get used to it. The men beside us made themselves rather disagreeable. The play "Here Comes the Bride", an insane series of situations played only fairly well by stock company. "Mit" and I had a nice talk - one of the reunion variety. Poor child! Jimmie is in France and life looks rather hard to her just now.

> Watching a play and chatting with friends, Marian can hardly imagine how hard life would be at the front.

Saturday, July 6, 1918 • Springfield, Massachusetts

A nice long auto ride with the Francis's in the afternoon. There were loads of wonderful flowers, yellow and white.

In the evening, we, as a family, went up to see "The Blue Bird" in the movies at the Phillips Theatre. It was beautiful and we had a feed afterwards.

> In the silent American movie, *The Blue Bird*, (Belle) two peasant children are led by a fairy in search of the elusive Blue Bird of Happiness. Along the way the children "become aware of and conversant with the souls of a Dog and Cat, as well as of Fire, Water, Bread, Light and other presumably inanimate things." (www.imdb.com) Happiness never seemed elusive for Marian.

Sunday, July 7, 1918 • Springfield, Massachusetts

Mother and I went to South Church to hear darling Dr. Gilkey preach. He was at Silver Bay, too. The South Church audience is so fearfully aristocratic and high bred. I should think the cool, middle-aged ladies, wreathed in pride, might frighten the adorable young minister who is so very much in earnest. The McKinnon's came over in the evening. It seemed funny to see Donald, a perfectly good young man and *not in the war*. His medical study is equally important, I suppose.

> Not only Marian, but most of America looked askance at men who did not serve.

This was another glorious day for Ida, with a sweet letter arriving in her mailbox from her son in Italy. Every letter would brighten her day in a way that nothing else could. S. Mitchell kept busy with war efforts at home raising money for Liberty Bonds; serving as Treasurer of the Columbia County Chapter of the American Red Cross; a member of the Columbia County Rationing Board; Treasurer of the Hudson Young Men's Christian Association; and a member of the board of managers of the Columbia County

Tuberculosis Hospital. But, as night would set in, the quiet would turn to thoughts of anguish and anxiety wondering about the future.

July 10, 1918

Dearest Mother,

I am wondering if it is as warm at home as it is here. It certainly is warm during the day but cools off some at night. Of course, we see some wonderful sunsets.

I was allowed downtown last Monday and spent the whole day just wandering around to the stores and seeing as much as we could in the limited time. I can not tell you what I saw for I know that it would not pass the censor. It would undoubtedly convey to you where I am and that seems to be what is most guarded against. For the first time since I left the States I had a good meal of my own choice. I had some splendid roast duck. Food is pretty scarce, therefore about twice as expensive as before the war. For instance, my luncheon cost 14 lire which formerly could be had for about 8. However, it cost $1.50 approximately for duck and Muscat which is not all expensive.

To-morrow morning, for the first time since I have been in a motor service, I am to be detailed as a motor driver. Whether it will be a big truck or a touring car I do not know but I much prefer the latter. This, however, is temporary and I am hoping to be put on an ambulance soon.

The meals in camp are really remarkable. We have quite a variety and it is very well cooked. If that old saying is true that a man must be fed well to be a good soldier we all ought to be fine soldiers. And, everything else is made just as comfortable as possible for us. I am glad now that I did not go to Plattsburgh, NY or any other officer's camp. I would not miss this experience for anything. I am perfectly happy, which fact may be some consolation to you.

I think it would be a good idea to number all the letters you send me and I will do the same to yours. This is #3. Mrs. H. used to do that to the Colonel's so he could keep track of how many were missing and let her know.

We are most fortunate in being able to get tobacco, etc. There seems to be an unlimited supply of American cigars and cigarettes. Chocolate also is plentiful.

Last night I heard a talk given by an American Y.M.C.A. man with the Italian Army. He was most interesting, telling us what we might expect and what he had already been through.

My love to all,
Your son, Howard

> Waiting for his post, Howard seemed preoccupied with food. Perhaps it was his age. Many soldiers, including Howard, enjoyed trying the variety of food in Europe, as many had never been across the pond before. Marian devoted a great deal of ink to what she ate too.

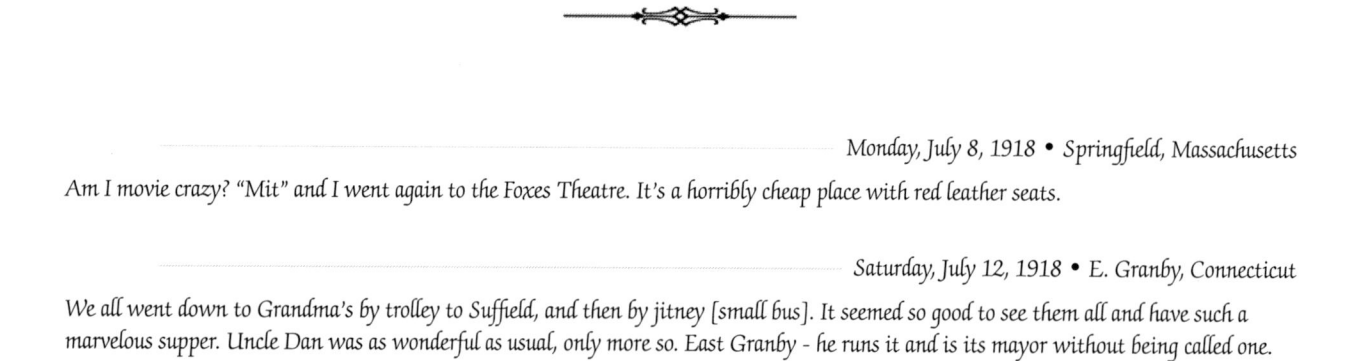

Monday, July 8, 1918 • Springfield, Massachusetts

Am I movie crazy? "Mit" and I went again to the Foxes Theatre. It's a horribly cheap place with red leather seats.

Saturday, July 12, 1918 • E. Granby, Connecticut

We all went down to Grandma's by trolley to Suffield, and then by jitney [small bus]. It seemed so good to see them all and have such a marvelous supper. Uncle Dan was as wonderful as usual, only more so. East Granby - he runs it and is its mayor without being called one.

Sunday, July 13, 1918 • E. Granby, Connecticut

I went to church with Grandpa and had to shake hands with everyone afterwards whether I knew them or not. The old minister is a dear — so simple and sincerely good. Theo came to dinner. Pardon me again for mentioning food, it was chicken. Father and I went home early. Mother was to stay a day longer.

Monday, July 14, 1918 • Springfield, Massachusetts

I'm in the Renewal Department this week. I can't endure my boss! And my job! Checking subtractions and filing endless cards. But, there are a lot of people in there I know — so there are a few breaks in the working hours.

I worked from 5 to 9 p.m. as always, at the Red Cross, taking in knitted articles. The socks and sweaters come fast. Six of us work on Monday nights. We enjoy it, and the cause is a glorious one.

War news is looking up. The Germans are in retreat across the Marne and the Americans are doing their bit bravely. We have a *million* men in France now and more to follow all the time. There won't be many of the youth of our land at home soon. But it's only right, where the fight to death for humanity and democracy are at stake.

> Marian thinks of war in grand terms. Howard will soon experience its grim reality.

Thursday, July 25, 1918 • Springfield, Massachusetts

"Pris" and I had a "bat" at the Broadway Theatre and saw *"How Could You, Jean?"* with Mary Pickford and William Desmond Taylor. It is adorable. Afterwards, we went to get fudge chocolate.

> This was one of William Taylor's last pictures with Mary Pickford because he was killed in 1922 in a famously unsolved murder.

Sunday, July 28, 1918 • Springfield, Massachusetts

A terrible bore this evening, in the shape of a call from a private whom I met at a soldiers' dance at the Y.W. a week ago. His talk is not highly elevating. Father told me to promise not to ever go out with him, so I killed that idea on the spot. He stayed until after 11 pm with perfect ease, although I yawned a great deal, and the clock was much in evidence. I hope I can fix it up so that he won't *ever* come again! There is some patriotism that I must stop at.

Week of July 29, 1918 • Springfield, Massachusetts

I worked two evenings at the Red Cross. We were very busy on both nights taking in articles, helping people who were mixed up, and answering every conceivable question. Tuesday and Wednesday, mother was at East Granby making raspberry jelly and other canning. Father and I had a great time keeping house. In the evening we tried making corn syrup fudge with poor success. It is "conservation" candy with brown sugar and corn syrup. We held it over a cake of ice, but no avail. Wednesday, Mother came home and I had a nice hot dinner waiting for her at 6.30 pm. I love to cook. It's the only branch of housekeeping that I favor. Saturday afternoon I spent my holiday time rewriting a story I wrote at college called "A Chance for Cinderella." I'm disgusted with my writing abilities. All day Sunday, I wrote and read. Quite a literary day. I love that kind. I can aspire, anyhow. Nobody should say "nay" to that.

Howard wrote letters to his Aunt Maude (Mary) Rainey, his father's older sister. She never married and did not have children of her own.

Before America entered the war, in September 1914, as Germany was rapidly approaching Paris, the French were in a desperate situation to get battle ready troops to the front. The rail way system was clogged and there were a limited number of army motor vehicles and drivers available. To try to expedite the troop transfer, the French General Gallieni came up with the idea of using 1,200 Paris taxi cabs for troop transport. Each taxi cab could carry five solders to the Western Front to help save Paris. Later, this idea became known as the legend of The Taxi Cabs of the Marne. The taxis were used again in 1916 to transport troops on the 45 mile Voie Sacre ("Sacred Way") road between Bar-le-Duc and Verdun (Meuse), with Souilly as the half-way point, towards the Battle of Verdun. Howard wrote home that his friend, Hubert, was driving taxicabs in Paris as part of the American Expeditionary Forces X-Ray Division from Williams College. In September 1918, he transferred to Echelon American Parc G and later to the USAAS section #SSU 544 where he saw more action driving an ambulance, which he preferred.

Howard's Pawling friend and golf team captain, Phil Carter, a Red Cross ambulance driver, was a superb amateur golfer who had won the North & South Men's Championship at Pinehurst, North Carolina in 1916. Not only did Phil have golfing ability, but he also had political connections. His uncle, Charles Evans Hughes, had been an unsuccessful candidate for President in 1916. In fact, Charles went to bed thinking he was president, only to learn the next morning of his defeat in California that had handed the victory to Woodrow Wilson. For these reasons, a young man such as Phil would have had the opportunity to play golf with Marshal Joseph Jacques Cesare Joffre. The French general Joffre was best known for "regrouping the retreating allied armies to defeat the Germans" at the strategically decisive and successful First Battle of the Marne in 1914. Joffre's "popularity led to his nickname *Papa Joffre*." (www.wikipedia.org)

August 16, 1918

Dear Aunt Maude,

This is my first chance to drop you a line. I am limited to a few letters a week and have been using that privilege to write Mother and Aunt Alice regularly each week. I have absolutely exhausted my line of news to them so I am going to write to a few of my relatives this week.

I received your very nice letters and am hoping for more. I know you are terribly busy but hope that you can find time occasionally to drop me a line or two.

When are you going to get a chance to come across the pond? I should think that your cause has been long enough to warrant it. By the way, if you want any more assistance from Colonel S., you know that he has been transferred from Hospital #1 in N.Y. to Fort Riley, Kansas. I also understand Major Elting's Base Hospital is stuck in England for the duration of the war. It seems a shame to keep as wonderful a surgeon as he, so far from the front.

We have had only about two hours of rain since we left the States. The weather has been ideal.

I had a letter from Hubert Grabau from Pawling the other day. He is stuck in France with the taxicabs, the most dangerous enemy. He is pretty disgusted for he wanted to get to the front with an old ambulance.

Was glad to hear that when you were home you had such fun motoring weather. I have been motoring too but not of the pleasant kind. I am testing motors now and have to test them out over the hills, etc. But, it is not much fun, for we have to sit on the gas tank to drive, and it is rather uncomfortable.

One of the Ansuldo hydro-aeroplanes (Italian) flew over camp the other day dropping leaflets of welcome to "their brothers from over the seas." The interesting part of it was the fact that it is supposed to be the fastest plane in the world. I think I got some good pictures of it that I can show you after the battle.

I heard of Major Mitchell's death shortly after it happened. We are very well informed, as we can get several good newspapers each day. The Chicago Tribune is about the best as far as news from the States and the London Mail for doings over here.

Have you heard anything from Uncle S.? I do not see how he can stay away now. He never did appreciate a good wife when he had one anyway.

I understand from some of the Red Cross drivers at this front that Jack (John) Lummis and Phil Carter from Pawling are here. I hope I can run across them. We might be able to have a few rounds of golf together. I know Phil has his clubs with him, for you know he has played General Joffre several times.

Ran across a Red Cross girl here from Great Barrington, NY. She knows several people in Hudson and went to Miss Hall's School for a year with Aunt Alice. She has been over here for four years.

Feeding wonderfully and feeling fine.
Love, Howard

Friday, August 23, 1918 • Windsor, Connecticut

Went to Doris Campbell's house. It was her 21st birthday. Poor child. She has been sick for three weeks. They didn't know what to call it but very hard pain. "Eth" and "Pris" and I trolleyed down. "Eth" is with me over the weekend. She is farming up at college. The girls are doing splendid work up there, canning and hoeing. There will probably be enough canned stuff to supply the college. I took Doris a little book I have found that I love —"*The Answering Voice*"— a collection of love poems by women. They are all so beautiful and yet very wistful. Why do so many inspired women sing of their unrequited loves? There was a birthday dinner, of course, and a regular feast. More chocolates than I have seen since the war began.

Mrs. Campbell took us home late in the afternoon in the new car - a Buick and a beauty. Father went up and got us some ice cream. Oh my home and my home folks! They are so wonderful.

"House of Dreams"

You took my empty dreams
And filled them every one
With tenderness and nobleness,
April and the sun.

The old empty dreams
Where my thoughts would throng
Are far too full of happiness
To even hold a song.

O, the empty dreams were dim
And the empty dreams were wide,
They were sweet and shadowy houses
Where my thoughts could hide.

But you took my dreams away
And you made them all come true-
My thoughts have no place now to play,
And nothing now to do.

Sara Teasdale

Sara Teasdale, an American poet, born in St. Louis, Missouri, edited the anthology of poetry, *The Answering Voice: One Hundred Love Lyrics by Women* (Teasdale) in 1917. In 1918 she won the Columbia University Poetry Society Prize, later known as the Pulitzer Prize for Poetry for her book *Love Songs*. Her work focused on romantic, classical verses which have a musical quality to them, as Marian said "why do so many inspired women sing of their unrequited loves?"

Sunday, August 31, 1918 • E. Granby, Connecticut

I spent this week at Grandmas and such a happy one! Aunt Theo and Umpa were up for all day Sunday. On Monday, father and I picked over grapes for grandma's grape juice. I read about all of "*Mr. Britling Sees It Through*", a book everyone else was reading three years ago. It is splendid; you can fairly see into the mind of Mr. Britling. We weep with him when his son, Hugh, is killed on the battlefront in France.

As Marian continued her fascination with war novels, she read the 1916 Bookman Best Seller "*Mr. Britling Sees It Through*" by H. G. Wells. (H. Wells) It is a tale about the unfolding events during the outbreak of the war in England. Marian attempts to experience war – through books and poems, her favorite way of gaining vicarious experience, although she admits she is late reading this book. Later in his career, from 1900-1920, H.G. Wells wrote more realistic novels. Mr. Wells was a science fiction writer, historian, and journalist.

France

Ambulance # 21 Section   World War 1

Howard Rainey, Standing, Fifth from Right

On August 24, 1918, Howard was selected – which was quite an honor – along with 31 other men from Section #521 of the USAAS to leave for the Western Front in France which was a bloody battle by now. The whole front was ablaze. They travelled on flat-cars, a railroad car without sides generally used for carrying goods rather than people. When the new smaller Section #521 crossed the Alps through the Modane Tunnel into France, Howard wrote home about the beautiful scenery, emphasizing the positive aspects of the experience to comfort his mother. In Rimacourt, France, they unloaded their ambulances at a Camp Hospital and then drove to Souilly, France where there was an American Military Hospital. Here Howard wrote that they were received with enthusiasm, "stopped many times on the streets, cheered and patted on the back." The next day they moved through Neufchateau, Ligny, and turned toward Verdun, France. In the pre-radio days, news from "over there" would come mostly by newspaper. Ida knew that Howard's move from Italy to France was going to be more dangerous than his time in Italy. News about the Western Front was covered in the American papers. She knew Howard would be in the thick of it all.

This poem gives us a glimpse into what life was like in the city of Artois, France where the front line ran through the province which caused a lot of destruction. There are French words interspersed throughout the poem. For clarification, "Comme Ci Comme Ça" translated means "like this, like that" or it can mean "neither good nor bad," or "so so." "Oui" means yes, and "Avez Vous" means "Have you?" Dit-il means "he says." I think my grandma loved poems that included another language, especially French which she studied in school. My grandfather spoke a little French also which probably helped him during the war.

"Comme Ça in Old Artois"

"I came over the border to a little French town,
Having only a couple of hours
For France, and with only a word or two.
Like oui, madame and avez-vous.
At the school gate, tired, I sat me down
And picked some simple flowers
And smiled at les enfants as they came through.

And some smiled back at me, but more
Were afraid of the stranger man.
A little chap fled when I called Voila!
But a fair little maid, when I said Comme Ça.
Presenting a flower with Je vous adore.
Danced off and cried, "Oh Suzanne!
Comme Ça, dit-il. Haha! ha ha ha!"

Darling coquette, pirouetting round
With hand on heart, like mine!
Then showing her flower. "Suzanne! Nannette!"
With a torrent of French that I couldn't get.
But the merry, melodious ripple of sound
Went to my heart like wine.
And her laughing eyes I shall never forget.

Thy tinkling bell then summoned in school
Away! But throwing to me
Sweet good-bye glances, Parthian-wise,
But of gay little heart, through merry French eyes.
Je vous aime, pretty nameless. Fanchette? Ursule?
Madelon? Je vous aime aujourd'hui.
For we change not our mind when we change our skies.

But, oh how changed thy skies, poor child!
What of thy school to-day?
Thy waters, the white village, the green pasture-lands.
When a world is harried by war's bloody hands;
While chargers thunder and shells shriek wild.
And the horse battle-trumpets bray.
And fierce ones scorn le bon Dieu's commands!

God grant it be not so, Cherie.
In that poor village home of thine,
The children lie crushed in many a street.
Ah, no comme ça, near thee, pauvre petite!
Jesus keep the dear innocent ones like thee
Close in His arms Divine.
But, let tyrants be ashes under His Feet!"

From "Monday Musings"

Howard's Ambulance "Esercito Americano"

After the Armistice, the censorship would be lifted and Howard would be able to write a more detailed account of his service. Souilly, France was the base hospital for all three major drives Howard participated in: St. Mihiel, Verdun, and the Argonne. First, his corps attended to the soldiers at the St. Mihiel battle September 12 - 15, 1918 "where we have been having no end of trouble with our cars. Our mechanics have been working all day getting the cars in tune. They are all new, of course, and are still pretty stiff." Next Howard's group attended to the wounded at Verdun. He wrote: "I have been in Verdun several times and that is the most interesting old place. It is entirely shot to pieces as is St. Mihiel." Howard's corps then moved to the Meuse-Argonne Sector the night of September 25, 1918, where they participated in the offensive from September 26th until November 11th; the day the Armistice was declared.

September 2, 1918

Dear Mother,

I suppose you think it queer that I have not written before but I have been sent to France for a change. A number of us were picked from our section to go to France and as you see I was among them.

Our trip over was a wonder. We came part of the way by flat car and the rest by continental driving. Our trip through the Alps was marvelous. We could look up from the valleys and see the snow-capped mountains.

I have been driving quite a bit as I am assigned to an ambulance. I signed up for the whole thing and have a man under me to do the cranking etc. for all that I am supposed to do is drive. This morning I had a rather funny experience. I started out at about 11:00 A.M. and got stuck along the road until after 5:00 P.M. I did everything to get started but no use. Finally, I got towed by a truck I missed my lunch but am getting used to going without a meal now and then. The roads are fine considering, and we can make pretty good time.

I have gone through several ruined villages and they certainly are ruined. Nothing left but a church here and there. It seems that the people might move back into their homes by putting up some sort of shack. The roads are lined with graves and all in all the sights are most sympathetic.

We are located in very nice barracks and are feeding finely. The camp is very nicely located and one only hardship is the lack of water. To be sure we can bathe once or twice a week and have real hot water. The other night I had my first warm bath since leaving the States and it surely felt fine.

Aeroplane battles are not infrequent here. It is often that we see several planes battling over us.

We have been having no end of trouble with our cars. Our mechanics have been working all day getting the cars in tune. They are all new, of course, and are still pretty stiff.

As far as I can see, we are just making a tour of the world. I have seen six countries and may see Italy again before I see the U.S.

My car will not be running tomorrow so I guess I will have an easy day, but I shall probably have to drive at night which is not much fun but all in the game. A little scrap going on overhead now, but really I am calloused to them already and pay no attention to them except to see the fun.

I am sorry if I have made you worry for not having received any mail from me but really, this has been my first chance. I cannot promise to write regularly but shall do so as often as I can.

Lots of love to all.
Your son, Howard

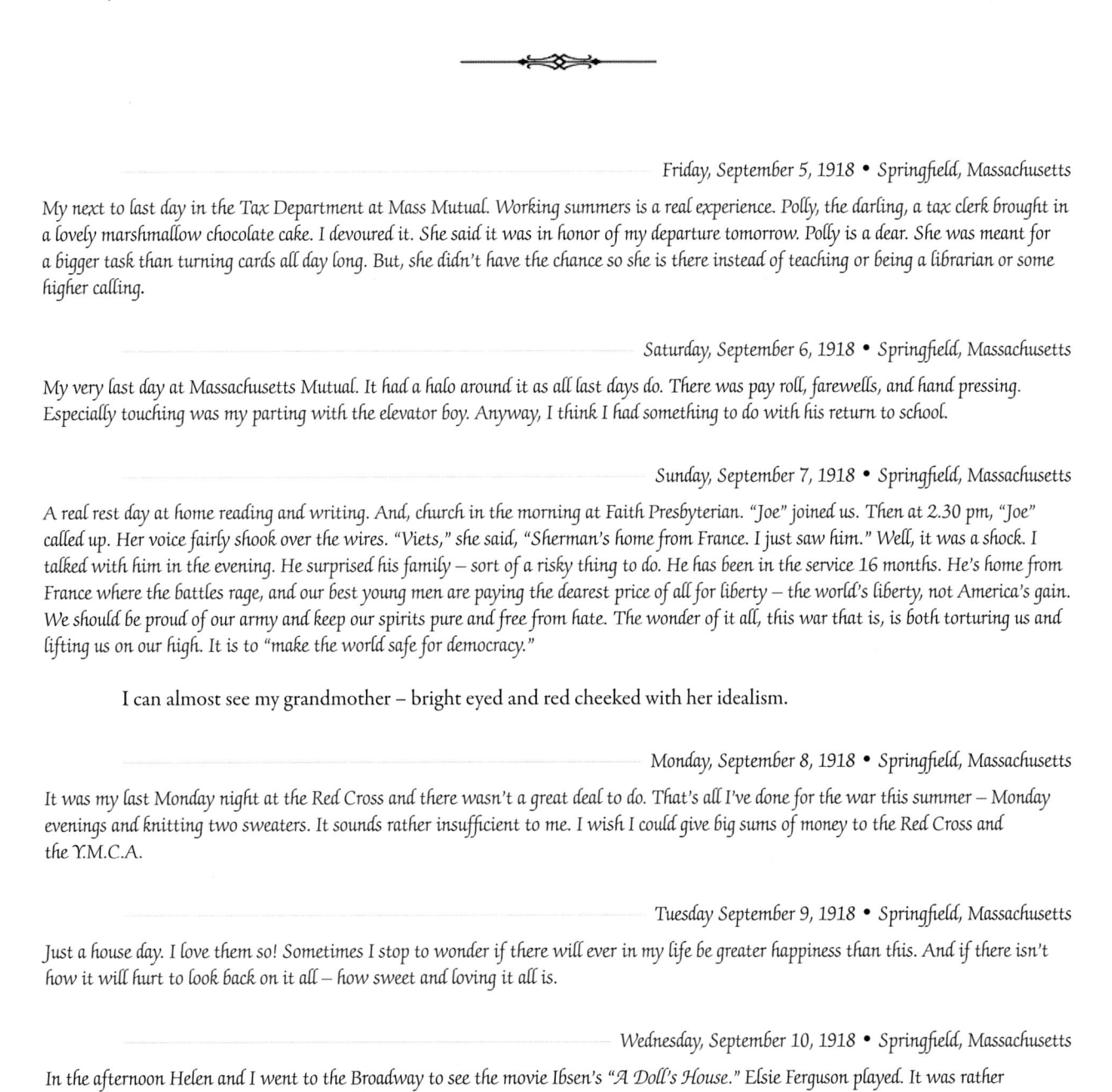

Friday, September 5, 1918 • Springfield, Massachusetts

My next to last day in the Tax Department at Mass Mutual. Working summers is a real experience. Polly, the darling, a tax clerk brought in a lovely marshmallow chocolate cake. I devoured it. She said it was in honor of my departure tomorrow. Polly is a dear. She was meant for a bigger task than turning cards all day long. But, she didn't have the chance so she is there instead of teaching or being a librarian or some higher calling.

Saturday, September 6, 1918 • Springfield, Massachusetts

My very last day at Massachusetts Mutual. It had a halo around it as all last days do. There was pay roll, farewells, and hand pressing. Especially touching was my parting with the elevator boy. Anyway, I think I had something to do with his return to school.

Sunday, September 7, 1918 • Springfield, Massachusetts

A real rest day at home reading and writing. And, church in the morning at Faith Presbyterian. "Joe" joined us. Then at 2.30 pm, "Joe" called up. Her voice fairly shook over the wires. "Viets," she said, "Sherman's home from France. I just saw him." Well, it was a shock. I talked with him in the evening. He surprised his family – sort of a risky thing to do. He has been in the service 16 months. He's home from France where the battles rage, and our best young men are paying the dearest price of all for liberty – the world's liberty, not America's gain. We should be proud of our army and keep our spirits pure and free from hate. The wonder of it all, this war that is, is both torturing us and lifting us on our high. It is to "make the world safe for democracy."

I can almost see my grandmother – bright eyed and red cheeked with her idealism.

Monday, September 8, 1918 • Springfield, Massachusetts

It was my last Monday night at the Red Cross and there wasn't a great deal to do. That's all I've done for the war this summer – Monday evenings and knitting two sweaters. It sounds rather insufficient to me. I wish I could give big sums of money to the Red Cross and the Y.M.C.A.

Tuesday September 9, 1918 • Springfield, Massachusetts

Just a house day. I love them so! Sometimes I stop to wonder if there will ever in my life be greater happiness than this. And if there isn't how it will hurt to look back on it all – how sweet and loving it all is.

Wednesday, September 10, 1918 • Springfield, Massachusetts

In the afternoon Helen and I went to the Broadway to see the movie Ibsen's "A Doll's House." Elsie Ferguson played. It was rather unsatisfactory I thought. And the vaudeville was cheap.

Next week we will be back at college!

The 1879 controversial play by Norwegian playwright Henrik Ibsen was critical of 19th century marriage norms. The play ended with the final revolt of the wife who had been treated as a plaything. Although Ibsen denied it, *A Doll's House* is often called the "first true feminist play." (www.wikipedia.org) How significant that my feminist grandmother did not like the movie.

Thursday, September 11, 1918 • Springfield, Massachusetts

I went over to the Rodgers's house to dinner tonight. In the evening, we saw a corking movie show at the Phillips Theatre: John Barrymore in "Raffles: The Amateur Cracksman" and the Japanese actor Sessue Hayakawa in "The Honor of his House." Movies these days in succession. This must stop. Carolyn told me that she was engaged and asked me to be her bridesmaid. It is a secret.

John Barrymore was a leading man in more than 60 films that spanned 25 years. He specialized in light comedies during the silent era, such as "Raffles" where he was a cricketer by day and a gentleman-thief, Raffles, referred to at the time as a cracksman, at night. Barrymore went on to more serious work when talkies debuted. (Barrymore) The Asian-American actor, Sessue Hayakawa's, popularity continued throughout the war; following World War 1, the economic slump, and a rise in Anti-Asian sentiment and immigration issues, his popularity declined. His movie career eventually came to an end and he returned to Japan. After the Second World War, he returned to Hollywood, re-launched his career, and eventually earned an Academy Award nomination in 1957 for Best Supporting Actor as the prisoner of war commandant in "The Bridge over the River Kwai." He retired to Japan in 1966 and became a Zen Buddhist priest while giving acting lessons. (www.wikipedia.org)

On September 12, 1918, the Americans launched an attack to free the Paris-Verdun-Nancy railroads with over a half a million Americans and 110,000 French soldiers on St. Mihiel. The U.S. forces under General John J. Pershing "were victorious in their first independent operation of the war, reducing the St. Mihiel salient." (Willmott) The Germans started to evacuate their positions before the Americans began the attack and the battle took only four days. Approximately 9,000 Allied soldiers were lost but 15,000 German prisoners were captured.

September 13, 1918

Dear Dad,

I do not doubt that you were somewhat surprised to learn of my arrival in France. It was more or less of a surprise to me, but in the army one can never tell what is going to happen to him in the next 5 minutes.

We have had a great deal of rain and do not dare step out of the barracks without a raincoat. We are getting fairly used to the rain and wind. The wind I think is worse than the rain. We have some trouble with our cars but manage to get around fairly well. I suppose it seems much worse to us coming from a warm dry country to a cold rainy one. For comfort, which I am not looking for particularly, they can send me back to Italy as soon as they wish. However, I guess I can stand inconvenience as well as the next fellow for I did not expect to find a bed of roses.

This morning I mailed you a German helmet. I do not know if you will ever get it or not but I hope you do. It is a real one and although it is dirty and bloody, I think it interesting. You can see where the old machine gun bullet went through.

Night before last I had my first real experience in night driving. I was on night duty and was sent down the line with a couple of patients. It was so dark that I could hardly see 25 feet ahead, and it was just by luck that I did not hit anything. Of course, we are not all allowed to carry a light of any kind. This night was a cold, rainy, disagreeable one, and as luck had it, I had two trips. I indistinctly saw an object ahead of me so slowed up, fortunately, for it was a convoy of big trucks. I got all mixed up with them in trying to get out of it all night. On the way back my assistant was driving, and just as we were nearing our camp we missed a French truck that was coming lickity-split the wrong side of the road. I was soaked when I got back but dried out somewhat and did not have the slightest cold.

The Americans certainly are a wonderful lot. I have seen them with arms and legs shot off and whistling Yankee tunes while waiting to be attended to. One fellow I shall never forget. He was a great big, strong, wonderfully built fellow who had his arm shot off just above the elbow but was happy, and his happiness seemed to inspire the rest. I do not mean that he was happy because he lost an arm but for the simple reason that it was all for a good cause he had done his bit.

My letters now are censored at the base so I can write more personal letters. I am pretty busy so cannot promise a regular correspondence but will do the best I can to all.

Tell Grandma Rainey I am going to write her soon. My ambulance is running very smoothly and hardly ever has any trouble. I picked up an empty 3 in. shell the other day. I kept it and hope that I can continue to keep it.

Lots of love to all,
Howard

Howard kept up a brave face in his letters, but he brought the grim reality of war home when he mailed his parents a bloodstained German helmet.

The helmet arrived safely at his parent's house and was passed on to his son, my dad. Growing up, my father loved to talk about the old German helmet, called a Pickelhaube (Pickel meaning point, and Haube meaning bonnet). It sat in the bookcase in our den as a constant reminder of the war. Inside the helmet is stamped "C. E. Juncker 1916," the manufacturer. The C. E. Junker Company of Berlin, Germany, was the "royal producer of medals and belts" (www.cejuncker.com) and military uniforms. The helmet is a rusted gun metal grey steel, with a bronze colored spike attached in a cloverleaf design. The Imperial Prussian Eagle crest is a lighter silver grey metal, signifying the regiment's province or state. The eagle has a crown on his head and holds a sword in one talon. Spread across the wings is a banner that says: "MIT GOTT FUR KOENEG UND VATERLAND" (translation: With God for King and Fatherhood.") The lobster tail back protected the soldier's neck. Despite the bloodstains in the leather lining, we used to try to put the helmet on our heads. It never fit. The Germans must have had small heads in the olden days, we thought.

During the early months of World War I, the Pickelhaubes were made solely of leather and did not measure up to the realities of trench warfare. In 1916, the new German steel helmet was introduced and German head wound fatalities decreased by 70%. (www.wikipedia.org) The conspicuous spike made soldiers a target in the trenches. Later models introduced a detachable spike, such as the one Howard sent home. After World War I, the Pickelhaube helmet became ceremonial wear.

Sunday, September 15, 1918 • Springfield, Massachusetts

We had a leisurely breakfast of pancakes cooked by father and a late dinner. I read Robert Louis Stevenson's' "Inland Voyage" (1876) and "Travels with a Donkey" (1879). They surely were delightful. He was such a dear, unconventional wanderer and didn't seem to mind if he was taken for a beggar at every Inn.

In the evening, we went to church — splendid sermon and good music. We love the "old First." Then, we all had ice cream. We ate some more after we reached home. We just work and play together, our little family, in spite of high prices and lack of money. No! Nothing can quell our happiness.

> Robert Louis Stevenson, a Scottish poet and author, wrote *An Inland Voyage* about his travels canoeing through France and Belgium in 1876. It was his first book and a pioneering travelogue of outdoor literature. The route itinerary has become popular with modern travelers to reenact Stevenson's voyage. Outdoor leisure travel was unusual at the time and Marian wrote that he was an unconventional wanderer and mistaken as a "beggar at every Inn." The book is a romantic work during a more innocent time period in Europe which painted a delightful atmosphere. The second travelogue, *Travels with a Donkey in the Cevennes,* was written in 1879. Stevenson travelled for 12 days in southern France with a donkey. In 1883, Stevenson wrote his most famous book, *Treasure Island*. Next year, Marian would be fortunate enough to hear Mr. Stevenson speak at Mount Holyoke about poetry.

Monday, September 16, 1918 • Springfield, Massachusetts

Miss Clarke sewed for me all day. She is making my old serge suit into a dress which we hope will emerge quite stylish and modern in appearance. All day I tried it on and when I didn't I gobbled Stevenson.

Tomorrow I go back to begin my senior year at Mt. Holyoke.

Howard tried to write home every week or two. Today was the last of four days of the St. Mihiel offensive. Howard was unable to write of their success, due to the censorship. No matter how long Howard's letters were, it didn't matter as long as Ida had any word from her only son that he was surviving.

September 16, 1918

Dear Mother,

I have told Dad all the news in his letter but there is one thing that happened yesterday that I know will be interesting as well as consoling. I ran into Major Elting. I was detailed to run my lieutenant's car, and who should be going along with him but Dr. Elting? He said that I had grown and filled out so much that he did not know me, but on second look, he remembered me. We had quite a talk together. He told me how wonderful you and Dad are. I already knew that, and also told me to be sure and send you both his love. He is right in my camp, and he said that he was going to keep his eye on me. He is the only one of his outfit that is here

Love,
Howard

Although Howard couldn't mention it in his censored letters, he was entering the "Big Push" in Verdun. Could he survive the long nights, difficult conditions, and constant bombardment? Simultaneously, Marian was anxiously looking forward to her senior year in college.

CHAPTER FIVE

"GO WHERE NO ONE ELSE WILL GO…."
MARY LYON

On Tuesday, September 17th, 1918, Marian wrote in her diary: "A-never-to-be-forgotten day." She could barely contain her excitement about the first day of her senior year; the day Marian had been dreaming about as long as she could remember. As a youth college seemed out of reach; her family could not afford the tuition for such a lofty goal. How could this dream ever come true? The Springfield Club had come to the rescue and offered Marian a scholarship. She was sure to make the club proud.

Despite Marian's joyful feelings upon arrival at Mount Holyoke that day, looming beneath the excitement and anticipation for senior year droned a constant undertone of concern and worry about the continuing war. All the while, Howard was experiencing the horrors of war on the European front.

Nevertheless, the Great War did not daunt Marion's youthful enthusiasm for the new adventures awaiting her, the fulfillment of so many wishes and dreams during her final chapter at Mount Holyoke. In the bedroom of her family's apartment on Belmont Avenue in Springfield, Marian and her mother finished packing her college trunk for the last time – surely a bittersweet moment for her mother. She was so proud that her daughter was starting her final year of college, but also sad that her only child would soon be leaving the nest.

After three years as a wide-eyed underclassman looking up to and admiring upper classman, faculty and mentors, now Marian would be a senior revered by the younger students. Marian wrote: "I simply can't realize that I'm a senior and that there's no class above us. Most of all it's hard to believe that all our bunch is in Porter Hall – "Dot" (Dorothy Williams), "Pop" (Emma Frazier),

"Hild" (Hilda Jones), "Pris" (Priscilla Spaulding), "Shep" (Florence Sheppard), and Doris Campbell. Oh! It's great." Doris was Marian's roommate senior year.

Later that morning, Doris "Dick" Gidley, an old and dear classmate at both Central High School (CHS) Springfield and Mount Holyoke, "called" for Marian and her mother in her car. Along the way they picked up another classmate, "Pris" Spaulding, and headed north to Mount Holyoke to join the other members of the class of 1919! Once on campus, the five of them stopped for a relaxing lunch in a grove of white birch trees, one of Marian's favorite spots on campus known as Upper Lake.

In her room in Porter Hall, Mother helped Marian unpack her shirt-waist (tailored blouse) box and get settled. When it was time to say their goodbyes, Marian's mother beamed with pride. Her daughter was one of the few fortunate women who would graduate from college, accomplishing what so many other women were unable to do. The words of Mount Holyoke Founder Mary Lyon written on her tombstone would continue to guide and motivate Marian throughout her life on her path to success - "Go where no one else will go, do what no one else will do."

As her mother departed to catch the 4:30 pm trolley back to Springfield, they both knew Mount Holyoke was the perfect place for Marian and were so grateful that Marian had the opportunity to pave the way for other women. Memories of Mount Holyoke and its strong bonds of sisterhood would inspire Marian her whole life. A hymn well known to all the students at Mount Holyoke aptly describes this legacy:

> "Blest be the tie that binds,
> Our heart in fervent love;
> The unity of kindred minds,
> Is like to that above.
> Amen."
>
> John Fawcett

This is the first verse of a hymn written by the ordained minister, John Fawcett, of Leeds, England in 1782. This hymn "was heard again on October 3, 1986 when members of the college and the town of South Hadley commemorated the one hundred-fiftieth anniversary of the placing of the cornerstone for the original seminary building." (Edmonds)

At Mount Holyoke, many traditions strengthen the ties that bind as they pass from generation to generation. *The One Hundred Year Biographical Directory of Mount Holyoke College 1837-1937,* listed at the time of the centennial 660 family groups with relationships in the direct line, eight of which represented four generations of students, and fifty-six of which had three generations."(Edmonds) Marian had watched the upper classmen participate in certain rituals reserved for seniors, such as Cap and Gown Day, Senior Dance, Senior Mountain Day, and the Laurel Parade, one event of the three days of activities around Graduation. Marian had earned her place as a senior to bask in the glory of her accomplishments. One senior role Marian particularly enjoyed was "no more waitressing!" At dinner a faculty member traditionally sat at every table in the dining hall and a senior sat "opposite" while underclassmen took turns waitressing. Marian continued to develop close relationships with members of the faculty, a group of powerful women. Many were Mount Holyoke graduates and shared the bonds of sisterhood and traditions, shared dreams, and a sense of pride in their institution. Marian stayed in contact with several faculty members following graduation, and Marian used Miss Stevens and Miss Snell as references for English teaching jobs.

Marian had to find a balance between academic excellence and her many social activities, such as church, vespers, Bible study, Debating Society, Llamadra yearbook, Dramatics Club, The Student's League, YWCA, The Silver Bay Club, Blackstick Literary Club, tutoring, Red Cross work, the competitive sing, and her many friends! Miss Woolley stressed that: "scholarship was a prime reason for attending Mount Holyoke." (Edmonds) As a result, in 1910, Miss Woolley abolished secret societies and sororities on campus and opened social events to everyone, saying "The social life should be distinctly a means to an end and not an end in itself, a recreation relieving the strain, rather than adding to it, an amusement, not a business." (ibid) I think it is a wonder how my grandmother successfully balanced all of her activities with academics, but she did and flourished doing so.

Yet despite the beauty and pageantry of Mount Holyoke's traditions, solemn purpose marked the school during Marion's senior year. Everyone on campus was urged to do her part for the war; these activities were time consuming. In addition to Red Cross fundraising campaigns, student war-relief work included fieldwork at the campus farm and nearby Skinner's farm, producing plays to raise money, and knitting for the soldiers. Marian did her part.

War, peace, and student obligations toward the war effort consumed discussions on campus. Marian wrote: "our best young men are paying the dearest price of all for liberty – the world's liberty, not America's gain. We should be proud of our Army and keep our spirits pure and free from hate. The wonder of it all – this war that is both torturing us and lifting us on our high. It is to make the world safe for democracy." The debate even spilled over into Marian's English papers. In her spare time, Marian chose to read books about the war, such as "*Pere Mabel*" and "*The Marne*" and also learned about events in Europe through movies. Though the cloistered college girls were sheltered from the depravity of combat, newspapers, magazines, and lectures provided glimpses into the Great War.

During the cataclysmic days of 1918, Marian and Howard led parallel yet contrasting lives. Marian's life was serene and safe, far from danger and the horrors of the conflict. Concentrating on her studies, she continued to play her small part in the war efforts as senior year began. Her personal search for identity and a place in society took place in the most nurturing, pleasant environment possible: Mount Holyoke College.

Howard's life, on the other hand, had nothing safe, serene, pleasant or nurturing. His life consisted of: mopping up blood after unending battles, equipment problems, disease, and the dirty, rotten business of war. In his letters home to his anxious mother, Howard was careful to give no indication of what it was like to be a volunteer ambulance driver in the middle of a war zone. Howard cared for soldiers on the battlefield, evacuated field hospitals and made runs from the battle lines back to base hospitals. He worked long hours without sleep despite perilous driving conditions near the western front in France. Howard's thoughts were survival mode: the other soldiers and his own. Every day he struggled to save lives and to escape injury and death himself. Dreams of a future back in America were nothing but a distant mirage at this point.

"In the Trenches"

"Oh, the tassled golden wheat uncut, the corn still green-
Pleasant fields of standing grain, and bread for all!
Then the war drum summoned me from
that fair scene.

Brother of the enemy, why came that call?
Oh, the clashing of the cymbal and the wild horn's bray!
Brother, did you hear them – clanging in the morn?
To the fever of the music then I marched away.
Brother, did you likewise when this hell was born?

Oh, the good wife and the children and the little farm!
Of all I may not see again I dream – day, night.
(And of the priest who married me, and blessed this charm!)
Brother, is it so with you? Why do we fight?

Oh, the unconsidered men who die that kings may gain!
Brother, armed against me, do you think as I.
Sodden in the trenches, in the lashing rain?
Hark! Is it the fall of kings the cannon cry?"

Gerald B. Breltigam

Marian's thoughts about the war were sometimes expressed more clearly in her poems than in her diaries. The poems she chose to enter into her diaries show a much deeper understanding of how the soldiers and families suffered in Europe. Although Marian was able to turn to the future: graduation, career, romance and children, she did not do so without sympathy for our Doughboys and our European Allies and their families.

Tuesday, September 17, 1918 • (A never to be forgotten day) Mount Holyoke

Mother and I packed my trunk in the morning at 11.30 am. "Dick" called for us. She was driving the car. We stopped for "Pris" Spaulding; then, off to college all together. We ate lunch in the favorite grove of white birches on Upper Lake at Mt. Holyoke; such good eats. I was so happy. I just knew how mother was enjoying herself. Then, we came back to my dorm room in Porter Hall to settle a little. I unpacked my shirtwaist box and the box in the basement and moved the furniture around. About 4.30 pm mother left on the trolley. "Pris" and I spent the evening together. "Shep" came late in the evening. I moved a cot into their room and slept there. The moonlight was glorious. We sat up by the window a long time talking.

Wednesday, September 18, 1918 • Mount Holyoke

Chasing freshman all day! I piloted one around with her father and all but bought their furniture. I have called on most of mine. Porter Hall is beginning to fill up. Thirty-four freshmen are to be here. Imagine! I simply can't realize that I'm a senior and that there's no class above us. And most of all it's hard to believe that all the bunch is in Porter Hall—"Dot", "Pop", "Hild", "Pris", "Shep", Freda, and Doris. Oh! It's great. I slept with the kids again tonight. Doris Campbell, roomie, got in this afternoon. Her mother helped us hang pictures and curtains.

Freda, "Pop", "Dot", and "Hild"

Friday, September 20, 1918 • Senior Freshman Party • Mount Holyoke

Tables are assigned, and I am Senior Opposite at Miss Morgan's [Zoology] table. It's a real treat not to be a waitress, as in the past three years. We gave our Senior Freshman party tonight. I hope the kids had fun while they were there. My trunk hasn't come yet. I attended the party in a borrowed rig.

Students lived in the dorms with the faculty which created close relationships between them. Marian enjoyed the opportunity to live and learn among her mentors. In the dining room, it was a tradition that each table of fourteen students was presided over by two faculty members. "The senior faculty member served the meat; the junior faculty member served the vegetables." (Edmonds)

On September 21, 1918 Howard was transferred with his unit from the St. Mihiel victory straight to Souilly, France where General John J. Pershing set up the First Army headquarters, which was strategically located west of St. Mihiel and south of the Argonne Forest. Howard's ambulance unit #521 would use Souilly as their base for operations. Ambulance drivers would evacuate the field hospitals as close to the front line as possible, with runs back to the evacuation or base hospitals. According to the records of the Medical Corps of the AEF, there were 144 Base Hospitals throughout France. Some were General Hospitals or temporary barracks, tents, or buildings. But, many were converted hotels, monasteries, chateaus, insane asylums, estates, seminaries, schools, colleges, and convents. Some base hospitals were specifically "Fever Hospitals" for flu patients only.

During runs in France, ambulances would take injured soldiers from dressing stations behind the front line to the base hospital located safely farther away. Model T ambulance drivers faced many challenges such as narrow and treacherous roads, inadequate brakes, darkness, mud, shrapnel and their own complete exhaustion. Since horse-drawn carts or mules were still prevalent, horseshoe nails in the roads wreaked havoc with tires. Although Model T ambulances were able to climb narrow mountain roads, soldiers had to drive backwards up the hills to keep gasoline flowing from gravity-fed gas tanks. Brakes could not handle steep grades so drivers had to look for trees to stop the ambulances if necessary. To further complicate matters, drivers were forbidden to turn lights on at night in order to remain undetected in combat zones. Since Howard and his comrades could barely see 25 feet ahead, scouts would sit on the front of the cars to guide them. Fortunately the Ford Model T sat high enough so that the ambulance could get through flooded roads inaccessible to lower-riding vehicles. And, the T was light enough that three or four soldiers could pick it up and move it out when it got stuck in a ditch or shell hole. Drivers would go for days and nights without sleep in order to run men on stretchers from the dressing station behind the front line to the field or base hospitals, back and forth as needed. Many ambulance drivers suffered nervous breakdowns. It was "not much fun but all in the game," Howard wrote as he tried to keep his spirits up while reassuring his mother, in particular, that he was handling the stress of his part in the war.

The need for ambulances and ambulance drivers was greater in 1918 than anticipated because "hauls were longer, wear and tear more severe, destruction by artillery fire was more frequent, and facilities for repair were less."(history.amedd.army.mil) I am so proud of my grandfather and of all of sleepless nights he endured while transporting injured soldiers as quickly as possible to field hospitals. Due to his efforts, many soldiers survived who otherwise might have perished. The rate of survival for an injured soldier improved depending upon the length of time it took to get treatment. Treatment started in the trenches and continued in the ambulances. Ambulance drivers were as important as doctors and nurses because they were often the first point of contact to administer first aid and to reduce the risk of infection for the wounded. Ambulances were not allowed to go to the front lines; they usually stopped at least 50 yards away near a dressing station. Injured soldiers walked or were carried on stretchers to an advanced dressing station behind the trenches. There they prepared for ambulance transport to field hospitals farther behind the battle lines. Soldiers were loaded on stretchers in the rear of the ambulance or even in the front seat to take them to the nearest field hospital. Field hospitals were usually located near railroad stations so the more severely injured soldiers could take trains to base hospitals.

Since Howard almost had to drive close to the battlefront, he experienced near misses with shrapnel and mustard gas. Howard wrote home that he had his "share of shot and shell but fortunately was not even scratched." Later he said, "Machine gun bullets have popped all around me and big shells have hit near me." Howard made it sound in his letters as if he had a magical protective shield around him; we could only wish this was true. How could it be that he dodged so much shrapnel? One day Howard went into a place that had been heavily gassed, and he reported receiving a "touch of gas" that made him sick for a couple of hours. Many soldiers had permanent lung damage from gas. Although Howard most likely kept news of many of the dangerous close calls out of his letters as required by the rules of censorship, he also did so to protect his mother from the reality of the war. Still his job was perilous.

Wednesday, September 25, 1918 • Mount Holyoke

It has rained all the week so far and everyone is getting the grippe [flu] there are at least 100 cases in college. The epidemic is all over the country, and there are many deaths around Boston and in the big military camps. We haven't the most serious kind here, but it's bad enough that the girls have high temperatures. Brigham Hall is opened for an infirmary. In the afternoon, I went to the cannery and peeled tomatoes. We have 15,000 cans of vegetables that the girls have done. I call it splendid war work - two sophomores are running the cannery now with no outside help.

In the fall of 1918, a deadly flu virus began infecting people all over the world. It started in either American Army camps in France or in the United States (U.S.). It was termed the Spanish flu because the Spanish government, a noncombatant state, spread the news about the pandemic. In America, the flu spread from soldiers arriving back in the United States through Boston and New York. (Because of Mount Holyoke's close proximity to Boston, 95 miles west, the campus was affected; fortunately, Marian never became ill.) From there, it spread through the U.S. The pandemic hit in two stages: the fall of 1918 and the spring of 1919. "This highly infectious flu turned rapidly into pneumonia, against which medicine had no defense." (Willmott) The constant movement of people throughout Europe and America, unsanitary living conditions, and ineffective medicine, increased the spread of the disease. The numbers were staggering. It is estimated that the worldwide death toll from the flu, or grippe (influenza), was between 20 and 50 million people, including 540,000 to 675,000 from the U.S. "In all, 62,000 American service personnel died of the flu—more than were killed in battle." (ibid) Mysteriously, in 1919 the flu disappeared completely.

A healthy Marian was able to work at the cannery and do her part farming at Mount Holyoke. "With the entry of the United States into World War I in April 1917, the faculty and students needed little more than President Woodrow Wilson's call to the country to propel the college's already sympathetic support for the Allies into a patriotic fervor of activity. Projected food shortages led to the proposal that some college land should be converted to a farm on which groups of student would work for a month at a time. During the summer of 1917, fourteen acres of the McIlwain property adjacent to Button Field were plowed under, and an additional fifteen acres were developed the following summer on the playing fields by Upper Lake. Corn, potatoes, beans, winter squash, and tomatoes were harvested for a college-run cannery or stored for winter consumption." (Edmonds) For Marian, farming was in her bloodline. She described herself as "an old conservative with 200 years of New England ancestors behind me, farmer folk who worked hard." Marian was not a stranger to hard work. It came naturally to her.

Thursday, September 26, 1918 • Mount Holyoke

More rain and more grippe. It never ceases.

Sherman Ellis came up to college in spite of the weather. He was quite grand in his Second Lieutenant of Aviation uniform. But, I found him the same old Sherman, and we can't get along together. His idea about girls I abhor. He disapproves of a college education for a girl; it makes her too independent, with too many new ideas. As if we hadn't a right to think! We spent all the time in the Porter Hall parlor with the rain tearing down in sheets outside. I wasn't thrilled at all except just before he came when I hoped I might find a different man after his 16 months experience abroad.

On September 26, 1918, General Pershing would launch the Meuse-Argonne offensive, nicknamed "The Big Show" by the soldiers. It would be the largest and bloodiest American battle with over a million soldiers in very rough terrain. The Argonne valley was "flanked by thick forest on one side and the Meuse River on the other."(militaryhistory.about.com) Howard would not be able to find time to write his mother until October 5th.

"Over there" in France, following the success at the St. Mihiel offensive, the United States was hoping the Meuse Argonne drive would end quickly which it did not. It was also known as the 100 Days Offensive. Unfortunately, the Meuse Argonne drive was also one of the largest, which stretched along the entire western front. There were 1.2 million soldiers in the 47 day battle with over 26,000 dead and over 96,000 wounded. It is here that Howard would witness the atrocities of war firsthand in difficult terrain and almost continuous rain.

The World War I battlefront descended into the lowest rungs of hell. At the outbreak of hostilities, armies expected the elaborate military maneuvers of the past, but new technologies - artillery and rapid-fire machine guns - had rendered these obsolete. The only way to survive these new weapons was to dig into trenches. From inside the trenches, armies fought over inches. Men remained dug in for months. Standing in mud and damp, soldiers' bodies literally rotted, falling prey to such conditions as trench foot and trench mouth. Unable to bury the dead, soldiers often fought alongside the corpses of comrades. April 22, 1915, the Germans inflicted a new weapon of a barbarity so horrendous it was later forbidden by the Geneva Protocol of 1925. The Germans gassed French troops with chlorine, blinding them and inflicting hideous suffering as their lungs imploded. After the war, doctors recognized a new condition to define mental illness caused by the suffering of war; they named it Shell Shock but we now call it Post-Traumatic Stress Syndrome. I cannot imagine the terrible things that my grandfather witnessed as he was transporting soldiers back and forth to hospitals. What horrid conditions and sleepless nights he endured.

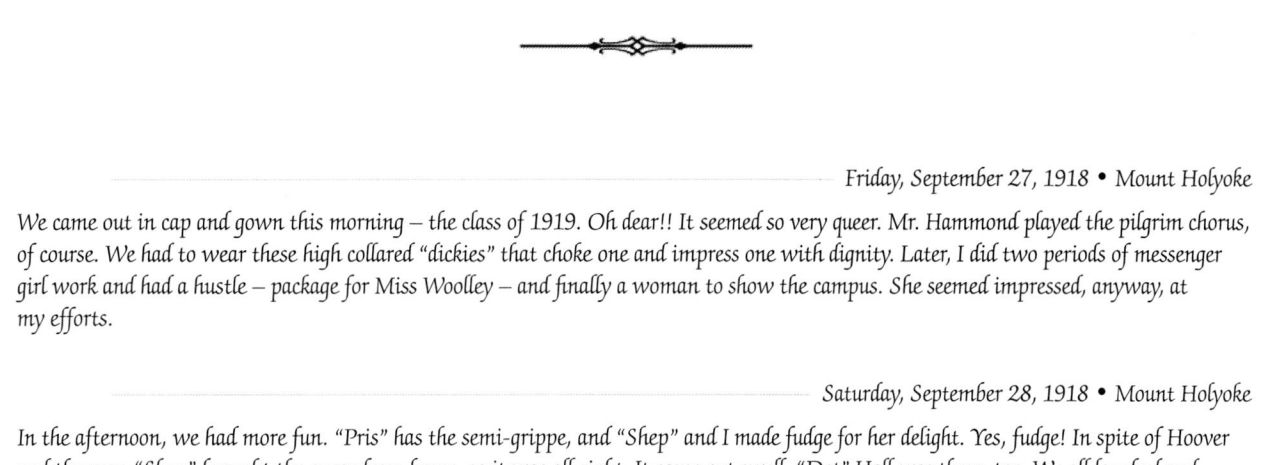

Friday, September 27, 1918 • Mount Holyoke

We came out in cap and gown this morning – the class of 1919. Oh dear!! It seemed so very queer. Mr. Hammond played the pilgrim chorus, of course. We had to wear these high collared "dickies" that choke one and impress one with dignity. Later, I did two periods of messenger girl work and had a hustle – package for Miss Woolley – and finally a woman to show the campus. She seemed impressed, anyway, at my efforts.

Saturday, September 28, 1918 • Mount Holyoke

In the afternoon, we had more fun. "Pris" has the semi-grippe, and "Shep" and I made fudge for her delight. Yes, fudge! In spite of Hoover and the war, "Shep" brought the sugar from home, so it was all right. It came out swell. "Dot" Hall was there, too. We all laughed and fooled like the big sillies we always are.

In the evening, there was a big mass meeting of the well ones among us in college. Miss Woolley said that we are now under quarantine and can't even go to the village stores. Also, no visitors can come here. And the faculty members are to carry trays to the sick girls in Brigham Hall because older people are more immune than "young fry." The faculty members are grand about volunteering. Anyone with a cold must isolate herself completely. The whole thing has its humorous side. We all went up to the store and called from outside for the things we wanted. I had to stock up in hairnets.

> President Woodrow Wilson appointed Herbert Hoover the head of the American Food Administration following the entry of the United States into the war. Hoover believed "food will win the war." (www.wikipedia.org) He set certain days to encourage Americans to avoid eating foods to save them for soldiers' rations: meatless Mondays, wheat less Wednesdays, and "when in doubt, eat potatoes." (ibid) All Americans were affected by the war in one way or another.

Sunday, September 29, 1918 • Mount Holyoke

In the afternoon, we all went for a walk. We were wandering through the cemetery when "Shep" and I conceived the idea of calling on Miss Woolley. It was such a grand bright day — all autumn colors and sunshine — we felt like doing something big and exciting. We did it. "Dot" and "Pris" wouldn't join us. Miss Woolley didn't seem at all surprised to see us. We talked before an open fireplace in her beautiful dark paneled living room. Then, horror of horrors, the other kids appeared with Doris delivering a paper to Miss Marks. We ignored their existence but left soon after. They gave us the deuce when we reached home. All through supper we laughed and fooled. All we do is act foolish, the whole bunch of us. After dinner, Miss Carr asked me in the faculty parlor for coffee and I went. Those heavenly faculty! Miss Smith is such a scream. But Elizabeth Adams in Zoology is a wonder – really thrills me till I can't see straight. Miss Comstock is cute and mischievous and Miss Carr!! Well words can't express it that's all. Later, Miss Carr played piano while we sang hymns; then, we sat in the darkness while she played for us. She is a great woman, and I worship the ground she walks on. Is that schoolgirl enthusiasm? All the evening we talked and fooled. Will we ever settle down to business? And we're Seniors with a little supposed dignity.

> Many of the faculty residents in Marian's dorm, Porter Hall, during her senior year were recent graduates of Mount Holyoke: Emma Perry Carr (1902), Miss Adams (1914), Alzada Comstock (1910), and Christina Smith (1915). Their closeness in age and their sisterhood bond, strengthened their trust and confidence in each other which Marian sorely needed. Dr. Morgan received her B.A. (1906) and Ph.D. from Cornell University. Marian realized that the faculty residents in the Mount Holyoke faculty dorms had isolated social lives, especially regarding men and dating. Her dreams differed. Marian wanted to teach and have a family

without the responsibilities of dormitory life. Several years later, the Mount Holyoke faculty started moving from the campus houses to small apartments or rooms in the village, which afforded them more independence and privacy.

Monday, September 30, 1918 • Mountain Day

Mountain Day and a gorgeous one. We hastened to the gate to wait for our equipment. You should have seen us! We were huddled up as if for an artic voyage. Our Cadillac 8 and chauffeur arrived at one o'clock. Father had hired it for us. We went to Middlefield, Massachusetts, for a wonderful Berkshire Hill ride. We picked up apples on the way. When we reached Middlefield, it seemed as if my heart would burst at the sight of the dear little streets and the grand old mountains. I never knew that fall foliage could be so beautiful, so soft and full of rich tints. I hope some of our pictures will come out well. We went all around the fair grounds. We had to come right back, since time was money, and the machine was $3.00 per hour. Oh, it was such fun. The entire bunch was there except Hild. Dr. Morgan chaperoned us. Our bill was $15.00, which was quite cheap for such a treat. Oh, it was such a sleepy evening with burning cheeks and heavy eyes. It's such fun at Dr. Morgan's table. She is such an original little dear.

By October 4th, which was nine days since the Allied Offensive began; British, French and US forces broke the Hindenburg line and took 36,000 German prisoners of war, and 380 guns. The Germans were short of food, and had worn out clothes and boots. (www.wikipedia.org)

To his mother Howard wrote only that his section followed "our splendid infantry" and cared for the wounded in France. The insight his letters provide into the Great War is limited to Howard's experience of the ground war in France. Moreover, in his letters home he always tried to project a positive attitude to ease his mother's anxiety.

By now, Ida heard the news about the deadly flu virus spreading like wild fire. Her thoughts and memories must have intensified as she relived the horror of her brother's death in the Spanish American War in 1898 from typhoid fever. It was not just the battles in Europe that Ida worried about but the living conditions and diseases associated with them.

The following letter from Howard was the first opportunity he had to write to his mother since the Meuse Argonne offensive began on September 26, 1918:

October 5, 1918

Dear Mother,

This is absolutely the first chance that I have had to drop you a line in, as it seems, weeks. I have been awfully busy, going day and night. The other evening when I came in from all day runs, after 5 days and 5 nights without much sleep or even rest, I made up my mind to write you, but as I could hardly keep my eyes open went to sleep for at least 2 hours when I was called out again for all night. Last night too I worked until 5 o'clock, but I am determined to drop you at least a note for I know you are worrying not having heard from me in so long. But, I think that you can understand why I have not written before.

I hope that at the end of this month I am going to an artillery officers training camp. I cannot go, of course, as long as this big drive is going on, but as soon as it ends, I am leaving the ambulance section for a 3-month's course at this artillery camp. I may be able to pull a commission. I am hoping that I may for I would like to get up to the front lines with the rest of the boys.

"Gerry" (German air plane) paid us a little visit last night, but he did not do much damage. The searchlights played all over him and, although we could not see him, we could hear his motor very plainly. Once you hear the hum of a German plane's motor you can never forget or miss it for it has a very distinctive sound.

This surely is a lovely war, as the English say, but I guess it will be over soon. Hope to be home a year from Christmas. And well and happy.

Lots of love,
Howard

Unbeknownst to Howard and most soldiers, negotiations continued to try to end the war. With all their recent success, the Allies held a strong hand at the negotiating table. In January of 1918 President Woodrow Wilson presented The Fourteen Points to Congress as a public statement outlining what the Allies hoped to accomplish through a victory over the Central Powers. It laid out a policy for free trade, open agreements, democracy, and self-determination (www.wikipedia.org). The Fourteen Points was the only explicit statement of war aims and post war goals. The Germans sent a request for an armistice via the Swiss to President Wilson on October 4th, based on his Fourteen Points. In response, on October 8th, President Wilson demanded the withdrawal of Germans from occupied territories and, on October 14th, he demanded an end to German U-Boat offensives, and "recognition that peace could not be concluded with the existing German imperial and military authorities (Willmott)." "Wilson's third demand, for a change of regime, caused Hindenburg and Ludendorff to call upon the army to ignore the government and its negotiations. For this act of insubordination, Ludendorff was forced to resign by the Kaiser. Acceptance of the third demand was given on October 29 in a note that assured Wilson of the government's credibility." (ibid) The Germans made dismissive responses to the U.S. President's demands. The negotiations and the battles continued.

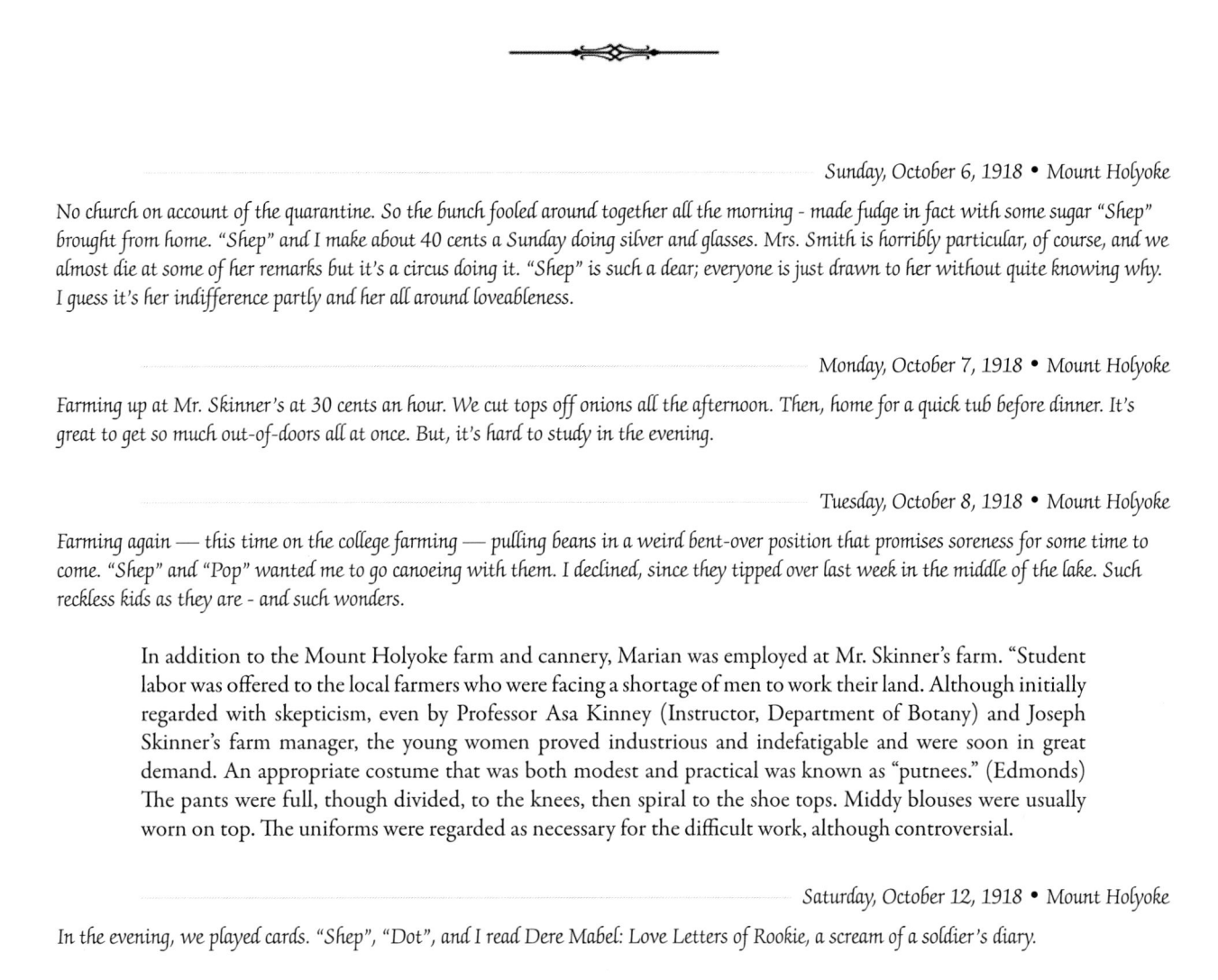

Sunday, October 6, 1918 • Mount Holyoke

No church on account of the quarantine. So the bunch fooled around together all the morning - made fudge in fact with some sugar "Shep" brought from home. "Shep" and I make about 40 cents a Sunday doing silver and glasses. Mrs. Smith is horribly particular, of course, and we almost die at some of her remarks but it's a circus doing it. "Shep" is such a dear; everyone is just drawn to her without quite knowing why. I guess it's her indifference partly and her all around loveableness.

Monday, October 7, 1918 • Mount Holyoke

Farming up at Mr. Skinner's at 30 cents an hour. We cut tops off onions all the afternoon. Then, home for a quick tub before dinner. It's great to get so much out-of-doors all at once. But, it's hard to study in the evening.

Tuesday, October 8, 1918 • Mount Holyoke

Farming again — this time on the college farming — pulling beans in a weird bent-over position that promises soreness for some time to come. "Shep" and "Pop" wanted me to go canoeing with them. I declined, since they tipped over last week in the middle of the lake. Such reckless kids as they are - and such wonders.

> In addition to the Mount Holyoke farm and cannery, Marian was employed at Mr. Skinner's farm. "Student labor was offered to the local farmers who were facing a shortage of men to work their land. Although initially regarded with skepticism, even by Professor Asa Kinney (Instructor, Department of Botany) and Joseph Skinner's farm manager, the young women proved industrious and indefatigable and were soon in great demand. An appropriate costume that was both modest and practical was known as "putnees." (Edmonds) The pants were full, though divided, to the knees, then spiral to the shoe tops. Middy blouses were usually worn on top. The uniforms were regarded as necessary for the difficult work, although controversial.

Saturday, October 12, 1918 • Mount Holyoke

In the evening, we played cards. "Shep", "Dot", and I read Dere Mabel: Love Letters of Rookie, a scream of a soldier's diary.

> Edward Streeter was an American journalist, war correspondent, travel writer and novelist. His humorous, *Dere Mable – Love Letters of a Rookie,* contained illiterate letters written home from a soldier, Bill. (Streeter) Fiction books about the war brought a lighter side to the war to everyone back home. The reality was a deeper, darker experience for the soldiers.

Sunday, October 13, 1918 • Mount Holyoke

An unusual and long-to-be-remembered day. We were wakened about 7 o'clock by an automobile load of soldiers tearing around campus and shouting, "The war is over! The war is over!" Everyone ran downstairs in nightgowns, bathrobes, and curl papers. Miss Carr was at the telephone, trying frantically to get connection with the outside world. We dressed hurriedly and most of us cut breakfast to get out, to run around wildly in search of news. One chapel bell was ringing and all the bells in the village. Finally, we saw Mary Vance Young (Ph.D Professor of Romance Languages), who told us that Germany had surrendered unconditionally and was ready to accept Wilson's peace terms. She said her source was The Republican (Springfield, Massachusetts newspaper).

By this time the whole college was gathered around the flagpole and Nina Babcock, Class of 1920 song leader, with a little flag baton, was leading us in singing "America," "The Star Spangled Banner," "Rule, Britannia" [a British Patriotic Song], and "The Marseillaise [The National Anthem of France adopted in 1795]." Then, in a body, we went to Miss Woolley's house and sang for her. John R. Mott, YMCA General Secretary, appeared on the piazza beside her. We expected him to speak, but he didn't. He only thanked us and said it was a fine early morning awakening. Even in the midst of our gay singing and enthusiasm, we had doubts in our hearts, doubts whether it could be so glorious and still so true.

The papers came. Something had happened. That was clear. Germany had proposed an armistice and would accept the peace terms, but Washington was doubtful. The wiser among the faculty seemed to hate the idea of peace when we are driving on so fast to a victory in the fields. It would be of great value to Germany now to have peace when they are in so dangerous a position. The enemy would escape with their skins, as it were, and not be beaten at all.

Dr. Mott was splendid in church. He spoke of the college student- the student who is thorough, earnest, energetic, and she who is lazy, content with half way methods, inefficient. He said the world needed now the best- the leaders who could do things well. He alluded to our new war news - as the beginning of the end - light healing – dawn - not the finish.

Doris and I went to walk with Miss Warner (Instructor, Department of English) in the afternoon. She had a little repast ready for us when we reached her little apartment — red jelly and white puffy popcorn. Later, we walked around upper lake, sat on the wharf, and discussed many things. She is bitter on the war, more so than I could believe her sweet, lovely nature could ever be. We do love her, Doris and me. We sat on her little porch when we came back and then she walked home with us to Porter Hall. She is so dear and friendly.

> The front page of the October 13, 1918 Springfield Republican erroneously proclaimed "Berlin Accepts US Terms." "Huns agree to evacuate all invaded territory." Underneath the headline was a box of text "Unofficial Text of German Peace Party." (Springfield Republican) It is not clear if the Springfield Republican was the only newspaper to make the error.
>
> From 1915-1928, Dr. John R. Mott was the General Secretary of the International Committee of the YMCA. "During World War I, when the Y.M.C.A. offered its services to President Wilson, Dr. Mott became the General Secretary of the National War Work Council." (nobelprize.org) "For the YMCA he kept up internal contacts as circumstances allowed and helped to conduct relief work for POW's in various countries." (ibid)

Monday, October 14, 1918 • Mount Holyoke

At dinner, we had a baby party. We all brought our baby pictures and tried to recognize them. They didn't have very good luck with mine, since I was only four months old. We had chocolate peppermints to celebrate. Today is Donald McKinnion's birthday.

Baby Marian, 4 Months Old

Tuesday, October 15, 1918 • Mount Holyoke

Mrs. Hopkins from Amherst came over today to instruct Bunny and me in the art of short story writing. I love the short story and am having more fun working over it.

> Marian's short stories must have been very good to inspire the wife of an Amherst professor, Arthur John Hopkins, a professor of Chemistry, to come instruct Marian. Mr. Hopkin's wife, Margaret Briscoe Hopkins, was a short story writer, playwright and novelist. She was also a patron and sponsor of young writers. Mrs. Hopkin's charismatic personality must have charmed Marian, as an interesting contrast to the serious faculty at Mount Holyoke. Mrs. Hopkins was a member of the Amherst School Alliance and the Amherst Civic League. She was opposed to woman suffrage. As much as she loved to write, Marian still felt such a pull towards teaching as to her future career.

Wednesday, October 16, 1918 • Mount Holyoke

I farmed today in the most glorious orchard, about half a mile back of Mr. Skinner's house and straight toward the mountains. It was a day of glorious fall colors and keen air. Florence ("Shep") and I worked together, climbing trees and packing the great luscious fruit.

Thursday, October 17, 1918 • An Extra Mountain Day!!

Imagine the angst faculty of this place granting such a thing! In the morning we all farmed – dug potatoes and beets and carrots. It was great. Then, we had a fishing party on Upper Lake for "Shep's" fountain pen that she dropped in a week ago. We didn't get it. About noon, we started to the mountain with lunch boxes - our bunch plus "Canary". We ate lunch down by the river with the sisters. How I did stuff! It surely was a terrible disgrace. We came home fairly early and rested before dinner. In the evening, late, the sophomores serenaded us. We hid under the couch covers on the front porch, then popped up when they said "Put your shades up, Senior Class!" Dear 1921, they are a grand class.

Saturday, October 19, 1918 • Mount Holyoke

The play, Alfred de Musset's, No Trifling with Love, was given up in the open-air theatre on Prospect Hill. The scene was lovely — just a conventional fountain, high back bench, and flower stand. The bare outline of the play was tropical, made relevant in parts by funny dialogue between the tutor and the priest. Some of us ushered in Red Cross regalia, and took up a collection of about $30, which, with the ticket sales, netted about $120.

In the evening "Dot" Hall and I were perfect fools. We went to the Library in hats of the Louis XIV period used in the play-great satin affairs of bright colors with tassels. We fooled around most of the evening away. Fun! But un-Seniorish - very!

> At Mount Holyoke, students "took an active part in selling War Saving Stamps and Liberty Loans and sponsoring fund-raising campaigns for war relief work, with an aggressive enthusiasm that brought in a total of $168,113.72, far exceeding the initial goals. A branch of the Mount Holyoke Chapter of the Red Cross was organized at the college in early 1917 and undertook the making of surgical dressings and hospital garments and the knitting of over 3,000 articles, such as sweaters, socks, helmets, and afghan blankets. After the war these efforts went to providing supplies for refugee children in Belgium." (Edmonds)

Friday, October 25, 1918 Mount Holyoke

Porter Hall went on a "bat" to the button field – a huge bonfire, hot dogs, and baked beans and apples. Then each class had a show and played games. I'll never forget "Pop" and "Dot" screeching at the top of their lungs "All Hail!! The gang's all here!" What dandy girls they all are – the darling old crowd – and there's no better anywhere in the world.

Saturday, October 26, 1918 • Mount Holyoke

Hockey games today and the dear old yellow worn. [Class of 1919 Color: Yellow, Flower: Daffodil]

In the evening I went down to the faculty house to dinner. The faculty are so sort of queer and lonesome - eccentric. They come in to their tables at odd times – and talk so excitedly. Elbows on the table is quite the thing – it seems. And, walking around between courses. I judged at a debate in the evening: "Resolved that German should continue to be taught in the high schools." The affirmative won. Margaret Gantt presides marvelously and is so dignified in cap and gown. Oh, for the cool logic of her well-ordered mind!

In Hudson, New York, S. Mitchell Rainey, was busy raising money for the troops through Liberty Loan bonds. The United States Secretary of the Treasury William G. McAdoo said that: "The greatest immediate assistance the American people can render in this war for universal freedom was to purchase the bonds and thus supply the government with such financial sinews of war." McAdoo awakened "a patriotic spirit in the American people, who were unused to saving through the purchase of government bonds, and floated four Liberty Loans to pay for the war." (www.treasury.gov) "The Act of Congress which authorized the Liberty

Bonds, is still used today as the authority under which all U.S. Treasury bonds are issued." (www.wikipedia.org/wiki/Liberty_bond)

The government used a variety of propaganda to sell the bonds and get their message out: posters, bond rallies, stickers in windows, buttons, and movie stars holding rallies, including Mary Pickford and Charlie Chaplin, air shows with Curtis J4 Jennys, and even the Girl and Boy Scouts with the slogan "Every Scout to Save a Soldier". (ibid) This was total war, with every element of society focused on victory from the Mount Holyoke girls working in farmers' fields to Boy and Girl Scouts selling bonds.

A preliminary meeting was held on May 18, 1917 at the Hudson City Savings institution where Howard's father, S. Mitchell, worked to discuss the campaign, with representatives from Hudson's four banks, the two newspapers, a minister, the President of the Civic league, and the City Clerk. S. Mitchell was appointed the committee head of the solicitation of "professional men". The first of four loan drives began Sunday, June 3rd, 1918 and took in $820,900 (over $8,500,000 in today's dollars) by June 15th.

The second loan drive kicked off with a big mass meeting held at the Playhouse on October 22, 1917 with speakers, and a Liberty Loan chorus. Liberty Day was observed throughout the country on October 24, 1917. Two days later, an aviator dropped "bombs" in the form of advertising for the loan down on Hudson. When the drive closed on October 27th Hudson exceeded their goal for a total of $1,431,800 (over $14,900,000 in today's dollars). A total of 5,500 people took subscriptions, and nearly $400,000 (over $4,150,000 in today's dollars) was bought on the last day alone, including the Hudson City Savings bank where S. Mitchell Rainey worked reported $100,000 sold, and individuals reported $100,500.

The third and fourth Liberty loan quotas were over a million and $1,952,850, respectively. When the returns were counted on October 21, 1918, the total subscriptions for the four Liberty Loan drives in Hudson were $5,305,500 (over $55,000,000 in today's dollars). For a small town, this was quite an impressive show of support for the troops and Howard's father was a large part of the successful campaign. Through the selling of Liberty bonds, the U.S. government raised approximately $17 billion. That figure represented an average expenditure of $170 ($1,760 in today's dollars) each for the 100 million Americans at the time. However, for the town of Hudson, of approximately 7,000 residents, they raised a total of over $5,300,000 or an average of $758 ($7,860 in today's dollars) per resident.

While the Rainey family was busy behind the scenes supporting Howard and the troops "across the pond", their son was involved in the Meuse Argonne offensive. It had been almost three weeks since Howard had time to write his mother. Could Howard survive the "big push?" As long as the letters kept coming, his mother could continue to hold out hope.

October 26, 1918

Dear little Mother,

I really have nothing much to say, but will just drop you a line to say that I am well and working hard. The old Americans certainly are a wonderful lot, knocking the spots out of the Germans on all fronts. We are paying for it though. However, I really believe that the end is in sight, and another big smash in the spring will at least end hostilities.

Day before yesterday I bought some very nice souvenirs. A Frenchman makes them entirely by hand and they are really quite wonderful. I bought a paper-knife, a combination ash tray and lighter, and a little table with a pitcher and six mugs. All of these things are made from old shells and take a very high polish. The table is the most wonderful of all. The top is the bottom of a French 75 with a machine gun shell coming down from the center and rifle bullets carving from that to make it stand evenly. The pitcher is a machine gun shell and the mugs are revolver shells each with a tiny copper wire handle.

You may have noticed in the casualty lists that Jay Van S. is "missing in action." As Buckley says, the Y.M.C.A. is fine but the Red Cross is still more wonderful. Behind the lines the YMCA is O.K.

Lots of love,
Howard

> "Little you'd care what I laid at your feet.
> A ribbon, a crest, or a shawl
> What if I'd nothing to bring you, Sweet,
> Nor maybe come home at all.
> Ah! But you'll know Brave Heart, you'll know
> Two things I'll have kept to send,
> Mine honor for which you bade me go,
> And my love - my love to the end."
>
> *Vermude*

Howard tucked this enchanting poem by the soldier-poet, Vermude, into his letter to convey his thoughts and feelings about the war to his mother in another voice.

Poetry was a powerful means of expression for many soldiers, especially on the Western Front. Whether the soldiers were in the trenches, on the front line, or driving ambulances, writing or sharing poetry gave soldiers another avenue to express the soldier's plight in the war to those back home. Soldiers wrote poems on scraps of paper in the trenches, on the back of envelopes, and in letters home. A large amount of "trench poetry" and songs were written by ordinary soldiers, published in trench newsletters or the Stars and Stripes newspaper.

One of the most famous World War I poems, "In Flanders Fields" (McRae) was believed to be written by a Canadian surgeon John McRae during the early days of the 2nd Battle at Ypres, Belgium. (Flanders Fields straddles the Belgian provinces of West Flanders and East Flanders). In the spring of 1915 when the weather began to warm up, poppy flowers miraculously began growing in the disturbed earth of the fighting zones, graves, and devastation of the Western Front providing the poet his inspiration. The poppy flower became internationally known as the symbol of Remembrance. Poppy seeds are disseminated by the wind and can lie dormant in the ground until the ground is disturbed, as it was in the spring and summer months of 1915, 1916, 1917 and 1918. For the soldiers who lived in the underground network of trenches, tunnels and holes, the poppies had to be a refreshing natural sight of beauty amongst the chaos.

At the end of the war, Poppy Day was also known as Armistice Day or Remembrance Day in the Commonwealth. In America, it is known as Veteran's Day and celebrated on November 11th each year. When my son and I went to the WWI Museum in 2012 the first experience we had was walking over a glass bridge of 9,000 poppies (One for each 1,000 soldiers who died). It was quite impressive and meaningful.

"In Flanders Fields"

> In Flanders field the poppies grow
> Between the crosses, row on row,
> That mark our place; and in the sky
> The larks still bravely singing fly
> Scarce heard amid the guns below.
>
> We are the Dead. Short days ago
> We lived, felt dawn, saw sunset glow,
> Loved and were loved, and now we lie
> In Flanders fields.
>
> Take up our quarrel with the foe:
> To you from failing hands we throw
> The torch; be yours to hold it high.
> If ye break faith with us who die
> We shall not sleep, though poppies grow
> In Flanders fields.
>
> Dr. John McRae

Dr. John McRae was "promoted as acting rank of Colonel on January 13, 1918 and named the Consulting Physician to the British Armies in France. The years of war had worn McRae down. That same day he developed pneumonia and later cerebral meningitis. He passed away at the Military Hospital in Wimereux, France on January 28, 1918, where he is buried with full military honors." (www.wikipedia.org)

Sunday, October 27, 1918 • Mount Holyoke

My Bible class met today for the first time. I have twenty sophomores; my subject is "Winning the War in Our Hearts." Well, I managed to get through the ordeal. I don't know just how twelve Sundays will come out. I do want to accomplish something.

Doris and I went down Morgan Road to Miss Alice (Department of German) and Miss Clara (Department of English) Stevens to dinner. We had a perfectly lovely time and a very nice dinner. Miss Clara Stevens and Miss Alice Stevens are surely the New England type of cool, pure, maiden ladies. Everything is just right — their speech careful, their starched white immaculate. We talked the first part of the afternoon with Miss Clara, who is so loveable and sympathetic.

I came home and worked hard on Mrs. Hopkins' work. Writing is such fun, and so hard and never quite satisfying. I read De Maupassant, a French author, and then tried to write a story of my own. How pitiful!

> Clara and Alice Stevens were both graduates of Mount Holyoke. Clara, a Professor in the English Department, became a mentor for Marian throughout the college years. Following Marian's graduation from Mount Holyoke, they remained close. In 1931, Marian listed Miss Stevens as a reference on her application for her College Graduate Certificate. By this time, Miss Stevens was retired.

Monday, October 28, 1918 • Mount Holyoke

I received permission to go home tomorrow. Oh joy of joys! Although we are still in quarantine, Miss Purington has let me go since Father will come up and bring me back in Mr. Jordan's little Ford. In the evening, the table gave me the sweetest birthday party with little black and white place cards, yellow flowers, yellow candles on chocolate peppermints, and yellow ice cream to cap it all. The dear kids! They put the party ahead a night since I was going home.

When I came up from dinner, an old shoe was on the door with a big white bow and a sign "Just Married." I went in, and there was the whole darling bunch - palms and ferns everywhere. I opened a big package on my desk, and there was a silk shirt and silk "panties." Oh! I had always wanted them so. I was a happy girl.

Tuesday, October 29, 1918 • My 21st Birthday

I am in disgrace — am 21 years old!! But, I just can't help it. Had a lovely box of notepapers from Florence ("Shep") and a poetry book from Helen.

Then, joy of joys — at 4 o'clock I met mother and daddy at the gate in Mr. Jordan's car. I hadn't seen them since September 17th. We rode through Granby and Belchertown where father had calls to make for work. We ate a picnic of sandwiches and apples. We reached home about 7:30 pm — the dear little house. We had a lovely picked up supper and best of all — a whole evening's talk.

"Youth"

"What do they know of youth, who still are young?
They but the singers of a golden song,
Who may not guess its worth or wonder —
flung
Like largesse to the throng.
We only, - young no longer, - old so long
Before its harmonies, stand marvelling -
Oh, we who listen - never they who sing.
Not for itself is beauty, but for us
Who gaze upon it with all reverent eyes;
And youth which sheds its glory luminous,
Gives ever in this wise:-
Itself the joy it may not realise.
Only we know, who linger overlong,
Youth that is made of beauty and of song."

Theodosia Garrison

Theodosia Garrison, an American poet who contributed poems and stories to *Everybody's Magazine* which was founded in 1899 and ceased publication in 1929.

Wednesday, October 30, 1918 • Springfield, Massachusetts

Miss Clarke sewed for me all day and finished my serge dress, which is dear, one of the new round-necked affairs with rows of braid and very tight sleeves and buttons. Mother went uptown to shop for me, as I promised Miss Purington I would not leave the house because of the flu quarantine. Mother bought me some comfy, dark, red bedroom slippers with Grandma's birthday money. Late in the afternoon, I came back to college with father. He bought me a box of Jensen's candy and some gorgeous chrysanthemums. He is a dear, dear father, generous and so companionable. I hated to leave him when we arrived back.

Meanwhile, across the pond, on November 1st, the second phase of the French – U.S. offensive began. The soldiers moved to the Aisne-Meuse front, a bit farther northeast of the Argonne-Meuse. Such a contrast!

Sunday, November 3, 1918 • Mount Holyoke

I "passed pie" at church in senior gown. I didn't drop it, either. Mr. Tweedy was splendid. His face is like the pictures of Christ. He spoke to us on having a better attitude toward church going — not going in that rushing fashion that gives you hardly time to catch your breath before the postlude, but going to church quietly and in the spirit of reverence and waiting for spiritual refreshment. In the afternoon, I had to haunt the library to work on my debate, "Resolved that U.S. Food Administration should be continued after the war." I'm affirmative.

Bunny asked me home for tea, and I went. Up in her cunning little room we let the little kettle purr and the toast brown. (It had cinnamon on it). We talked of everything under the sun. Bunny is such an anarchist, and I am an old conservative with 200 years of New England ancestors behind me, farmer folk who worked hard, But, my dear father broke away, came to the city, and loved it. He had new ideas and wouldn't go back to the old way. I think I'm like him; yet, here in college I'm an old conservative, going to every class and studying in my free periods.

"Tea, whether in the formal parlors or in individual student and faculty rooms, was the focus for social gatherings in the 1920's. Each room had the requisite round table, embroidered tablecloths, and appropriate tea service." (Edmonds) This was an important part of Marian's social life at college.

It is interesting how Marian has absorbed the family history and turned it into an archetype: "Father broke away and came to the city and loved it. He had new ideas and wouldn't go back to the old way." She has a premonition of her future: "I think I'm like him."

Monday, November 4, 1918 • Mount Holyoke

Austria gives in and surrenders. We had a celebration with the chapel bell peeling and we all acting like "loons." Miss Woolley spoke. "It seems" she said "that the end is near." She spoke on the war drive and our part in it to make good.

On November 3rd, 1918, Italy and Austria-Hungary signed an Armistice near Padua.

Tuesday, November 5, 1918 • Mount Holyoke

We had a tea for Mr. Chapman, a Y.M.C.A. Secretary in England. He spoke to us on the work of the Y.M.C.A. in France. He says it means everything to the men – home, and homefolks, and goodness.

> "On November 5th, Wilson informed the German government that negotiations could proceed on the basis of the Fourteen Points, and advised that an armistice would have to be secured from Foch." (Marshal Ferdinand Foch, Commander in Chief of the Allied Armies) (Willmott)

Wednesday, November 6, 1918 • Mount Holyoke

Reverend Edward Lincoln Smith of New York spoke here at chapel. Well, there's nothing left to do but give our utmost. He said it was our last chance to sacrifice, our last chance to help at the end. I have decided to give $10.00. I don't' know just where it will come from — spelling pupils, messenger work, a little domestic work, and Skinner farming — quite a nice little sum in all. But the cause is worth it. It is the great alliance of societies this time: The YWCA, the YMCA, the Jewish Order, the Library Association, the Camp Community Service, and the Salvation Army. The war, we all believe, will soon be over; then, demobilization and the men, released from the nervous tension of war, will feel a letdown. Oh, these societies will marshal all their forces to keep our soldiers from the scares that lie in the French cities as in all others under the sun. We will fail to return a clean army of men to America if we fail in this enterprise.

In the evening, we held our mass meeting, and together from pledges given on the floor we raised $16,000 in the college for the War Relief Fund. It is our quota and represents a very large per capita gift. Our slogan is not "Give until it hurts," but "Give until it feels good."

> "Sixteen thousand dollars for the War Relief Fund raised by the students directly supported six workers for overseas service, of which there were many alumnae representatives." (Edmonds) Marian was very perceptive - realizing that the war is not over for the soldiers when the fighting stops. And, her $10.00 was quite a sacrifice for her meager lifestyle.

> On November 8th, German Armistice negotiators arrived at Compiegne, France, a clandestine location, and were given the armistice terms to end the fighting. On November 10th the Kaiser authorized acceptance of the armistice terms, then abdicated and crossed the border into the Netherlands after losing support of the German army and navy. On November 10th, the combined French and U.S. offensives were able to seize the cities of Mezieres, Charleville, and Sedan in the Meuse sector, pushing the Germans and the western front farther back.

Sunday, November 10, 1918 • Mount Holyoke

In the afternoon, "Pris", "Shep", and I went to ride with Doris and her mother and sister. We rode all around Amherst College and saw the men everywhere. A bunch of them passed us in a machine. They slowed down again until we caught up and then passed us again with many grins and salutations. It's tantalizing to see real men once more.

Miss Morgan had Miss Warner to dinner. That surely graced the dinner. Miss Carr played piano after the dinner in the parlor - the lights all out and dear familiar tunes one after the other. Then we read out loud - or rather I did - Edith Wharton's "The Marne" in the Post - a mightily strong piece of writing. We had a feast of squash pie, cider, and chocolate cookies.

> Edith Wharton (1862-1937) was a celebrated American author considered one of the great female novelists of the early 20th Century. During World War I, Edith Wharton spent much of her time assisting refugees and orphans in Belgium and France and writing about her experiences. Her book, *Fighting France*, in 1915 was a collection of her essays and diary entries from her firsthand experiences in the war efforts. In 1918, she wrote the book *The Marne*. Wharton's war novella "concerns a young American Francophile who serves in the

ambulance corps to aid the French, and, in his view, civilization, while participating in the climactic Second Battle of the Marne." (www.answers.com) The Second Marne offensive was from July 15 to August 5, 1918 and was a significant Allied victory. The Germans lost a lot of ground during this offensive. This timely piece was of particular interest to Marian and her fellow classmates as they struggled to understand the raging war in such a distant place. In 1920, Edith Wharton won a Pulitzer Prize for her novel, *The Age of Innocence*.

While Marian was reading this fictionalized account of an ambulance driver, she was unaware that Howard was experiencing the horrors firsthand as a USAAS ambulance driver in France. Marian's desire to read so much about the war would be an advantage later, helping her to understand Howard's experiences.

Monday, November 11, 1918 • Armistice Agreement

This afternoon the bells rang and classes were called off at 11 o'clock. Germany signed the armistice agreement and the WAR IS OVER!! At nine o'clock in the evening, the whole college formed a long torchlight procession. We marched by halls, everyone with a tin pan, a huge dinner gong, a whistle, or at least a comb to blow upon. Then, there was a bonfire on the ruins of "Willy" (Williston Hall was destroyed by a fire in 1917), and we all stood around it and sang all sorts of patriotic songs and watched the bright sparks shoot up in the night. What a great day this is for all history—a day of rejoicing. I telephoned Father. The demonstrations in the city are frightful with talcum powder over everything, bells ringing, and old tin tubs on the back of automobiles. Everyone, he said, is crazy. It seems almost too solemn a time to act so wild—the end of slaughter and pillage, and terrible blood shed. Of course, in these after-years, we shall surely reap from the horror that is past; but it will be at least constructive.

At 11:00 am on the 11th day of the 11th month, November, 1918, the Armistice would be signed. "Foch advocated peace terms that would make Germany unable to pose a threat to France ever again." (www.wikipedia.org) It took six months to negotiate the Treaty of Versailles, the treaty that marked a victory for the Allies and a complete defeat for Germany. Although Foch declared the treaty an armistice for twenty years, Germany was allowed to remain a united country. Germany, however, had not surrendered; an armistice is merely a call for a cessation of hostilities. Unfortunately, this treaty also sowed the seeds of World War II; Germany emerged embittered by the settlement.

In some ways, Marian would "reap from the horror that was past" most of her adult life for it had set its mark upon the man she would love.

Tuesday, November 12, 1918 • Parade • Holyoke, Massachusetts

This morning the college marched in the parade at Holyoke, Massachusetts. This is a state holiday. We seniors were in cap and gown - and we marched four miles steadily. The Holyoke trolley men are on strike so we had to walk to the city of Holyoke. But, Mr. Skinner and Mr. Towne, our guardian angels, sent trucks after the greater part of us and we rode into the city - cheering again and again and singing. Everyone seemed to recognize that we were college girls. Oh, the crowd in Holyoke! The street was lined with foreigners. We sang the "Marseillaise" lustily and "Battle Hymn of the Republic." It was easy to march and sing with hearts as light as ours. When the parade ended, Mr. Skinner had hot chocolate for us at the church. Oh! It tasted good! And we were home by noon.

The Skinner family was an important part of life at Mount Holyoke and came to the rescue again. They were more than donors, they were friends. Mr. Skinner served as a board trustee from 1905-31 "with wisdom and generosity." (Edmonds) The city of Holyoke is fourteen miles away from Mount Holyoke College, where the Skinners had a silk manufacturing company. Mount Holyoke had an "800-member contingent in the Armistice Parade through the streets of Holyoke." (ibid)

In the afternoon, "Dot" Hall and I dozed while the heroine "Pop" read out loud from Harper's. We had a supper party up in "Dot's" room, and made some grand fudge as an "after the war" treat.

Later that day, back in her dorm room, Marian enjoyed reading the *Harper's* Magazine which debuted in 1850 as America's general interest monthly magazine. It provided readers "with a unique perspective on politics, society, the environment, and culture. The essays, fiction, and reporting in the magazine's pages come from promising new voices, as well as some of the most distinguished names in American letters." (Harpers.org) Harper's was an important resource for inquisitive Marian and her friends.

In the evening, Coningsby Dawson, a British Army Officer and author, spoke to us on "The Soldier's Peace." We were all disappointed - in him - or rather most of us. He seemed so radical and rather extreme.

Coningsby Dawson, was an Anglo-American author and poet who joined the Canadian Army at the front in 1916. After being wounded in the war, he wrote about his war experiences. In 1917, he compiled personal letters in *Carry On: Letters in Wartime*. In 1918, he wrote *The Glory of the Trenches* where he was quoted: "The glory is all in the souls of the men - it's nothing external." Following the end of the war, Mr. Dawson went on lecture tours in the United States which is when Marian heard him speak. "In 1918, he investigated for the British Ministry of Information on the American military preparedness in France. The following year, he visited and reported on the devastated regions of Central and Eastern Europe at the request of Herbert Hoover" (www.wikipedia.org/wiki/Coningsby_Dawson) who was the U.S. Secretary of Commerce. The following poem from *The Glory of the Trenches* is about Dawson's experiences in the hospital following his injury:

"In Hospital"

Hushed and happy whiteness,
Miles on miles of cots,
The glad contented brightness
Where sunlight falls in spots.
Sisters swift and saintly
Seem to tread on grass;
Like flowers stirring faintly,
Heads turn to watch them pass.
Beauty, blood, and sorrow,
Blending in a trance -
Eternity's tomorrow
In this half-way house of France.
Sounds of whispered talking,
Laboured indrawn breath;
Then like a young girl walking
The dear familiar Death.

Coningsby Dawson

Saturday, November 16, 1918 • Mount Holyoke

My mamma came today — the first time since college has opened. We were alone together until about 4 o'clock - then adjourned to "Pris's" room. Her mother was up too — and we gave a little tea for them. I'm always so very proud of mother!

Tuesday, November 19, 1918 • Mount Holyoke

Mrs. Hopkins came over from Amherst College. Bunny and I enjoyed it, as usual. I am anxious to write. She says I can't teach and write, too: the first will crowd out and smother the second. Well, I must teach to earn money and have the joy in a job. Miss Woolley spoke at 4.45 pm on the "need of the college in the church." "We are needed always in our home churches," she said, "to give new inspiration and new ideals."

Mrs. Hopkins seems to take Marian's writing talent seriously. Her opinions helped sharpen Marian's resolve about her future career.

Wednesday, November 20, 1918 • Mount Holyoke

I farmed at the Skinner's and on the way home took a flying leap from Doris's bicycle to the sorrow of both palms of hands, both knees and one elbow. Oh, I was a mess! I washed my wounds and did my knee up in plaster strips and surgeon's gauze.

Although Marian had some bad luck with her borrowed bicycle, the independence a bicycle offered women was one of the most significant symbols of the transformation of women's lives. In the 1895 book, *How I learned to Ride a Bicycle*, the author, Frances Willard, longtime head of the Women's Christian Temperance Union, stated that the bicycle made her "master of the most remarkable, ingenious, and inspiring [vehicle] ever devised upon the planet." (Collins) It changed the way women dressed and offered them independence. By 1900, there were "more than 10 million bikes on the road with models specifically manufactured for women. " The bicycle craze took over the nation so quickly that people barely had time to go through the traditional soul-searching over whether cycling would make women nervous or endanger their reproductive systems." (ibid) Women stopped wearing corsets while bicycling. Skirts became shorter so they wouldn't get caught in the spokes. This was the beginning of major changes in the fashion industry for women. The picture below is of Marian's mother, Gertrude Viets, (right) riding her bicycle.

Gertrude Viets (right)

Helen and I took Dr. Morgan to the YWCA dinner. Miss Woolley was there. At 8 o'clock in the Chapel Mr. Powys the poet spoke very picturesquely and feelingly on the work of Emily and Charlotte Brontë.

> John Cowper Powys was a charismatic British lecturer, writer and poet. He lived in the United States from 1904-1934, serving as an "itinerant lecturer" for the American Society for the Extension of University Teaching (www.wikipedia.org). Following graduation from Mount Holyoke, Marian lectured to groups on the Brontë sisters from England and her love for their work. The Bronte sisters published works in 1842 under the male pseudonyms of Currer, Ellis, and Acton Bell because they lived in an age when there was prejudice against female writers. Although Marian seemed to have many battles ahead of her as a woman; women behind her had already succeeded in ways that benefited her, including something as seemingly simple as a bicycle, or writing a poem.

Thursday, November 21, 1918 Mount Holyoke

I was fearfully lame today from my fall off the bicycle. I can't bend one knee and can't go down stairs worth a cent

Friday, November 22, 1918 • Mount Holyoke

Went to Skinner's farm this afternoon and earned 50 cents. Joke! I took Doris and she earned 50 cents also! Bless her heart! It isn't her fault she hasn't earned money. She has never had to. We raked leaves and it was terribly cold. The rake handle felt like ice.

Saturday, November 23, 1918 • Mount Holyoke

I heard Helen Fraser speak tonight. We can never appreciate what women across the seas have done in this war. The women of America have not suffered so - for us it has been only parting and fear of bad news. We went up to shake hands with her afterwards.

> Helen Fraser was a British botanist who was appointed the chief controller of the Women's Army Auxiliary Corps in 1917. In 1918, she became the head of the Woman's Royal Air Force.

While in Europe, the "doughboys" read the official newspaper of the American Expeditionary Forces (AEF), The *Stars and Stripes,* as a source of invaluable communication. From February 8, 1918 to June 13, 1919, it was distributed by trains, automobiles, and a motorcycle to deliver the news to over 500,000 "doughboys", American soldiers. (memory.loc.gov/ammem). The newspaper provided hope and inspiration to homesick soldiers with news from home, cartoons, sports news, poetry, and a sense of unity for scattered troops. The newspaper was eight pages long and came out every week on Friday.

Although Father's Day was not yet an official holiday in America, President Wilson verbally approved a Father's Day without signing a proclamation. The *Stars and Stripes* newspaper wanted to honor fathers with a letter writing campaign on November 24, 1918 between fathers at home and their sons in Europe. The intent of Howard's letter, as suggested by the newspaper, was one of sincere gratitude to his father for his stoicism (particularly when his mother was anxious) and for his financial support, especially his work with the Liberty Loan bonds. Howard's father undoubtedly read all of his mother's letters. But, this letter was specifically addressed to "Dad"; father to son, man to man. Howard respected and loved his father.

Many years later, in 1966, President Lyndon B. Johnson issued the first Presidential Proclamation designating the third Sunday in June as the official Father's Day. It wasn't until 1972 that President Richard Nixon actually signed Father's Day into law, making it a permanent holiday.

Howard wrote the following letter specifically to his father in commemoration of Father's Day:

November 24, 1918:

Dear Dad,

Today is Father's Day and our strict censorship has been raised so I am writing you and telling a few things I have been unable to tell before. I cannot begin to tell you all that I have been through and shall have to save most of my career over here until I get home. By the way, it is rumored that I will be home pretty soon. I am in the finest army and that is the finest home. I guess we are leaving here in about a week for the south. So rumor hath it.

Well, the Huns [derogatory terms for German soldiers] are licked for good and although I did not do much I am glad to say that I had a part in it. I have had my share of shot and shell but fortunately was not even scratched. Machine-gun bullets have popped all around me and big shells have hit near me. One day I had just a touch of "gas" but it had no other effect than making me sick for a couple of hours. I went into a place that had just been heavily gassed and the gas was still lurking around.

Well, as you know, we landed safely in Italy at Genoa, the birthplace of Columbus. I passed his house often and it is no wonder he looked for another house in America. While in Italy we saw no active warfare and set up our ambulances, etc. By the way, on our way over we stopped for 24 hours at Gibraltar where we cooled, landing at Genoa, June 27th. Just out of Gibraltar in the Mediterranean we missed a submarine by 15 minutes but our English convoy chased it away without further excitement. We came over on the "Giuseppe Verdi" the second fastest and largest passenger steamer of the Italian Government. I have told you of our reception in Genoa.

On August 24th we left Genoa for an unknown place in France. We came most of the way to France by flat-car, driving only from Riu au Court to Souilly. Souilly has been our base ever since but we took active part in the St. Mihiel Battle, Verdun and Argonne drives, following our splendid infantry and caring for their wounds.

Our trip from Italy brought us through the Alps. We came by way of Turino, the last city in Italy being Bardonecchia and the first one in France being Modane. Between the two cities is an 8 mile tunnel (Col du Mont Cenis), going into Italy and coming out in France.

I have the honor of being one of the American soldiers in Metz, France. That was the first city in months that I had seen that was not in ruins. We were stopped many times on the street, cheered and patted on the back. In one of the stores I found a woman who spoke English had quite a visit with her. She could not understand why we had sided with the Allies instead of with Germany. I gave her a few good reasons and she then said that German had the Allies beaten until America stepped in and saved the day.

I have been in Verdun several times and that is the most interesting old place. It is entirely shot to pieces as is St. Mihiel. In St. Mihiel I started to go across the Meuse River and found that there was no bridge; it had been entirely shot away. So, I waited until a new bridge was built and went across.

I have beaucoup souvenirs taken from dead Dutchman but I am sure that I cannot carry all of them home. I have seen any number of aerial combats in which for the most part we have come out ahead. The French people are so glad to get back to their old homes, even if their houses are not there. They just build little wooden shacks inside of their old stone home and live on. On the whole the people, especially the women, are very appreciative of what we have done for them, and they waste no words in expressing the same.

The night that the armistice was signed was one of wild excitement. Every Frenchman was drunk and I was in the ditch most of the time trying to keep out of the way of their trucks. Near St. Mihiel a bunch of Frenchman got out in a field and started throwing hand grenades at each other.

Well, this is Dad's day and Dad's letter but I should like to make it also a family letter and have you all read it for I send my love to all.
Your son. Howard

Wednesday, November 27, 1918 • E. Granby, Connecticut

At 4.10 pm, I met father at Court Square and we boarded the Suffield trolley together for E. Granby. We talked so hard all the way down. Umpa met us with the canopy top, and we drove eight, cold, dark miles. It was cheerful to see the little lights shining out of the huddled farmhouses. And it was so thrilling to reach Grandma's where there was such a warm welcome. We had our regular Thanksgiving Eve supper — a big steaming chicken pie. Oh, so good! It was an entirely satisfactory evening all together.

Thursday, November 28, 1918 • Thanksgiving Day

All the morning was lazy - reading and talking. Families are so nice and full of love. I know I'm growing older because sometimes I long so for that family of mine that may be some day.

The dinner was grand. Umpa and I waited on the table. Oh Umpa! He is a love — one of the dearest on earth. Such a dinner - a long line of vegetables, squash, turnip, turkey-pie, jellies, and fruit cocktail. That's all a jumble and in the wrong order but it's the way it is in my mind. In the afternoon, late, we left for home. It always seems so sad to leave the two old people again, standing there at the doorway while their children drive away in different directions. They come home for so short a time and are off again. But, it's the way of the world.

"Growing Old"

"A little more tired at close of day:
A little less anxious to have our way.
A little less ready to scold and blame.
A little more care for a brother's name:
And so we are nearing the journey's end.
Where time and eternity meet and blend.
A little less care for bonds and gold:
A little more zest in the days of old:
A broader view and a saner mind.
And a little more love for all mankind:
A little more careful of what we say:
And so we are faring a-down the way.

A little more love for the friends of youth:
A little less zeal for established truth:
A little more charity in our views.
A little less thirst for the daily news:
And so we are folding our tents away
And passing in silence at close of day.

A little more leisure to sit and dream.
A little more real the things unseen:
A little bit nearer to those ahead,
With visions of those long-loved and dead:
And so we are going where all must go.
And the place the living may never know.

A little more laughter, a little more tears
And we shall have told our increasing years:
The book is closed, and the prayers are said.
And we are a part of the countless dead.
Thrice happy, then, if some soul can say,
"I live because he has passed my way.""

From the Railroad Telegrapher

Friday, November 29, 1918 • Springfield, Massachusetts

Mother and I spent the morning up town. I bought a new winter coat — grey with a big black fur collar and lined with a fancy silk. I revel in its newness.

Another Thanksgiving is over, my 21st, and all of them so happy. Wish I didn't keep wondering if the next 21 would be as sweet. I keep probing the future like the little fool that I am, wondering and wondering. Will it be the love of a man or the call of a career or a humdrum existence without even the right to be called a career? Yet, I am strong enough to bear children and want them. It isn't strength that makes a man woo a woman - and I don't seem to have attracted men so far. That's what makes me doubtful.

> Marian stood at the first swell of the women's movement. In her time, most women longed for a family and did not even consider the possibility of a career unless they were so unlucky as to remain single.

Saturday, November 30, 1918 Springfield, Massachusetts

Mother and I had a quiet afternoon and evening together. I studied some but saw no one outside. Doris blows me for being so shut up in my family that I don't call up my friends when I'm home. Perhaps it's true - but I feel that I owe them this time when I am all they have and they do so much for me.

Tuesday, December 3, 1918 • Mount Holyoke

Mrs. Hopkins came over this afternoon to give Bunny and me our writing lesson. Then, we invited her to stay to supper. She came to Porter Hall with me, to Miss Morgan's table, and in the faculty parlor afterward where she entertained everyone. She's a great talker. How she hates science. The sparks flow between her and Miss Carr (Ph.D Professor of Chemistry).

Bunny and I took Mrs. Hopkins to Blackstick where Fanny Stearns Davis, the poet, talked. She begged us to write while we are in college and have the encouragement and the time to do so. She is charming with her crown of auburn hair.

Mrs. Hopkins discouraged me about teaching school, saying it would smother my writing. She can't sympathize with my great longing for a job. I want to earn money and work and be independent and, above all, useful. The world doesn't need my pen scratches.

> The class of 1919 founded "Blackstick," a literary organization for the purpose of encouraging original writing in the college. As a guest speaker, Fanny Stearns Davis Gifford, a 1904 graduate of Smith College, spoke about her two volumes of poetry, *Myself and I* (1913) and *Crack O' Dawn* (1915). Fanny Stearns Davis's poem "*The Hermit on the Dunes*" from *Myself and I*, was one of Marian's favorites and she specifically chose to enter this poem into her diary:

"The Hermit on the Dunes"

Low water low water silence on the sea,
Across the moors the Sunday bells ring warm and drowsily.
Low water low water dim and smooth and pale.
Across the moors the windmill waves an idle Sabbath sail.
Low water low water plover peeping faint,
Across the moors the church-doors swing for sinners and for saint.
Low water low water silence on the sea, -
Across the moors they pray to God, while here He breathes on me.

Fanny Sterns Davis

> Marian enjoyed Mrs. Hopkins visits and admired her writing. She published numerous short stories, and serialized fiction in periodicals such as *Harper's Bazaar* and *The Outlook*, in the late 19th and 20th century. Mrs. Hopkins also published six books which were compilations of previously published works. She encouraged Marian to publish her own work instead of teaching others to write. In Marian's mind a publishing career could not guarantee a steady salary. Mrs. Hopkins viewpoint was completely different than Marian's; she grew

up with private tutors in her home, and did not attend college, which wasn't done in the "circles" she grew up in. I don't think Mrs. Hopkins was aware of Marian's financial struggles.

Wednesday, December 4, 1918 Mount Holyoke

At the YWCA meeting, we read The Christmas Rose by Selma Lagerlof. We sang carols, too. So thrilling. Then I went to an open meeting of College Settlements. A social worker spoke on the need for our help – and the fact that wealth consists, after all, in diversity of interests. Then, I am wealthy – if money is out of it. We must broaden the interests of everyone.

> Selma Lagerlof was a Swedish-born stylish novelist, who in 1909 became the first woman writer to win the Nobel Prize for Literature. *The Legend of the Christmas Rose*, a religious fable, was published in Good Housekeeping in 1907. A Christmas rose (commonly known as Hellebores) is an evergreen perennial that magically flowers from December to April in cold weather, reminding us of the miracles of life. Marian definitely believed in miracles!

Friday, December 6, 1918 • Mount Holyoke

I took a long cold walk in the snow this afternoon and went to a meeting of the Woman's Land Army. The speaker told us that farmers are greatly needed for the coming summer.

"Merely Mary Ann" (play) was given in S.A.H. at 7:00 pm. Doris Campbell had the leading role – Mary Ann - and was fine. I sat in the third row from the front since I went with Mrs. Campbell. I did enjoy it thoroughly. Doris had many congratulations afterwards and she deserved them. She is so interested in dramatics – our room is full of roses. The scent of them is delicious. I shine by reflected glory from my little star.

Sunday, December 8, 1918 • Amherst!

Oh! A day! In the afternoon, Bunny and I took the 4.10 pm car for Amherst to Mrs. Hopkin's house for dinner. We reached there about 4.30 pm. No other guests had yet arrived. The parlor was all candle light and little, individual, gilded tables. Then, the guests began to come: a Professor, an essayist, two young sophomores, 3 lieutenants, and a mob of others — quite distinguished. Bunny and I ate with the three lieutenants and the sophomores. They were fascinating fellows.

Mrs. Hopkins started a discussion on college education for girls. She spoke against it. Then, she informed us that we should be married. And, the girls should have had children by now. Bunny and I were thrilled with the haze of cigarette smoke, men's voices, and just their being there was a joy.

> This is what the incipient feminist was up against. The very Mrs. Hopkins, who so ardently urged Marian to pursue her writing, tells her she shouldn't go to college but should be married.

Tuesday, December 10, 1918 • Mount Holyoke

Chapel was a thriller today. Mr. Towne, a trustee and an honorary of the class of 1919, has presented us with the eight flags of our allies, silk and beautiful, draped about the chapel. We had a dedication for them. Louise, our president, presented them formally. Then, Mr. Hammond played the national anthems of those nations. Oh, our allies! We must never forget them: their heroism, and the part they played in this big struggle. This war has meant so much about sacrifice and adherence to great ideals.

Wednesday, December 11, 1918 • Mount Holyoke

I copied my new story all day. "Pride" is the name. It's a sort of silly affair without a breath of war in it; fortunately, since Mrs. Hopkins insists that I must get over this war excitement that tears through my stories. In the evening, Dr. Morgan came down after me. I went up to her room, and we talked futures, etc. I had to tell her how Mrs. Hopkins is upsetting me over my writing. She doesn't want me to teach and I want to. Miss Morgan is a very dear friend.

Thursday, December 12, 1918 • Mount Holyoke

Mrs. Hopkins came over today. We had a nice talk over vacation reading. She is a dear, for all her upsetting remarks to me. What does she expect — that I will stay home with papers strewn about and rejected manuscripts falling out of a stuffed wastebasket? No, I can't bite the end of a pen next year, not unless I correct high school papers and bite in the sheer wrath at the stupidness of my pupils. I must work. Bless Miss Morgan! She is on my side in this mix up.

Marian depended on the support and understanding of her faculty mentors, especially Dr. Ann Morgan (Professor of Zoology) who resided in Porter Hall as a faculty resident. Marian confided with Miss Morgan about her conflicts with her writing career and consternation created by Mrs. Hopkins. While Mrs. Hopkins nourished the creative side of Marian; faculty mentors provided a realistic viewpoint of careers for working women.

Marian also relied on insight from famous authors such as Horace Greeley, an editor and the Founder of the New York Tribune. This quote was taken from "*The Book of the World's Classics – Restricted to Prose*" (Volume X – America – II), 1909. Horace's contribution to the book was specifically in regards to his profession as an editor, *The Fatality of Self Seeking in Editors and Authors*. The following is the second to last paragraph of the article. It was always interesting for me to discover which specific paragraphs, out of so many, Marian chose for hallowed space in her diary that had special meaning to her. Becoming an editor instead of a teacher deserved serious consideration.

"But if you are sure that your impulse is not personal nor sinister, but a desire to serve and ennoble your Race, rather than to dazzle and be served by it; that you are joyfully to "shun delights and live laborious days," so that thereby the well-being of mankind may be promoted, – then I pray you not to believe that the world is too wise to need further enlightenment nor that it would be impossible for one so humble as yourself to say aught whereby error may be dispelled, or good be diffused. Sell not your integrity; barter not your independence, beg of no man the privilege of earning a livelihood by Authorship."

Horace Greely

Saturday, December 14, 1918 • Mount Holyoke

I gave Miss Morgan her handkerchief today – one with a little blue butterfly that mother had picked out. She thanked me for it so sweetly. My but I love her!

Sunday, December 15, 1918 • Mount Holyoke

A heavenly day! Special Christmas music at church and an attractive young minister from Providence, Rhode Island. The chapel was beautifully decorated with wreaths and bunches of hemlock all around the gallery and, of course, the allied flags.

At my Bible class, I read van Dyke's "The Other Wise Man," and we talked a little about the Christmas spirit. I am so thrilled with it all, but I wonder if I ever convey anything to my students.

In Henry van Dyke's book, *The Story of the Other Wise Man*, he added a fourth Magus, named Artaban, who sets out "to see the newborn ruler carrying treasures to give as gifts to the child." (www.wikipedia.org) This became one of his most popular Christmas writings. Dr. Van Dyke, a Presbyterian minister, is best known for his "Hymn of Joy" ("Joyful, joyful, we adore Thee…" 1907) sung to the tune of Beethoven's "Ode to Joy". (ibid) Marian loved Mr. Van Dyke's poetry throughout her life.

Marian chose this special book to share with her Bible class. The following meaningful poem is before the preface:

"Who seeks for heaven alone to save his soul
May keep the path, but will not reach the goal;
While he who walks in love may wander far,
Yet God will bring him where the blessed are."

Henry Van Dyke

In the afternoon I took Miss Snell to Christmas Vespers. The music was so sad - especially *"Night Dance"* – sung from the back gallery – about a hundred picked voices.

Monday, December 16, 1918 • Mount Holyoke

This day is very long to be remembered, at least the evening part of it.

At dinner, we had our grinds [funny poems or sayings imitating each other] and table party. Miss Morgan had given us a big basket of red carnations for the center and dear little place cards all around. The grinds were screaming: Miss Morgan, a bottle of nerve tonic; Helen, a set of Shakespeare, etc. I had a hair net and a cute verse, which was:

> "There is a young girl at our table
> Who ne'er in the world will be able
> To avoid meeting her fate
> As a school-marm, sedate
> O, this charming young girl at our table
> The boys, oh indeed, they'll adore her,
> With the rolls on the side
> And her smile so wide
> Perhaps a hair net may save her."

We had ice cream with chocolate marshmallow sauce. Then, we all went upstairs for a party in another room for toasted marshmallows, popcorn balls, social whirls, and maple hearts. We played all kinds of games and didn't leave the festal scene until just before 10.00 o'clock. Doris and I sat up a while. Such excitement always reigns the night before going home — a delicious, suppressed feeling of happy things to come. I do love it!

Tuesday, December 17, 1918 • Mount Holyoke

We were awakened by the Cowles (dorm) sophomores singing Christmas carols – a long procession of them in white night gowns, streaming hair, tinsel, candles and the same dear old carols. Then, many goodbyes and at 11:30 am Doris and I left for home.

Stop! Look! Listen! We walked to High Street to the palmist to have our palms read. So thrilling. I must tell mine. I'll write it as she said it in the second person:

"You should have been born a man, for you aim high and want to do big things which you will not do now, for they look too great to you as a woman. You will not consider it worth your while to go on. You will teach, only a year or two, no longer; then will be chosen for reconstruction work — abroad perhaps — for you will be much on the water. You should indulge in water sports — learn to swim well. Men are awed and impressed by you, but they are afraid of you, also. You should have men instructors; they would give you very high marks and let you convince them. They would be rather helpless before you. In five years, a man will come into your life and will want to marry you. He will love you passionately. He will be all that a man should be. You will not love him, but you will respect him and you will honor him. You will marry him.

"Still, you will go on in organizing, executive work outside your home. You may have 4 children, but only after an operation has been performed. You will have a broad, full life and have few hard knocks. You will write but only for commercial reasons. It is your passion to earn money. You would be more likely to be an editor. You would not be content to write for the love of it, to revise and revise and then to have it accepted. Your own ideas are better than what you get out of books. Abide by your first impressions, your first judgments. They are the best. You take after your father's side. Your proud and haughty ways you inherit from your mother's family. Your father is easier to meet. You shall never be home again after next year."

Well, that is my reading, all for 50 cents. There is some of it I would adore, such as the nice husband after I have tried my wings.

> The palmist made a big impression on Marian for she wrote down much that she told her. She must have felt the palmist's observations had some accuracy. Certainly Marian has expressed her desire to look into her future many times as well as her fear that men do not respond to her. How perceptive of her to tell an ambitious feminist that she should have been born a man. Perhaps in Marian's world, her fate would have

been easier that way. The palmist picked up on both her teaching and her writing. I wonder if her father was easier to meet than her mother. And what she said about the husband that Marian longs for, would that come to pass?

Thursday, December 19, 1918 • Springfield, Massachusetts

Spent the night with "Mit" Woodin – the dear child. "Mit" is such a love - so pretty and dear. She is to have her engagement ring for Christmas. Jimmy sent the check from France.

Friday, December 20, 1918 • Springfield, Massachusetts

Mother and I "Christmas shopped." My card list is atrocious - about fifty and then not nearly all I might remember. I'm not buying any presents except for Father, Mother, and Grandma. I bought Grandma some hyacinth bulbs. She does love to watch things grow.

Monday, December 23, 1918 • Springfield, Massachusetts

More shopping and now it is done. My cards have begun to arrive. It is such fun lying in wait for the postman. I studied some today. College work follows one even in vacation. Our reading, H.G. Wells "Research Magnificent"– such an unnatural thing - it seems to me - a man fighting against sex - even with his wife.

H.G. Wells was an English writer best remembered for his early works from 1895-1901 in science fiction, including: *The Time Machine*, (1895) *The War of the Worlds* (1898), and *The Invisible Man* (1897). He was a pacifist and outspoken socialist writer of fiction and non-fiction.

Tuesday, December 24, 1918 • Christmas Eve

The very busy day before Christmas! Mother has invited the McKinnon's for dinner tomorrow. I made fudge for Grandpa and ourselves. In the evening, we had our presents on the dining room table. Mother gave me some beautiful, black silk stockings with white embroidered socks, and father gave me some Crane's notepaper, Jensen's chocolates, money for a waist, and a wooly kitty that he bought at a toy store. Father gave mother a handsome pocket book that I picked out for her, and I gave her a chemise, some talc, and a little hankie. Also, I have some dishtowels to hem for her. We gave father gloves and linen initialed hankies. Mrs. Bemis gave mother and me very handsome waists. "Mit" gave me a holder for photo films; and "Joe", a hankie. I didn't remember those girls at all.

"The Empty Stocking"

There's an empty stocking hanging
From many a little bed,
Where a God-blown dream hangs over
Each sleeping curly-head;
And the vision gathers nightly
If a day that's soon to come
Where little feet should patter
To the music of the drum.

There's an empty stocking hanging
By many a wind-blown door,
That must wait in vain for Christmas
In the gray haunts of the poor;
And eyes that now shine brightly
Shall, through a rain of tears
See nothing there on Christmas
But the sorrow of the years.

> But out where splendor centers
> In the mansions of the Great,
> No call will go unanswered-
> No tot will vainly wait;
> The Christmas horn will summon-
> The Christmas drum will roll
> The tide of Joy in magic
> Thru the gateway of each soul.
>
> But where one gift would brighten
> The dark of weary days,
> No reindeer's hoof will thunder
> Out poverty's dreary ways;
> And so for God's white season-
> For some wee dreamer's cause-
> Don't you think that you might whisper
> Just a word to Santa Claus?
>
> Grantland Rice

The poet Henry Grantland Rice (1880-1954) was an "early 20th Century American sportswriter known for his elegant prose. His writing was published in newspapers around the country and broadcast on the radio." (www.poethunter.com). His campaign to collect contributions to help fill empty stockings on Christmas morning ran in newspapers across the United States. Mr. Rice is best known for being the writer who dubbed the great backfield of the 1924 Notre Dame Fighting Irish Football Team "The Four Horsemen of Notre Dame" (www.wikipedia.com)

Wednesday, December 25, 1918 • Christmas Day

Such a happy day! All the morning was spent in preparing the dinner, rescheduled for two o'clock. And such a feast! Soup, turkey, potato, turnip, onions, cranberry sauce, olives, celery, fruit salad, ice cream, cookies, coffee, and nuts. Donald brought us more Jensen's chocolates, and I had fudge on hand. Father and Mr. McKinnion played rum, 55 hands. The McKinnions left about 8 o'clock. We all did the dishes, a pile of them. Such happy hearts, for we love one another.

While Marian spent Christmas with her family, Howard was overseas far away from his family. Even though the Armistice had been signed, there was still work to be done. Howard made ambulance runs to hospitals, and spent time guarding cars. There was still an element of risk for Howard. It had been almost a month since Howard wrote his mother. Finally this letter arrived.

December 26, 1918

Dearest Mother,

I intended to write you yesterday, but I was unexpectedly on the road until dinnertime and after that had to go on guard over the cars. We had a fine Christmas. Although, I was down in southern France at the Bar-sur-Antibe over Christmas Eve looking up some of our mail, incidentally my Christmas box, so that we could have mail for Christmas Day. Some one hung up my sack, and when I came back found it filled with candies and cakes.

I have now in my possession two officers helmets. The better but not polished one is the prettiest. It is made of steel and belonged to an officer of the Franciscan guard. The other made of patent leather with the coat of arms in brass belonged to an officer of infantry rather than the F.G. I am not going to attempt to send either home for I am afraid that it will be lost, and I would sooner lose my clothes.

We are at our stopover house and are going to make another in about a week. We are now at the city of Fenay in eastern France and hope soon to be on our way to a sea port.

I wanted to buy you a pair of French silk stockings but have forgotten what size you wear so it was impossible. However, I have something small for each you and Dad. It is so hard to get anything nice, but the trinkets that I have, have some interest attached to them. Aunt Mary sent me some cigarettes, which came through O.K. By the way, I have part of some poor German's skull that I am going to bring home.

Mrs. Evan's death was very sad and I was most sorry to learn of it. Thank goodness you have all escaped "flu", etc. There seems to have been so much of it. Even more than over here, where it has been bad enough.

Please do not worry any more. I will write when I can but often our mail is delayed. There is absolutely no cause for worry for the war is over.

Our barracks are all decorated with holly, Christmas trees, and mistletoe that we went to the woods and picked. Can you imagine stepping outside and picking holly?

Lots of love to all,
Your son

Monday, December 30, 1918 • Springfield, Massachusetts

Mother and I shopped. She bought a lovely dress. I am so happy. She has so little and is so unselfish. The dress is café au lait charmeuse with jet beading — very stylish. I bought a dark blue georgette with Grandpa's Xmas check. In the evening, we all went to the Court Square Theatre, a great event for the Viets family. But, it is Dad's and Mother's anniversary — their 22nd. We saw Come out of the Kitchen, a light farce, which was good and entertaining.

Wednesday, January 1, 1919 New Year's Day

New Year's Day and a steady drizzle. Mother and I stayed in all day dusting, studying, etc. This is an eventful New Years' day. 1919 should be full of happenings. In the great world, it will see the Peace Conference and settlement, reconstruction, and readjustments. For me — how unimportant just one human being — the end of college and the entrance into a job. And now President and Mrs. Wilson are "doing Europe" with royal honors.

> Following the Armistice, the work began on peace treaties. President and Mrs. Wilson arrived in London in late December, 1918, on their way to Paris for the Peace Conference at Versailles. On January 18, 1919, negotiations began between the Allied Powers at the French Foreign Ministry.
>
> This was one of the largest diplomatic meetings in history with over 30 nations attending. The "Big Three" presided: President Wilson, Prime Minister David Lloyd George of Britain, and Premier George Clemenceau of France.

Friday, January 3, 1919 • Mount Holyoke

Came back to college this morning. It all seemed very homelike and natural to settle once again in Porter and attend the round of classes and be a messenger. We are in quarantine for a week and no entering other dorms.

Sunday, January 5, 1919 • Mount Holyoke

The bunch took a long walk around the river road. It was hard walking through deep snow. We took a lot of pictures. We can NEVER forget one another.

Tuesday, January 7, 1919 • Mount Holyoke

"Dot's" birthday. The bunch gave her red roses – a dozen. We entered the room at the stroke of the rising bell while she was still in bed. Mrs. Hopkins was over. We talked literary work. She is encouraging – but I remain unfooled.

Saturday, January 12, 1919 • Mount Holyoke

We took Miss Ellis (Ph.D., Associate Professor of History) home after Debating Society and she invited us down to sit around her fire. It was so cozy in her little parlor, and we had a good lively discussion of Wilson and the Peace table. I wish I knew half what she does. My deplorable ignorance.

Tuesday, January 14, 1919 • Mount Holyoke

Oh, Miss Morgan is such a love! I really feel that I am coming to know her well. She has a way that is irresistible – a certain sweetness and simplicity in the midst of such real nobility of character.

Saturday, January 18, 1919 • Mount Holyoke

Bill C. came over from Amherst and we danced in S.A.H. He is a dear and lots of fun to talk to. It seemed great to see a man.

Tuesday, January 21, 1919 • Mount Holyoke

The last classes before exams. In the evening was a Big League meeting. Miss Woolley spoke on "Reconstruction." A vote against smoking here in college was taken and passed.

Then, Louise, class president, spoke and our class brought out Mr. Wicks (Revered Dr. Robert Russell Wicks, pastor of the 2nd Congregational Church of Holyoke, Massachusetts) as an extra honorary member for senior year. Slips of paper were thrown from the gallery, with a real lamp wick attached and the words "Wicks for a Student Lamp." We had some cute songs, and the whole thing went well. We established a precedent for the odd-year classes in the future.

Miss Woolley's talk tonight was sorely needed, a sort of waking us up to work and a reconstruction of our attitude toward our work. "Now practice it!" I resolved, but will I? Exams are ahead. Work is sure.

> Miss Woolley motivated Marian to continue her hard work at college. As Marian would soon leave her youth behind, she looked forward to her dreams. She would be ready to leave home and start a career. Marian fittingly entered the following poem from *The Works of Robert Louis Stevenson Volume Fourteen* by Robert Louis Stevenson into her diary:

"To Will H. Low"

YOUTH now flees on feathered foot,
Faint and fainter sounds the flute,
Rarer songs of gods; and still
Somewhere on the sunny hill,
Or along the winding stream,
Through the willows, flits a dream;
Flits but shows a smiling face,
Flees, but with so quaint a grace,
None can choose to stay at home,
All must follow, all must roam.
This is unborn beauty: she
Now in air floats high and free,
Takes the sun and makes the blue;—
Late with stooping pinion flew
Raking hedgerow trees, and wet
Her wing in silver streams, and set

> *Shining foot on temple roof:*
> *Now again she flies aloof,*
> *Coasting mountain clouds and kiss't*
> *By the evening's amethyst.*
> *In wet wood and miry lane,*
> *Still we pant and pound in vain;*
> *Still with leaden foot we chase*
> *Waning pinion, fainting face;*
> *Still with grey hair we stumble on,*
> *Till, behold, the vision gone!*
> *Where hath fleeting beauty led?*
> *To the doorway of the dead.*
> *Life is over, life was gay:*
> *We have come the primrose way.*
>
> Robert Lewis Stevenson

Marian's diaries skipped from January 21st to March 21st. Many pages have dates on them but the pages are blank. And, Marian cut out many pages, for reasons unknown. My father said that his mom went through a "cutting phase" later in her life as her dementia worsened. She cut photos, post cards, and her diaries. It is unfortunate that she was unaware of what she was doing to her treasures.

The mail service was slow from Hudson to Europe. It took two to three months for Howard to receive his letters from home.

Jan. 27, 1919

Dear Mother,

Still in the same uninteresting place. There has been some excitement in the form of a French wedding. It lasts for 3 days. The wedding procession paraded around the town yesterday and tonight there is a dance that I have just left. It is lots of fun. The music is a fiddle, and the musician knows but 2 pieces.

I received quite a bunch of letters the other day, mostly from you. The next day I received one that you wrote on October 13. Tell Dad that I received his in the bunch. In it he said that it was a Christmas letter and that I would in all probability get it about the middle of January. He wins. I received it Jan. 23rd.

This afternoon I was "deloused" That, I figure, is a step in the right direction. It is essential that each man have this tick bath and his clothes sterilized before he boards the ship for the U.S.A. It is rumored that we are leaving for the U.S. about March 1st. This seems, from all outward appearances, like good dope, but, of course, no one around here knows for sure. We are all hoping.

Love to all,
Howard

Feb. 10, 1919

Dear Mother,

Still nothing exciting to write about. The rumor about our leaving soon seems to have passed over, and now it seems that we will be here for some time yet. I am growing quite impatient for it seems such a waste of perfectly good time.

We have had some snow and quite cold weather. The seeming lack of wood does not make things any easier, but we manage to survive.

The last two nights I have gone for long walks. The evenings have been beautiful, perfectly clear and a wonderful old moon. The moonlight and the snow have made it perfectly beautiful and the clear crisp air has made walking a pleasure. I am going to walk to a small town today to try to locate an army doctor for a poor old man who looks about all in. His old wife wanted me to see what I could do for him, and as that was a little out of my line the best that I can do is to find a doctor for him.

I am about due for a 7 day's pass. It is my turn next; a bunch left this morning. The pass takes us to Southern France around Nice. The boys who have come back from there have said not to miss it and I am not going to if I can help it. The other ambulance drivers went to Monte Carlo, etc. and enjoyed it very much. All expenses are paid by Uncle Sam; that is, travel, food, and lodging in the good hotels. I have decided not to send anything but will try to carry it all with me. Just received a letter from Grandmother.

Lots of love,
Your son

Feb. 20, 1918

Dear Mother,

We have moved again but this time a distance of only about 2 kilos. I do not think that we will be here long, but of course I know nothing about it. Why can't they get us all home? The name of this town is Joinville, France, but as far as I can see it is joined to nothing but hard work.

I have sent 2 packages and am going to send 2 more. The first 2 I sent this morning and the other 2 are ready and will be sent tomorrow in all probability. Keep a look out for the packages and do not open any of them for they might contain surprises. Any way, I would rather show you the things. I hope they will all get there O.K.

Tonight Miss Margaret Wilson, President Wilson's daughter, is singing downtown so I guess I'll go down and take it in.

I still have nothing of interest to tell you. This is the most uninteresting and impracticable life that I have ever lived and hope that I never have to do it again.

Love to all
Your son

There were two evacuation hospitals in Joinville, France. Evacuation hospitals functioned as general hospitals, providing modern surgery. Howard continued to run soldiers from field hospitals to evacuation or base hospitals for months after the Armistice.

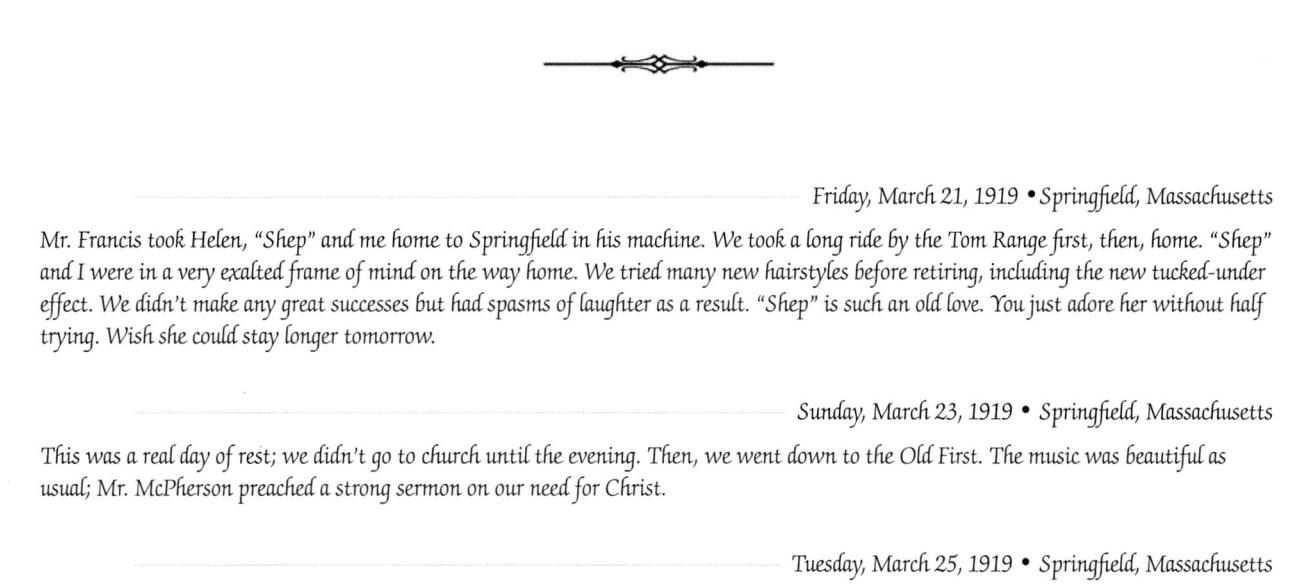

Friday, March 21, 1919 • Springfield, Massachusetts

Mr. Francis took Helen, "Shep" and me home to Springfield in his machine. We took a long ride by the Tom Range first, then, home. "Shep" and I were in a very exalted frame of mind on the way home. We tried many new hairstyles before retiring, including the new tucked-under effect. We didn't make any great successes but had spasms of laughter as a result. "Shep" is such an old love. You just adore her without half trying. Wish she could stay longer tomorrow.

Sunday, March 23, 1919 • Springfield, Massachusetts

This was a real day of rest; we didn't go to church until the evening. Then, we went down to the Old First. The music was beautiful as usual; Mr. McPherson preached a strong sermon on our need for Christ.

Tuesday, March 25, 1919 • Springfield, Massachusetts

Mother took me to an open meeting of her club over at Cousin Helen's. Rabbi Price spoke on the Jewish commonwealth. It was very good.

Wednesday, March 26, 1919 • E. Granby, Connecticut

I took the 6.40 a.m. train to East Granby and spent the day with the dear folks. Uncle Dan pitted me with questions about Amherst. I came back on the 5.17 p.m. and went up to "Joe's" to dinner.

Thursday, March 27, 1919 • Springfield, Massachusetts

In the evening, Aunt Mame had Mother, Father, and me over for a "rabbit." She had a young sprig there for me, and we danced together. He invited me to the Polis Theatre Saturday evening. He's rather attractive, but I was not susceptible.

Friday, March 28, 1919 • Springfield, Massachusetts

I visited Central High School English classes and enjoyed it. I hope I can amount to something next year as a teacher. I know I shall be partial to the boys in my classes. They are so interesting and have some good ideas. The girls seem silly and indolent.

Saturday, March 29, 1919 • Springfield, Massachusetts

This afternoon, I went down to the YWCA with mother for the big party given for the poor children. Mother has been managing that work all winter. The children marched and sang, and there was entertainment for them – a piano solo by Margaret Ellis, songs, and a solo dance. Then, came the eats: striped ice cream and cake, and ladyfingers. Oh, the children were so happy!

Sunday, March 30, 1919 • Springfield, Massachusetts

In the evening Nelson came over. We fooled around while, and then went down to Carolyn's, where we knew we'd find her fiancé who was up from Yale for the weekend. I wanted to have another look at him. We didn't get home until late.

Monday, March 31, 1919 • Springfield, Massachusetts

I visited two of Miss Anthony's classes at Central High School. She's a corker and fascinating in her way. Came home and toiled at the flat iron and trunk. Back to college tomorrow for the last 10 weeks of college. Oh, my youth is departing. I read Riley's poem, "There, little girl, don't cry!" with real feeling. "Life and love will soon come by," the poet goes on. Will it come to me? Not - I fear - when I heartily disapprove of every fellow I meet. Oh, I did get so furious at Nelson last night! I felt like a cat and just wanted to claw and scratch. Isn't that a nice Christian spirit?

"A Life Lesson"
"There Little Girl Don't Cry"

There! little girl; don't cry!
They have broken your doll, I know;
And your tea-set blue,
And your play-house, too,
Are things of the long ago;
But childish troubles will soon pass by. --
There! little girl; don't cry!

There! little girl; don't cry!
They have broken your slate, I know;
And the glad, wild ways
Of your schoolgirl days
Are things of the long ago;
But life and love will soon come by. --
There! little girl; don't cry!

> *There! little girl; don't cry!*
> *They have broken your heart I know;*
> *And the rainbow gleams*
> *Of your youthful dreams*
> *Are things of the long ago;*
> *But Heaven holds all for which you sigh. --*
> *There! little girl; don't cry!*
>
> James Whitcomb Riley

As Marian's school girl days were almost over, she wrote in her diary about her private worries about whether she would ever find love. The American poet, James Whitcomb Riley, seemed to give Marian some reassurance about her life dreams, even though she disapproved of men she had met so far.

Riley's poetry stemmed from his own experiences growing up in the Midwestern state of Indiana. He is best known for his children's poems which were humorous and sentimental and "fostered the creation of a Midwestern cultural identity."(www.wikipedia.com) Ironically, Riley's own childhood was less than idyllic. Riley's father enlisted in the Union Army during the American Civil War and returned partially paralyzed and was unable to "continue working in his legal practice and the family soon fell into financial distress." (ibid) Riley's mother died from heart disease in 1870 which prompted Riley to move out of the family home, following much consternation with his father. Riley began working a variety of jobs, while continuing to pursue his writing and poetry. After much persistence and effort, by 1890 Riley became a bestselling author with his book, *Rhymes of Childhood*, which sold millions of copies. By 1895, Riley toured on the lecture circuit earning $1,000 per week. "His works became staples for Ivy League literature courses." (ibid) He was influential in helping other poets launch their careers, including Edgar Lee Masters who Marian was so fond of. Following his death in 1916, many memorials were established including the James Whitcomb Riley Hospital for Children in Indianapolis and the James Whitcomb Riley Museum House which is preserved as an historical site.

Tuesday, April 1, 1919 • Mount Holyoke

Came back to college rather rebelliously but was happy when I struck the place. Bless the dear old crowd! They did all look so good to me. Of course, "Dot" Hall April-fooled me unmercifully.

The glorious day finally came for the Rainey family! On April 13, 1919, Howard's USAAS Section #521 boarded the USS Manchuria, a troop transporter, with about 3,000 other anxious soldiers for home. The troop transporter made nine round trips to New York from Saint-Nazaire, France following the Armistice bringing home a total of 39,500 troops. Each voyage took approximately 10 days.

Howard was heading home to America to reunite with his family and loved ones. He would go back to a new life and one that would never be the same again. He was a changed man but grateful that he had escaped injury, illness, or death.

It had been over five long months since the signing of the Armistice. The war was not officially over until the peace treaties were signed. Slowly troops were heading home in anticipation of peace.

Howard arrived safely in the U.S. on April 23, 1919, much to the delight and relief of his parents. Howard E. Rainey, Private First Class USA Ambulance Service Section #521 was honorably discharged from The United States Army at Camp Dix, NJ on the 26th of April, 1919 at the age of 23 years and 8 months. It was less than two years from enlistment October 12, 1917 to discharge April 26, 1919. Yet, Howard played his part in the war and would have a lifetime of memories, good and bad, to carry with him.

Howard's discharge papers read:

Enlisted: Oct. 12, 1917 at Allentown, PA
Serving in: First enlistment period at date of discharge
Prior Service: None
Noncommissioned officer: Never
Marksmanship, gunner qualification or rating: Unqualified
Horsemanship: Not mounted
Battles, engagements, skirmishes, expeditions: St. Mihiel offensive September 12, 1918 to Sept 16, 1918. Meuse-Argonne offensive September 26, 1918 to November 11, 1918
Knowledge of any vocation: Broker
Wounds received in service: None
Physical condition when discharged: Good
Typhoid prophylaxis completed: January 18, 1918
Paratyphoid prophylaxis completed: January 18, 1918
Married or single: Single
Character: Excellent
Remarks: USA Ambulance Service, Section 521. Oct. 12, 1917 to April 16, 1919. Served in France and Italy. Left US June 13, 1918. Arrived US April 23, 1918

Signature of soldier: HOWARD E. RAINEY
James G. Knight, Major Inf. USA
Certified statement to Preston Gilmore, Notary Public
Springfield, MASS
August 28, 1924

Camp Dix, NJ April 26, 1918
Paid in full $95.81
Including Bonus Pay

Of the 11,750 ambulance drivers of World War I, 182 were killed and another 320 wounded or gassed for a 1.5 percent casualty rate. While this compares favorably with the 7.1 percent casualty for American troops in the war, my grandfather put his life at risk in his ambulance to make the world safe for democracy.

Howard played his important role on the stage of a unique military organization, the United States Army Ambulance Service. The Ambulance Service came into being in 1917 and disappeared from the ranks of the armed forces in 1919. (History of the American Army Ambulance Service).

All of Howard's mother's wishes and prayers came true. Her only son survived the war and came home in good shape physically. She knew there would be an adjustment for Howard back in the U.S. But, there was plenty of time ahead for the family to be together again.

Saturday, April 26, 1919 • Competitive Sing

Senior picture was taken on the steps today. In the afternoon, singing for competitive sing took up most of the time. "Canary" felt rotten; she could hardly stand up to lead us. The pieces are difficult — "Kiplinger's Recessional," "Carry me Back to Old Virginia," "The Alma Mater," and an original serenade (sung to Mr. Hammond).

Well, I can't wait to write it: we won the serenade, 1919! We did try hard! And darling "Canary" received the baton given up by 1920. We left S.A.H. with our caps tipped drunk. We sang to "Canary" after we reached home and just celebrated with shouts and thrills of delight. We were a bit intoxicated. Many of the 1917 girls were back, which made it all the sweeter to have the victory. "Dot" Hall slept with me in Doris's absence. We talked later – over lots of things – our class, and the dear old bunch.

> While Howard was leaving the service, Marian would soon be leaving college. Both had been molded and changed by their experiences. Still, what a contrast!
>
> As soldiers returned to America, many found they needed assistance adjusting to their new lives. One organization, the non-profit American Legion, was chartered by Congress in 1919 as a "patriotic veteran's organization. Of the almost four million American Veterans to set foot safely back on American soil approximately 260,000 soldiers were wounded and would need care for many months, years, or a lifetime. Congress authorized some disability compensation but for many it was not enough. Focusing on service to veterans, service members, and communities, the Legion evolved from a group of war-weary veterans of World War 1 into one of the most influential nonprofit groups in the United States." (www.legion.org/history) The American Legion held a caucus in St. Louis, Missouri on May 8-10, 1919, to adopt the organization's official name. A Hudson, NY post was founded in 1919 for financial, social and emotional support for soldiers, including Howard. Fortunately, Howard was not wounded physically but any emotional scars were concealed.

Sunday, April 27, 1919 • Mount Holyoke

Reverend Harry Emerson Fosdick, New York, New York, preached today. He was so young and enthusiastic. It was a beautiful day! We all dressed in white. In the afternoon, we took a blanket down by the lake and read and bathed. Oh, Sundays at college are numbered!

Tuesday, April 30, 1919 • Springfield, Massachusetts

Florence ("Shep") and I went home at 3 pm. "Joe" and "Mit" were up to dinner. We danced and talked to our hearts' content. "Joe" has just returned from New York where she met Roger, back from France.

Wednesday, May 1, 1919 • Springfield, Massachusetts

Miss Clarke came to make my yellow taffeta today. In the evening, Florence and I went to the Polis Theatre. More fun. Sort of gay and unchaperoned. The picture was adorable with Constance Talmadge in The Secret Curtain. The vaudeville was mediocre, but we enjoyed it. There's something about college that, when one gets away, you enjoy anything as long as it's different. And the Polis is different from cool, chaste South Hadley!

Thursday, May 2, 1919 • Mount Holyoke

We came back this morning early. At 4.45 pm, Mr. Towne's class on "Teaching English to Foreigners." At 6:00 pm, Porter Seniors gave Porter Juniors a dinner.

Sunday, May 7, 1919 • Junior Top Spinning

The juniors spun tops today at 5 o'clock. Nina Babcock, junior, was the top in red, white, and blue. They ran in a single file line and wound round and round like a ball of string. "Joe" Lane was up visiting, and we all went in canoes for a picnic afterward.

In the evening I had a rehearsal of the Italian dance for May Day. May Day is in the hands of the seniors this year. We are giving a pageant called the "Spring Festival." It is based on the idea that spring comes to all the countries and that youth wanders through all these countries in search of beauty. The May Queen arrives at the end of his search.

Saturday, May 10, 1919 • Senior-Freshman Picnic

Senior-freshman picnic was scheduled for today, but it poured so the picnic was called off. At 5 o'clock, we went down to S.A.H. with our picnic supper. We ate and danced, and then the freshmen gave a series of shows. The rain was coming down in torrents. We waited until 9 o'clock for Miss Ellis. Finally they had a machine waiting for us. It was a wet dark ride down to the cottage by the river. Miss Ellis retired early, but the girls talked in front of the fire until most daylight.

Friday, May 16, 1919 • Senior Dance

The great day dawned bright! My flowers for the dance came in the morning. They were sweet peas of two shades of pink. We hated not being able wear them until the dance. A sophomore dressed me. Mother and Mrs. McCord stopped in the room for a minute. They came up to look on for a while.

At 3.30 pm, we left in Burton's car for the dance – Bill and I, "Hild" and Sherman, Doris and Burton. (I should have mentioned us last) in the auditorium. The decorations, of course, were simple. We had Wittstein's (Eddie Wittstein and his Yale Prom Orchestra) for 20 dances and 5 extras. We walked outside after each dance. It was such a dream of an evening, and the apple orchard back of S.A.H. all blossomy and sweet smelling. The banquet at 7.30 pm was downstairs. And, the place was like paradise with hanging crepe paper, wisteria, and subdued purplish light. I sat between Bill and George Sheppard. George is a dear; we got acquainted so fast!

After the dance, we talked until 2.30 am in "Canary's" room.

> This is the first mention of George Sheppard, the older brother of Marian's dear friend Florence "Shep" Sheppard. George already graduated from Yale College and was working in their home town of New Jersey. He fit right in with the "bunch." Marian's date to the Senior Dance was Bill, but she seemed to prefer getting acquainted with George.

Saturday, May 17, 1918 • Senior Pageant and Play

Pouring rain! Poor Doris on whom the afternoon pageant and evening play so largely rests. Well, the girl went to pieces. Her nerves just gave out. She held her control just long enough to give orders for having the Senior Pageant indoors - then she came home and tore around the room like a wild thing. The pageant was given in S.A.H. Mother came up with Mrs. Bemis and Aunt Mame. I think it went off well. The dances were smooth. Then, we went to the play, Romeo and Juliet. We had grand seats, due to Doris and "Dot" Hall who managed cast choice. Doris, "Dot" Hall, and "Shep" paced the stage and were real Elizabethan gentlemen. We left right after the play for the house party.

Sunday, May 18, 1919 • Senior House Party

At the house party and a heavenly day! We danced on the porch until 3:30 am. The river is shimmering and glorious, and the mountains clear. We girls all dressed in white. Breakfast was served on the front piazza. It tasted so good. Almost everyone went to church. I sent "Pris" with Bill. George Sheppard and I sat on the hill instead and talked. George and I had the grandest line – a tale he made up about "The Yale" valley where gold is easily dug and money comes fast. He wants me to go with him, across the continent on donkeys named Penelope and Buttons. In the afternoon, we danced, played winkum [musical chairs], hop scotch, threw pennies, took pictures, etc. At 6.30 pm, we left for supper at the Croysdale Inn; then, took a ride afterward out toward Amherst. At 8.30 pm, the men left for their trains. It was a glorious weekend.

> Once again, Marian passed her date, Bill, off to "Pris" so that she could spend time alone with George Sheppard. At last a man who was not afraid of Marian. Would George Sheppard stay in Marian's life?

Tuesday, May 20, 1919 • Mount Holyoke

I went out for an auto ride with Bill at 4.30 pm. A Chi Phi brother of his has a car, and we were included in the party. We went all around Amherst's campus. There were men all over frat house verandas, without any apparent duties whatsoever! At 6 o'clock, Miss Warner (Instructor, Department of English), and I went for a picnic supper on the lake. We talked about everything under the sun: college, graduating, and teaching. Oh, I hope I can make good as she has! And I wonder if I'll love it well enough for a life job. She surely means to become established in it.

> Miss Warner took a keen interest in Marian and her future. Marian's drive to succeed was easily identifiable. Miss Warner was a Mount Holyoke 1911 graduate. She was very close in age to Marian and felt comfortable giving advice. Miss Warner and Elizabeth Crane Porter edited *A Mount Holyoke Book of Prose and Verse* (Warner, 1912) which was a "collection of work from the college magazine at Mount Holyoke between 1891 to 1911, including the best of what Mount Holyoke graduates have written" (ibid). Among the book entries were several poems from two of Marian's favorite English teachers at Mount Holyoke, Frances Warner (1911) and Alsada Comstock (1910), when they were students themselves. The book coincided with the 75th anniversary of the founding of the college in 1887, and had alumnae interest. The sales of the book at $1.35

prepaid, benefited the Student Alumnae Building Fund. How reassuring it had to be for Marian to receive such valuable and encouraging advice from one of her mentors who chose to make teaching English her career and made "good."

Thursday, May 22, 1919 • Senior Reception

Miss Woolley's reception to the seniors was at 5 o'clock. "Pris", "Shep", "Dot" Hall, and I went together. "Dot" Hall is beaming. She has just returned from four days at New York. Howard Fish returned from two years in France Tuesday morning. "Dot" stayed at the Commodore Hotel with Howard and his father and mother. They were glorious days for her. How she loves and is loved. And, how it brings the light of heaven into a girl's eyes.

Friday, May 23, 1919 • Mount Holyoke

The last day of classes. I can hardly realize it! Bed felt pretty decent at the end of the day. With classes over, I feel almost like a B.A. At least, my school days are a thing of the past.

Saturday, May 24, 1919 • Springfield, Massachusetts

I studied all day on history with only intermissions for ice cream. At 6 o'clock, I took the trolley for home. I didn't study in the evening. But I am so tired, just weary and sort of at the end of my rope. But, my own little room, my big, comfy bed, and my dear, dear mother will help a heap.

Sunday, May 25, 1919 • Holyoke, Massachusetts Senior Vespers

I studied at home all the morning, and early in the afternoon Mother and Dad and I left for Holyoke and a 4 o'clock Vespers in Skinner's Chapel (United Congregational Church) for the senior class. Mr. Wicks preached, and Mr. Hammond played, and the choir sang. Oh so beautiful - the chapel with its gothic arches and its many-colored, studded windows, the glory of the music, and the angel heads in the ceiling. Mr. Wicks gave us a real message, and our hearts responded. I shall never forget it!

Tuesday, May 27, 1919 • Mount Holyoke

Teacher's English exam in the p.m. The exam was hard, comprehensive no end. But, Miss Stevens, (Professor, Department of English) is a dream!

Wednesday, May 28, 1919 • Mount Holyoke

The Literature exam was fair and square, and I told Miss Harper so [Ph.D., Associate Professor, Department of English Literature]. I meant it too. She has roped me in on the job of getting senior pictures for The Delineator, which is to contain the article on our questionnaire. I'll earn $10.00 if I can do it.

The Delineator, A Journal of Fashion, Culture, and Fine Arts, was published from 1873 to 1937 by The Butterick Publishing Company, New York. Marian was always looking for ways to make extra spending money and Miss Harper must have known.

Sadly in December of 1919, Miss Harper became ill on a Wednesday evening after meeting her classes that day. She was operated on the next day in a hospital in Greenfield, Massachusetts and died on Saturday. She received her B.A. from Mount Holyoke and her M.A. from Radcliffe College. Marian was fortunate to have had her as a teacher and mentor her senior year. "She dropped a few very choice pieces of advice" to Marian when she needed them the most.

Friday, May 30, 1919 • Memorial Day

The exercises in honor of Memorial Day were at 9.30 am in the chapel. Faculty and seniors were in cap and gown. Mr. Mauer gave the address on "Nationalism and Internationalism." He was a chaplain with the American Army and was at Chateau-Thierry and the Argonne Forest. He warned us to overcome the nationalist's spirit and love the whole world instead. We marched to the village green where the civil war veterans and troops back from overseas were gathered. The school children recited the Gettysburg address. Then, we marched back through the entrance gate – between ranks of soldiers.

In the afternoon Doris and I left for Springfield and had dinner at the Ellis's. At 7.30 pm, we left in the National (National Motor Car) for the Windsor-Senior Prom at the Campbell school in Windsor, Connecticut. Sherman and I, Burton and Doris, picked up "Pris" and Bill. The prom was grand fun. Afterwards, we drove to Hartford.

Saturday, May 31, 1919 • Windsor, Connecticut

I'm continuing here about the ride after the dance, since it was this morning. After doughnuts and coffee, we started to ride again. It was a dream of a night. I have refused Sherman so many times before, so this time I let him love me a little. But he is over passionate and puts too much feeling into it. It isn't good for one. At 6.30 am we arose, breakfasted, and at 7.30 am started back in the National. They dropped Sherman and me in Springfield. Mother met me at 9 o'clock. We picked out a lovely wristwatch, which was Grandpa's graduation present to me. It is beautiful! We shopped almost all day.

Sunday, June 1, 1919 • Mount Holyoke

A very quiet day. I read the "Atlantic" and devoured Rickard's "The Light Above the Cross Roads." Both were entertaining and a rest from study.

The *Atlantic* is an American magazine founded in Boston in 1857. It was created as a New England literary magazine (www.wikipedia.org). The magazine's founders were a group of writers that included Harriet Beecher Stowe, Ralph Waldo Emerson, Henry Wadsworth Longfellow, among others.

Jessie Louisa Rickard (1876-1963), an Irish literary novelist, was one of many prolific female writers of World War I novels. Her husband, Lt. Colonel Victor Rickard of the Royal Munster Fusiliers, died in May of 1915 as he led his Irish regiment in battle. "The shamrock, which forms part of the cap badge of the Royal Munster Fusiliers, was first introduced, in February 1915, by Lieutenant-Colonel Rickard, in the Second Battalion, with the object of giving a distinctively Irish emblem to all ranks of the Regiment. It is now worn by all the battalions of the Munsters." (Rickard) As a widow with a son to support, Rickard turned to writing to support her family. During her career, she "became a versatile writer who produced over forty novels." (ibid) In her book, *The Story of the Munsters* (1918), Mrs. Rickard dedicated the book to her husband, Victor Rickard and his comrades in all ranks of the Munster Fusiliers, who fought and fell in the Great War 1914-1915:

"One who never turned his back but marched breast forward,
Never doubted clouds would break,
Never dreamed, though right were worsted, wrong would triumph,
Held we fall to rise, are baffled to fight better, sleep to wake."

Jessie Rickard

Monday, June 2, 1919 • MountHolyoke

Back to college! Doris is awfully tired. Well, all of us are, more or less. I brought back a lovely tea apron scarf that we girls are going to give "Dot" Hall for an engagement present. We are going to make up a little poem about our "engaged girl."

Tuesday, June 3, 1919 • Mount Holyoke

We had a sing at 4.40 pm. We have some beautiful songs for the Step Exercises on Alumnae Day June 7th [College Songs, Senior Class Song, Senior Step Song and "Alma Mater"], and for the Grove and Ivy, Exercises [Memorial Song, Planting Class Ivy, Ivy Song, and Ivy Orations] on Ivy Day June 9th. The Ivy Orations! Horrors! I must learn it.

Marian was chosen by her class to write and deliver the Ivy Oration speech at the graduation ceremonies which is a part of the graduation traditions which was quite an honor. This is the beginning of Commencement Week for the class of 1919; a weeklong celebration.

Thursday, June 5, 1919 • Senior Mountain Day

We left at 5 p.m. for the mountain — four truckloads of us, all in cap and gown, and very happy. The sophs gave us a good send off, carried our suitcases, and sang lustily. We reached the mountain about 6.30 pm and had supper at 7.00 pm. There were toasts all through the meal and improvised songs for the occasion. After supper, for an hour we danced. Then, we had stunts. Grace did some screaming imitations of faculty. "Canary" and "Hild" did their song-and-dance stunts.

This was followed by class meetings. After the junior class meeting, we all went upstairs and put on our lovely nighties and our caps and gowns. Then came senior class meeting, after which the class roll was called for engaged girls. We only had 13 answer "guilty." Four of them were class secrets: Fran, Fern, Marcia and Pechie. Gretchen was the only new announcement that was not secret.

After midnight we went to bed. Doris and I had a mattress on the floor in "Dot" and "Pop's" room and "Pris" and "Shep" had a mattress there too. We didn't sleep a great deal.

For the night at the mountain, undergraduates made nighties for their senior sisters. Attired in their nighties, to be worn only on this special occasion and never again until marriage, "the seniors answer "guilty" or "not guilty" to a midnight roll call as to whether or not they are engaged." (Edmonds) Marian secretly wished that she would be engaged someday.

Friday, June 6, 1919 • Summit House

The seniors spent the night at the Summit House on Mt. Tom in the Mt. Holyoke Range. Shows before breakfast, and toasts all through breakfast. I had to give a toast on "My Experiences at the Movies." After breakfast, we danced and had a sing. At 11.30 am, the mail came up. And, such a deluge of notes! They were so dear, too. George Sheppard wrote to the entire bunch perfectly killing notes.

At 2:00 p.m. came the very formal banquet with Miss Woolley and the honorees present. They all arrived in Mr. Towne's machine and came up to the hotel singing "Hail! Hail! The gang's all here." Yes, even Miss Woolley shouted, "What in the deuce do we care." The honorees did some wild stunts after the banquet. Mr. Towne led a sing (an imitation of "Canary"). Then, Miss Woolley had a class meeting among the honorees. Toasts were given. They were splendid, but, most of all, Mr. Wicks gave us some splendid advice about after-college friendships, warning us against exclusiveness and in favor of the "cross section of life policy."

The sophs gave us a hearty welcome when we reached South Hadley at 7.30 PM. We sang on the steps.

Monday, June 9, 1919 • Ivy Day

Ivy Oration, by Marian Viets"

"The planting of the ivy is a tradition with graduating classes. Our class, in following the tradition, is seeking again to leave behind a symbol of its loyalty to the college, and its desire for class expression, along with the others that have gone before. And upon this occasion, in other years, other classes have said, "We are leaving the protection of these college walls to face new problems which will confront us in the world. May we be faithful to the ideals of Mount Holyoke, and keep her name ever glorious." If all classes have expressed the same sentiments, then wherein lies the unique entrance of any class onto the world stage? It is in the problems that confront us – wherein we are unique; for upon world problems plays an ever-changing light, reflecting new developments and new phases to us.

During our four years of preparation, the Class of 1919 has witnessed gigantic events and turbulent history. We have gone about our work and study here, while the world was on fire with war and intrigue. We constantly assured ourselves that it was best to work quietly on to the completion of our college course. First came the war in Europe; then the entrance of America, which gave so vast an opportunity for women to serve at home and abroad. Our friends, outside college, were assuming these new tasks; we remained at college and tried to do our bit in the big drives, and in the war work that was carried on here. And in college was fostered the spirit of patriotism, the love of service, and a strong conviction that America and her allies were in pursuit of a right and just cause. Then, finally, in our last year, came the armistice, and we are graduating into a world where the Great War no longer rages. But the pathway to peace is still obscured by new conflicts and great perils. Reconstruction, the new world, international friendship – these words are constantly on our lips. We are entering upon a world where idealism is not unpopular. It has always been a criticism that the college graduate is over-idealistic. She cannot adapt her soaring theories to everyday practice. Will there be a place, now, perhaps, for an expression of these ideals, an outlet for the waves of enthusiasm that have gathered during the four years of our preparatory training? And at the same time may we realize our responsibility to make our ideals useful and workable for the purpose of real service.

We plant with tender care the ivy, in the hope that it will grow sturdily, and will increase in luxuriant beauty as the years pass by. So often shall we turn back lovingly to thoughts of this place, and to the patch of earth where the roots of our ivy cling and find nourishment. The ivy, reaching ever upward, should symbolize the hopes we have in ourselves; for hope lies justly where there is growth and development. In the spirit of reconstruction, in the desire for upbuilding and uplifting, may we adapt our happy idealism to a world that is not scorning the practical application of idealism to all vital problems of the day."

MARIAN G. VIETS

Marian expresses beautifully the struggles of these conscientious girls studying in their ivory tower while "the world was on fire with war and intrigue." Are they too idealistic? Will their studies achieve "practical application" in the new world order? She manages to tie her thoughts to the tradition of planting ivy, striving upward to "symbolize the hopes we have in ourselves." What a masterful teacher she must have been. No wonder her classmates chose her to speak for them. The carefully chosen and meaningful words Marian spoke about ivy would stay with her and serve as an inspiration when times were tough in the years ahead.

On Tuesday, June 10, 1919 Marian Gertrude Viets proudly graduated from Mount Holyoke with a Bachelor of Arts degree with majors in English and English Literature at the 82nd Commencement at Mount Holyoke. She was the first woman in her family to receive a college degree. Marian was a brave, strong, warrior.

Following graduation, Marian secured a job teaching English at Hudson High School in Hudson, New York for $800 per year, where she would fulfill her lifelong dream of being an English teacher. Dean Purington helped place her in this position. A 1918 Mount Holyoke graduate, Sonny, took a job in Hudson last year and she thought it would be a good fit for Marian.

After spending four years in a very special place named Mount Holyoke, these uncommon women became "sisters" by encouraging and supporting each other every step of their journey. Along the way they shared their triumphs and challenges as trailblazers for all women. In their quest for a college degree they depended on each other as like-minded women could only do. The bonds of the "sisters" would endure for many years to come. Marian wrote in her diary on January 5th, 1919: "we can NEVER forget one another."

As the "sisters" were ready to spread their wings and fly away to the next step of their lives, they would be separated by miles, but they would stay in contact through their "Robin's Gang" (Doris, "Canary", "Pris", Helen, "Dot", "Pop", Florence "Shep", and "Hild", and of course Marian) circulated letters. Each woman found her passion, whether it was dramatics, music, teaching, writing, or physical education. Only one "Robin" was engaged before graduation, "Dot" Hall, but there would be many marriages and children to follow.

While Marian chose to accept a teaching job in Hudson, NY, Helen, Marian's dear roomie freshman year, Helen Francis, was returning to Springfield to teach high school English. "Pris" also returned home to Springfield and served as the Society Editor at the "Springfield Union" newspaper from 1919-1923; Marian's dear roomie senior year, Doris Campbell, who managed the Mount Holyoke Senior Pageant and Play, *Romeo and Juliet*, returned home to Windsor, CT to teach drama and writing; "Canary" who lead the Class of 1920 to winning the baton at the "Competitive Sing" took a job with the Girl Reserves (a movement for young teen age girls in the YWCA) in Indiana; "Dot" moved to Pennsylvania following her marriage; "Shep" returned to her home town of Passiac, New Jersey; "Hild" taught physical education in Rochester, NY; and "Pop" taught physical education in Illinois "teaching others how to be healthy" and rode her bike 500 miles through England and Scotland in the summer of 1927.

The gang knew that in ten years they would assemble once again as tradition dictated at their Mount Holyoke reunions, stay in the dorms, and reminisce!

Nothing would keep them apart.

On June 28, 1919, the Treaty of Versailles, one of the peace treaties negotiated at the end of World War 1, was signed. Negotiations had been conflicted and took six months to resolve at the Paris Peace Conference to conclude. Germany was required to accept the responsibility for "causing all the loss and damage" (www.wikipedia.org) during the war. As a result, no country was contented, least of all Germany. A discontented Austrian housepainter would soon find a new vocation expressing the German's need to prove their superiority over those who had chained them to debt and despair. Soon enough he would throw the world into the cataclysm once again.

This is Marian's final diary entry as she prepared to head to Hudson, New York to start her teaching career:

Saturday • August 30, 1919 • Springfield, Massachusetts

Mother left early for East Granby. Grandma is ill. I kept house all day, cleaned, and baked. "Dot" Woodin came to dinner — talking mostly of her two babes. She is a dear. One day more before Hudson.

CHAPTER SIX

THE NEW MARIAN

When I first started going through my grandmother's private diaries, I thought Marian was a goody two-shoes. Until I read her 1919 - 1920 journals, I thought she was not my type of girl. After I made the acquaintance of the new Marian, I found my grandmother much more attractive. She knew how to have fun.

Leaving safe and familiar Mount Holyoke behind, Marian stepped out into the world and her first teaching job in Hudson, New York during the school year of 1919 - 1920. Marian was a "New Woman," a nickname coined by the media to describe changing attitudes of women at the turn of the century. The "New Woman" was confident, independent, aggressive, and able to take care of herself, more so than her Victorian predecessors. "The country was fascinated with them, although people didn't always agree on what a New Woman was." (Collins) Serious as she was, Marian also had a touch of the flapper – the even newer woman who danced her way onto the American scene after World War I. The country survived the war, and now everyone wanted to cut loose a little – especially these flapper girls. "The American woman was transformed after the war. They seemed to embody the changes going on in the country." (ibid)

Once upon a time, a woman worked and a lady did not. The "New Marian" turned her back on the old ways. She was ready to take her fate into her own hands as a college graduate looking for a promising career, securing the right to vote as a woman, and enjoying the freedom to discover life's mysteries. Not all her rebellions were serious; she also wanted to wear more comfortable clothes – to throw away her corset, put on make-up (powder at least), spend more time with the opposite sex and fall in love, and smoke a few cigarettes. Gone was the staid student at the cloistered all-female, private-college campus; the "New Marian" was a more independent and competent woman as she started her new life.

Even as the world changed around her and she changed into a "New Women," Marian held fast to her core. Now that the war was over, soldiers were returning to America to start their lives once more. The Peace Talks continued, but people at home breathed a sigh of relief that America could begin again. This fervor for new beginnings motivated Marian to take up her service and passion: teaching.

Still, like most "New Women," Marian went through "a career crisis" – they "could marry, or they could become professionals – teachers, librarians, social workers. Almost no one felt they could do both." (Collins) Many college-educated women chose jobs over husbands, families, children and love. "For most women, work was a brief interlude between school and marriage. They made much less than men; in 1927, the average weekly wage for a man was $29.35 and for a woman it was $17.34. Women were also likely to be overqualified for the work they could get." (ibid) "Only about 10 percent of women kept their jobs after marriage, and most were working-class wives who could not afford to quit. Even within the elite women's colleges, attempts to combine family and careers were mostly confined to those who opted for work and childless marriages. But a great many more women were dissatisfied with their choices." (ibid) Men were leery of marrying the "New Woman" type "although they enjoyed her company." (ibid) Men hoped that the "New Woman" "was sexually liberated."(ibid)

Marian yearned for more than success in her career. At church one Sunday in November, the sermon was about "Service." Marian said it was "the most inspirational meeting I ever attended. The love of Christ was there and it was a sort of holy thing. I was deeply moved… I needed it, for I feel so uncertain about life. Perhaps it's because I'm grown up, or perhaps it's just that I'm scanning the future too searchingly. I'm wondering if always and forever I shall teach or whether I shall have love. And, above all else, shall I have children, dear little mites, whom I can unfold in my arms. I want them so, and I want them <u>now</u>."

Marian was not a typical "New Woman" because she knew she would not choose a job over a family; she wanted both. Marian hoped to have a career and to find a man who would love the "New Marian" she had become. Now that she was out of college, Marian watched with envy as many of her friends got engaged, married, and started having children. Love meant everything to her; the love she had for her parents made her want to share her love with a man and a child of her own. After Marian's mother visited her at her boarding house, Marian wrote in her journal "It was great to have mother kiss me goodnight. I wonder if I shall ever be somebody's mother. I'm rather weakening in my conviction that a career is the only thing, and that I want my freedom forever. Sometimes I want arms about me, and love on which I may build a home."

As advanced as she was intellectually, Marian was a late bloomer romantically. As a young 21 year old, Marian hadn't dated much nor had a serious boyfriend yet. But she made up for lost time when she got to Hudson. As important as a career was to Marian, she also wanted to find true love but often doubted whether she would ever marry and have a family. She decided to do some "fooling around" in the meantime. She realized "the sex life in me has awakened rather late, and I am sorely tempted. Especially as the real loved one may never come. I shall be good during vacation." So, she started dating incessantly to make up for lost time. She started experimenting with men and sex. The "new national pastimes were necking and petting - terms that seemed to cover behavior ranging from nuzzling to everything short of intercourse." (Collins) With the advent of the privacy of an automobile, nice girls "allowed their boyfriends to put their hands and mouths places that previous generations would never have considered - or at least never admitted to." (ibid)

"New Women" were supposed to find out all about dating, relationships, and sex by reading articles and books. Marian, however, got her sex education from an unlikely place, a fellow boarder nicknamed "Grandma." For 23 years, "Grandma", Miss Anderson, had been a nurse, a profession that gave her insight into the body. Marian wrote that: "she knows what she knows. Especially she has advised me in sex matters, telling me not to let men love me and kiss me. I have been careless this last year." Even though birth control was available, social mores dictated that women wait to have intercourse until they were engaged or married.

On September 1, 1919, the "New Marian" and her father boarded the B & A train on the way to Hudson, New York, about four hours from home, the trip that was the beginning of a new life. Despite all of the obstacles society put in her path 100 years ago, Marian was a success story. Her prior five years of journaling chronicled her path to this point. My grandmother was filled with hopeful enthusiasm and ideals of real service through her career as she embraced the possibilities for her new life in the small river town. Little did she know that she was going to have lots of fun and quite a bit of excitement too.

Upon arrival, Marian and her father's first impressions of Hudson were positive. "My abode is lovely. We finally reached it after tramping indefinitely. It is a sort of English cottage like of two stories and my room is in the front, very fresh and sweet with white painted furniture." Hudson was a small, friendly city of about 8,000, ideal for the young teachers. Located on the Hudson River, 120 miles from the Atlantic Ocean, Hudson was settled by New England whalers and merchants who came primarily from Nantucket and Martha's Vineyard. The city was laid out on a grid with Warren Street the main thoroughfare amid shops, restaurants, and theaters. In the book *Historic Hudson An Architectural Portrait* by Byrne Fone, he writes that Hudson has historic and architectural treasures including: "Nantucket-style saltboxes, Federal, Greek Revival, Gothic Revival, mid-century Victorian, towered and turreted late Victorian, Italianate, stick-style houses of the 1880's, Second Empire, Queen Anne and Colonial Revival homes of the 1890's, Romanesque, Academic revival, Arts and Crafts bungalows of the 1920s and 1930s, as well as less grand early-twentieth-century "comfortable homes" of shingle, stucco and brick." (Fone) Hudson has been described as "a dictionary of American architectural design" (ibid) where one can see "nearly every type of residential architectural style invented or adapted in America." (ibid)

After dining with her father, meeting her principal, Mr. Knapp, getting a tour of her school, and checking out her eating joint, Sheldon's, her father left on the 5:30 pm train back to Springfield. Marian was feeling quite anxious as she wrote, "I went to bed early for the first time in my little home. My, I felt queer, sort of stranded like. Yet it is the work I have chosen to do and I shall love it I'm very sure. It's what I've always aspired to. Now here I am. I <u>must</u> make good. Oh, I shall try!!!"

The next day, Marian met up with her friend Sonny, a fellow Mount Holyoke alumna, and class of 1918, who had taught at Hudson High School the year before. It was quite a comfort for Marian to see a familiar face. Sonny ate her meals at Sheldon's with Marian but lived in a different rooming house.

Marian started her teaching job on September 3, 1919. The next week school shut down as the whole town turned out for a parade to welcome home the troops. Howard Rainey was home from the war now. He was putting the pieces of his life back together and started a freight company with his Pawling Prep friend, Hubert. Indeed, the Great War was never far from Marian's thoughts. Some of her students were returning veterans older than she. Whereas Marian and the rest of America had suffered from a dearth of men for the last two years, suddenly Marian and the country confronted a mass of returning soldiers, men forever changed by what they had experienced "Over There." Sometimes it seems as if Marian had left the cloister of Mount Holyoke to jump into the arms of men, quite a few men.

Flash forward 89 years to the summer of 2008, as my daughter and I made the drive into the Hudson River Valley in search of the allure that Hudson had held for my relatives. We were struck by the natural beauty of the river and the mountains. I remember visiting the Catskills as a child. Coincidentally, my daughter's only wish for this part of our trip was to hike the Catskill Mountains which I couldn't have been happier about. So, after we checked into our room, we put on our hiking gear and headed towards the park. Along the way, we stopped in a log-cabin gift shop in the mountains and bought a pocket map with expert guidance to the best trails. Our hike would take about four hours, so we needed to rush to beat the sunset. As we hiked, we came across spectacular views at several designated outlooks on rock formations beside the Hudson River. The markers told us that famous Hudson River Valley artists used to paint in the surrounding area, including the Catskill, White, and the Adirondack Mountains. It was easy to see why the Catskills were a favorite subject for artists.

The Hudson River School was a nineteenth century American school of landscape painters, including Thomas Cole, Frederic Edwin Church, Asher B. Durand, and Thomas Moran. These painters "depicted the American landscape as a pastoral setting, where human beings and nature coexist peacefully." (Wiki.org) "Frederic Church studied with Thomas Cole in Catskill, New York" (www.olana.org) from 1844 to 1846. Church completed his very unique house in 1891 with fantastic views of the Hudson River Valley and the Catskill mountains. Unfortunately, the house, Olana, south of Hudson, was closed the day we were there. After seeing the brochure, I was anxious to see Olana because of the unique "mix of Victorian architectural elements, and Middle Eastern decorative motifs." (ibid) In June of 1967, Olana became a New York State Historic site on approximately 250 acres open to the public. I can see why my grandparents loved living in Hudson so much. The natural beauty of this area as depicted so beautifully by these painters tugged at the heartstrings of Marian, Howard, and their descendants.

As my daughter and I continued exploring the city of Hudson, we found that many of the physical landmarks mentioned in Marian's diaries still exist today. While some of the 100-plus-year-old buildings were dilapidated, they have survived nonetheless. I saw the house where my grandfather grew up; I visited Hudson High School (now Hudson Junior High School) where my grandmother taught and my father matriculated on his way to play baseball at Amherst College; we went into the Presbyterian Church; we saw the building where my great grandfather worked, walked through the train station on the riverfront where Marian came and went in her diaries, and drove by the house my grandparents lived in that I used to visit as a child. Gone are many of the restaurants and shops that my grandmother talks about in her diaries; but, with Hudson's rebirth, these places are being replaced with new and trendy enterprises.

There are many family memories in the little river town of Hudson, but, most important to me, are the valiant steps my grandmother took there as a trailblazer for all working women. She demonstrated to future generations of women that it is possible to successfully combine a family and a career and live one's dreams, with the right man. This was Marian's gift: follow your dreams, work hard, be thankful for the love in your life, and become all that you want to be.

Marian entered another favorite poem by Henry Van Dyke about schools into her diary. As Marian was about to begin her teaching career, the poem seemed to comprehend the feelings Marian had about wanting to be a teacher because she loved "the teacher's task."

"Spirit of the Everlasting Boy (Verse IV)

"What constitutes a school?
Not ancient halls and ivy-mantled towers,
Where dull traditions rule
With heavy hand youth's lightly springing powers;
Not spacious pleasure courts,
And lofty temples of athletic fame,
Where devotees of sports
Mistake a pastime for life's highest aim;
Not fashion, nor renown
Of wealthy patronage and rich estate;
No, none of these can crown
A school with light and make it truly great.
But masters, strong and wise,
Who teach because they love the teacher's task,
And find their richest prize
In eyes that open and in minds that ask;
And boys, with heart aglow
To try their youthful vigor on their work,
Eager to learn and grow,
And quick to hate a coward or a shirk:
These constitute a school,--
A vital forge of weapons keen and bright,
Where living sword and tool
Are tempered for true toil or noble fight!
But let not wisdom scorn
The hours of pleasure in the playing fields;
There also strength is born,
And every manly game a virtue yields.
Fairness and self-control,
Good-humour, pluck, and patience in the race,
Will make a lad heart-whole
To win with honour, lose without disgrace.
Ah, well for him who gains
In such a school apprenticeship to life;
With him the joy of youth remains
In later lessons and in larger strife!"

Henry Van Dyke

Monday, September 1, 1919 • Hudson, New York

Father and I left home at 7.20 am and took the 7.54 am B & A train to Hudson, New York. We reached Chatham about 11:00 am and changed trains there. Father is such a darling. He gave me a little talk in psychology first and told me many things I feel very sure are going to help. We reached Hudson at 12. Well, it's an unusual city! Very quaint and oh so different from anything I've ever seen in my life — houses tucked right on the streets, steps spilling onto the sidewalk, and beautiful homes beside squalid tenements.

My abode is lovely. We finally reached it after tramping indefinitely. It is a sort of English cottage of two stories. My room is in the front, very fresh and sweet with white painted furniture. Then, father and I sought a hotel for dinner. After that, we went up to (the) high school, saw the superintendent, Mr. Williams, and the principal, Mr. Knapp, who showed us all over the building. It's very well equipped for a small school.

My "eating joint," Sheldon's, was the next place we looked up. Funny! It's a regular boarding house over a store, up a dark stairway, and there you are. Father left about 5.30 pm, after fixing the electric fixture in my room and taking notes on everything to write mother who is in East Granby taking care of Grandma.

At dinner, I met two Wellesley girls, also teachers, who have not been at it long (since 1917, in fact). We looked for Sonny every minute, but she didn't appear. We called at her rooming house later. Mr. Williams met us and took us to his home in his car. He has a beautiful home. I am to have his daughter, Alice, in some of my classes! We imagined that Sonny had gone out with a man somewhere. Last year she had so many — so the Wellesley girls said. She's so sweet and beautiful; how could she help it?

I went to bed early for the first time in my little home. My, I felt queer, sort of stranded. Yet, it is the work I have chosen to do, and I shall love it I'm very sure. It's what I've always aspired to. Now, here I am. I must make good. Oh, I shall try!

> "And thus ever by day and night, under the sun and under the stars, climbing the dusty hills and toiling along the weary plains, journeying by land and journeying by sea, coming and going so strangely, to meet and to act and react on one another, move all we restless travelers through the pilgrimage of life."
>
> Charles Dickens, From "Little Dorrit"

Tuesday, September 2, 1919 • Hudson, New York

I had breakfast at the 'joint' where I saw Sonny for the first time. Bless her heart! At 8 am we reported to school, where instructions were doled out by the cartload. At 8.30 am, I was established in the advisory room to receive my mob. That's the system in this school. Each teacher has an advisory group the first thing in the morning from 8.30 to 9 am. They're a bit difficult to manage at that peppy hour, I imagine. Classes were only kept a short time this morning. And, in the afternoon we just came back to give out books and locker keys.

Let me characterize some of the teachers:
Mr. Knapp, Principal, a real gentleman, and very clear about his directions.
Miss Dowsland, Elocution, thin, grey haired, enthusiastic and girlish
Then, the two Wellesley girls, Katherine Ferris and Margaret Talmage
Sonny (Mount Holyoke)
Quite a bunch and Mr. Williams to top it off.

Wednesday, September 3, 1919 • Hudson, New York

The first real school day with four classes. A sea of faces, but so interesting. The seniors are so grown up and quite adorable. I can see easily that it's the boys I adore. I'm rather desperate; since I must order the classics they read from and teach without books until the publisher sees fit to send the books from New York. I have 35 students in my sophomore advisory group, which meets with me before school starts in the morning and in the afternoon. They are a bunch of active kids, and the boys are regular vaudeville performers, if they aren't squelched.

Saturday, September 6, 1919 • Hudson, New York

I studied today and went up to the library, which is an impossible collection supervised by the D.A.R. I was rather furious at Hudson for not having anything better. The streets of Hudson are thronged on Saturday afternoon. People come in from the country to shop, and everybody is out on general principles. The boarding house will surely finish me. The food is good and the people high class, but the whole environment of the place is different.

> The Daughters of the American Revolution (D.A.R.) was founded in 1890, and chartered in Hudson in 1896 as the Hendrick Hudson Chapter at 113 Warren Street. Today the Hendrick Hudson Chapter maintains the Robert Jenkins House Genealogical, History, and Reading Room. In order to be a member of the DAR, one has to "prove lineal descent from a patriot of the American Revolution." (www.dar.org) The societies' "objectives are: Historical Preservation, Education, and Patriotism (to cherish, maintain, and extend the institutions of American freedom, to foster true patriotism and love of country, and to aid in serving for mankind all the blessings of liberty)" (ibid) The DAR provided a place for women, that were excluded from men's organizations, to show their patriotism and memories of their ancestors. Since its founding the DAR has admitted more than 950,000 members.

Marian could trace her genealogy to her great-great grandfather, Captain James Viets, from Copper Hill, E. Granby, Connecticut, who served in the Revolutionary War as a Private from 1775 to 1783 in the 18th Regiment Militia of Connecticut. The Viets family "did good service for the patriot cause by keeping Tory prisoners at Newgate Prison" (Viets) in E. Granby which served as a Revolutionary War jail. Marian was very proud of her family legacy and their service. Marian took her lineal descent seriously and met the objectives of historical preservation, education, and patriotism.

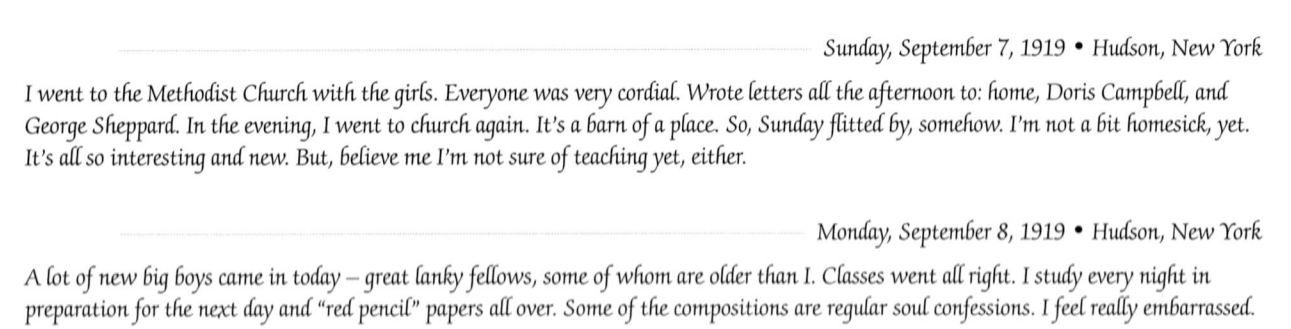

Sunday, September 7, 1919 • Hudson, New York

I went to the Methodist Church with the girls. Everyone was very cordial. Wrote letters all the afternoon to: home, Doris Campbell, and George Sheppard. In the evening, I went to church again. It's a barn of a place. So, Sunday flitted by, somehow. I'm not a bit homesick, yet. It's all so interesting and new. But, believe me I'm not sure of teaching yet, either.

Monday, September 8, 1919 • Hudson, New York

A lot of new big boys came in today — great lanky fellows, some of whom are older than I. Classes went all right. I study every night in preparation for the next day and "red pencil" papers all over. Some of the compositions are regular soul confessions. I feel really embarrassed.

World War I Welcome Home Celebration September 8th and 9th, 1919
Hudson, New York

Everyone was catching the fervor sweeping the country! All across America, home towns held "Welcome Home Celebrations" for the nearly four million discharged World War Veterans. On August 19, 1919, the weekly newspaper of Columbia County, New York (population 38,000) *The Columbia Republican,* (1881-1923) ran an article "271 Veterans Have Accepted the Invitation" to parade in uniform at the home-coming events. One veteran decided not to attend the events because his name was left off "Hudson's Roll of Honor" erected in town. This would be one of the greatest events ever held in the Columbia County Seat of Hudson. The committee raised $7,600 and big plans were underway. The city was going to be transformed into a maze of electrical lights, red, white and blue. On September 8th and 9th, 1919 the city of Hudson, NY had two days of festivities for the Veterans. In the souvenir program the celebration was dedicated:

> "To the Soldiers and The Sailors, to The Men and Women who did their share in the Great World War whether on this side or on the other; to the memory of those who sleep because they loved their country better than themselves; to the heroes who have endured and have come through the crucible which truly tried men's souls, this little book is dedicated."

Howard had been home for over four months now. This was surely a bittersweet celebration for Howard. Of the 1,005 registered soldiers from Columbia County (Hudson and the vicinity), 94 were casualties: 39 were killed in action or died of disease, 55 were wounded or gassed. Howard lost classmates, friends, and neighbors. In the program the following poem was next to the pictures of the honored Hudson men that lost their lives:

"The Peacemaker" (Verse II)

"What matter death, if Freedom be not dead?
No flags are fair if Freedom's flag be furled.
Who fights for Freedom goes with joyful tread
To meet the fires of Hell against him hurled.
And has for Captain Him whose thorn-wreathed head
Smiles from the Cross upon a conquered world."

Sergeant Joyce Kilmer

This poem written by the American poet Alfred Joyce Kilmer (1886-1918) honored the dead. Tragically, Kilmer was killed in the line of duty in France on July 30, 1918 at age of 31. He left behind a wife and five children. His publication in 1913 of *Trees and Other Poems* was the most well received of his work. His poetry was described as exhibiting a deep respect for God and nature.

"Trees"

I think that I shall never see
A poem lovely as a tree.
A tree whose hungry mouth is prest
Against the earth's sweet flowing breast;
A tree that looks at God all day,
And lifts her leafy arms to pray;
A tree that may in Summer wear
A nest of robins in her hair;
Upon whose bosom snow has lain;
Who intimately lives with rain.
Poems are made by fools like me,
But only God can make a tree.

Alfred Joyce Kilmer

Howard was one of the lucky ones. He was here to celebrate the homecoming with his family and friends in his quintessential small town America, Hudson, a tight knit community that supported each and every soldier every possible way they could. Howard was grateful for everything that the town of Hudson had done for the war efforts, yet he struggled with survivor's guilt, watching the families mourn their deceased sons, as he questioned why he was one of the soldiers that survived. Howard brought home with him many horrible memories of the wounded soldiers he transported to the hospitals. Talking about those memories was difficult. Howard was a quiet and reserved man, and he wanted to leave those memories locked in a box and throw the key away. Howard was not the same man that he was before he left for the war. And, he never would be. He was changed forever.

As Howard reentered the work force, he decided not to return to stock brokerage, but he took a chance and started a new venture in freight management with his Pawling friend Hubert Grabau. Howard struggled to find out where the "New Howard" fit in. Many "doughboys", the nickname for WWI veterans, found that the jobs they left before the war were no longer available when they returned home. And, because there were so many returning veterans looking for jobs, unemployment was high. Many soldiers went from job to job, never quite figuring out their purpose. Government programs were not in place yet to support the troops return home.

The celebration was eventful for the entire Rainey family. Howard's father was instrumental in the successful Liberty Loan drive, serving on the Committee representing the Hudson City Savings Institution where he was the treasurer and a trustee. And, Howard's mother could finally relax that her son was home out of harm's way.

The festivities began on Monday night September 8th, Howard and his parents attended the Banquet tendered to World War Veterans at the Armory, followed by a Presentation of Honor Medals. There were more than 615 medals for Hudson heroes. Then at 10:00 P.M. there was a Block Party with dancing on the street pavement at Union and 4th Street, with music by the Hudson Band.

On Tuesday, September 9th, whistles blew and bells rang to officially open the half-holiday of the big celebration proclaimed by the mayor of Hudson. Parade goers came from neighboring counties and lined the streets. At 1:00 pm there was a Monster Street Parade which consisted of: World War Veterans, Civil and Spanish American War Veterans, Red Cross, Fraternal Organizations, 10th Regiment, New York State National Guard, School Children, fifty Floats, Hudson Fire Department and Visiting Fire Companies. At 4:00 P.M. there was a Concert of Massed Bands of 300 pieces and a concert by the chorus composed of the school children of the city, in Washington Park. In the evening, there was vaudeville entertainment at the Playhouse, and a Victory Ball at the Armory for World War Veterans and their guests.

"America's Welcome Home"

Oh, gallantly they fared forth in khaki and in blue,
America's crusading host of warriors bold and true;
They battled for the rights of man beside our brave Allies,
And now they're coming home to us with glory in their eyes.

> *Oh, it's home again, and home again, America for me!*
> *Our hearts are turning home again and there we long to be,*
> *In our beautiful big country beyond the ocean bars,*
> *Where the air is full of sunlight and the flag is full of stars.*
>
> *Our boys have seen the Old World as none have seen before.*
> *They know the grisly horror of the German gods of war:*
> *The noble faith of Britain and the hero-heart of France,*
> *The soul of Belgium's fortitude and Italy's romance.*
>
> *They bore our country's great word across the rolling sea,*
> *'America swears brotherhood with all the just and free.'*
> *They wrote that word victorious on fields of mortal strife,*
> *And many a valiant lad was proud to seal it with his life.*
>
> *Oh, welcome home in Heaven's peace, dear spirits of the dead!*
> *And welcome home ye living sons America hath bred!*
> *The lords of war are beaten down, your glorious task is done;*
> *You fought to make the whole world free, and the victory is won.*
>
> *Now it's home again, and home again, our hearts are turning west,*
> *Of all the lands beneath the sun America is best.*
> *We're going home to our own folks, beyond the ocean bars,*
> *Where the air is full of sunlight and the flag is full of stars.*
>
> Henry Van Dyke

Marian did not write in her diary on Tuesday which I found quite surprising because she so enthusiastically wrote in her diaries about the Armistice Parade in Holyoke, Massachusetts during her senior year of college. School was closed for the day, as many of her students participated in the parade and band.

Wednesday, September 10, 1919 • Hudson, New York

I went to the Woman's Home Missionary meeting with Katherine Ferris. Imagine the dissipation [amusement]. It's queer to what straits one may be driven. It was interesting, as always, to study the women as they sat around. I helped serve tea.

> Woman's Home Missionary Societies were voluntary associations for the advancement of Christianity. The associations were dominated by white, middle-class women who were demonstrating their new voices in public affairs.

Saturday, September 13, 1919 • Hudson, New York

I went to the movies with a man from the boarding house, Bill. We walked up to the reservoir afterwards and then went to Dayton's Restaurant, of course.

Sunday, September 14, 1919 • Hudson, New York

Methodist Church again. I sat with Miss Dowsland, a fellow teacher at Hudson. I don't know how I shall like it. The people are the plainest imaginable, somehow not at all worldly looking. They have the converted look.

September 14 - 20, 1919 • Hudson, New York

I surely have missed Sonny this week, but am glad she's staying away after her mother's death, to gain in strength and poise of mind. School really thrills me through and through. I love to stand before my classes and feel them respond. But, my inexperience is surely an ever-present fact. Each day is such a new-fledged thing, a sort of abyss. I never know just where I'll land. New pupils keep coming in, and they get older, it seems, every time. My senior English class is up to 30 now with the addition of two enormous youths who had been away to school and now are back again. I work after school to help the laggard ones and am dead weary at the end of each day. I always lie down between 5 pm and 6 pm, then rise and go to supper, then back at work, studying or correcting compositions.

I went to a dance in the mid-week with Bill. All my high school upper class boys were there, very nearly. I danced with many of them. We ate at the Lincoln Restaurant afterward. Pie a la mode is the thing in this town for midnight fare. Saturday night Bill took me out to play cards. The nerve of Bill! On this brief acquaintance, he tried to kiss me. The very idea! Men are such idiots!

Sunday, September 21, 1919 • Hudson, New York

Sonny came back! She is in mourning. I found her at the boarding house at suppertime when I returned from a walk up Mt. Merino with Bill. We lost our way and tramped miles and miles before we finally reached home. How backwards I am talking about this, but I went to the Presbyterian Church this morning, and like it ever so much. I am to sit with Miss MacMaster, principal of a grammar school and a dear.

Marian would soon become part of the social life at the Presbyterian Church with her friend Miss MacMaster at her side. Marian knew that the First Presbyterian Church in Hudson was a fit for her. Even though she attended Congregational churches in Springfield with her parents and in E. Granby with her grandparents, she instinctively knew something was right about her new church. With Marian's outgoing personality, doors unexpectedly opened for her. Miss MacMaster would play a crucial role in Marian's success providing her connections in the future. The pieces were all falling into place in this little river town for Marian. The attraction of the natural beauty of the Hudson Valley was a natural fit for Marian in her new environment. Mt. Merino is a mountain summit just south of the city of Hudson with a majestic view of the city against the backdrop of the Catskill Mountains. In 1835, Oliver Wiswall, a successful Hudson businessman, built a distinctive Greek revival mansion on this imposing location with views as far north as Albany, New York. Mr. Wiswall imported Merino sheep to Hudson for their fine merino wool; hence Mt. Merino was named.

Friday, September 26, 1919 • Hudson, New York

Sonny and I are wretches. We go up and down Warren St. after supper in search of excitement. This time, it was two of our pupils, Harold and Frank, who picked us up, and whirled us off for a ride. It was a wild one, because Harold speeded, yelled at the car as if it were a stubborn horse, and steered crazily on purpose. They took us off into the country and once trailed off into a cornfield. Sonny and I laughed until we were limp and weak — regular dishrags. They are cute boys, wanted to impress the teachers, I guess.

Saturday, September 27, 1919 • Hudson, New York

Sonny and I walked up toward the river. We stopped at a little violin store. She picked up all shapes and sizes of fiddles and played on them, so divinely that a crowd gathered outside the stuffy little shop to hear her. And, I might add, to watch her, for was there ever a lovelier face? She was trying to find a fiddle to buy for Cyrus who she is to teach.

Sunday, September 28, 1919 • Hudson, New York

The Williams's took Sonny and me for a glorious ride in the country. We sat on the back seat with their daughter Alice and gossiped. We bought loads of candy at a cheap little store and threw most of it away, preferring to give ourselves a better chance at life. The autumn colors were perfect, and the Catskills Mountains were glorious in the yellow sunlight. Alice is an attractive girl — not at all the type to be the daughter of the superintendent of schools, if there is a type.

Thursday, October 2, 1919 • Hudson, New York

Mark arrived at the Worth House, took me to the Shirly Restaurant for dinner and a show, and we walked up to the reservoir afterward. The Hudson River and the mountains in the starlight were beautiful. Fool! Fool! I'm talking to myself. I submitted to his urging, and he kissed me, not once but many times. He was free with his compliments, all right.

Saturday, October 4, 1919 • Hudson, New York

Saturday evening found Sonny and me, as usual, on Warren Street. We wandered up to Scientto's fruit store. Sonny wanted to try Eugene's violin. Well, there was a new glimpse of life — an Italian family over a fruit store and Eugene, who went to high school last year and played the violin divinely. They played duets, he and Sonny. You can see he adores her and wanted to give her music, 9 strings bass guitar, everything he could lay his hands on. We ate candy galore, brought up from the store below by his fat Italian mama who was wearing earrings. The Bill incident is in the past. I went out with him seven times, but he is not my sort.

Monday, October 6, 1919 • Hudson, New York

George Sheppard writes the Princeton game is all O.K. on November 8th. I can hardly believe it. Imagine, leaving here that Saturday morning on the 7.47 a.m. train for New York. Oh, I shall be thrilled!

> Marian was going to take a trip to the Princeton football game in Princeton, New Jersey with her friends, the Sheppards. Marian met Florence's brother, George Sheppard, at the Senior Dance at Mount Holyoke. George graduated from Princeton in 1917, and served in France as an Army officer. George was showing a lot of interest in Marian. Would George be the one?

Wednesday, October 8, 1919 • Hudson, New York

Sonny, Miss MacMaster, and I went to see "Mickey", a real dissipation. It was a clever picture. Sonny got wildly excited and clutched me for dear life. We reveled at Dayton's afterward, the tired teacher's Paradise. "Tired teachers" is a good alliterative phrase. Mrs. Hopkins told me I'd have no time nor pep to write. It's true. I have positively no time and no pep. I haven't a spark of originality after giving out to the kids four or five periods a day.

> *Mickey*, produced by Mark Sennett of the The Mabel Normand Feature Film Company in 1917, was a six-reel comedy, melodrama, and romance, starring Mabel Normand as Mickey. Sennett presented Normand with her own product company to appease his former sweetheart and restless top star! This was the first and only film to emerge from the production company. Movies were Marian's escape from reality. She was such a dreamer!

Friday, October 10, 1919 • Springfield, Massachusetts

I skipped out early to get the 4.55 pm train for home. I made the express and secured a "chair," so the ride was very comfortable. I arrived in blessed old Springfield at 8.10 pm. Father met me, and greatest surprise of all, Uncle Dan, also. Father took me right up to Memorial Church for a rehearsal of "Mit" Woodin's wedding. It was all over when I got there, but I received instructions. "Mit" looked very sweet and all excited. Is it any wonder? I hadn't seen Jimmy since his return from France. He looked fine. "Mit" gave her bridesmaids beautiful gold thimbles with the Greek key design. It was so exciting to arrive home. Theo was there. She and Umpa were on their eighth anniversary trip — to Niagara Falls, this time. We talked very late. I couldn't keep still about school. I was certainly tired.

Sunday, October 12, 1919 • Springfield, Massachusetts

We took a beautiful trip with the McKinnions over to Jacob's ladder (a 33-mile trail of Route 20 between Russell and Lee, Massachusetts.) The fall colors were just right. The dear old Berkshire Mountains just touch my heart. Nothing can ever be quite like New England to me. We came home around 5 o'clock and had a wonderful dinner at the Highland Hotel. Tuesday is Donald's birthday, and mine comes very soon, so the fathers and mothers of the families said we should have a birthday dinner. We had wine to begin and one fine dinner, private dining room and all. It was such fun. It is very comfortable to be with an old a friend as Donald, whom I have known since babyhood, and with whom I can be entirely at ease. We slam each other terribly but always recover good-naturedly. We took another ride after dinner, then up to our house for more eats. Such a happy day! My schoolteacher mantle has dropped away completely.

Monday, October 13, 1919 • Springfield, Massachusetts

A quiet morning at home and a chicken sent by Grandma for dinner. It is a holiday, Columbus Day, so Father was home. How mother and I did visit!

I took the 12.40 pm train for Albany, New York on my way back to Hudson. Father couldn't get a chair for me, so I was stowed away in the sleeper, riding backwards. My "opposites" were meek looking souls, man and wife, with an untraveled air. I saw on an envelope the man held in his hand addressed to a reverend in Amherst, Massachusetts. No wonder he is meek living on a minister's salary. It would squeeze the pep out of the most daring. His wife had the air of one forever denied things. She was wearing a plaid silk waist, plain and durable, a rather rusty black velvet hat, and a complexion fresh and untainted by the touch of a powder pad. In the course of conversation, I found that she was Mt. Holyoke College, 1890 something. So, we had a bond in common, although my nose was powdered.

> The New Women, including Marian, started to wear make-up as part of their new freedom of expression. The cosmetics industry had become "the fourth biggest business in the United States-behind cars, movies, and bootlegged liquor."(Collins) Women began to wear rouge and face powder. They started carrying compacts in their purses. Women were bombarded by the advertising industry "with products to make them more beautiful." (ibid)

Friday, October 17, 1919 • Hudson, New York

I haunted the post office today, but no evening dress arrived. Therefore, I went to the senior dance with one of my students, Bob, in my rather ill-looking yellow taffeta. He is a mighty fine youth, class president, destined for Yale, and clever. It was so funny for me to be a teacher at the high school dance. I had a fine dance program and a fine time, but it was different. I can't deny it. Jeff insisted that I jazz with him, Joe threatened cheek to cheek, and Sam - the nerve - squeezed my hand to which I paid not an atom of attention, naturally. I must be more the schoolteacher if I am to succeed.

> Today a teacher would never attend a dance with a student. That situation could lead to conduct inappropriate for a teacher-student relationship.

Saturday, October 18, 1919 • Hudson, New York

At 5 o'clock, the folks came in Umpa's car — Theo, Mother, and Father. We drove around Hudson for a while; we even went into the school. I was rather proud to show them around the dear old place. Then we had dinner at the Worth Hotel. It was so nice to sit down with the family again. After dinner, we walked up to the playhouse and saw Hearts of the World. It was very good.

It was great to have mother kiss me goodnight. I wonder if I shall ever be somebody's mother. I'm rather weakening in my conviction that a career is the only thing and that I want my freedom forever. Sometimes I want arms about me and love on which I may build a home.

> Following the success of Filmmaker D.W. Griffith's movies, *Birth of a Nation,* about the Civil War in 1915, and *Intolerance,* an epic film about the effects of intolerance in four different historical periods in 1916, he was persuaded by the British Government to make a propaganda film, *Hearts of the World,* with the hopes of encouraging the American people to come to the aid of the beleaguered French and British in their desperate fight against the Germans. Set in France, it is the portrait of a village overrun by German soldiers. Although it was filmed in California, it included a "brief prologue with footage of Griffith touring the battlefields in France, where some documentary footage was shot." It also showed Griffith "meeting with British Prime Minister David Lloyd George." (www.answers.com/hearts-of-the-world) As the story progresses, it becomes a love story between the two main characters, Lillian Gish and Robert Harron. By the time the film was released in 1918, the United States had already entered the war. And, by the time Marian saw the movie the war was over.

Sunday, October 19, 1919 • Hudson, New York

I dined at the Worth Hotel for breakfast with the folks. It's a glorious day. We walked up to the reservoir, and it was never more beautiful — so clear and the usual wide sweep of view that I love. Sonny has gone on the Mohawk Trail today with Harold F. He surely must adore her; at least it looks that way to me. The folks left at 12:30 pm — I boned on my Woman's Club paper.

> The Mohawk Trail of New York, also known as the Iroquois Trail, is a scenic drive that extends from Albany west to near Tonawanda at the eastern end of Lake Erie, where Buffalo is now located. Marian was envious of Sonny's adventures with men seeing the sights of New England.

Tuesday, October 21, 1919 • Hudson, New York

Woman's Club meeting at Mrs. Williams. I gave my talk without mishap. And Miss Dowsland, Catherine, and Margaret read part of Oscar Wilde's "Lady Windemere's Fan." They did it cleverly. Several of my pupils were there, to my horror. I was so tired when I reached home that I fairly dropped into bed.

Lady Windermere's Fan: A Play About a Good Woman is a four-act comedy by Oscar Wilde. It was first produced in 1892 at the St. James Theatre in London. (www.wikipedia.org) It is a satire on the morals of Victorian society, particularly marriage, a subject which Marian was always dreaming about.

Thursday, October 23, 1919 • Hudson, New York

Sonny and I went up town after supper. We stopped at Mr. Bergeron's drugstore. He's a Frenchman, wears diamonds galore, and even one in the filling of a tooth. Sonny and he fell to talking French. He was delighted to talk. Then, he showed us a portfolio of pictures of his wife, Eva May Allen, the actress. She died of the flu last year. It wasn't so pleasant to be forced to look at all of them since Eva May was an over-fat, rather coarse-appearing lady. We adjourned to the playhouse, sat and waited, learned it was vaudeville, and demanded our money back at the door.

Friday, October 24, 1919 • Hudson, New York

I'm writing this October 24, 1919 wondering how it will sound June 30, 1920 when my year is over.
Every day I start to school with joy in my heart that I'm a teacher.
I enjoy every class, and love to exert my utmost to get things over.
I'm happy in Hudson, although I can't say that I've made many friends as yet.
I'm *not* lonesome for college.
I have one terrible fault: I like to feel that I'm well-groomed when I start for school, because (this is terrible) I feel that the boys look at me approvingly (Isn't that horrible?)
I give out too many themes.
I like the boys better than the girls and find them more interesting.
I'm *not* crazy to get married (added Dec. 5).

Saturday, October 25, 1919 • Hudson, New York

Virtue shineth like a beacon. I mended all day long when I wasn't asleep.

The Princeton game, November 8th, with the Sheppards is a surety, followed by a bat in New York in the evening. I wrote to Margaret Gantt (Mount Holyoke Class of 1919, a Statistician at Metropolitan Life) in New York City and hope to stay with her that night.

Sunday, October 26, 1919 • Hudson, New York

Church in the morning, as usual. I enjoy it ever so much at the Presbyterian Church. Miss MacMaster and I have acquired a pew of our very own. In the afternoon, I went to ride with Arthur. We went to Kinderhook, New York, where we had some eats. He called me a "chicken," which I resented, and begged me to leave the school teaching profession and not become an old maid.

Wednesday, October 29, 1919 • 22nd Birthday!

Mother came today. I hurried down from school to meet the train. She looked so dear when she stepped off, all flushed and excited. It's my birthday today — twenty-two — and I am wretchedly conscious of the fact. I took her to Sheldon's to supper. She loved the girls, especially Sonny whom she rather adored right off. Anyone would fall for her looks. All evening we visited. Father sent me chrysanthemums all the way from home. Mother brought brownies, and we had a feast with Miss Anderson and the girls. Mrs. McCord sent me a cake. I felt so thrilled with mother here. The room seems smaller than ever with two of us to bump about in it. But, it's a dear room, and the Lyons are angels, too good for such as I. Mother and I slept together. We are so happy, and we love each other, oh so much! I'm beginning not to like birthdays.

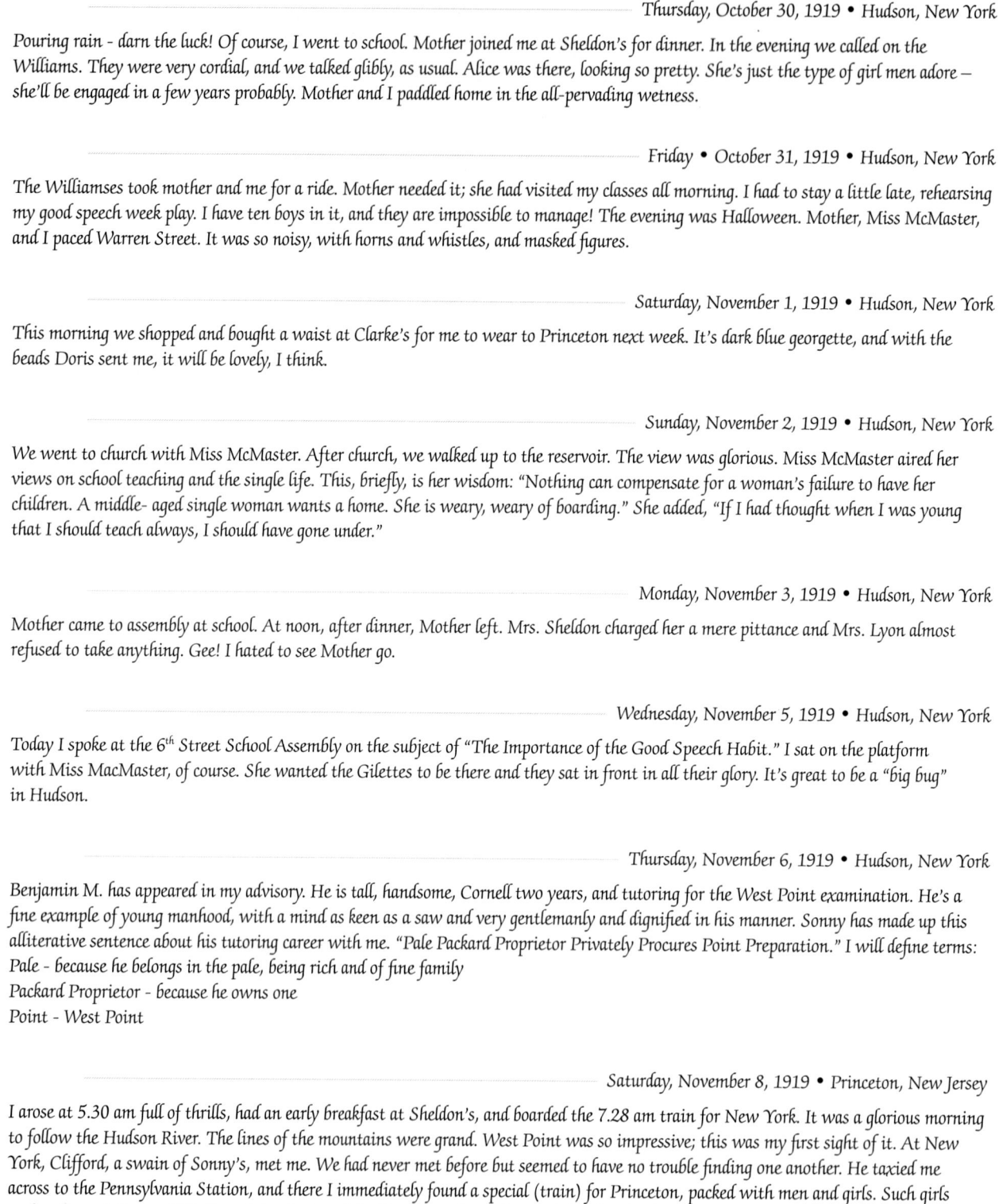

Thursday, October 30, 1919 • Hudson, New York

Pouring rain - darn the luck! Of course, I went to school. Mother joined me at Sheldon's for dinner. In the evening we called on the Williams. They were very cordial, and we talked glibly, as usual. Alice was there, looking so pretty. She's just the type of girl men adore — she'll be engaged in a few years probably. Mother and I paddled home in the all-pervading wetness.

Friday • October 31, 1919 • Hudson, New York

The Williamses took mother and me for a ride. Mother needed it; she had visited my classes all morning. I had to stay a little late, rehearsing my good speech week play. I have ten boys in it, and they are impossible to manage! The evening was Halloween. Mother, Miss McMaster, and I paced Warren Street. It was so noisy, with horns and whistles, and masked figures.

Saturday, November 1, 1919 • Hudson, New York

This morning we shopped and bought a waist at Clarke's for me to wear to Princeton next week. It's dark blue georgette, and with the beads Doris sent me, it will be lovely, I think.

Sunday, November 2, 1919 • Hudson, New York

We went to church with Miss McMaster. After church, we walked up to the reservoir. The view was glorious. Miss McMaster aired her views on school teaching and the single life. This, briefly, is her wisdom: "Nothing can compensate for a woman's failure to have her children. A middle-aged single woman wants a home. She is weary, weary of boarding." She added, "If I had thought when I was young that I should teach always, I should have gone under."

Monday, November 3, 1919 • Hudson, New York

Mother came to assembly at school. At noon, after dinner, Mother left. Mrs. Sheldon charged her a mere pittance and Mrs. Lyon almost refused to take anything. Gee! I hated to see Mother go.

Wednesday, November 5, 1919 • Hudson, New York

Today I spoke at the 6th Street School Assembly on the subject of "The Importance of the Good Speech Habit." I sat on the platform with Miss MacMaster, of course. She wanted the Gilettes to be there and they sat in front in all their glory. It's great to be a "big bug" in Hudson.

Thursday, November 6, 1919 • Hudson, New York

Benjamin M. has appeared in my advisory. He is tall, handsome, Cornell two years, and tutoring for the West Point examination. He's a fine example of young manhood, with a mind as keen as a saw and very gentlemanly and dignified in his manner. Sonny has made up this alliterative sentence about his tutoring career with me. "Pale Packard Proprietor Privately Procures Point Preparation." I will define terms:
Pale - because he belongs in the pale, being rich and of fine family
Packard Proprietor - because he owns one
Point - West Point

Saturday, November 8, 1919 • Princeton, New Jersey

I arose at 5.30 am full of thrills, had an early breakfast at Sheldon's, and boarded the 7.28 am train for New York. It was a glorious morning to follow the Hudson River. The lines of the mountains were grand. West Point was so impressive; this was my first sight of it. At New York, Clifford, a swain of Sonny's, met me. We had never met before but seemed to have no trouble finding one another. He taxied me across to the Pennsylvania Station, and there I immediately found a special (train) for Princeton, packed with men and girls. Such girls and such men! One could feel youth in the air. I felt old and wondered if I was labeled "school teacher" anywhere. I didn't want to be. The men or boys, whichever is more appropriate, looked spoiled and somewhat easy. The girls were adorable, rather "made up" and over anxious to please.

I reached Princeton before the Sheppards, so I waited around for them at the little crowded station. I had reached there almost an hour before they expected me. At last, I saw "Shep" and her mother, then George on the platform. George told me afterward that he almost kissed me; he forgot "all the world besides," he said. We went immediately to Princeton's Palmer Stadium. Our seats were marvelous, of course, on the Princeton side. Mrs. Sheppard had put up lunch for me, which I munched joyously. The game was a thriller. Princeton led 7-0 until the last quarter; then, 10-3; then, after a touchdown for the Harvard Crimson, it was 10-10. The Princeton boys were cruelly disappointed. We went right up to George's club (Gateway) and had a little supper to hold us until our arrival in New York City. We took in the campus very hastily. It's so beautiful–artistic, varied, and rich. It looks like money, money, money, plus good taste. We took the train for New York at 5 p.m. but didn't reach the city until 7.30 pm. Our train waited a long time on the tracks without any apparent logic about it. We had a bite to eat; then, saw *The Royal Vagabond* at the Cohan and Harris Theatre. We had box seats next to the stage. After the theater, we went to Murray's where we ate and ate ... and I smoked.

> Marian was heading to Princeton to meet her friends the Sheppards to attend the Princeton vs. Harvard football game in Palmer Stadium. Palmer Stadium was built in 1914 to hold 42,000 fans. It was demolished in 1996 to make way for the Princeton Stadium. The Sheppards, including Marian's Mount Holyoke classmate "Shep", lived in New Jersey. Following the football game, Marian and George toured New York City. George was Marian's first love, she thought. The eating clubs at Princeton, such as Gateway, were both dining halls and social houses, where the majority of Princeton's upperclassmen took their meals. Marian definitely enjoyed her "eats" and was very impressed with the riches at Princeton. The clubs were private institutions and not officially affiliated with Princeton University. The Gateway Club was in operation from 1913 to 1937 until it was demolished. It is now the site of the Center for Jewish Life.
>
> *The Royal Vagabond*, produced by Cohan and Harris, was a musical in three acts. The theatre was located at 226 W. 42nd Street in New York and seated 1,200 people. The theatre was built by Coca-Cola magnate Asa Candler and was leased to Cohan and Harris until 1920, when they ended their partnership. Eventually, the theatre was demolished in 1996 to make way for the new 42nd Street.

Sunday, November 9, 1919 • New York, New York

I'm starting this at 2.00 a.m. because it's Sunday morning all right. We left Murray's and taxied to West 29th where Margaret Gantt lives. George kissed me goodnight, of course; there was no use to protest. He claims it as his right. How he did make love to me, all this long evening. And, he was so complimentary. It's foolish. Margaret and I talked late. At 10.00 o'clock in the morning, George called for me. We took a bus and did Riverside Drive and 5th Avenue. We argued! Is it right to indulge in the kiss when one is not engaged? Of course, he is all for it. I took the other side. We settled nothing. We had dinner at the "Pennsylvania," a marvelous place. Then, we had to hurry frightfully to make the 3.30 pm train. All the way back to Hudson I thought and thought about my wonderful time.

> I found it interesting that Marian packed her diary into her suitcase to take with her on her trip to New York City to meet George. Then, she stayed up into the early morning hours writing about her escapades. No wonder she saved her diaries all of these years. Her diaries were her confidante, soul confessionals, and record of her life. The scenic Riverside Drive is a north-south thoroughfare in Manhattan, running parallel to the Hudson River. The Pennsylvania Hotel was built in 1919 by the Pennsylvania Railroad in the neo-Renaissance style at 401 7th Avenue at 33rd. At the time, it was the largest hotel building in New York with 2,200 bathrooms and 3,537 beds and with the world's first high-rise elevator system. The hotel has kept the same telephone number since 1919, which was immortalized in the 1938 Glenn Miller hit "Pennsylvania 6-5000." The hotel still stands today.

Monday, November 10, 1919 • Hudson, New York

I was glad to teach again, glad to see the kids, glad to be on the job. Yet, I am a bit tired, and it looks as if this week might be a long and hard pull. When I came into the house before supper Mrs. Lyon said, "Call from the Worth House." I went right down, of course. Aunt Mame was sitting in her room, with a box of fancy chocolates beside her. Bart and I went to the Playhouse, then he went around to the garage for the car and we went riding. We stopped on a little country road and Bart acted like a crazy thing. I had to speak sharply, like a school teacher, to straighten him around. Of course I allowed the moderate amount but no more.

Sunday, November 16, 1919 • Hudson, New York

I went to a little Christian Endeavor service taught at the Methodist Church. Catherine Ferris led, and it was on the subject "Service." It was quite the most inspirational meeting I ever attended. There were only a scattered few present, but the love of Christ was there, and it was a sort of holy thing. I was deeply moved. I began to probe my selfishness, my self-centeredness, and my love of material things. In prayer, I concentrated myself anew. I needed it, for I feel so uncertain about life. Perhaps it's because I'm grown up, or perhaps it's just that I'm scanning the future too searchingly. I'm wondering if always and forever I shall teach or whether I shall have love. And, above all else, shall I have children, dear little mites, whom I can enfold in my arms. I want them so, and I want them now. I believe that George Sheppard loves me, but I don't love him, not even a little wee bit.

Thursday, November 22, 1919 • Hudson, New York

I saw Grace George tonight in *Quick Work* at the Playhouse. She was very attractive and it was a clever play – a war marriage comedy. These days at school are fiercely hard. I'm dead weary.

> For a small town, Hudson was able to attract top rate entertainers and productions. Marian always took advantage of cultural events at home, college, and now in Hudson. Grace George, 1879-1961, was a popular actress with more than 50 stage roles. She popularized many of George Bernard Shaw's plays in the United States. *Quick Work* was her first play under the management of Charles Frohman, Inc.(www.picturehistory.com) Frohman controlled five theaters in London, six in New York City, and over 200 throughout the rest of the United States. Frohman died in the 1915 sinking of the RMS Lusitania by the German submarine U-20.

Friday, November 21, 1919 • Hudson, New York

Sonny and I were a bit incensed today. It's Senior Show night at (Mt. Holyoke) college, and we want, oh so badly, to be there! Well, I was a judge at the prize-speaking contest held in High School Hall. There was mighty good speaking, and hard to choose the best.

Then – oh fool – I've suffered enough for it since. My imagination has pictured all sorts of horrors to me. At 11.15 pm, after my ordeal at the contest, Harold M. called and asked me to go for a ride. Imagine! At that hour! I went and we rode until 2.30 a.m. And suddenly, and without warning, the boy kissed me – me, a teacher.

> This event tortured Marian for months. After succumbing to the kiss from a student, Marian was guilt ridden and nervous about losing her job. We all make mistakes, but, up until this point in the diaries, I doubted whether Marian would ever make one. She always seemed to do the right thing, remain positive, and see the best in everyone. It was somewhat refreshing in an odd way to realize that Marian actually was a normal human being who stumbled now and then and learned from the hard lessons in life. She had set her bar so high, trying to be the perfect teacher, that it was difficult to meet her own standards. She knew it was wrong for a teacher to be intimate with a student in any way. Yet, according to her diaries, teachers were more than merely chaperones at school dances; they fraternized and danced with the students. Moreover, although she does not say so, the student was most likely a returning soldier, older than and worldlier than Marian. These activities plus closeness in age created a grey area of blurred and confused boundaries between teachers and students for Marian.

Saturday, November 22, 1919 • Hudson, New York

Oh dear! I'm going through mental agony today. I don't know when I've suffered so. Fool!!! If Mr. Williams (superintendent) ever knows this, I'd be run out of town. Me, riding at midnight on lonely country roads, and being kissed by a pupil. Well, it's unforgivable of me. I blame, blame, blame, myself. I feel like running somewhere to hide my face in utter shame. How can I face anyone again, and him at school? Horrors! What will the future bring? Fortunately, I had to work all day at school and work hard, putting on marks. I couldn't get the horrible thing out of my mind. And, I'm tired, oh so tired. This job is aging me.

Last night's unfortunate episode taught me one big lesson — that when one is a teacher, it isn't one's own affair alone how one's life is to be governed. It is like the minister's family. You belong to the public; your business is thoroughly hashed over and discussed; and you must, above all else, be an example, shining and perfect. My impulsive lack of correct conservatism is out of place. I'm thinking I ought to get out of this type of job unless I can live up to it.

Monday, November 24, 1919 • Hudson, New York

Sonny is engaged to Harold F. Imagine that! He is handsome, rich, and a lawyer. She is beautiful, gifted, and lovable. I'm glad she is so happy. He will give her everything. This is her last year teaching, without any doubt. I wonder how that feels. I feel as if I should go on forever and ever. Really, marriage doesn't seem my line at all. But, I believe that I do rather want it for all of that.

Only one day of school this week. I'm rather glad, since I have a beastly cold and of course feel rotten discouraged with this trouble weighing me down. I feel as if my job hangs in the balance. And, I'm horribly shifty eyed before Mr. Williams. If that man ever knew, I'd be bounced –positively. I'm sure of that.

I've written barrels of letters tonight. Wish I loved George 'cause I know he does me. I don't care for him. Just now my heart has every lastingly gone over to the "Pale Packard Proprietor"– a mere boy whom I tutored in English for West Point. He's a dream … positively. I'd rather write in this dear book than see a show.

Tuesday, November 25, 1919 • Americanization Meeting Albany, New York

We took the early train for Albany, New York. The Hudson station was thronged with teacher folk, jamming up to the door of the ticket window to get round trip tickets with forty cents knocked off. No accommodation for us at the YW in Albany, so we tramped the streets to a boarding house near the Capitol called "Ole Marian." Sonny and I had a room next to Catherine and Margaret on the top floor. There was no elevator. But, what can you expect for $1.00 per room? I went to the Americanization meeting. It was very worthwhile. The immigration commissioner spoke. It is great new work.

Teachers, including Marian, played a large role in the Americanization Movement by encouraging immigrants and their children to attend public schools and to learn English. Americans assumed that immigrants would be easily absorbed into the population, but assimilation required work from the public and private sectors. For example, of the five million Italian immigrants who came to the United States between 1876 and 1930, four fifths were from the South, including Sicily. "The majority (two thirds) were farm laborers or laborers, or contadini (an Italian peasant or rustic). (www.mtholyoke.edu). "About 50% of Italians repatriated, which meant that often times the immigrants did not care about learning English or assimilating into American society because they knew that they would not remain in America permanently." (ibid) The Federal Bureau of Education, the Immigration and Naturalization Service, the General Federation of Women's Clubs, and the U.S. Chambers of Commerce joined forces for Americanization work. By 1921, as each state provided educational opportunities for immigrants, the movement subsided.

Despite the seriousness of the Americanization Movement, Marian copied this light hearted poem into her diary. "Donna" is a title or form of address for an Italian woman. Palermo is a city on the island of Sicily.

"Sicilian Immigration Song In New York Harbor"

"O – OH –HE! La La!
Donna! Donna!
Blue is the sky of Palermo,
Blue is the little bay;
And dost thou remember the orange and fig
The lively sun and the sea breeze at evening?
Oh –eh- Li! La La!
Hey – la!
Donna! Donna!
Gray is the sky of this land.
Gray and green is the water.
I see no trees, dost thou?
The wind is cold for the big woman there with the candle.
Hey – La!
Donna! Donna! Maria!"

William Carlos Williams

Wednesday, November 26, 1919 • Springfield, Massachusetts

Rose very late, skipped breakfast, and attended the modern language meeting with Sonny. It was pouring rain, so we bought a cheap umbrella, but I had no rubbers and a fierce cold — one of the breathing-through-the-mouth perpetually variety. We taxied to the station — luncheon there, and I caught the 12.30 pm train for home.

Marian spent Thanksgiving in East Granby, Connecticut with her extended family and did not write in her diary.

Sunday, November 30, 1919 Hudson, New York

I took the 12.40 pm train for Albany after spending such a happy holiday with the folks. One train was filled with Vassar girls. I was fortunate in getting a chair. I watched the Vassar's with much interest. They were a rich crowd, all in possession of fur coats and stunning serge dresses. And, I made a careful study of their rings. How differently I went through college. And, their talk was not unlike the college conversation the world over. My dear, hectic! It was weird —positively weird. My dear!

Monday, December 1, 1919 • Hudson, New York

Back on the job and glad as ever to be just here. I wish the pay was more, for I feel like a pauper. I wore my new shirt and was quite thrilled about it.

Wednesday, December 3, 1919 • Hudson, New York

Women's Club vaudeville was in the evening. It was clever and rather shocking, too, for a D.A.R. Hall and little Hudson. Helen sang Tosti's (1881) "Goodbye." Her gown was scarlet and scarce (alliterative).

Friday, December 5, 1919 • Hudson, New York

Sonny and I played bridge at Miss MacMaster's with Helen, a girl of wealth and social position. Sonny was adorable as always. She wears Harold's DKE pin now, concealed. She doesn't seem quite so thrilled now over her engagement. And, she's nervously used up.

Sunday, December 14, 1919 • Hudson, New York

After church Mrs. Gillette invited Miss MacMaster and me to dinner. It was a glorious treat, four course dinner, exquisitely served, and oh so non-Sheldon like. Their house is so rich too, the best of everything, and an air of refinement over the whole.

The Terry-Gillette house, at 601 Union Street built circa 1850, after a design by architect Richard Upjohn. (Fone) The house has many window forms which frame the remarkable views of the Catskill Mountains. Mr. Upjohn was famous for his Gothic Revival churches and was the founder and the first president of the American Institute of Architects. (www.wikipedia.org) "An early owner was William H. Terry, a prosperous local merchant, who purchased the villa in 1872." "The next owners were John Westfield Gillette and his wife Grace Field James. Grace was the niece of Marshal Fields, founder of the Department Store. She grew up in Williamstown, MA where John attended Williams College. Grace and John met when he rescued her when she had fallen through the ice while skating." John Gillette "returned to Hudson to take a position at a company partially founded by his father, the Allen Paper Car Wheel Company. After his death in 1921, Grace Gillette retained the property, but eventually sold the building to the Hudson Lodge of Elks in 1935." (www.historichudson.org) Today the Terry-Gillette house is known as the Hudson House which can be rented for special events. Marian was fortunate to be invited into many of the architectural gems of Hudson.

Tuesday, December 16, 1919 • Hudson, New York

The "Pale, Packard, Proprietor" came to tell me of his appointment at West Point, and I went to ride with him afterwards. Bless his heart! He passed with a 98 average. He's just a dear and so handsome and splendid.

Thursday, December 18, 1919 • Hudson, New York

The next-to-last day. I shopped all the evening and packed. I also called on "Grandma" and helped her do up packages. She's a dear, and has helped me just loads in every way. It is so Christmassy everywhere, and I'm thoroughly thrilled to be alive and have the vacation ahead.

I'm going to think over some of the things "Grandma" has told me. She has seen life from a nurse's standpoint for 23 years, and she knows what she knows. Especially, she has advised me in sex matters, telling me not to let men love and kiss me. I have been careless of that this last year. I believe the sex life in me has awakened rather late and I am sorely tempted. Especially, as the real loved one may never come. I shall be good during the vacation.

Friday, December 19, 1919 Christmas Vacation • Springfield, Massachusetts

Everyone wished everyone else a merry Christmas. It was very jolly all around. It was a hustle to get to my train; my hands nearly froze. Indeed they would have if one of the boys hadn't offered to carry it for me. Katherine and I travelled together all the way. Father was at the station. Bless his heart.

Saturday, December 20, 1919 • Springfield, Massachusett

Shopping almost all day. The stores were mobbed fearfully. I had lunch with mother at the Y.W. after her school was out. I met "Pris" Spaulding at 2:30 pm. She is on the Springfield Union newspaper staff (Society Editor) and loves the work.

Monday, December 22, 1919 • Springfield, Massachusetts

I bought a suit at Forbes Department Store. It is really handsome, dark brown wool velour, and it was marked to $40 from $55.00. At 12.45 pm, I went to the Commercial High School at Mr. Ellis's summons. I visited an English class and saw the head of the English department. I had a semi-offer from Mr. Ellis for next fall. How am I ever to decide??

I came home and Doris Campbell was here. Oh it was a meeting! The dear little roomy. We went over to "Pris" Spaulding's in the evening. It was "Pris's" birthday and she saved the cake for our arrival. I'm always so thrilled over candles and lights. We talked over the bunch singly and collectively. "Pris" looks well; she has a new dignity and poise that becomes her. Dick B. called up about the reunion. It seemed great to hear his voice again.

Tuesday, December 23, 1919 • Springfield, Massachusetts

Again I was up town – looking this time for a semi evening affair for the reunion. Doris lent her advice – but no use. I couldn't find a thing. We met "Pris" Spaulding for lunch, then I went up to Central High for the graduation exercises. Dick B. and I sat together. The exercises were fine - well worked out and attractive costuming. It was great to see all the old friends on the faculty, now hailing me as a fellow of the profession.

Dick B. came up in the evening. We discussed all the pros and cons of the C.H.S.'s (Central High School) fifth reunion and all sorts of other topics. He's had many interesting experiences since 1915 when we left the high school stage, especially last summer when he and another Harvard friend took a long trip, earning their way as they went. And, as for a specimen of manhood, Dick B. is a corker — handsome, polished, and perfectly splendid. I thereupon resolve not to fall if grace be given me to withstand.

> During the war, many young men had their college careers interrupted by their service. Dick B. spent time in the Navy and would graduate from Harvard a year later. Dick B. held a special place in Marian's heart as her first high school crush. Clearly she still admired and respected him five years later. She expresses more excitement about Dick B. than she did about poor George who loved her so. Marian was living and working in Hudson where she was meeting new people and starting a new life. Would Dick B. continue to be a part of Marian's future as more than an esteemed classmate?

Wednesday, December 24, 1919 • Christmas Eve Springfield, Massachusetts

Christmas cards are coming in an avalanche, and many from unexpected sources. Bart came over in the evening with Aunt Mame. We went out to ride alone. More foolishness. I must make new resolves for 1920.

Thursday, Christmas • 1919 Springfield, Massachusetts

I made some calls on Spruceland Avenue in the morning. It is an ideal snowy Christmas, crisp and cold. First, I called on "Joe". She has her engagement ring. Then, to the Coe's house, the Ellis's house, and Aunt Mame's house. At the Coe's prosperity reigned supreme. It added to all the excitement to be wearing my new suit.

About 2 o'clock, Donald called for us in the sedan and we met the McKinnon family at the Kimball. Donald's Harvard medical friend is a dream of a chap, the sort one never can forget because his smile is so winning and he is such a gentleman. Donald is very much older and more dignified.

The dinner was delicious — almost too rich, but very fascinating. I shall think back upon it when I get back to Hudson fare. After dinner, we rode out over the Boston Road. The sunset was glorious on the snow and in back of the dark woods. We returned to the McKinnion's house and played around until 9 o'clock. I had the usual fight with Mr. McKinnion and Father over the cigarette, which ended in my usual yielding to their wishes. But, it's no credit to me. I have to yield. We went home very late. A happy Christmas.

Friday, December 26, 1919 • Springfield, Massachusetts

More cards today and more presents. I have two crepe de chine waists (pink), a dream of a camisole from Doris, handkerchiefs (8 in all and sadly needed). Also, some books, a picture frame, woolen stockings, a bathrobe (from dear Umpa), some underwear, and money. Santa was generous!

Mother and I shopped today. Mother got a dress, a blue satin, and, I purchased a hat (satin trimmed with fur) to match my suit. We lunched uptown. In the evening, Bart took me to Court Square to see the play, "Ready to Occupy," a screaming bedroom farce with Ernest Truex in the chief role. We sat way front, surrounded by people whom I knew and hadn't seen for ages. Then, a little ride after the theater. Again, I was foolish.

It seems the Viets' family finances have improved judging by the gifts given this Christmas.

Saturday, December 27, 1919 • Springfield, Massachusetts 1915 Class Reunion

At 5:30 pm Dick B. called for me, and we called for all the patronesses.

Well, the 1915 Class Reunion was thrilling! Just to be in the dear old building and meet old friends whom I hadn't seen for ages. I was thrilled to see all the old crowd. After the banquet Dr. Law spoke, Dick B. presented the cup, and I gave the history of the class. Dr. Law was received with much enthusiasm. She was dear, too, and said just what we wanted her to say. After dinner we began the dancing — mobs of girls without partners and the same few dancing all the time. I had some wonderful dances. Then, about 10.30 pm, I danced with Sydney, and we continued together. My, but he could dance. We sort of fell for one another. He held me closer and closer, holding his check against mine. I loved it! We talked very little, and we danced perfectly together. I wonder if I shall see him again? Went home with Dick B. and the patronesses. I think the reunion went off well. Of course, I've fallen hopelessly for Dick B. But, no other man in the class appealed to me – except Syd in a romantic way. And Malcolm is wonderful to talk with.

Sunday, December 28, 1919 • Springfield, Massachusetts

Bart and Aunt Mame took me down to East Granby. They were out for pine boughs. We stopped and visited the folks on the way back. Grandpa and Grandma have grown so old, and they seem so weary. Who would not? After years of early rising, and late lying down, and no time in between to draw a quick breath. Grandma was, as ever, the cordial hostess, serving us rich hot chocolate and cream.

In the evening, Bart brought me back to Aunt Mame's to sit around the fire, eat nuts and apples and Christmas candy, and play the vic incessantly. At 9.30 pm, we left and rode along the river road in the cold, clear starlight. I was weak and let Bart love me, as I shouldn't have done. Then, he said when he took me home "You have made me think of you, as I know I shouldn't. Oh God! I wish I had never seen a woman."

Monday, December 29, 1919 • Springfield, Massachusetts

Mother and I "house worked." We have let things go in the Christmas rush. About 3.30 pm I went up town, met "Pris" Spaulding for a shine, and thence to the Kimball for Bodiene's tea. Such an elegant affair with such a glad array of sleek, prosperous girls with heavy fur coats and smooth velvets underneath. Bodiene was wonderfully made up as to hair, carefully cared for skin, sapphire blue velvet, and daintily attired feet. It was all very formal, and the food was rich and elaborately concocted. What is society anyway? Its outside is insincere and mocking. Inside, it must be sometimes true and fine. I feel so like a cynic, surveying it all, for I am not "in the swim" after all.

Tuesday, December 30, 1919 • Springfield, Massachusetts

This noon I went to lunch with dearest "Mit" (Woodin). She had all her new wedding things on the table and such a dainty lunch. Her mother's home is a love. Ruth is so happy and loves Jimmy so. The happiness just radiates from her smiles. Oh, she's a dear friend. All the afternoon, we visited in front of a slow fireplace fire and played sweet, haunting things on the "vic." It was all so intimate and nice; she had news of her sister "Dot" and her babies. I was full of Hudson tales.

Tonight we went to the theatre – the Viets family intact. This is Dad's and Mother's 23rd anniversary, so we are truly celebrating. It was a beautiful play, with William Hodge in "The Guest of Honor." Hodge is so high-minded in his acting.

Wednesday, December 31, 1919 • E. Granby, Connecticut

Early – oh very early before the dawn — I started for the station to take that early riser, the East Granby train. The stars were out when I took the trolley. And, on the train I saw the sunrise very beautifully over the snowfields and the river. I spent a very quiet day at East Granby. Theo came in the afternoon, and the doctor came to see Grandfather, who is not at all well and shows his age only too evidently. Dr. Carver said I looked much like mother, which thrilled me, of course. He said, "She's put her stamp on you, so that she can never lose you."

In the evening, we went over to Aunt Mame's house to watch the Old Year out. Bart and I played the vic and danced. We toasted marshmallows by the fire. Then, we had a wonderful midnight supper — rabbit, cocoa, ice cream, and little cakes — and some wine for a real 1920 welcome!

New Year's Resolutions for 1920:

I shall maintain a better dignity in my profession (remember Nov. 21). I shall be more thoughtful of my home folks.
I shall keep Sunday more truly a Lord's Day.
I shall be more loyal in my friendships.
I shall spend more time in Bible reading and in prayer.
I shall be more careful in the spending of my money.
I shall try to keep my thoughts high and thus conquer the passions which are lower and rise within me.

I shall try to observe the following health rules:

Eat more slowly
Give up coffee
Take more baths
Sleep 8 ½ hours
Get more fresh air
Do simple exercise
Concentrate better – so that my work will not hang on so
Be less intense
Eat meat once a day only.

I hereby transcribe — my feelings of shame and sorrow for the events of Nov. 21st. I'm not worthy of the teaching profession. I've confessed to no one but Doris, to whom I wrote it all. She would understand, I'm sure. But, if C.S.W. ever found out, I'd be a "dished woman" and would probably be consigned to the Hudson station with an invitation to depart without delay. If June comes and I am undiscovered I shall consider myself lucky beyond all hope – and far better off than I deserve.

Marian and Her Mother, Gertrude

Thursday, January 1, 1920 • Springfield, Massachusetts

1920 is here. What will it hold, and how will it end? I should almost like to be engaged before '21 walks in. But, I don't believe I shall be. And why do I want to be, since I love my work? I reviewed 1919 rather quickly when I got into bed about 2 am. It has been a great year — the frosting on the cake of four years of college, graduation, my trip in June, camp, my job, and this glorious vacation almost completed. I met George and Bill in 1919, and I renewed my friendship with Dick B. They are three fine, splendid men. Of them all, Dick B. appeals most, just now. At 5 pm, I went to the Blue Cross tea with "Pris" Spaulding, and I spent the evening with the family haranguing against society and the wild pace of the youthful set.

Friday, January 2, 1920 • Springfield, Massachusetts

I went over to Cousin Helen Bemis's. I stayed to lunch. It was so luxurious, served out in the solarium. We gossiped fearfully, especially about Aunt Mame and her relations with Bart. In the evening, I went to the Polis with Bart. We rode afterward, but I refused to let him kiss me, for such is my New Year's Resolution, applying to all men.

Saturday, January 3, 1920 • Springfield, Massachusetts

I had to make a hurried trip up town for a few last necessaries. I met "Pris" Spaulding for a little farewell chat. Then Mother and I went to lunch. In the evening, I went to the Bridgeway Hotel with Sherman Ellis, an unexpected invitation, and really great fun. We ate and danced and gazed upon the gay ones. So many painted faces, so much of the extreme shining! Oh! Ye evil world.

Sunday, January 4, 1920 • Hudson, New York

I boarded the 12.40 pm with Katherine Ferris. We reached Albany at 3.45 pm and decided to wait for Margaret's train at 7.00 pm. The station was thrilling; it was so crowded, full of Cornell and Hamilton boys, some of them quite attractive. One, we called "dappie," short for dapper. He was huge; fur coated, and carried many big suitcases, mandolin cases, etc. I went to bed early after glancing over some belated mail that had arrived here. It's great to be back in many ways. But, it's fearfully cold!!!

Monday, January 5, 1920 • Hudson, New York

Katherine Ferris is engaged and sporting a diamond she has kept the secret all the fall. Imagine that! I never could. And, Sonny has smashed her engagement, which she had thought so ideal and perfect a month ago. She's a queer duck, that girl. I can't comprehend her.

School seemed so natural. Study hall is even more so. I was truly glad to be back, even to Sheldon's. I feel very much at home here now. The Lyons are dear; I am fortunate to be so situated. "Grandma" and Miss MacMaster are my other two loves besides the Wellesley girls and Sonny, of course. C.S.W. and Mr. Knapp are good scouts, too, but whenever I see them, my conscience still reminds me of that horrible event with Harold. If that boy keeps still all the year, I shall be a fortunate girl indeed. Everything depends upon his discretion. Here's hoping!

> While Marian continued teaching, the negotiations for peace following the Great War continued. On January 10, 1920, the League of Nations came into existence, ratified by 42 nations, as a result of the Paris Peace Conference. Its mission was to maintain world peace. While these were lofty goals, it was difficult to enforce, as they were divided by their deep differences. The United States Senate declined to approve acceptance of the League of Nations. The ineffective League of Nations lasted for 26 years until it was replaced with the United Nations at the end of the Second World War.
>
> By the end of the Great War, four major imperial powers ceased to exist: The German, Russian, Austro-Hungarian, and Ottoman Empires. "The successor states of the former two lost substantial territory, while the latter two were dismantled. The maps of Europe and Southwest Asian were redrawn, with several independent nations restored or created." (www.wikipedia.org/wiki/World_War_1)
>
> Could the League of Nations prevent a repetition of another horrific conflict in the future?

Saturday, January 10, 1920 • Hudson, New York

Alice Williams and I walked downtown and we fooled around until Harold M. picked us up in his car. Horrors!! Harold M.! Shades of that ill-starred evening.

Sunday, January 11, 1920 • Hudson, New York

At 4 o'clock, we went over to Margaret and Catherine's for supper. "Grandma" was there, and Miss MacMaster. We cooked a simple supper over Canned Heat and read aloud Daisy Ashford's "Young Visiters." Also, we gossiped very extensively about all things but………….. Margaret divulged that she is engaged! It is to the soldier man who came in the fall. My first two encouragements in teaching came yesterday and today — yesterday, from that dear "Packard Proprietor," and, today, from Miss MacMaster. It was something Mr. Williams had said. I won't quote it here, because I don't believe it, and I shan't think of it, but it did thrill me and make me very, very happy.

Daisy Ashford's full name was Margaret Mary Julia Ashford (1881-1972). She wrote the novella, *The Young Visiters, or Mister Salteena's Plan*, parodying the upper class of society in the late 19th century England, when she was nine years old. So, the spelling is incorrect purposely.

Wednesday, January 14, 1920 • Hudson, New York

A lull in this busy week came tonight when I went down to the Womens' Club open meeting at the D.A.R. Really this has been such a hard week and we're only half way through the mess now. Tests are the cause of the trouble, and tutoring after school for Regents tests which will be ahead.

I forgot to say that on the way home from the D.A.R. "Granny" and the two "Old Reliables" took me in to Daytons, treated me to eats, and announced my engagement to Bergeron, he of the diamond tooth! Ye gads!!!

The first Regent Examinations in the state of New York were administered in 1866. In 1878 the system was used as a way to assess the curricula taught in secondary schools in the state of New York, including Hudson. A passing score on the "statewide standardized examinations in core high school subjects" are required for a Regents Diploma. "Regents Diplomas are optional and typically offered for college bound students." (www.wikipedia.org) Marian tutored students to help them pass the exams which were given after half year or yearlong courses. New York is the only state to conduct Regent exams. Marian's dedication to her students and her commitment to helping them pass these exams made her the kind of teacher every student would be lucky to have. I am so proud of my grandmother for all of the sacrifices she made to help her students succeed and have better lives.

Friday, January 16, 1920 • Hudson, New York

This was a day! The last five week test was held, tutoring, and a howling mob after school in my room. Then, I fled to Miss MacMaster's office in the 4th Street School and there, at her summons, found a cake stirred in chocolate, fresh baked, and frosted in layers. "I'm reckless" says that lady principal, posing a pen knife over the dainty. We fell to! We ate it all but a scrap hardly worth mentioning.

In the evening, Sonny and I went to the Episcopal Parish House dance and had *more* fun. Lots of partners, high school boys and otherwise. I danced long and often with Harold. Heavens! How have I the nerve? The boy is evidently planning all sorts of spring parties and rides, tennis, etc. Help me to have judgment! I haven't much, and I'm impulsive. I danced with several older men who were attractive, rather, but very silly. I am failing to impress my schoolboys with age and dignity – positively failing. I seem to be able to handle them academically, but they have no right to be so flirtatious in off school hours.

Saturday, January 17, 1920 • Hudson, New York

I tutored Alice Williams and Elbert all morning, preparatory to English III Regents exams. They were very wide awake and satisfactory. I spent the evening with dear Miss Mac. We read poetry and talked, etc.

Monday, January 19, 1919 • Hudson, New York

More snow and continued cold. Gee! This is some climate. I'm continually frozen. In the morning I tutored. Two of the country boys couldn't get in – bad drafts, etc. There is an air of exam taking in the school. In the afternoon was the ordeal of proctoring my students in Study Hall taking their exams, with the help of three other teachers, but the sinking heart was mine.

I hurried to correct the tests. Two out of 20 failed. Hooray for the other 18. But I couldn't bear to have two fall below 75. This has been a day! My three English III people passed in the 80's. They all phoned me tonight – bless their hearts. I fall hard for Elbert. Alice Williams was dear over the phone too. She's a sweet child when she doesn't talk in class.

Thank God for this job I love, even if my salary is a mite.

Tuesday and Thursday, January 20 and 22, 1920 • Hudson, New York

Such days proctoring the Regents exams. There is a great influx of kids from the country who try preliminaries in English, geography, and history. They're such raw, crude little individuals, unpolished and afraid of their new surroundings. My English Grammar people passed 7 out of 9 on the Wednesday morning exam. Sonny and I proctored spelling in the afternoon and Mr. Williams bothered us to death with much useless teasing. He's weird!

Wednesday, January 21, 1920 • Hudson, New York

"The Family" met in "Grandma's" room for a rabbit supper. I read aloud. The two "Old Reliables" knitted. We had the worst time opening the cans containing the new variety of rabbit. After we ate, we stayed until 12.30 am. "Grandma" regaled us with bits from her experiences. She's rich in them. She's brought so many babes into the world, has closed so many eyes in death. She has made friends everywhere, too. If ever women needed friends, it's she, for she has no living relatives.

Sunday Evening January 26, 1920 • Hudson, New York

We had coffee and doughnuts tonight up in "Grandma's" room. Sonny was there for a wonder, I had written a fool poem about our "engaged girls" and that was read at the proper moment. We read aloud from the Atlantic Narratives, and then talked, "Grandma" again holding the floor on her experiences.

Wednesday, January 28, 1920 • Hudson, New York

We took a walk after school tonight - the two "Reliables" and I – over across the snowy fields, beyond the fireman's home. It was very, very cold, but a glorious walk; and the sunset over the mountains were clear and flaming. I saw a little low hill that looked like Prospect at Mt. Holyoke; it made me gulp a bit for the "dear old place." Supper at Sheldon's tasted so good to hungry souls! It's a dear old world. How completely men are out of it just now for me! I don't get any mail these days either except from home, Doris, and George. The girls seem played out, or else are too very busy!

Friday, January 30, 1920 • Hudson, New York

At six o'clock, I knew I was surely going to a dance at the Worth House. Alice Williams phoned me at Sheldon's and said that I was to go with one Harold B., former captain in the army. At 9 o'clock, he called for me. I wore my pink evening dress that has seen so many good times, including prom at Amherst and Mt. Holyoke, and finally "Mit's" wedding. Well, it was a very speedy party with drinks galore. The Mac Wardle's orchestra was fine and I had some good dances. And, I found that Harold B. was dangerous. He wanted me to make a fuss over him when we got home and even said quite boldly that he had no limit to his loving. He's a man of the world and a bad egg. Mother would loathe him.

Saturday, January 31, 1920 • Hudson, New York

This morning I signed the contract to return to Hudson, for the salary they offered me was $1,100 and I really do want to stick by Hudson. I've grown so attached to the school and the way things are done. I did get some letters written in the evening and read some Thackeray. I can't realize I've signed up to stay here, but it's true because I can look at the visible contract. The folks phoned me last night. They weren't over pleased it seemed to me.

In the afternoon, Sonny and I assisted at Miss MacMaster's card party given at Mrs. Gillette's. We punched scores and helped serve and incidentally took a good look at many of Hudson's elite. After the rest had gone we sat around the fire and ate on chicken patties and nuts, and all the goodies. The ever adorable Mrs. Gillette was there.

Sunday, February 1, 1920 • Hudson, New York

A freezing cold day – almost unbearable. It was uncomfortable at church and Sunday School. I did get some letters written in the afternoon and read some Thackeray.

Letters from Doris Campbell are so thrilling. We tell each other everything about events, ambitions, thoughts, ideals, oh, all the list of things! It's good that no one can x-ray the paper. Bless her! I wonder what will become of her. Will it be the stage or marriage or something less appealing? We wonder together what that future holds. We peer down the road of future days. I can't see a step beyond June 1921. I'm in Hudson until then; that's a certainty now. But beyond? Will a man's love enter in? Men seem sort of alien to me now. I'm getting used to high school boys again. With them, I flourish, but there seems to be no older men in Hudson. Not real men whom I can admire and respect. Ain't it fierce?

Wednesday, February 4, 1920 • Hudson, New York

I slept with Sonny and had a horrible nightmare. I rose up in bed and announced decisively that my arm pained me. She was anxious, piloted me to the bathroom, tried to administer hot water and salve, and rubbed it to get up circulation. Finally, I came to and laughed hysterically! We didn't sleep much, I'll confess!

Friday, February 6, 1920 • Hudson, New York

The senior play, "Green Stockings", arrived. The attendance at school was slight due to impassable roads. In the evening, I went to the Parish House dance. Had a good time dancing with all the high school boys. Billy startled me by asking my age, which I refused to tell, then he announced my age accurately. "Oh, we all know," he said assuredly.

Saturday, February 7, 1920 • Hudson, New York

Margaret's brother was here today. We went over to school in the afternoon for a feast of music, he at the piano, Sonny with the violin. "Grandma" came too. Also, we who were not performers devoured marvelous chocolates. Such a treat to have candy. I'm so poor this month, having sent home my suit check that I can't even buy a chocolate bar. Stamps and laundry are all I can spend for.

Sunday, February 8, 1920 • Hudson, New York

I went to church in the evening to hear a Home Missionary who has worked 35 years in the states of our great West. Shall I have any record of service when I die? I shall try to begin now when I'm young and strong and eager to do something for my master's kingdom.

Wednesday, February 11, 1920 • Hudson, New York

"Green Stockings" (1916 comedic play by A.E.W. Mason) tryouts resulted in a decision on all but the leading man. Margaret is my assistant. Thank heavens I don't have to decide alone.

Saturday, February 14, 1920 • Hudson, New York

A very eventful day. I worked at school awhile in the morning. Then I tore home to finish my original Valentine for the Women's Club luncheon at the Worth House. At one o'clock we girls arrived. The luncheon was lovely – Valentine decorations throughout: heart place cards, hearts fluttering ceiling ward, kewpie dolls standing about coquettishly, red carnations, and red candlesticks. The luncheon was good, too, four courses, peppered with orchestra music and a buzzy general gab. The original valentines followed the luncheon. My! They were good. K. Ferris recited a French Canadian love song. Margaret and Miss Dowsland did "Sam Weller's Valentine" from Pickwick Papers (Charles Dickens). My foolish thing went well. It was entitled "The Modest Proposal." Then the Albany Women's' Club President spoke very incoherently on butterfly collections, care of roads, and Women's Club affairs.

> Marian didn't enter her original Valentine "The Modest Proposal" into her diary. She shared it with her friends at the luncheon. I wish I she would have shared it with me also. But, Marian did share another famous Valentine poem, "Daisy's Valentines" by the English poet Henry Austin Dobson in her diary. Mr. Dobson was born in Plymouth, England in 1840 and turned his attention to writing poetry in about 1864. In this particular poem he references the ancient city of Troy, near the Dardanelles, which was thought to be near Anatolia in modern Turkey. A Dardanian is a Trojan boy.

"Daisy's Valentines"

All night, through Daisy's sleep, it seems,
 Have ceaseless "rat-tats" thundered;
All night through Daisy's rosy dreams
 Have devious postmen blundered,
Delivering letters round her bed, —
Suggestive missives, sealed with red.
And franked, of course, with due queen's-head
 While Daisy lay and wondered.

But now, when chirping birds begin,
 And Day puts off the Quaker, —
When Cook renews her morning din,
 And rates the cheerful baker, —
She dreams her dream no dream at all,
For just as pigeons come at call
Winged letters flutter down, and fall
 Around her head, and wake her.

Yes, there they are! With quirk and twist
 And fraudful arts directed;
(Save Grandpapa's dear stiff old "fist,"
 Through all disguise detected):
But which is his, — her young Lothair's —
Who wooed her on the schoolroom stairs
With three sweet cakes and two ripe pears,
 In one neat pile collected?

"Tis there, be sure. Though, truth to speak,
 (If truth may be permitted,)
I doubt that young "gift-bearing Greek"
 Is scarce for fealty fitted;
For has he not (I grieve to say)
To two love more, on this same day,
In just this same emblazoned way,
 His transient vows transmitted?

He may be true. Yet, Daisy dear,
 That even youth grows colder
You'll find is no new thing, I fear;
 And when you're somewhat older,
You'll read of one Dardanian boy
Who wooed with gifts a maiden coy,-
Then took the morning train for Troy,
 In spite of all he'd told her.

> But wait. Your time will come. And then
> Obliging Fates, please send her
> The bravest thing you have in men,
> Sound-hearted, strong and tender,-
> The kind of man, dear Fates, you know,
> That feels how shyly Daisies grow,
> And what soft things they are, and so
> Will spare to spoil or mend her.
>
> Austin Dobson

Thursday, February 19, 1920 • Hudson, New York

My dearest father's birthday. Wish I could see him! He's 52 today, and I know is furious about it; he loathes getting old. I sent him a pack of cards, so that he may pursue "rum" with clean instruments. Mother says his pet pack is now vile and chewed in appearance. I tried to think of Father all day, but it was so busy that I couldn't. The first rehearsal of the senior play was at 3.45 pm, and I had to summon all my pep and courage for that. It went fairly well, although the entire cast was not there. I fell into bed early, forgetting papers waiting for the red pencil. I was utterly weary.

Friday, February 20, 1920 • Hudson, New York

This week has been almost the busiest of my life, and this Friday night, I am more than relieved that it is over. First, the Lyons succumbed to grippe Sunday. We had a blizzard too. Then, lack of money worries me. I haven't had a cent this month, due to check for $45.00 that I sent home for my suit. So, this week I charged rubbers, a shirtwaist, and a plant for the Lyons, and more. Also, my watch stopped this week. I'm penniless and timeless. But, I'm full of the joy 'o life.

Sunday, February 22, 1920 • Hudson, New York

The birthday of the noble George.

At the mass meeting for Armenians, my heart was simply torn with pity for those starving martyred folk. I stopped in with Miss "Mac" and we talked until late, as usual.

> I found it very touching that my grandmother continued to be so concerned about the Armenians and their plight following the end of the war. The Armenian Genocide, also known as the Armenian Holocaust, resulted in the loss of over 500,000 Armenians between the years of 1914-1918 during World War I. The genocide was "centrally planned and administered by the Turkish government against the entire Armenian population of the Ottoman Empire." (Armenian-genocide.org) "The Armenian people were subjected to deportation, expropriation, abduction, torture, massacre, and starvation." (ibid) The international community condemned the Armenian Genocide.

February 27 and 28, 1919 • Utica, New York • Visit to "Dot" (Woodin) and Paul

I taxied to the train station. It is a wonder I got there at all. There were so many kids clamoring for attention after school. The train was on time at 4.55 pm. Paul met me at the train in Utica and we were soon at 1411 Oneida. Such a cold night!! "Dot" - oh it was great to see her. She expects her third baby in the summer. Paul wakened Betty – so sweet and sleepy. Betty was a circus playing with my "powder face" and key case. All her T's are P's so it's "rock a bye baby in the pee pop." And, little Ted had his bottle. The apartment was homelike, as "Dot" would have it always. I'm glad Paul has done so well - he's getting $3,000 now. We played hearts – I smoked.

Tuesday, March 2, 1920 • Hudson, New York

Horrors! I spoke before the school – on books – very thrilling, I assure you. It's over, thank heavens, so I'm satisfied, or partially so. These days are so strenuous. George is coming Saturday. I hope I shall have some "pep" left. But, I am so very, very happy in my beloved work. Each day I love it. Even the kids seem dear, when they're not trying.

Saturday, March 6, 1920 • Hudson, New York

Dear memory book! My first proposal came tonight from George in Mrs. Lyon's little parlor. He was so sweet about it. "You'd make a wonderful wife for a businessman," he said. But, I told him I didn't know and might not know for ages, and then my answer might be, "No," because I can't tell. And, he's not at all the Prince Charming of my dreams. Of course, he's a good man and can make money, I truly believe. And, he'd be a good husband to me, and the Sheppards are a fine family. But, I don't love him, and that's necessary. He says he adores me and is unhappy when away. What shall I do? I told him he might have to wait a year and then I might not be able to say yes to him. All of this is very true. I shall tell my dear mother and father. Oh dear! How can a girl ever decide?

Sunday, March 7, 1920 • Hudson, New York

(In all, since George came, I've smoked 10 cigarettes.)

The day dawned clear and cold. George came over from the hotel right after breakfast. We talked and took a walk over the hospital way. We took the 12.48 pm to Albany, and had a dream of a turkey dinner at the Hampton. I smoked two cigarettes at dinner. After hot chocolate and cake, we hurried to the station. Our train landed us in Hudson at 8.10 pm.

All the evening, again, we talked. George was very thoughtful and gentle. He talks of marriage so sensibly, so splendidly. "Each year would be more wonderful with you," he said. We talked of children, etc. Then, we discussed whether it was wrong to hug and kiss. We decided that it was wrong in one respect — that so many could not control themselves. How passionately he kissed me. Oh! He loves me! And, when he went he just took me in his arms and held me very close. Then, he kissed me. Oh! I never felt like that before. All the vitality seemed squeezed out of me. I was limp. And, I couldn't sleep.

Monday, March 8, 1920 • Hudson, New York

George left today. I'm in a queer frame of mind. It is new to me that I am the object of a man's love.

In the evening, Mr. Williams had me speak at the general teachers' meeting on the old subject of Tuesday morning tests. C.S.W. spoke at length and earnestly on better teaching to meet better salaries, etc. I was tired unto death, simply dead somehow with no life. Bed is my heaven these days, where I lose myself and not have to think in the endless round.

Tuesday, March 9, 1920 • Hudson, New York

Of course, I worked on school matters in the evening. Miss Mac had some wild strawberry jam and crackers, so altogether we had a feast. I had written to Mother about the events of the weekend.

Thursday, March 11, 1920 • Hudson, New York

I had a letter from George, the dearest letter. He said returning to Norristown, NJ was like going from the ethereal to the sordid. Oh dear! Is this life — that such a love be offered and I care not to take it?

Saturday, March 13, 1920 • Hudson, New York

Such a full day! We rehearsed the one act play for the Woman's Club in the morning. It's a Barrie war play, "The New Word."

> J.M. Barrie (1860-1937) was world famous for his play and story about Peter Pan in 1904. *The New Word*, a one-act play, only 40 minutes long, is a fairy tale of sorts for adults in a country gone to war. Written in 1915, the play is about a British father and his nineteen year old son during World War I trying awkwardly to convey their feelings to each other. There are only four characters in the play and I think Marian played the part of the Mother.

Tuesday, March 16, 1920 • Hudson, New York

It is Mother's birthday. I phoned her in the evening. Dear mother! This is the first time I haven't been with her on her birthday. She and Father had been downtown to dinner and a show. I'm so lucky in my family!

Wednesday, March 17, 1920 • Hudson, New York

Oh! I was so tired before the play, "The New Word", at the Woman's Club! Sonny came home after supper and did my hair high. We powdered it. Oh! It was classy and really becoming. The play went well. I was ready to fall into bed when I reached home. Such days as these are. Little Hudson is taking the toll of my youth and bloom.

Friday, March 19, 1920 • Hudson, New York

We repeated "The New Word" in school this morning. Oh! How we hated to do it. Again my hair was powdered. We lived through it, and I taught with silver locks. Wild! I was dead weary at close of school. I came home to sleep and rose to a late supper. Then sought bed again and became as one dead.

Sunday, March 21, 1920 • Hudson, New York

Church was somehow beautiful today. There was a splendid sermon that has preached itself in my ears ever since. Miss Mac and I took a walk in the sweet spring sunshine. The warmth is so welcome. In the afternoon, Margaret and I walked again, through the mush underfoot, out the Stottville Road. The Catskill Mountains were a queer blue, yet dear. They have the more graceful line, when compared to my own best-loved Berkshires.

We spent a heavenly hour at Anna's breathing in the beauty of her home and playing the vic to my heart's content. We were regaled with strawberry ice cream and an abundance of macaroons. Supper at Sheldon's was a severe anticlimax. Somehow, life always deals you a jolt like that.

> As Marian's interest in the Presbyterian Church continued to grow she knew there was a connection to the people and it felt right for her.

Monday and Tuesday, March 22 and 23, 1920 • Hudson, New York

Both evenings we had the Green Stockings play rehearsal. Harold H. is behaving better. My, but he's touchy; he whines at the least correction from Margaret or me. I'm glad the vacation will intervene. We're all tired and cross and doing poor, slow work and wasting time. "Courage, girl, courage," I say to myself after each rehearsal. I wish Doris Campbell were here to advise.

Wednesday, March 24, 1920 • Hudson, New York

No play rehearsals tonight. A little respite. They come so seldom. The play worries me horribly. I feel utterly inadequate to run the thing and dread the presentation horribly. The kids do well, but Green Stockings is quite an undertaking. It will be such a relief to be home one week from tomorrow to cast off my responsibility for a change and live lazily and with no one special. The first part of the time will be entirely minus social engagements. I shall revel in the restfulness. Then, the arrival of George to upset things again.

Thursday, March 25, 1920 • Hudson, New York

This day was full of many things. The kids balked on long lessons. They refused to respond to the music of Stevenson's prose in his "Travels."

Saturday, March 27, 1920 • Hudson, New York

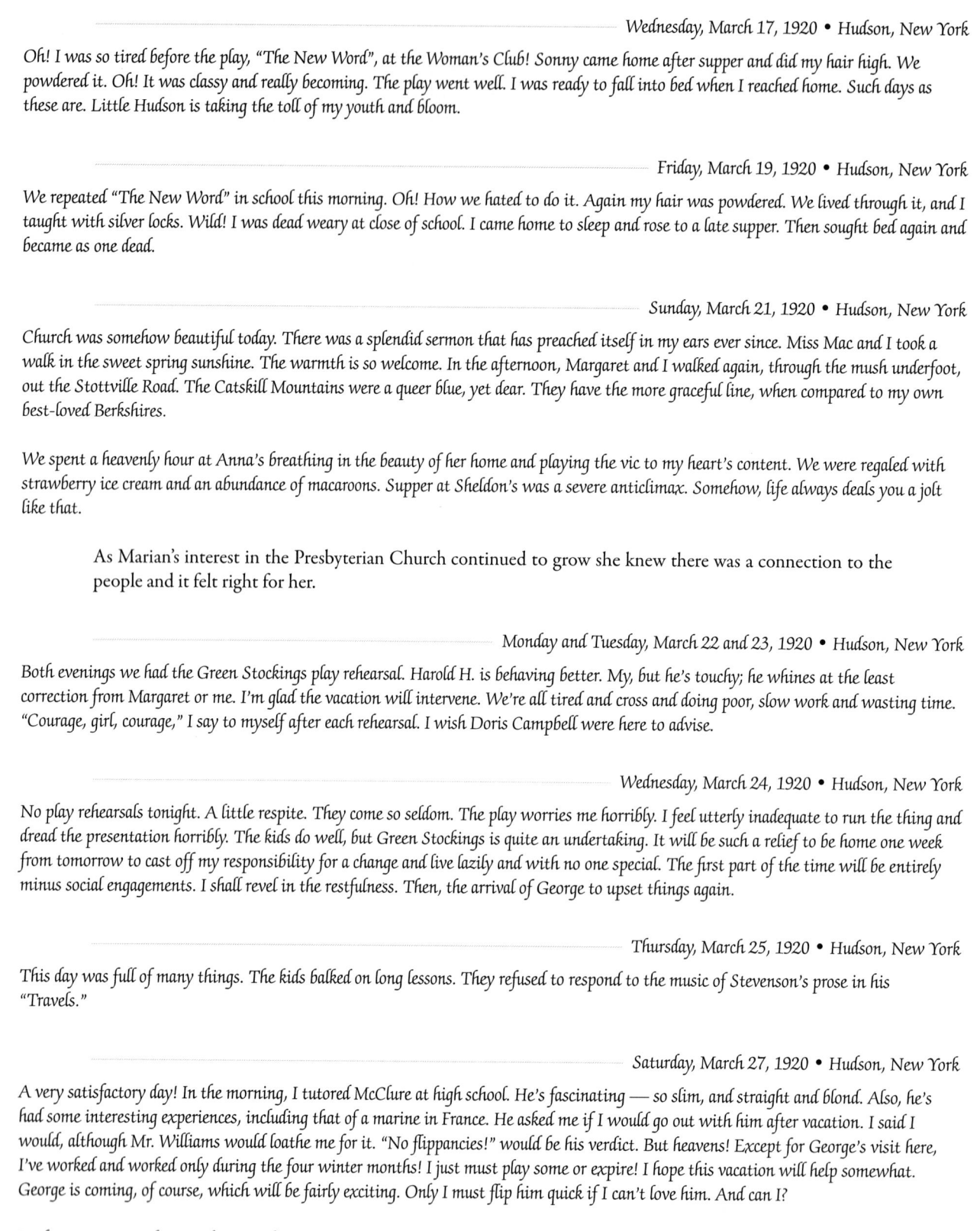

A very satisfactory day! In the morning, I tutored McClure at high school. He's fascinating — so slim, and straight and blond. Also, he's had some interesting experiences, including that of a marine in France. He asked me if I would go out with him after vacation. I said I would, although Mr. Williams would loathe me for it. "No flippancies!" would be his verdict. But heavens! Except for George's visit here, I've worked and worked only during the four winter months! I just must play some or expire! I hope this vacation will help somewhat. George is coming, of course, which will be fairly exciting. Only I must flip him quick if I can't love him. And can I?

In the evening, I took "Grandma" to the movies. Everyone in Hudson was at the Playhouse. Such a mob. A week from tonight I'll be home! So much has happened since I last saw the folks – regrets, snow galore, debate, Woman's Club play, George, Utica, etc.

Wednesday, April 11, 1920 • Hudson, New York

This was a day. In the evening we all went to the big gym exhibit at the Armory. It was fine; Hudson school in full array and such a mob of spectators. After the exhibit Miss MacMaster and I went up to Daytons. Suddenly out of the clear sky my student Clifford B. appeared. In a calm steady voice he said, "Will you chaperone a little party of us tonight at Jim's?" "Sure" I said. "Be around in fifteen minutes." I took Miss Mac home.

It was a wild affair and perhaps I have made a conquest of Jim, it looked that way. He's attractive and rich. We went to his house in Columbiaville. His family is southern. We had cocktails first, danced to the "vic" and later coffee and hot dogs in the kitchen. Jim's brother, a noted wild one around town, appeared. He's a dream looker but dangerous. We didn't start home until two am. How he did kiss me when we said goodnight. "Little girl," he said "you're all right. We'll have fun this spring." Yet somehow I doubt it I will ever see him again.

I couldn't sleep - heard the Presby clock strike five am.

Thursday, April 12, 1920 • Springfield, Massachusetts

I was a fag for school today.

We left on the 4.55 pm train, K. Ferris and I. I was so excited about getting home. Father was at the station. How I did hug mother! They're curious to see George next weekend. My vacation has begun. So, soon, it will be over.

> This was the last diary entry by Marian. I will never know why she stopped so abruptly. There was so much left to tell. Did other journals somehow get lost? We will never know.
>
> Fortunately, I was able to put puzzle pieces of Marian's life after 1920 together with the help of the archivists at Mount Holyoke. In the years following graduation, the college stayed in contact with Marian through confidential address lists, directory information, Alumni Registry, and most importantly personal letters from Marian to Dean Purington and Miss Voorhees of the Placement Bureau, which they kept in her file. These letters provided a new layer of understanding about my grandmother and her life after the diaries ended.
>
> I am grateful to the archivists. The mission statement at the bottom of their emails says it all: "The mission of Mount Holyoke College Archives and Special Collections is to help people transform their lives and our communities through active participation with history, culture, and creativity." Once again, I learned why Mount Holyoke meant so much to my grandmother.
>
> Would Marian get engaged to George? Would Marian's dreams come true? Would Marian fall for a "Doughboy"? The Epilogue follows them through the good and the bad times.

CHAPTER SEVEN

EPILOGUE

Optimism was in the air! The "Roaring Twenties" in post-war America, known for flappers, jazz, and gin, brought economic prosperity, as well as cultural and artistic dynamism to Americans. This era witnessed notable milestones, particularly for women.

On August 18, 1920, the long awaited Nineteenth Amendment to the United States Constitution was ratified: "The rights of citizens of the United States to vote shall not be denied or abridged by the United States or by any State on account of sex." When women went to the polls to vote for the first time in 1920, they "made up an estimated one-third of the voters. Mainly, they voted for Warren Harding, who turned out to be one of the worst presidents in American history. He had stuffed his platform with female-friendly promises like equal pay for equal work, an end to child labor, and more women appointees to government positions – none of which came to pass. "But his attraction was probably the same for both sexes — the promise of a return to "normalcy" after the war and the turmoil that followed it." (Collins)

Technology altered post-war lifestyles in America, including the introduction of the radio in 1921. "By 1929, a third of all American households were listening to the radio, the vast majority every day." (Collins) No longer were American lives spent in silence at home. The car continued to radically change American's lives as well. "In the 1920's most American families acquired cars, and there was no real question whether women would be allowed in the driver's seat." (ibid) Strangely for someone so independent, Marian never learned how to drive a car; she continued to take cabs or public transportation the rest of her life.

Despite her participation in all of the changes and advances for women, Marian continued to crave a traditional lifestyle. In earnest, Marian continued to search for the right man, sometimes doubting whether she ever really would find him. She had decided that George Sheppard was not the one for her and told him so. In fact, her Mount Holyoke friend, "Pris" Spaulding, who was working for the newspaper in Springfield, started dating George after Marian and George parted ways.

Marian had a contract in hand for another year of teaching at Hudson High School and believed her dreams were coming true. She loved teaching and "wanted to stick by Hudson." Maybe she could finally put her constant money worries aside, embrace the twenties, and start a new chapter in her life. Marian knew she loved teaching but wanted more. Outside of school, Marian attended the First Presbyterian Church with her dear friend, Miss MacMaster, the principal of a grammar school. She was a friend whom Marian enjoyed "ever so much." She wrote: "Miss MacMaster and I have acquired a pew of our very own." As Marian met more church members, she knew the First Presbyterian Church was the right place for her. Still, Marian's search for true love was always on her mind. She carefully copied this poem by the poet Henry Van Dyke into her diaries. The title is a French word which means to "meet." Marian probably thought she might meet someone special in her future, by a chance encounter or "recontre" at a feast day or "en fete"!

"Recontre"

Oh, was I born too soon, my dear, or were you born too late,
That I am going out the door while you come in the gate?
For you the garden blooms galore, the castle is en fete;
You are the coming guest, my dear,--for me the horses wait.
I know the mansion well, my dear, its rooms so rich and wide;
If you had only come before I might have been your guide,
And hand in hand with you explore the treasures that they hide;
But you have come to stay, my dear, and I prepare to ride.
Then walk with me an hour, my dear, and pluck the reddest rose
Amid the white and crimson store with which your garden glows,--
A single rose,--I ask no more of what your love bestows;
It is enough to give, my dear,--a flower to him who goes.
The House of Life is yours, my dear, for many and many a day,
But I must ride the lonely shore, the Road to Far Away:
So bring the stirrup-cup and pour a brimming draught, I pray,
And when you take the road, my dear, I'll meet you on the way.

Henry Van Dyke

Unbeknownst to Marian, former ambulance driver Howard Rainey, a WWI Doughboy who had returned from the war almost one year before, was sitting with his family in a pew nearby at the First Presbyterian Church. Howard was discharged on April 26, 1919 but Marian did not mention a single word about him in her diary before she entered her last page almost a year later on April 20, 1920.

The Rainey families were lifelong members of the First Presbyterian Church of Hudson which was founded in 1793. In the 1800's, the Robert Rainey family found exactly what they were looking for in America: a church where they could worship freely. Howard's father, S. Mitchell, was a member of the church since 1888 (when he was 17 years old). He became a Trustee in 1913, a Treasurer in 1920, and a member of the Board of Ruling Elders, known as The Session, until his passing in 1960. The Rainey family roots were firmly planted in the First Presbyterian Church. Marian instinctively felt the warmth from the members at the First Presbyterian Church. Something pulled her there that would influence her life.

After returning to Hudson in the fall of 1920 to begin her second year of teaching, Marian and Miss Mac continued to faithfully attend Sunday service at the Presbyterian Church. It was during this school year that Marian finally had her chance encounter with Howard. I am sure Marian's attraction was immediate. With the image of ambulance drivers romanticized in novels and movies, Marian was curious about Howard's worldly adventures. He was what she had been looking for: attractive, polished, educated, and respectful – a real gentleman. He had a quiet and reserved nature that didn't push Marian too quickly. As the only child of S. Mitchell Rainey, a banker in town and a respected member of the church and community, he already enjoyed a position in small town Hudson society. Howard was a businessman working in freight management after the war. Since both of them were only children, they understood the importance of close family ties. Two lonely souls were each looking for the love of his and her life.

Marian's decision to stay in Hudson for a second year of teaching proved to be the right one. When she signed her contract in February of 1920, Marian was hesitant about being away from her parents for another year. Marian wrote in her diary: "I can't realize I've signed up to stay here (Hudson), but it's true because I can look at the visible contract. The folks phoned me last night. They weren't over pleased it seemed to me."

After spending more time with Howard and his family, Marian knew he was "the one." She needed a husband who would accept and love her for the strong woman she was. And, Howard was that man. Perhaps on some level it appealed to her that she could be the strong one, the ambitious one. The war had changed Howard in ways that exposed his vulnerabilities

Marian loved this poem by Henry Van Dyke that speaks so clearly about the kind of man Marian found in Howard:

"Four Things"

Four things a man must learn to do
If he would make his record true:
To think without confusion clearly;
To love his fellow man sincerely;
To act from honest motives purely;
To trust in God and Heaven securely.

Henry Van Dyke

Marian and Howard were destined to find each other and become the best they both could be on life's journey together. It was not going to be a traditional journey. For her day, Marian wanted more than most women: to be able to work full time. Howard was just the man to support Marian along the way. It all seemed so simple back then. It was their religious faith that brought Robert Rainey to America, and that same faith brought Howard and Marian together. In April of 1921, Marian and Howard proudly announced their engagement.

Marian and Howard 1921

Marian tucked this quote by Bishop Jeremy Taylor (1633) into her diary which described his outlook on love and marriage. The quote gives a sense of reality for the future without presenting overly optimistic expectations for married life. Marian must have thought there was an element of truth to his opinion or she wouldn't have saved it so carefully.

"Marriage hath in it less of beauty but more of safety, than the single life;
it hath more care, but less danger, it is more merry, and more sad;
it is fuller of sorrows, and fuller of joys;
it lies under more burdens, but it is supported by all the strengths of love and charity,
and those burdens are delightful."

Bishop Jeremy Taylor

After living and working in Hudson for two years, Marian returned to Springfield to live with her parents, teaching English at Buckingham Junior High School from 1921-23. Howard followed her there, renting his own apartment. At the time of their engagement, Howard was working in Springfield as a broker at Myron S. Hall, Investment Bankers of New York. His salary was $3,900 per year ($3,900 in 1923 dollars would be worth $54,166 today). The job opportunities for Howard in Springfield with a population of 130,000 were greater than the small river town of Hudson with a population of 7,000.

As a stock broker, Howard experienced one of the greatest bull markets recorded in U.S. history from 1922 to 1929. During this time period, the Dow-Jones Industrials Average (DJIA) rose from 91 points in 1922 to 290 points in 1929, a 218.7% increase in value. "This is equivalent to an 18% annual growth rate in value for the seven years."(economichistory.net) Share prices continued to rise, which encouraged buying. Many bought on margin, with borrowed money, creating problems when the market crashed. Marian had no reason to doubt Howard's ability to support their family.

The big day finally arrived! On September 29, 1923, Marian and Howard were married in an intimate ceremony, surrounded by family and attendants, at the Viets' favorite church, Faith Congregational Church in Springfield, Massachusetts. The following poem is from Marian and Howard's wedding keepsake book:

"Our Bridal Chimes"

"Down from the gray old steeple,
Where the swift-winged swallow dwells.
Softly floats the music
Of the joyful bridal bells;
While on the kneeling lover,
Before the altar place,
Falleth the primal blessing,
With its sweet abiding grace."

Adelaide S. Jordan

Marian entered this poem into her diary with hopes that Howard would envy her and long to love her as his wife.

"Lover's Envy"

"I envy every flower that blows
Along the meadows where she goes,
And every bird that sings to her,
And every breeze that brings to her
The fragrance of the rose.

I envy every poet's rhyme
That moves her heart at eventime,
And every tree that wears for her,
Its brightest bloom, and bears for her
The fruitage of its prime.

I envy every Southern night
That paves her path with moonbeams white,
And silvers all the leaves for her,
And in their shadow weaves for her
A dream of dear delight.

I envy none whose love requires
Of her a gift, a task that tires:
I only long to live to her,
I only ask to give to her
All that her heart desires.

Henry Van Dyke

Simultaneously, Marian's dear friend Priscilla "Pris" Spaulding who had been working at the newspaper in Springfield since graduation from Mount Holyoke became engaged to Marian's previous suitor, George Sheppard. Coincidentally, "Pris" and George were married the same day as Marian and Howard. Many years later, "Pris" wrote my dad a letter saying that she and George "attended the Viets-Rainey wedding by waiting over the few hours in between." Pris and Marian had been friends since high school and the Mount Holyoke days and stayed in touch as part of the "Robin's Gang" with their round robin circulated letters. Marian and Pris would always be dear sisters and "Robins!" Now they would always share a very special day: their wedding day.

Following their wedding, Marian listed her present occupation as "Household Management" in the Mount Holyoke 1923 Alumnae Questionnaire. She taught a summer session at the high school in 1924 in Springfield, Massachusetts, but she put her full-time teaching aside to be a traditional wife to Howard, volunteering at the YMCA just as her mother did.

Joy of joys! My father, Clarke Mitchell Rainey, was born on August 1, 1927, in Springfield, Massachusetts. It was not an easy delivery. As a result of an emergency procedure performed following his delivery, Clarke had no belly button – a distinction that marked him as unique from birth. (If someone didn't believe my dad, he would always pull up his shirt to prove it!) Marian was also told that Clarke must be her only child, for safety's sake. Marian and Howard were both only children, so the tradition continued. Marian copied this poem into her diaries about having a son - probably quite an eye opener for Marian, especially after attending an all-female college and lacking brothers.

"The Way of a Boy"

This is the way a boy comes home,
and the way it shall ever be:
A scamper of feet through the leaf and loam
And the chase of a vagrant bee;
A coat cast off and quite forgot,
A whistle and ringing cheer.
And a romp near every well-known spot
On the way from There to Here.

This is the way a boy makes haste,
And the way it has ever been:
A squirrel seen is a squirrel chased.
And a top is made to spin;
A tree's to climb and a brook's to wade,
And the shade is a place to lie
After the zest of the game that's played
When the sun is hot and high.

This is the path a boy calls straight:
By every winding way
Where berries are or wild birds wait
Or squirrels dart at play;
By banks that bid you sit and cool
Two dusty feet and brown
In the pebbly shallows of the pool
That's on the way from town.

> This is the errand swiftly done,
> As doing shall ever be:
> An ounce of care to the pound of fun,
> And an hour that grows to three;
> A fence to climb and a rail to stride,
> With berries to hunt and share.
> And a breathless quarter hour beside
> A timid woodchuck's lair.
>
> And this is the thing that a boy calls Care
> And the thing it shall ever be:
> An old straw hat that's lost somewhere
> In the shade of some far-off tree;
> A shirt that's damp or trousers rent,
> A bruise or a hornet's sting
> And lagging footsteps choreward bent
> In the soft twilights of spring.
>
> So these are the ways that boys all know,
> And so may they ever be;
> Fancies as fickle as winds that blow,
> And dreams as wide as the sea;
> Heaven above where the blue sky smiles,
> With no day overlong.
> And a whistle of merry tunes that whiles
> A whole world into song.
>
> James W. Foley

While Marian loved her time spent as a wife and full-time mother, she grew restless and wanted to teach again. In 1928, Howard's job would take the family to Albany, New York, the state capital, about an hour and half away from Springfield. My dad, Clarke, was only a couple months old at the time. Marian was trying to plan ahead to have a job in place when she arrived in Albany. She contacted the placement director at Mount Holyoke for assistance but unfortunately, no positions were available at the time. Marian would continue in earnest to try to find work while Howard worked as a broker to provide for the family. Still, it was not Marian's nature to let her career end. She wanted to keep her finger in the pot and remain active.

That spring, in May 1928, Marian updated her classmates in the Mount Holyoke publication, *The Ninth Wave*, about her important milestones since graduation nine years ago. Marian wrote, "Marian Viets (Mrs. Howard Rainey) of Albany, New York, is the mother of Clarke, born August 1, 1927. During the last year she gave talks to women's clubs on Willa Cather and the Bronte sisters." Although Marian was not working, she kept active giving talks, continuously enriching her knowledge of literature, especially American and British novels. Marian loved reading about her Mount Holyoke sister's lives. She always valued her friendships as if they were family, through all of life's ups and downs they were there for her. This letter from Bishop Jeremy Taylor in 1657 was in reply to "The Most Ingenious and Excellent Mrs. Katherine Phillips" about friendships. Marian clipped it out of a newspaper and pasted it into her diary. I left the words exactly as they were written several hundred years ago.

"The Imperfect Grace of Our Friendships"

> "So that to your question, how far a clear and perfect friendship is authorized by the principles of Christianity?- The answer is ready and easie. It is warranted to extend to all Mankind; and the more we love the better we are and the greater our friendships are, the dearer we are to God; let them be as dear, and let them be as perfect, and let them be as many as you can; there is no danger in it; only when the restraint begins, there begins our imperfection; it is not ill that you entertain inane friendships and worthy societies; it were well if you could love and if you could benefit all mankind; for I conceive that is the summe of all friendship.

I confess this is not to be expected of us in this world; but as all our graces here are but imperfect, that is, at the best they are but tendencies to glory, so our friendships are imperfect, too, and but beginnings of a celestial friendship, by which we shall love everyone as much as they can be loved. But even so we must love in our proportion, and indeed that is it that can make the difference; we must be friends to all: that is, apt to do good, loving them really, and doing to them all the benefits we can, and which they are capable of. The Friendship is equal to all the world, and of itself hath no difference but it is differenced only by accidents, and by the capacity or incapacity of them that receive it."

Marian would never lose the bond of her imperfect friendships with her Mount Holyoke sisters. She would love them as much as if they were blood sisters, although distance separated them more and more.

As Marian was beginning her new life in Albany, she was unable to visit her grandparents in E. Granby as often as she wished. When she was able to travel to the Clark farm, she noticed how much her Grandma and Grandpa Clark aged. In 1928, Marian received sad news of dear Grandma Myra Smith Clark's passing at the age of 82. Grandma Clark's love for her only grandchild was unconditional. She nurtured Marian throughout her life to follow her dreams. Grandma Clark attended Mount Holyoke College for one year as a member of the class of 1867; she was not as fortunate as her granddaughter to call herself a Mount Holyoke graduate. But, they always shared the "sisterhood" bond.

Gertrude Clark Viets, B.P. Clark (seated), Marian Viets Rainey and Clarke Rainey
October 7th, 1928

During this era, Americans increasingly moved away to cities, forsaking the agricultural lifestyle that was Marian's relatives livelihood. B.P. Clark's two sons, Charles and Daniel, were both tobacco farmers on the Clark land in E. Granby but neither had children to pass on their legacy. With changing times, only 30% of the population farmed in 1920, compared to 49% of employed persons who farmed in 1880. Marian wrote in her diary after a visit to E. Granby in 1918: "Grandpa and Grandma have grown so old, and they seem so weary. Who would not after years of early rising, and late lying down, and no time in between to draw a quick breath?"

With failing health and no one to inherit his farm, B.P. Clark made the decision to sell the cherished Clark family house (and contents), which had been in the family for five generations. The house, built in Turkey Hills, Connecticut in 1737 by Joel Clark (B.P.'s great grandfather), was such a classic example of Americana that it ended up in a museum. B.P sold it to a New York investor and collector of antiques, Francis P. Garvan, an 1897 Yale graduate. Garvan had the house "carefully dismantled and he donated six of its rooms to the Yale Art Gallery" (Springman) where two rooms displayed as "strikingly good examples of the best architecture of upper class homes of their period." (ibid)

One year after grandma's passing, in 1929, her husband, B.P. Clark passed away at 89 years old. All of the hard work, long hours, strenuous labor, and stressful weather conditions on the farm provided a very long life for Marian's grandparents whom she loved so deeply. It was here in the town of E. Granby, Connecticut – the offspring of three towns, Windsor, Simsbury, and Granby - and the successor to Turkey Hills, that families passed on land to their children and grandchildren for generations – a way of life, which Marian witnessed.

With all of life's changes, Marian, Howard, and Clarke peacefully enjoyed their first year and a half in Albany, New York, including the frigid winters. Howard supported the family as a stockbroker while Marian raised Clarke. Being a mother meant so much to Marian. She learned patience, "remembered to bless" and unconditionally loved her little mite. This poem expresses Marian's love for Clarke so beautifully:

Clarke and Mother February, 1929

"With The Child"

They are such dear, familiar feet that go
Along the path with ours — feet fast or slow
And trying to keep pace: If they mistake,
Or tread upon some flower we would take
Upon our breast, or bruise some reed,
Or crush poor hope until it bleed,
We must be mute,
Not turning quickly to impute
Grave fault: for they and we
Have such a little way to go — can be
Together such a little while along the way —
We will be patient while we may.

So many little faults we find!
We see them, for not blind
Is love. We see them, but if you and I
Perhaps remember them, some by and by,
They will not be
Faults then — grave faults — to you and me,
But just odd ways — mistakes, or even less —
Remembrances to bless.
Days change so many things — yes hours:
We see so differently in sun and showers.
Mistaken words to-night
May be so cherished by to-morrow's light.
We must be patient: for we know
There's such a little way to go.

George Kringle
In the Christian Advocate

Unexpectedly, the lives of many Americans were turned upside down on October 29, 1929, otherwise known as "Black Tuesday," when the Dow Jones Industrial Average fell 23 percent." (topics.nytimes.com) The market dropped from an average high of 290 in 1929 to an average of 225.8 points in 1930. Howard's career as a stock broker was precarious. The euphoria of the "Roaring Twenties" was over.

The stock market crash was only the beginning of the Great Depression; a worldwide economic crisis ensued. "From 1929 to 1932, about 5,000 banks went out of business. 13 million people become unemployed. In 1932, 34 million people belonged to families with no regular full-time wage earner." (Wikipedia.org/wiki/Great_Depression) Industrial production fell by nearly 45% between 1929 and 1932. "Some 6,000 street vendors walked the streets of New York City in 1930 trying to sell apples for 5 cents. Thousands of homeless families camped out on the Great Lawn at Central Park in New York City, which was an empty reservoir during the Great Depression." (great-depression-facts.com) Concerns over how long this would last pervaded society. Since Marian and Clarke depended on Howard's livelihood as a stockbroker, this was a crushing blow to their family.

The Depression continued, and Marian and Howard were running out of money. Howard borrowed against their life insurance policies for income. The unemployment rate in America had soared past 20 percent, and Howard had become a part of that statistic. The DJIA continued to fall to an average of 134.1 points in 1931, with hopes of a recovery looking bleak. "From 1929 to 1932 stocks lost 73% of their value." (economichistory.net) Unbeknownst to Howard, the stock market wouldn't return to pre-depression levels until 1954. Howard's chosen field would not allow him to earn enough to support his family. Although reinventing himself would be difficult, he needed to find an alternate career. Marian had grown up watching her father struggle to provide for their family. While her mother did not have the skills to find employment to ease the stress, Marian knew she was different. She had a college degree and several years of full-time teaching experience. Out of necessity, she had to become the stable provider for her family.

A poignant song, titled "*Brother Can you Spare a Dime*?" popularized by Bing Crosby hit the charts in 1932. It was an anthem representing the shattered dreams of Howard's generation in the Depression era. The composer, Jay Gorney, wrote the song "to make people think." (www.wikipedia.com) The men who built the nation and fought in the war, such as Howard, were no longer needed and "find themselves abandoned and in bread lines?" (ibid) Had the system failed this generation? Howard and over four million Doughboys "sludged through hell" with "guns to bear," as the lyrics aptly said, only to return to their own personal nightmares. The Doughboys became the forgotten soldiers from the forgotten war, and Howard was one of them. It had been Howard's dream to serve his country, but the reality of the war and its aftermath were brutal. There weren't many programs in place to help soldiers find jobs; offer tuition to go back to college; or get other needed support. Moreover, many Doughboys suffered silently from depression, shellshock, and anxiety after the horrors they saw in Europe.

The following poem by John Masefield spoke to Marian as she and Howard struggled to be truthful about the Great Depression and how it was affecting their family.

"Truth"

Man with his burning soul
Has but an hour of breath
To build a ship of truth
In which his soul may sail —
Sail on the sea of death,
For death takes toll
Of beauty, courage, youth,
Of all but truth.

Life's city ways are dark,
Men mutter by; the wells
Of the great waters moan.
O death! O sea! O tide!
The waters moan like bells;
No light, no mark,
The soul goes out alone
On seas unknown.

Stripped of all purple robes,
Stripped of all golden lies,
I will not be afraid,
Truth will preserve through death.
Perhaps the stars will rise —
The stars like globes;
The ship my striving made
May see night fade.

John Masefield

No longer was it a choice whether Marian would work full time or not. Howard was out of work and out of time. It was a harsh reality, but one that she embraced.

In the spring of 1932, no longer able to afford to rent a place in Albany, Marian and her family moved home to Springfield to live with her parents. If Marian could find a job, her mother could take care of Clarke. They felt fortunate to have a place to stay. During the depression, many people "drifted from town to town looking for non-existent jobs. Many more lived at the edges of cities in makeshift shantytowns their residents derisively called Hoovervilles" (topic.nytimes.com) nicknamed after President Hoover.

Clarke was almost five years old now and starting school. Marian longed for some stability for her son so she again contacted Miss Voorhees at Mount Holyoke searching for a job, to no avail. Teaching jobs were scarce. By 1932, Marian was becoming more and more anxious about the Depression. When would things get better? The Presidential election in 1932 brought hope for America.

Herbert Hoover, elected in 1928, spent three out of the four years of his term with the country mired in the Great Depression. Franklin D. Roosevelt (FDR) ran his campaign promising progressive reform known as "The New Deal." On Tuesday November 28, 1932, incumbent Republican President Herbert Hoover lost the election in a landslide to FDR. Roosevelt took office on March 4, 1933. With an unemployment rate of almost 25% where 13 million people became unemployed, and a banking crisis, Americans were counting on FDR for a turn around. From 1933 to 1944, FDR gave 30 Fireside Chats. Americans listened intently to these speeches on their radios, hanging onto every word. His infamous declaration that "the only thing we have to fear is fear itself" stuck with Marian as she stoically did her best to face the future. Marian would not let fear destroy her family.

In the winter of 1933, Marian's dear father Samuel died unexpectedly of a heart attack at 64 years of age. At the time of death, as an insurance agent working on a commission basis, Samuel had seen his income drastically diminished. As the Depression worsened, Samuel was overcome by hopelessness and illness.

The following poem by Mr. Longfellow is appropriately entered into the preface of the *Genealogy of the Viets Family* (1902) as it so aptly refers to the loss one feels following a death. In the sixth stanza, Mr. Longfellow is referring to the death of his wife, Mrs. Longfellow, in 1835.

"The Footsteps of Angels"

When the hours of Day are numbered,
And the voices of the Night
Wake the better soul, that slumbered,
To a holy, calm delight;

Ere the evening lamps are lighted,
And, like phantoms grim and tall,
Shadows from the fitful firelight
Dance upon the parlor wall;

Then the forms of the departed
Enter at the open door;
The beloved, the true-hearted,
Come to visit me once more;

He, the young and strong, who cherished
Noble longings for the strife,
By the roadside fell and perished,
Weary with the march of life!

They, the holy ones and weakly,
Who the cross of suffering bore,
Folded their pale hands so meekly,
Spake with us on earth no more!

And with them the Being Beauteous,
Who unto my youth was given,
More than all things else to love me,
And is now a saint in heaven.

With a slow and noiseless footstep
Comes that messenger divine,
Takes the vacant chair beside me,
Lays her gentle hand in mine.

> *And she sits and gazes at me*
> *With those deep and tender eyes,*
> *Like the stars, so still and saint-like,*
> *Looking downward from the skies.*
>
> *Uttered not, yet comprehended,*
> *Is the spirit's voiceless prayer,*
> *Soft rebukes, in blessings ended,*
> *Breathing from her lips of air.*
>
> *Oh, though oft depressed and lonely,*
> *All my fears are laid aside,*
> *If I but remember only*
> *Such as these have lived and died!*
>
> Henry Wadsworth Longfellow

Samuel was buried in East Granby near his parents and family members. Marian had identified with and admired her father throughout her life because he took a risk to branch away from farming and try a new career in the city. Marian drew strength from her father to take risks of her own and have a career when most women did not, and her father supported her in her endeavor. Even though Marian's father was not very successful, Marian never resented their meager lifestyle. Nevertheless, Marian desired a more stable lifestyle for her family than her father was able to provide.

Amongst all of the papers my dad left behind, I found Samuel's estate papers. He left approximately $14 (today's dollars only $256) in cash, dividends and commissions, and $2,560 ($45,542 in today's dollars) in personal property in his will to his wife, Gertrude. Samuel's death, and the little money that was left after paying for the cost of the funeral, flowers, doctor bills, and fees, forced his widow to downsize to a smaller apartment without room for Marian and her family. It surprised me that an insurance agent left his widow without an insurance policy. Likely they did not have the funds to keep a policy active. This unfortunate circumstance left Marian and her family homeless again and jobless.

The tone of desperation became stronger and stronger in Marian's letters to Miss Voorhees at Mount Holyoke. With her father's passing, Marian realized she became responsible for her mother also. With Howard unemployed, their family was surviving on Marian's substitute teaching positions, which did not even pay enough to rent an apartment of their own. Their only option was to move to Hudson to live with Howard's parents. In March of 1933, the young Rainey family moved in with Howard's parents. They hoped it would be temporary until they could get their feet back on the ground. Clarke would start a new school in Hudson. By now he was in first grade. Marian continued her job search in earnest.

> *March 22, 1933*
>
> *426 Allen St.*
> *Hudson, NY*
>
> *My dear Miss Voorhees,*
>
> *Again I am writing in the hope that the Bureau may have a position for me this spring. The hope is faint, I know, for teachers are not changing or resigning. I was in Springfield through the winter and had some substituting in the high schools. My father died in January and on the first of March mother broke up our home and I had no place to stay in Springfield. I could not afford to pay room and board with uncertain times from irregular teaching days.*
>
> *Now my need for a position is all the greater for I must contribute to the support of my mother. She can go with me wherever I could find a position.*
>
> *I appreciate all your interest and help and realize how hard it is to find positions for any graduates now.*
>
> *Sincerely yours,*
> *Mrs. Marian Viets Rainey*

Despite all of Marian's fear and desperation, she remained always hopeful for her family's future. By example, her father had taught her to persevere in the roughest of times. With mounting pressure to support her mother as well, Marian remained graceful, determined and optimistic. I am so grateful I discovered Marian's diaries and was able to learn what a strong woman she was.

The Great Depression reached its depths in 1933; Marian and Howard continued to feel the effects. They struggled to get by, without a house or apartment to call their own, searching for almost non-existent work in Hudson. Howard's parents had graciously offered Howard, Marian, and Clarke, and Marian's mother, a temporary home with them. The Rainey's two-story, Queen Anne home, built in 1900, stood on Allen Street, one of the coveted historic streets in Hudson. With four bedrooms, the house provided ample room for everyone. Marian and Howard were fortunate to have such a lovely home to live until they found jobs and were settled in a place of their own. And, they were equally fortunate that the Raineys had lived a successful yet frugal lifestyle over the years in Hudson. Howard's parents had always supported him throughout his life and now continued to support him, as well as his extended family, in these extremely difficult times. To get through these hard times Marian and Howard had to believe in themselves and their "work done squarely" and the quality of their characters, as expressed in this poem:

"Under The Old Elm Tree" (Verse VI)

The longer on this earth we live
And weigh the various Qualities of men,
Seeing how most are fugitive,
Or fitful gifts, at best, of now and then,
Wind-wavered corpse-lights, daughters of the fen,
The more we feel the high stern-featured beauty
Of plain devotedness to duty,
Steadfast and still, nor paid with mortal praise,
But finding amplest recompense
For life's ungarlanded expense
In work done squarely and unwasted days.
For this we honor him, that he could know
How sweet the service and how free
Of her, God's eldest daughter here below,
And chose in meanest raiment which was she.

James Russell Lowell

James Russell Lowell (1819-1891) was an American Romantic poet, critic, professor at Harvard, editor and diplomat. He was associated with the group known as the Fireside Poets of 19th Century American poets from New England. These poets used conventional form in their poetry, making them suitable for families entertaining at the fireside. They believed that they could use poetry as reform, and a critic of society. In 1857, Mr. Lowell was the first editor of the *Atlantic Monthly* with the "stamp of high literature and bold speech on public affairs." (www.wikipedia.org) "Under the Elm" was read at the 100th anniversary of Washington taking command of the American Army under an elm tree at Cambridge.

Following FDR's inauguration on March 4, 1933, the first one hundred days of his administration saw sweeping legislation move the country in the right direction, particularly within the banking industry. As fear and panic set in across America, many people had rushed to banks to cash out their accounts and then stuffed their money under their mattresses for safe keeping. To ease this panic, on March 6, 1933 President Franklin D. Roosevelt declared a banking holiday, temporarily closing all U.S. banks. Great changes would be made in the banking industry to give individuals more security and to restore faith in the institutions.

Fortunately, the Hudson City Savings Institution (HCSI) where Howard's father, S. Mitchell Rainey, continued to effectively serve as Treasurer and Trustee was somewhat of an anomaly during the Depression. The HCSI "remained open, sound as ever, with total assets exceeding $11 million and reserves of $800,000." (HudsonCitySavingsBankonline.com) Following in his father's footsteps, my great grandfather, S. Mitchell, was well respected in the city of Hudson for his conservative banking policies at the HCSI. Chartered in 1850, the HCSI was the 19th oldest savings bank in the State of New York. Members of the Rainey family, including S. Mitchell's father, Samuel Rossman Rainey, had been active at the bank since its formation. Samuel R. was a member of the Executive Committee and elected Chairman of the Executive Committee in 1898, a position which he held until his death in 1900.

While many U.S. banks were failing during the depression, HCSI was in the unique position to not only be surviving but also thriving. HCSI was a mutual savings bank which differs from a commercial bank in its method of ownership. The members who subscribed to the common fund were the owners, without any capital stock issued. Profits after deductions were shared between the members (www.wikipedia.com). The HCSI provided a safe place for members to save and invest; here the Hudson community felt secure. In 1934, the bank had 11,233 accounts with deposits of over nine million dollars. The bank had an excellent surplus: over 20%, at investment value. I can definitely see a link between my father and his grandfather, S. Mitchell, regarding their conservative fiscal policies. My dad, Clarke, was fortunate to have a remarkable role model while growing up under the auspices of his grandfather.

As noted in the book, "*Historic Hudson,*" there was also a bleaker side to the Hudson economy during this time period. "Hudson's economy was almost entirely dependent on one industry alone – the cement plants which made it even more difficult to find a job. The mills had closed and Prohibition (1920-1933) had brought an end to C. H. Evans & Co. Brewery. The city had, in effect, become a company town." (Fone) Neither Hudson nor America would recover from the Great Depression for more than a decade. One industry that did continue to flourish and even expand in Hudson in the 1930's was the long-established house of prostitution. "What had been founded as a Quaker town in the eighteenth century became known as the Northeast's bordello in the twentieth." (ibid) It wasn't until 1950 that a police raid shut down the city's brothels and gambling dens. I cannot imagine the frustration and humiliation my great grandfather, S. Mitchell, suffered as a conservative banker in this small river town that he and his family loved for so many years, seeing their town's reputation so tarnished.

In the fall of 1933, after seven long years of searching and worrying, Marian received word from her Hudson friend, Miss MacMaster: that a position was coming available for the January 1934 school year at Central Grammar School in Hudson where Miss MacMaster was a principal. A teacher was going to be dismissed for unknown reasons. Marian preferred teaching high school, but she did not have the luxury of turning away a junior high school position this time. All of her hopes and dreams were answered. Marian started her position as the Head of the English Department overseeing three other teachers of 7th and 8th grade English at Central Grammar School for the salary of $1,450 (equal to $25,000 in today's dollars). Even with Marian employed full time, their total income for a family of four was at poverty level. I wonder how they were able to survive on so little money. I think Howard's mother and father helped out however they could. Marian wouldn't let this job out of her tight grasp. She could finally breathe a sigh of relief and put some of her worries behind her. Clarke was seven years old now and could finally settle into one school without the prospect of being uprooted again. Across America, the unemployment rate was heading down slowly. Marian would never have another job. She did not want to put her family through the turmoil of uncertainty and moving from place to place again. Their roots were firmly planted in Hudson. And, with all the love and support from their family, Hudson was a great place to raise their son. Marian's determination and positive spirit kept the hope alive for her family that better days were ahead for them.

It had been a very difficult path back to Hudson, but one filled with promise for a better future. Marian knew Howard was a broken man probably from what he witnessed in the war, and as a result he was unable to hold down a job. But, their enduring love for each other survived the difficult times. As Marian became the main breadwinner for the family, Howard would dabble in stocks and run the household and take care of Clarke, his parents, and Marian's mother. Howard was assuming an unusual role for a man during this period of time. Marian loved Howard for what he gave to the family and for what a great father, son, and husband he was. They were each other's "love and light."

"Love and Light"

There are many kinds of love, as many kinds of light,
And every kind of love makes a glory in the night.
There is a love that stirs the heart, and love that gives it rest.
But the love that leads life upward is the noblest and the best.

Henry Van Dyke

Until I researched my family genealogy, I never knew how much the Depression affected my dad the rest of his life. Of course, he never talked about it. Maybe it was too painful. My dad's family had been living below the poverty level for many years now, moving from house to house where they were welcomed by family. As teenagers we used to snicker at our dad when he tipped the valet parking attendant a quarter. We were so embarrassed! But, knowing how much a quarter meant to my dad his whole life, he probably thought he was being fair. We never knew the hardships our dad went through, never knowing where he would live next, or what school he would attend. After reading about his childhood, I can understand the quarter tips! I think my dad grew up thinking he always had to be the strong one on the outside but he was forever changed by his childhood memories.

Uncommon Sisters

Marian always kept her hope alive that her family would be able to support themselves in the future. She saved her Mount Holyoke yearbooks which held the memories of her Ivy Oration graduation speech which served as her motivation and inspiration for the rest of her life. I am sure it was a relief to Marian when she was able to write positive news in the publication *"Letters from the Class of 1919 in 1937"* eighteen years following graduation. In it, Marian submitted information about her job teaching English in Hudson and her son, born in 1927. Her entry sounded rather plain and uneventful compared to her friends. Conspicuously absent from this biography of her life was her husband's career. At this time, Marian confidentially listed their family income with the Appointment Bureau as a total of $2,000; $1,500 of which came from Marian's teaching salary. Marian was the main breadwinner; Howard dabbled in investments, bringing in his share of $500 a year. In today's dollars that is a household income of $32,787.00.

Marian's uncommon "sisters" lead very interesting lives and Marian lived vicariously through their travels and wealth.

The love of her "sisters" helped her endure the difficult times in years past. Their friendships were rich in love no matter how old they were or how many miles separated them. When I ran across this poem in Marian's diary I knew why she clipped it out and saved it. There was always potential in their friendships because each "sister" wanted it as much as the next one.

"The Word"

My friend, my bonny friend, when we are old,
And hand in hand go tottering down the hill,
May we be rich in love's refined gold,
May love's gold coin be current with us still.

May love be sweeter for the vanished days,
And your most perfect beauty still as dear
As when your troubled singer stood at gaze
In the dear March of a most sacred year.

May what we are be all we might have been,
And that potential, perfect, O my friend,
And may there still be many sheafs to glean
In our love's acre, comrade, till the end.

And may we find when ended is the page
Death but a tavern on our pilgrimage.

John Masefield

Marian enjoyed reading the "letters" about her friends in 1937, although most told of lives seemingly unaffected by the Great Depression. Many of Marian's Mount Holyoke friends travelled to Europe and owned several homes. Marian and Howard had not yet been able to purchase their first home. None of that seemed to matter to Marian; this was nothing new for her. Growing up, Marian's family moved out of their house and into an apartment during her senior year of high school. The Viets' family never owned a home again. As long as their family was together, whether in an apartment or a house, they were happy.

Marian's Mount Holyoke "sisters" came from families of wealth yet Marian did not seem to feel any jealousy. Rather, she felt sorry for her friends who never had to work. During senior year in 1919 when Marian took Doris Campbell to Skinner's farm one afternoon she wrote: "I took Doris and she earned 50 cents also. Bless her heart! It isn't her fault she hasn't earned money. She never had to." Marian found joy reading the Alumnae news from "cover to cover," catching up on friends' lives and staying close to one another.

By 1937, most of Marian's friends who were married and had children worked part time outside of the home if they worked at all; some continued their studies. Three of Marian's friends, Helen Francis, Elizabeth "Canary" McNarey, and "Dot" Williams, remained single eighteen years following graduation. They had careers or took care of their parents.

"Pris" Spaulding, who had married George Sheppard, combined work and family, gave violin lessons, and played in the Spartanburg and Greenville Symphonies. They owned the Carolina Suburban Gas Company in Laurens, South Carolina. Another friend, Margaret Gantt combined marriage, work and travel, as a statistician for Metropolitan Life. She spoke of an exotic trip to Dutch Guiana visiting the Saramaccaner Tribe.

Marian's senior roommate in Porter Hall, Doris Campbell (Mrs. Holsworth), continued her love of dramatics by coaching plays and pageants, acting, writing and teaching! During Marian's first year of teaching in Hudson, she wrote confidential, soul confession letter to Doris. "We tell each other everything, events, ambitions, thoughts, ideals - oh all the listing of things! It's good no one can x-ray that paper. Bless her! I wonder what will become of her – the stage or marriage, or something less appealing. We wonder together what that future holds. We peer down the road of future days." Doris was a dear lifelong friend to Marian. "Dot" Hall (Mrs. Howard Fish) raised their four sons and wrote "I'm rather proud of the above and feel no need as yet of an avocation." Hilda "Hild" Jones (Mrs. A.J. May) was a Director of Physical Education at the Eastman School of Music of Rochester, NY until she decided to stay home with her children. She wrote of: "The indoor sport of much entertaining with one maid, and the outdoor sport of keeping up with the boys."

In the summer of 1936, Marian "completed 6 hours in Education at the N.Y. State College for Teachers, Albany, and will finish the work next summer for my certificate, including Methods in Teaching Literature, Methods in Teaching Grammar, and Educational Psychology." In 1937, Marian received her New York State Teachers License, a necessity for her job.

Marian's thirst for learning would never end. In 1941, 1943, and 1946, some twenty years after graduation, to further her craft of writing, Marian attended summer sessions to work toward her Master's Degree in English at Middlebury's summer graduate school, Bread Loaf School of English, in Vermont. "The Bread Loaf Writers' Conference is one of America's most valuable literary institutions." (www.middlebury.edu) I am fortunate to have one of Marian's books *Shakespeare Criticism* from her time spent at Bread Loaf in 1941. The workshops, lectures, and classes, are held in the shadow of the Green Mountains. Bread Loaf "introduced generations of participants to rigorous practical and theoretical approaches to the craft of writing, and given America itself proven models of literary instruction." (ibid)

Education, service, family, and "sisters" were always more important to Marian than money.

Cooperstown

Growing up in small town Hudson, Clarke was doted on by both parents and three grandparents. Clarke was the only grandchild on both sides of his families. Of course, Clarke was fortunate to have one of the best teachers in town in his own house. The constant adoration and attention he received as an only child helped Clarke develop into a very self-confident young man, possibly even a bit over confident at times. Clarke proved a good student and a voracious reader, just like his mother.

During Clarke's elementary school years during the Great Depression, his family moved from town to town and Clarke moved from school to school. When the family finally settled down in Hudson in 1934, Clarke was seven years old. He should have been in second grade but he placed into third grade, essentially skipping a year. From outward appearances, Clarke looked older than most boys his own age, so being younger than his classmates never mattered.

When Clarke was twelve years old, his father heard on the news about a commemorative baseball game Monday, August 21, 1939 in nearby Cooperstown, New York. The Yankees were playing the Newark Bears to celebrate the 100th anniversary of baseball. After the game, Clarke had "the thrill of a lifetime" when the great Yankee Joe DiMaggio, consented to pose for pictures with him and give him his autograph. Joe DiMaggio was on the cusp of becoming one of the best baseball players in history, unbeknownst to Clarke. DiMaggio played for the Yankees from 1936-1951 and helped the New York Yankees to win nine World Series titles. He was inducted into the Baseball Hall of Fame in 1955.

The local news picked up on the story and ran an article in the *Hudson Daily Star* with the heading "Yankee Star Poses with Hudson Boy" - big news! Clarke looked very young standing next to a professional player in the picture, with his zipper partially open. This would be the first of many articles in the local paper about my dad.

Clarke and Joe DiMaggio 1939

World War II

America was headed to war again! World War I had been called the "war to end all wars" but apparently that wasn't true. For America, World War II began on December 7, 1941 when Japan attacked Pearl Harbor. War had been going on for years elsewhere. For the Chinese, "war began in 1931 when Japan invaded northeastern China, setting up a Japanese state called Manchukuo." In Europe, the "war began in 1939, when Germany invaded Poland." (nationalgeographic.com) Three days after the bombing at Pearl Harbor, Germany and Italy declared war on the United States. Just as America had tried to stay out of World War I, Americans had hoped to remain neutral during WWII. On December 8, 1941, President Franklin D. Roosevelt addressed Congress with his speech: "For a Declaration of War against Japan." Americans listened intently on their radios. It was only 22 years ago that Howard had returned home from Europe. Many Americans did not support another war; it seemed the First World War had not accomplished enough to prevent the second one.

In 1941, Clarke was only 14 years old, too young to enlist. The thought of sending her only son off to war frightened Marian. She could certainly relate to her mother in law's worries during WWI. Many of Marian's friends had older sons who enlisted while the mothers watched anxiously. While Marian's friends had started having children in their twenties, Marian was almost 30 years old when Clarke was born, making Clarke that much younger than her friend's children. Temporarily, Marian could escape the anxiety and worry that troubled mothers of soldiers in war. How long would World War II rage on?

As one can imagine, the apple didn't fall too far from the tree: Clarke excelled at Hudson High School. His activity list read as long as his mother's did when she was the same age. He participated as: the Class Treasurer, a Bond Salesman, a staff member on the *Owl* newspaper, an Honor Roll student, a "Charlatans" drama member as well as serving on the Nominating Committee, Dance Committee, and Service Committee. In addition, Clarke played Varsity tennis in the spring (which precluded him from baseball), Varsity Basketball in the winter, and interclass football in the fall. In the yearbook, his nickname was "Ace" and his main interest was "sports." It was obvious by the end of high school that Clarke was given a natural athletic gift; nevertheless, a gift alone is not enough unless it is nurtured. Combining his natural athletic ability with his self-confidence, he was a standout athlete.

In January 1944, with high school graduation on the horizon, Clarke decided to apply to Amherst College, a private liberal arts college with high academic standards, located in Amherst, Massachusetts, a few miles down the road from Mount Holyoke, where his mother went to college. Clarke had grown up admiring his great uncle Dan Clark who lived in E. Granby and was an alumnus of Amherst College. Dan reminisced with Clarke about his fond memories of Amherst College: music, speaking as the Class Ivy Orator, dramatics, and Phi Kappa Psi Fraternity. Following graduation, Dan had carried on the business of the family tobacco farm in E. Granby, Connecticut. He attended his Amherst Triennial class reunion and kept in touch with his friends, teachers, mentors, and the President Stanley King. Dan also served as a member of the Connecticut State Legislature in 1935 and 1937, a fact that Clarke also admired. Although Dan married, he never had any children so Clarke was a sort of surrogate child for Dan. Over the years, Dan convinced Clarke that Amherst was a very special place. If he ever had the chance to go to college, Amherst was where Clarke hoped to go.

On April 7, 1944, Clarke received his eagerly anticipated acceptance letter from Amherst College to start the summer term in June 1944 as a freshman. While Clarke would be several years younger than some of his classmates, his school record was satisfactory. As happy as Clarke was to be accepted, his mother was even happier. Instinctively, her son's Amherst acceptance caused conflicted emotions for Marian. She knew the numbers didn't add up for their family to be able to afford the tuition without aid. At this time, her teaching salary was $1,650 per year; not nearly enough for the $900 yearly tuition ($450 per semester) at Amherst. Howard's income was questionable and couldn't be relied upon to make the payments.

Realizing that scholarship money was scarce, Marian contacted her great uncle Dan "Umpa" Clark, to enlist his help finding Clarke scholarship money. Uncle Dan retained close ties to the right people at his alma mater. Without hesitation, Dan wrote a personal letter to President Stanley King, asking him to give Clarke's scholarship request his personal attention. By April 21, 1944, Dan received a response from "Stanley," as he called him, which Dan forwarded to Marian, writing: "I am enclosing this letter which I have just received from Stanley which lets you know he is giving your case his attention."

Great Uncle Daniel Clark, (Umpa) Amherst College Class of 1904

Luckily, Clarke received a scholarship from Amherst College of $175.00 per semester, enough for him to begin freshman year at the age of 16 years old. My instinct tells me that Uncle Dan participated financially with Clarke's tuition. Dan never had any children of his own, nor did his brother. And just as the Clark family doted on their only grandchild, Marian, the same was true for my dad, their only grandnephew and the only member of his generation.

In June of 1944, Clarke received not only his high school diploma but also his College Entrance Diploma from the University of the State of New York Education Department. Clarke also satisfactorily passed examinations at Hudson High School issued by the Regents. Three weeks after Clarke received word that he received a scholarship, he was setting off for the little town of Amherst, the all-male college cohort to his mother's beloved Mount Holyoke. My dad looked up to and respected his mother as the strong and accomplished woman she was. Howard was barely successful as a business man. He was a great father and son, but Howard just wasn't Clarke's kind of guy.

His mother had cut out the quaint poem about Amherst in 1915 and entered it into her diary not knowing that her son would be lucky enough to go to college there almost thirty years later. Quite a premonition!

"Little Town of Amherst"

"The little town of Amherst,
Set in the Pelham hills.
With four gray clocks to strike the hours.
And elms and daffodils:
Within this town of Amherst
The air with sunshine hills.

The spring comes back to Amherst
To foot it on the green.
Full many a lucent emerald
Upon her breast is seen;
She walks at dusk in Amherst,
Gypsy, but a queen.

And I have seen in Amherst
The lads stroll up and down
Singing songs in Amherst,
The summer-girded town.
The full, deep-throated choruses
Oblivion cannot drown.

The little town of Amherst,
She lies beneath the stars;
She kindles high endeavor
In ruddy avatars;
Her level-visioned sons go forth
To unexpected wars.

But she has struck upon them
The sword's touch of surprise.
And, set the flame unwithered
In their deep-seated eyes;
The little town of Amherst,
How peaceful still it lies!"

Willard Wattles

On June 27, 1944, Clarke packed his bags for Amherst, which probably took only a few minutes. I doubt there was very much to pack, given the scarce amount of clothes my dad ever wore; probably a couple of shirts and a couple pairs of pants was all he had or needed. My dad was one of those guys who never wore a coat. He never seemed to get cold. He would throw snowballs in our back yard in St. Louis without gloves or a hat. We always told him his hands would freeze! My dad was tough!

Clarke enthusiastically arrived at his dormitory as a wide-eyed, underage freshman at 16 years old. Since he was two years away from being eligible for the draft age of 18, it provided a unique opportunity for Clarke to attend Amherst College as a member of a larger than normal freshman class during war time. Attending Amherst College was a dream that barely seemed possible for his family. And, it was one that my dad appreciated his whole life.

As an all-male college, Amherst College was far from normal during the war: athletic teams, Glee Club, the Olio yearbook, "Masquers" theater performances, and fraternities were all put on hold. Only twelve students graduated in the class of 1944. Due to low enrollment, Amherst's budget was tight, but the school still tried to offer as many scholarships as possible to keep a quality student body. By 1945, they had 470 regular students, approximately one-third of the pre-war student body.

In the fall of 1944, Clarke walked onto the football team. In the winter he played on the basketball team. Clarke played both sports in high school so he was familiar with the games. During the war, teams were filled with students like Clarke, younger than 18 years old, or students who were unable to serve, and soldiers who had already returned from the war. In the spring of 1945, Clarke took a risk and decided to veer away from his high school sport of tennis to try something new. Clarke did not know too much about the game of baseball but decided to try out for the catcher position. The timing was right: there wasn't a lot of competition during the war. During spring training, Coach Eckley said it looked as if Clarke would be the club's backstop. However, at the last minute, the team's pitcher was called away by the draft. Desperate to find a mounds man, Eckley conducted an experiment to see who could throw the ball the hardest. "Rainey was chosen hands down, and then and there his career behind the plate came to an end." (The Amherst Student June 7, 1958)

According to the *Olio* Yearbook, "The 1945 baseball season opened on a wing and a prayer last year, with hardly enough candidates appearing to make two full teams. But when the season was completed, any pessimism on the part of the Jeff [Amherst is named for Lord Jeffrey Amherst] faithful was found to be totally unjustified for two reasons. The first and most important one was that the team completed a five game informal schedule without a defeat. Second, and almost equally important, was the outstanding pitching of Clarke Rainey. According to the comments of Coach Eckley, Rainey was one of the best pitchers he has ever seen at Amherst." (Olio Yearbook) This was the first undefeated (1.00) Amherst baseball team. Clarke ended his season with a 0.62 earned run average, an excellent record meaning he gave up less than one run per nine-inning game. The gamble that Clarke had taken trying a new sport paid off. The scouts were circling Amherst.

The Bomb

On August 6, 1945 the United States dropped the world's first uranium gun-type bomb on Hiroshima, Japan which immediately wiped out 90 percent of the city and "killed 80,000 people; tens of thousands more would later die of radiation exposure. Three days later, a second B-29 dropped another atomic bomb on the city of Nagasaki, Japan." (www.history.com) This horrific bomb killed an estimated 40,000 people. "Japan's Emperor Hirohito announced his country's unconditional surrender in a radio address on August 15, citing the devastating power of a new and most cruel bomb" (ibid) which would forever change the course of history.

After spring semester ended in 1945, shortly before he turned 18 years old, Clarke left Amherst College to enlist in the U.S. Navy, entering boot camp at Sampson Naval Base near Seneca Lake, New York. Prior to the end of boot camp training, he was accepted in the U.S. Navy V-12 Program and entered the Naval Unit at Ohio State University as a seaman, Second Class. World War II ended in Europe in May of 1945.

Due to Japan's surrender, Clarke never saw active duty and was honorably discharged in June 1946, much to Marian's relief. He returned to Amherst as a junior in the fall of 1946. Amherst allowed him to transfer one semester of credits from Ohio State. By 1946, fall enrollment at Amherst increased to a total of 1,174 students, of which 735 were veterans and approximately 22% received scholarship aid. (www.amherst.edu) Following the end of the war, America was in a rebuilding and reorganizing phase, as was Amherst College.

As a veteran, Clarke was authorized by the Veterans Administration to receive $65.00 towards his college tuition. Depending upon their eligibility, veterans received such government aid as: compensation for disabilities, hospitalization, home, farm and business loan guarantees, readjustment allowances, insurance, rehabilitation and vocational training, educational courses, assistance in obtaining employment and provisions for your dependents. Quite a difference in the level of support that veterans received after World War II compared with the almost nonexistent benefits for his father and other soldiers in World War I. Maybe Howard's life path would have been different if he had received similar aid.

After the war, the student body at Amherst slowly returned to prewar levels. Clarke played basketball and baseball in 1947 and 1948. His performances throughout his college years earned him election to the All-Amherst Baseball Team, First Team Pitcher - quite an honor, as only four pitchers were named from the first 100 years of baseball at Amherst. July 1, 1859 marked the first intercollegiate baseball game when Amherst College played against Williams College at a neutral site in Pittsfield, Massachusetts. Paul Eckley, baseball coach (1923-1965), and Charles Cole, College President signed the award, presented at the Centennial of Intercollegiate Baseball on May 16, 1959 at Amherst, Massachusetts.

At college and in summer leagues, Clarke's real talents were revealed on the baseball mound. Reporters touted Clarke's as: "a young hurler with a variety of tricks, including a sharp-breaking drop," a good "fast ball that was hopping," and a "fast breaking hook that had the opposing batters backing up." Clarke was "ripe material for the big league scouts – and they were watching him." In fact, when Clarke was 19 years old and a junior at Amherst, the Boston Red Sox drafted him as a pitcher, but his father said "no," firmly telling Clarke he had to finish college. (In these days professional baseball players did not make the money they do today.) Not bad for picking up the sport only three years before.

Doting father Howard was Clarke's biggest fan. In a folder marked "Clarke" I found many brown, crinkly, musty smelling articles that Howard had meticulously clipped and dated whenever his son was mentioned. Having been a baseball player himself who manned third base at Pawling, Howard was vicariously living his dreams through Clarke. Via newspaper stories, Howard managed to follow Clarke's games from town to town.

While Clarke was at Amherst, Howard took a subscription to the Amherst *Jeff* newspaper, which kept him up to date on all the news, including sports scores. Howard collected articles covering Amherst baseball games out of town: the *New York Times* covered the Yale and Williams games; the Yale games also appeared in the *Herald Tribune*; the Dartmouth games were covered by the *Springfield Union*; and Colgate (Hamilton, New York) games were covered by the *Knickerbocker News* (Albany, New York)

While home from college in the summer, Clarke also played on various Columbia County League Teams. In 1946, just back from the Navy, Clarke pitched for the town of Claverack, New York. On June 26, Clarke struck out twelve men in seven innings against Philmont. In 1947, he pitched for Hudson's Gifford Wood team. An article in the Hudson newspaper, *The Daily Star*, "Rainey Fans 13, Giffords Blank Hollowville 3-0," noted Clarke's strike-out record (13) for the league. Later that summer Clarke played on the Columbia County All-Star Stuyvesant Falls, New York team as the "big gun" against the Albany County McEnanys (Macs) of Albany, New York. It would be difficult to miss the attention Clarke received: Clarke was big news in Columbia County.

One of the most humorous old newspaper articles Howard clipped appeared in the *Hudson Daily News*. Apparently, my dad achieved celebrity status in small-town Hudson. When Clarke returned home from college to go bowling for an afternoon of fun with some friends in December, 1947, a reporter picked up on the "news." The following article appeared: "Clarke Rainey Hits 286 Single, Records 10 Straight Strikes. Clarke "excels in almost any sport he undertakes," and he tried his skill on the maples. After "ten straight frames Rainey chalked up a strike mark alongside his name but on the 11th ball, with most of the other bowlers anxiously looking on, rooting for the youngster to clean the pins" he came up with a split. Knowing my father, I am sure he found humor in these articles also.

The proud day arrived for the Rainey family. Their only child graduated on Sunday, June 20, 1948. As part of the graduation festivities, Amherst played a baseball game against Williams on Pratt Field on Saturday, the day before the ceremony. It was Clarke's last game at Amherst; his dad wrote on the scorecard that Clarke pitched in the 8th inning. Williams won 3-1 before an Alumni Day crowd of 2,000 fans. I have a picture at my dad's Amherst graduation with the very proud family: my dad in his naval uniform, his proud mother, Marian's mother, Howard's mother and father, and Clarke's great Uncle Dan with his wife, Theo. It was a joyous occasion, as such milestones are for all families, to see Clarke graduate from such a wonderful college.

Sadly, Uncle Dan suffered a cerebral hemorrhage in September of 1948, just three months after Clarke's graduation. Dan was seriously handicapped up to the time of his passing on July 14, 1949, at his home. Fortunately Dan was able to see his grandnephew graduate from his alma mater that he so dearly loved. I am thankful that the college provided my dad the opportunity to be a part of the Amherst heritage.

Following graduation from Amherst in 1948, my dad started a training course at General Electric (GE) in Schenectady, New York. My dad was determined to be a successful business man, unlike his father. He roomed with Dot Hall Fish's (Marian's close Mount Holyoke friend) son, Henry. After one year, Clarke was transferred to the General Electric headquarters in New York City. After completion of the General Electric Business Training Course in 1951, he came to St. Louis to work for Laclede Gas Company, after an Amherst alumnus recruited him for the position. My dad used to tell us that he thought New York City was too big and too dirty and that two years was enough. He wanted a smaller city with more opportunities. Although he would miss the mountains of New England, and his family, St. Louis would become his new home. St. Louis seemed like just the right size town, with plenty of career opportunities for Clarke.

St. Louis and Ginny

From the small river town of Hudson, New York my dad was headed to the larger river city of St. Louis, Missouri on the mighty Mississippi to begin a new career at the public gas utility company. My dad was determined to make his mark and be a successful businessman. The promise of a steady job at the gas utility company was its allure. He only knew a few Amherst alums in St. Louis casually. My dad jokingly said that he considered the job in St. Louis because "any town that has a major league baseball team is worth looking into." He found a semiprofessional baseball team to play on in St. Louis, which he thoroughly enjoyed. After visiting Hudson, I can understand why my dad did not settle down in his hometown. St. Louis offered more opportunities for a stable career for Clarke, opportunities which his own father never had.

Many years later when I was talking to one of my dad's baseball friends, he asked me if I knew why my dad stopped playing semiprofessional baseball after college. I said I did not know and was curious. How could he give up something he loved so much? His friend proceeded to tell me that in one of the last games my dad pitched, he beaned a player in the head so badly that the player was seriously injured. After that incident, Clarke didn't think he could ever pitch again. My dad would have never intentionally hit a batter. He looked tough on the outside but on the inside he was very respectful. The use of batting helmets was not mandatory in Major League Baseball until 1970, despite the death of a Cleveland batter hit by a Yankee pitcher in 1920 – an incident Clarke surely knew about it.

Shortly after arriving in St. Louis, my dad met my mother, Ginny, on a blind date, an arranged meeting that would change his life forever. My mom was almost six feet tall, athletic, thin, and blond. When they met, she was in her sophomore year at Washington University, studying Physical Education. My mother was quite an athlete; she played field hockey at Washington University, which I am sure impressed my dad. Ginny's talents weren't limited to the athletic fields; she was a talented seamstress also. But, her most endearing qualities were her positive attitude and her compassion that inspired her to help people.

From outward appearances, my mom appeared to have a charmed life. In 1934, when she was two years old, she was adopted from a small town in southern Missouri in Bollinger County, to a prosperous radiologist, Lex, and his wife, Vera. They lived in a large house on approximately sixty acres in a suburb of St. Louis named Ladue, escaping the city smog for a bucolic life in a prosperous farming community. Lex commuted from work at the Firmin Desloge hospital in the city, full of pollution from the burning of bituminous soft coal used to heat homes, power factories, and for transportation. The story goes that my mom's biological mother was an unwed teenager who wanted to give up her baby for a chance at a better life. The adoption records are sealed and we never could know anything about her biological parents. My mom's biological mother chose a family who were unable to have children of their own. I have a picture of my mom taken on her "day of adoption December 20, 1934." She is an adorable blonde haired blue eyed little girl. I was curious why the family waited almost two and half years to give my mom up for adoption. Was she placed in foster care her first few years of life, or worse yet in an orphanage? Was my mom loved the way she should have been at such a young age? I seemed to be more curious about my mom's background than she was. And, my mom said she never had any desire to know who her biological parents were because she was with a family that loved her, or so she thought. My mom loved her life in Ladue and would tell me stories of chickens, geese, and peacocks on their land, tea parties in her garden, and once even a helicopter landed on their property.

Tragically, in March of 1939, when my mom was only seven years old, her adoptive father, Lex, died suddenly of a heart attack. In the pictures of him he was a very large man, a bit overweight, and seemed so full of life. I wonder if all the pollution played a part in his ill health. My mom only knew her adoptive father for about five years of her life but I have many happy, smiling, pictures of him holding his little tow head girl. The family was able to afford to stay in the family home in Ladue following Lex's passing for many years. My mom told me that she took the "Clayton 04" trolley which stopped almost in front of her house on Conway Road to her grade school at Price School (the first grade school in Ladue); to church at Ladue Chapel Presbyterian Church; and ultimately to the first private coeducational school established for 7th through 12th grade students in the 1920's, John Burroughs School. To continue their life in this wealthy community, without Lex's income, it required the family to sell off acres of land, as needed. In fact, the street called Mayfair Road used to be their driveway. Mom said when they sold that particular parcel of land; they put their driveway on the other side of the house. I guess my mom's father bought the land as a sort of insurance policy and security for his family.

Growing up, when I would complain to my mom that she was too strict she casually would tell me that her disciplining was nothing compared to how her mother, Grammie, disciplined her during her childhood. Apparently, my mom said when she misbehaved she was beaten with a brush and locked in the dark basement. Parents couldn't get by with behavior like that today. But, to me it was also a sign of her mother's instability. My mom always tried to gloss over negatives and see the positives in people. My mom did not know what was ahead with her adoptive mother's erratic behavior.

When I was doing my research on the background of my mom's private college preparatory school, John Burroughs School (JBS), I thought I was going to find out very philosophical and intellectual reasons for the founding and naming of the school because it so highly respected across the country. But, according to the book *A Way of Life: The Story of John Burroughs School 1923-1973* by Martin L. Parry, seventeen and a half acres located on Price Road were purchased for thirty-five thousand dollars. A committee met to decide a name and legend has it that around midnight Mr. Stix who woke up from a nap exclaimed "Oh hell, call it John Burroughs and let's go home!" The naturalist John Burroughs had died just a year earlier and he typified many of "the ideals they were seeking for their children. He loved personality for its own sake." (Parry) "He coupled the appreciation of beauty with a rugged spiritual sturdiness. He radiated self-reliance, usefulness, brotherliness. Particularly he admired leadership founded on high motive." (ibid) It was here at John Burroughs that my mother fell in love with her school, friends, and teachers and mentors. She graduated in the class of 1950 from this very special place of higher learning and carried with her the dream that her own children someday would be able to experience the excellence of JBS.

Following graduation from JBS, my mother matriculated at Washington University. By this time the family had run out of money, sold the house and what acreage was left, and moved to an apartment close to college. Ginny was awarded a part-tuition General Scholarship for $400 where she played field hockey. Ginny and Clarke shared an understanding and sense of gratitude for the kindness extended by their respective colleges to allow them to attend. They in turn paid it back throughout their lives.

After dating for two years, Ginny and Clarke fell in love, announced their engagement in January of 1953, and married in August of 1953. During their first year of marriage, my mother finished her senior year of college. Her best friend's father walked her down the aisle. My mom was beautiful in a wedding dress she had designed and sewed herself. Two of my mom's closest friends from John Burroughs were her bridesmaids. My dad had several ushers including two friends from St. Louis, a friend from Amherst, Brian Sullivan, and "Dot" Hall Fish's son, Henry. Howard and Marian were present in good health to see their only child get married - a very proud moment.

Clarke and Ginny 1953

After my mother taught physical education for several years, she and my dad saved up enough money to buy their first house. My dad must have been so proud to own his own home at such a young age. His parents were unable to buy a home until after my dad graduated from high school. The closing documents for their first home were included in his old papers. My dad was determined to give his family a better life than he had, financially. With great joy, the first of three daughters, Jean, arrived in 1955. My mom loved staying at home, and my dad was so proud of her. My mom was involved in every volunteer project possible: Girl Scouts, Pi Beta Phi, Washington University, John Burroughs School, Warson Woods Swim Team, Warson Woods School library, and many more. She helped found the Sign of the Arrow gift shop run by Pi Phi volunteers to benefit charities, which is celebrating its 50th anniversary in 2016.

My dad's career seemed to be moving along very well. Although I always thought we were poor, this was far from the truth. Both of my parents grew up in families where money was tight. As a result, our family life was very simple and basic. To save money, my mom sewed many of our clothes. At first I wanted to be like everyone else with store-bought clothes. In grade school, she made all three sisters matching dresses. Since I had to wear my older sister's hand-me downs, it meant I wore the same dress for four years! Then I realized that what I had was unique and crafted with love as we picked out fabric and patterns for my dresses. Years later, even if my mom felt sick from her chemotherapy treatments, she managed to sew me a one of a kind prom dresses. My mother spent a lot of time passing on all of her skills to me; we were a do-it-yourself family. I cherish the time we had together working on these projects.

Today I understand my parents' frugality. As an adolescent, it was difficult for me when I was surrounded by wealth at my private high school and could not be a part of it. Yet, my parents taught us life lessons that I have passed onto my own children. When I turned sixteen in 1973, many of my JBS friends were given cars but I had to buy my own car with my sister, a Galaxie 500 for $425. I appreciate that my parents instilled in us a strong work ethic and a sense of what is really important in life.

Marian's Dear Mother

Meanwhile, back in Hudson, Marian and Howard continued their lives in the small town they loved so much. Marian was such a warrior: she survived two world wars, struggled through the Great Depression, earned the right to vote, supported her mother for over twenty years, and managed to "have it all" as a full-time salaried teacher, wife, and mother while always maintaining her upbeat spirit and zest for life.

Marian's mother's health continued to worsen the last couple years of her life. Sadly, in 1959, Marian's mother, Gertrude Clarke died at the age of 88. Nevertheless Gertrude was lucky to see her only grandson graduate from college, get married, and meet one great grandchild, Jean.

Perhaps musing on her mother's passing, Marian entered a mid-nineteenth century poem about the afterlife into her diary, *The Chambered Nautilus*, by Oliver Wendell Holmes. The nautilus, a sea creature, that lives inside a spiral shell, is a metaphor for the human soul, "sailing through the dangerous waters until it is wrecked." (encyclopedia.com) As it grows, the nautilus makes new, larger chambers of its shell in which to live, closing off the old chambers and gradually forming a spiral, emphasizing that people should grow and develop throughout their lives. At the end of the poem, Holmes emphasized "the idea that humans expand their horizons until they achieve the spiritual freedom of heaven or the afterlife." (ibid)

"The Chambered Nautilus" (Verse IV)

"This is the ship of pearl, which, poets feign,
Sails the unshadowed main,—
The venturous bark that flings
On the sweet summer wind its purpled wings
In gulfs enchanted, where the Siren sings,
And coral reefs lie bare,
Where the cold sea-maids rise to sun their streaming hair.
Its webs of living gauze no more unfurl;
Wrecked is the ship of pearl!
And every chambered cell,
Where its dim dreaming life was wont to dwell,
As the frail tenant shaped his growing shell,
Before thee lies revealed,—
Its irised ceiling rent, its sunless crypt unsealed!
Year after year beheld the silent toil
That spread his lustrous coil;
Still, as the spiral grew,
He left the past year's dwelling for the new,
Stole with soft step its shining archway through,
Built up its idle door,
Stretched in his last-found home, and knew the old no more.
Thanks for the heavenly message brought by thee,
Child of the wandering sea,
Cast from her lap, forlorn!
From thy dead lips a clearer note is born
Than ever Triton blew from wreathèd horn!
While on mine ear it rings,
Through the deep caves of thought I hear a voice that sings:—
Build thee more stately mansions, O my soul,

As the swift seasons roll!
Leave thy low-vaulted past!
Let each new temple, nobler than the last,
Shut thee from heaven with a dome more vast,
Till thou at length art free,
Leaving thine outgrown shell by life's unresting sea!"

Oliver Wendell Holmes

Marian's Retirement

Marian was proudly able to fulfill her lifelong goal to teach high school English. As a teacher she nurtured hundreds of students throughout the years. When Marian announced her retirement in June of 1960, her students wanted to do something really special for this beloved teacher so they issued the following proclamation:

"Whereas, Mrs. Marian Rainey has faithfully served for 28 years in Hudson High School as a teacher of English, head of the English Department, and advisor to the Blue and Gold (Yearbook) and in doing so has constantly encouraged respect for learning and high standard of academic achievement, of journalism, and of good citizenship.

Whereas, after 28 years of continuous service, Mrs. Rainey has announced her retirement; therefore, be it Resolved: that, the Student Council expresses the appreciation of the entire student body and extends best wishes for a very happy future and be it further Resolved: that this resolution be recorded in the minutes of the Student Council and that a copy be presented to

Mrs. Rainey this 13th day of June, 1960.
John Frentino, President
Hudson High School Student Council"

In the 1961 Hudson High School Blue and Gold yearbook the following dedication was made:

"To Mrs. Rainey, Hudson High School presents its deepest and most sincere appreciation for her years dedicated to the service and education of young people. We have known her as a sincere friend who has been interested in every individual, both in and out of the classroom. She was always willing to help with any problem, no matter how large or how small."

My grandmother saved her Hudson High School yearbooks all of these years to reread the kind words from her students that had meant so much to her. Her selfless nature always wanted to better others' lives through her love of teaching English. Many of us had that special teacher during our school years that made us want to learn, helped us figure out our passions, guided us in positive directions, and made a difference in our lives. Marian always found time for her students, putting in that extra effort. My grandmother wasn't a famous teacher; she never published any of her writings. Where would she have found time for herself? Still she was well known in her own right in the town of Hudson to her hundreds and hundreds of students and their parents. I wish I had been one of her lucky students. Maybe during retirement Marian would finally find the time to write a book, poetry, or short stories.

S. Mitchell and Ida Rainey

The passing of Howard's parents overshadowed the initial joy of Marian's retirement. First, my great grandfather, S. Mitchell Rainey, passed away in October 1960, at 89 years old. His only son, Howard, took care of him up until the last minute. S. Mitchell was associated with the Columbia County banking profession for more than half a century and was very active in the community. He lived his whole life in Hudson. On his 88th birthday in 1959, he attended the Hudson Rotary Club meeting. In his last 26 years, he had never missed a meeting of the organization for 1,352 consecutive meetings! - big enough news to warrant a photo and write up in the local newspaper.

The next spring, on May 2, 1961, Howard's "dearest little mother," "dear mother," Ida Rainey died after a long illness in a nursing home in Hudson. Howard had the good fortune to be able to be there for both his parents when they needed him. Fortunately in 1954, S. Mitchell and Ida had quietly observed their 60th wedding anniversary despite Ida's recent ill health. Howard was devoted to his mother throughout his life, as evidenced in his WWI letters that she had saved all of those years. Howard was a good son who took good care of his parents.

This poem by an Irish poet and lyricist Joseph Campbell (1881-1944) says goodbye to Howard's mother, the woman with an aged face. Campbell used the Gaelic form of his name, Seosamh MacCathmhaoil.

"The Old Woman"

"As a white candle
In a holy place,
So is the beauty
Of an aged face.

As the spent radiance
Of the winter sun,
So is a woman
With her travail done.

Her brood gone from her,
And her thoughts as still
As the water
Under a ruined mill."

Joseph Campbell
(MacCathmhaoil)

Howard and Marian

In 1963, several months after Marian's serious taxi accident, my dad drove our station wagon to Hudson, New York and strapped his dad in the back with the seats down. It seemed unkind to me, but dad said he had to tie his father down so he wouldn't try to escape from the moving car. Clearly, his father's dementia or PTSD was worsening and Marian could no longer take care of him or herself. My dad let his father stay with us for a few days while he tried to find a nursing home for my grandpa. It was not going over very well with my mom. I remember on about the third day my dad came home and my mom didn't waste any time or mince any words about how she felt watching my grandpa. She said "I have three other children to take care of during the day and taking care of your father is like taking care of a two year old. I have to watch him every minute. Either he goes or I go!" The next day my grandfather was gone.

It makes me very sad that those are the last memories I have of a grandpa who was so kind to me. Only twice do I remember visiting their house in Hudson. It was a long drive. I remember a huge weeping willow tree in their front yard where I would hide. If I got scared I raced out to my grandpa, and he would hold my hand and protect me. On one visit to Hudson, we drove across the river to the beautiful Catskill Mountains and went to the Catskill Game Farm to feed the animals. When I tried to feed the animals a bottle, they were so aggressive that I was scared, but my grandpa helped me. In 2008, when my daughter and I were in Hudson, I wanted to show her the Game Farm and tell about all of my fond memories, but it was permanently closed.

There is a poem in Marian's diary that she clipped out of a Boston magazine called *"Our Dumb Animals"* in February 1917. Published by the Massachusetts Society for the Prevention and Cruelty to Animals and the American Humane Society, it was a national and international magazine whose motto was "We Speak for those that Can't Speak for Themselves." I was kind of surprised at the name because it was not representative of what the organization was accomplishing. Thankfully, in 1979 it was renamed *"Animal Magazine."* This poem reminded me of my grandfather's gentle ways with people and animals.

"The Man Worth Knowing"

"There are many pleasant people
Whom one would like to know:
Editors and barbers
And men who shovel snow.
There are laymen, there are draymen,
[a person who delivers beer]
But, the ones I like to meet
Are the men who pat the horses
When they pass them on the street.

It's a jolly, on the Avenue
To bow and raise your hat
To someone so distinguished
That your comrade says "Who's that?"
But the man I really honor
When the stinging north wind blows
Is the man who always stops to stroke
Some horses frozen nose."

Christopher Morley

He was the only grandpa I ever had. Looking back now, I think he found his purpose in life by taking care of all the people he loved. It wasn't a typical path for a man, and probably one that did not earn him the same respect as other men, but he found his way.

"The Way"

"Who seeks for heaven alone to save his soul,
May keep the path, but will not reach the goal;
While he who walks in love may wander far,
Yet God will bring him where the blessed are."

Henry Van Dyke

After a short time in a nursing home, my grandpa died in January 1964 at 69 years of age. It seems strange to me that my grandpa lived only four years longer than his own father. I was only seven years old. None of this made sense to me. My father said grandpa died from diabetes, but I think he died from being so confused. I knew Grandpa served in the war, but I never once heard him talk about it. I wish I knew more, but maybe it was too painful for him to bring up those memories. I am sure he suffered more than we will ever know from what he saw in his ambulance during the war, but no one will ever really know.

When I reflect on the non-traditional marriage my grandparents had, I believe that each of them found their purpose in life: Marian worked full time while Howard took care of the house and family, even though it seemed to upset my father that his dad did not work full time. In Marian's diary she quoted a paragraph from the novel, *Felix Holt, The Radical*, about a man's fear of failure. Felix Holt preferred a life of "working class poverty" in England in 1832 over a life of comfortable wealth" (www.wikipedia.org) Howard was not a failure because he knew his purpose. The following quote is from Chapter XLV:

"But I'm proof against that word failure. I've seen behind it. The only failure a man ought to fear is failure in cleaving to the purpose he sees to be best. As to just the amount of result he may see from his particular work – that's a tremendous uncertainty:
The universe has not been arranged for the gratification of his feelings as long as a man sees and believes in some great good, he'll prefer working towards that in the way he's best fit for, come what may."

George Elliot

Mary Anne Evans used the male pen name George Elliot to ensure her works would be taken more seriously. She was one of the leading writers of the Victorian Era, including, *Middlemarch, A Study of Provincial Life,* in 1872. Significant themes in her work included the nature of marriage, the status of women, idealism, religion, and education, among others which were meaningful to Marian.

Shortly after Howard's death, my dad moved his mother and all of her boxes and belongings to St. Louis so she could live close to him in an assisted living nursing home where he could keep his eye on her. As a result of her brain injury, dementia set in. Despite the fact that she wasn't quite herself, she seemed to handle the move well. At first, Grandma had all of her furniture, oriental rugs, books, china, silver, and diaries in her cozy assisted living apartment downtown near Dad's office. Around the corner, she found a Presbyterian Church within walking distance. She loved it and made lots of new friends there. I really enjoyed having Grandma Rainey in town to spend time with us. She came out to our house for dinner every Sunday night. I didn't really know much about her except that she was an English teacher. She loved to read, which I did not. She would say, "Let's read a book." But I only wanted to go outside and play. Still, she was fun to have around the house. She loved telling me about this fabulous college she went to called Mount Holyoke.

After she suffered a terrible fall, my dad moved my grandma into a full service nursing home that was a lot different from assisted living. In the nursing home, she spent time in a hospital bed and a wheelchair and seemed to lose sight of who she once was. It was obvious Grandma couldn't take care of herself anymore. It was very sad when we went to visit her every Sunday after church because she seemed confused. Except for my dad, she did not know who we were; I went with my mom to Grandma's old apartment at the assisted living to pack up all of her belongings to be placed in storage. I felt so sad to realize that Grandma would never see her things again. If it wasn't for the taxi accident, we would have had many more years with her.

My dad managed all of my grandma's finances. Her mail came to our house, including her New York Teachers' Pension checks. My dad was proud of how hard she had worked as a teacher to support their family as the primary breadwinner. My dad never spoke of how proud he was of his own dad. I guess my dad lost respect for his father when he saw that Howard couldn't hold down a job or make enough money to support his family. My father was old fashioned and thought the man of the house was responsible for the family, although that is very different today. When checks came in the mail my dad showed them to me and explained that she got the checks because of the length of her service teaching, making the point that staying with a job can definitely have its rewards. Even though that is the way that my dad saw the situation, I do not think my grandmother would have been happy if she was the one who had to stay home without a career.

We Lost the War

It is still difficult to write these words, but, on Thursday, May 15, 1975, my mom died from AML leukemia. She had battled the disease with massive amounts of chemotherapy for four years. I was seventeen years old and have never gotten over it; I just had to learn to deal with it. My little sister, Alice, was only eleven years old, and Jean was nineteen.

I was lucky to be able to say goodbye to my mom on Mother's Day, which was the Sunday before she died. She was in the hospital, completely bed ridden. When I went down to the hospital to give her the Mother's Day card I had written out for her, she couldn't speak any more. I read it out loud and she squeezed my hand. I will never forget that Mother's Day as long as I live.

Earlier that day, I went to church looking for answers about what was happening in my life. The minister started to speak about my mom anonymously to the congregation in his sermon. He said that he went to the hospital earlier in the week thinking that he was going to be able to offer some comfort and solace to my mom as her days were numbered. But, instead, he said that the opposite happened and he learned so much from her, especially her considerate and graceful nature which made him feel like he was on the receiving end of her faith. I was sitting in the balcony and I felt like he was staring at me the whole time he was talking. No one else knew who he was talking about but me. The minister's words of comfort, hope and inspiration were exactly what I needed at that time. It helped me understand how amazing my mom was and how grateful I was to have been able to call her my mom.

Mom fought the battle with all her might, even going into remission several times, but ultimately lost the war. She was only 42 years old. My mother always put on a positive face. I learned from this experience, that while someone might look happy on the outside, you never know how that person could be suffering on the inside. So, I learned to always try to treat people with kindness. Many times it is too hard for those silent sufferers to talk about their pain inside. And, a little kindness can go a long way to aid someone who is hurting.

The last six months or so before my mom died, she was in a hospital bed on the first floor of our house. Since my bedroom was right above hers on the second floor, one of our neighbors installed a doorbell up to my bedroom. If my mom needed anything in the middle of the night, she could ring me. Many days in high school I didn't get much sleep as I was up taking care of my mom. I put makeup on to hide my puffy eyes. I cried myself to sleep often because I knew that my mom was near the end when she was down to seventy pounds.

Losing a mother at such a young age is devastating and humbling for a child. My life dreams were shattered. I wasn't at all like other girls who had mothers. There was a void in my life that no one could ever fill. Of course I could only wonder what it was like for my mom to live the end of her life abandoned by her adoptive mother and never knowing her biological mother. I wished my mom would have shared more about her feelings with me but I know the kind of person she was. She never would have wanted to burden me with her sadness, if there was any. My mom knew she had us and all of our unconditional love every day of her life. Taking care of her was not a chore, it was the least I could do for all that my mom had given me through all my ups and downs growing up. I remember one day I came home from grade school hiding my report card. I had to have my parents sign the report card and take it back to school the next day but I was embarrassed to show it to my mom. I got A's in physical education and math but B's in all my other subjects. My mom knew something was wrong by my erratic behavior. She asked me what was wrong and I finally got up the nerve to show Mom my report card. I started crying because I didn't think I was as good a student as my parents would want me to be. My mom sat me down and said that everyone has their strengths in life in different ways and grades were not the only measure of a good person. She said I would find out a way to use my strengths. I was so relieved that she loved me for what I was even though she emphasized that I had to continue to put my best foot forward in school. I wasn't off the hook completely. Even though it was hard for me to sit still for so long in classes, I had to give it my best effort. As comforting as my mom's words were, I knew she wanted me to be the best I could be and have a bright future.

During my mom's illness, I lost part of my adolescence during the four years from ninth grade until graduation from Burroughs because I was busy taking care of her. I didn't care because I would do anything in my power to help my mom feel better. When we found out mom was sick, my sisters and I walked up to the shopping center in our neighborhood together and bought our mom a teddy bear to keep her company in her hospital bed. We didn't want her to be lonely. None of us were old enough to drive yet. It made mom so happy when we gave it to her. She was always so appreciative of everything we did for. But, in reality, she was the one that was giving to us. I still have that teddy bear to this day. He was there for her when we could not be.

My mom's illness motivated me to spend my free time trying to cook food that appealed to her to try to put some weight on her. Mom was skinny to begin with, so it was quite a challenge. My desire to help my mom eat healthy food, eventually lead me to my undergraduate major in college, a Bachelor of Science in Food and Nutrition, Dietetics.

All of our efforts could not save my mom's life. After mom died, my dad took me with him to pick out my mom's casket and burial plot. I helped choose the dress that we wanted her buried in. That was a horrible experience at seventeen years old but it certainly helped put closure on a difficult situation. She always looked so gracious in her dresses. At my mom's funeral at Ladue Chapel, the church she loved so much her whole life, it was standing room only. My mom touched so many lives. The minister at the church gave a lovely speech and said she was a beautiful Christian person. He said that she was in a realm of tranquility now. Her spirit exists peacefully. I thought at the time that it was for the best for her that she did not have to suffer any more. Her body was released from her spirit, he said.

Grammie, my mom's estranged mother, showed up at the funeral. My dad sternly asked her where she had been the last four years when we needed her help. He said "you never sent a card, flowers, food, or even made a phone call." My dad did not let them sit in our family pew in the front row. I was proud of my dad for being so tough with Grammie. She did not deserve the honor of sitting with us. We needed help and Grammie was absent from our lives. I think Grammie was not a thoughtful person and certainly not a loving mother. I wondered if my mom changed her mind and wished she had known her biological mother since her adoptive mother abandoned her later in life. Although my mom would never tell me, I believe there had to be a hole in her heart that she didn't have a mother at all. It took such strength for my mom to keep up her positive attitude. I am in awe of her perseverance throughout her short life.

After the funeral, my dad told me that "life is for the living" and that as difficult as it would be, I should try to live my life in a way that would make my mom proud. He wanted me to carry on in school, and keep moving forward. While all of that sounds very logical and peaceful, in reality it was not. I wanted my mom around for all the little and big things in life. Or I would have relished a grandmother or aunt, but I didn't have that either. I was the only girl I knew who didn't have a mom. I felt isolated and misunderstood. Mother's Day was always very difficult as was Mother's weekend at my sorority. My dear friends offered to share their mom, but that didn't work for me. I know my dad wanted me to be as strong on the outside as he appeared to be but it wasn't possible. Many years later some of my friends told me they didn't see me smile a lot during high school and college. And, I told them I didn't have too much to smile about. Although my dad never shed a tear, he didn't do very well following my mom's death. I wasn't fooled.

In the summer after the mom's passing in 1975, I went to my swimming meet with all my friends to try to keep my life as normal as possible. As I stood on the blocks, I looked up in the sky and said to myself "Mom, I will break a record for you." I swam as hard as I could. When I got out of the water, the timer said to me: "Great race. You won and you broke a pool record." I knew my mom was always watching me, guiding me, and supporting me. I never told anyone about that incident. I needed a sign from her that things were going to be all right without her here on this earth standing by me, supporting me, and loving me unconditionally. Even though I always have her in spirit, I will always wish my life had gone differently.

As hard as it was, I have always tried to be positive my whole life, as my mom would have done. But, I think I am more open and honest with the realities and hardships of life with my children because I felt that I wasn't prepared for my mom's death. Up until the last minute she was still praying for a miracle. I was looking for help to deal with her death. I read a book about when bad things happened to good people to try to make some sense of why my mom was the unlucky one who tragically died so early in life. Why was my mom the one who got the bad virus that the doctors thought caused the leukemia? Eventually, I learned to be grateful for every day and live life to the fullest. I attribute my positive attitude in life to my mother. I was lucky to have two beautiful children in 1985 and 1989. I was determined to be around for my children when they were growing up. I couldn't let history repeat itself. I hoped and dreamed that someday there would be a cure so that other children did not have to go through what we went through.

One of my mom's dreams was for all of her three daughters to attend her private school in St. Louis, John Burroughs School (JBS). Although my dad thought it was unnecessary to pay for a private school, he understood my mom's wishes. Ironically, my grandmother was fond of John Burroughs' writings about nature, religion and literature. Burroughs lived in the Catskills for a period of time, near his birthplace of Roxbury, New York where he grew up on the family farm, very close to Hudson, New York. The school that we went to in St. Louis was founded on the principles of his writings. Although there is no way that my grandma could have known how much John Burroughs School meant to my mom, Grandma copied this poem into her diary. This poem is about John Burroughs "serene acceptance of life."

"Waiting"

"Serene, I fold my hands and wait,
Nor care for wind, nor tide, nor sea;
I rave no more 'gainst time or fate,
For lo! my own shall come to me."

John Burroughs

Burroughs wrote *Waiting* in 1862, when the thought came to him that "what belonged to me in time, if I waited - and if I also hustled. So I waited and I hustled, and my little poem turned out to be a prophecy. My own has come to me, as I never expected it to come. The best friends I have were seeking me all the while." (Burroughs)

All three Rainey girls graduated from JBS, but my mom was only able to live long enough to see her oldest daughter, Jean, graduate. My mom was determined to witness my graduation even if she came in a wheelchair. She died two weeks before my graduation ceremony in June of 1975. I tried to imagine that she was there and hold back my tears. Despite all of our sadness, I am glad we were able to fulfill her wishes that all three of her daughters graduated from JBS, even if she could not be there physically to enjoy it.

Goodbye Grandma Rainey

In August of 1975, less than three months after my mom died, Grandma Rainey died at 77 years old. I felt as if I had lost so much within such a short period of time. My dad dropped me off at college in August of 1975 and flew straight to Hudson with my little sister, Alice, to bury his mother next to his father in the Hudson Cemetery. There was an even greater void for me. Now that I have read my grandma's diaries, I know that she lived a great life.

After Marian's passing, "Pris" Spaulding Sheppard gathered all of the information from my dad to forward to "Dot," Marian's closest Mount Holyoke friend. "Dot" Hall Fish, wrote the memorial for the alumnae newsletter. When I was going through all of my grandmother's papers I found a copy of her Last Will and Testament dated 1968. In it she bequeathed to the trustees of Mount Holyoke College $1,000. For a woman coming from meager means, this was a lot of money. It showed how much she loved and appreciated Mount Holyoke. Marian wanted to pay it forward for other women in her financial situation who might not get to attend a college of such caliber without aid.

Though he never showed it outwardly or even talked about it, losing his wife and mother within three months of each other had to be very difficult for my dad. My dad had to be the strong one for us. Despite the Rainey family's strong Presbyterian faith, my dad was never a religious man. I am not sure why. Nevertheless, after my mom died, my dad continued to drive my little sister Alice to Sunday school every Sunday at Ladue Chapel. Yet, he would sit in the car in the parking lot, drink a can of soda, and read the newspaper.

For over four years, the two most important women in his life had declined simultaneously, and he took care of both. Just as thirty years before Clarke found the courage, strength, and mental toughness on the pitcher's mound, now he needed to channel that same energy towards mending his family following these tragedies. Dad seemed strong on the outside although we never really knew what was going on inside his mind. I think my dad learned at a young age that he had to be strong and never admit weakness.

Being an only child had to be lonely; he had no siblings to share the responsibility of caring for aging parents or to support him when he lost his spouse. My dad never had a sibling to reminisce about the good old days, as I do with my sisters. I think my dad saved the boxes of memorabilia and treasures he inherited as a comfort for his losses. These papers probably filled a void in my dad's life since he loved history, especially our family lineage. He was very proud of sharing bits and pieces of stories with me about his relatives. After he died, the papers were passed on to me, even though I was unaware at the time, and I discovered a lot more information about his family that he never mentioned. My dad never said anything about the diaries, letters, and other evidence of the lives of Howard and Marian. These treasures filled a void for me also but in a different way. Studying them, I was able to get to know his mother and father better. After so many losses in my life at a young age, I was grateful to be able to research my genealogy. My love for my grandparents grew when I was able to get to know them so intimately.

Ironically, after all of the hardship and sacrifice that Marian endured in her life, she left enough money in her estate to provide college tuition for all three of her grandchildren. My dad said most of the money came from the insurance settlement from her taxi accident. How bittersweet to be given such a wonderful gift. Grandma wanted us, her granddaughters, to complete our college educations so that no matter what happened in our lives we would be educated enough to support ourselves if necessary. Ironically, I ended up needing to support myself in the years following my divorce. Fortunately, I was a strong woman as both my grandmother and mother were in times of hardship. I have strength in my genes.

To continue to pay it forward, upon his death my dad left enough money for all his grandchildren to attend college – another testimony that education was always of utmost importance to our family. Because my grandmother, father, and mother had to worry about competing for scholarship money in order to complete their college educations, they were proud to be able to relieve their grandchildren of that burden.

As grateful as I am for all the loan-free college education I received, I would have traded anything to have my mother alive instead. I wouldn't have cared if I had to work to get a scholarship if she could have been there to share my life with me. Although Marian's parents were unable to pay for her education, they emotionally supported her through college. Lack of money never seemed to squelch her happiness. Marian had what I wished for in my own life. Because we had no control over my mom's illness, I realized that we are all vulnerable and the things we love so much can be gone in an instant. Money could not buy the one thing I wanted in my life: my mom's health.

On the last page of my grandmother's diary written in 1907 was a poem by Jean H. Watson. It must have had special meaning to her so I wanted to share it. We had a lot of grief in our lives but we always pulled ourselves through by staying in touch with our hope and faith.

"Out of Touch"

"Only a smile, yes, only a smile,
That a woman o'er burdened with grief
Expected from you.
'Twould have given relief,
For her heart ached sore the while;
But weary and cheerless she went away,
Because, as it happened, that very day
You were out of touch with your Lord.

Only a word, yes, only a word,
That the Spirit's
small voice whispered, "Speak,"
But the worker passed onward, unblessed, and weak,
Whom you were meant to have stirred
To courage, devotion and love anew,
Because, when the message came to you,
You were out of touch with your Lord.

Only a note, yes, only a note,
For a friend in a distant land.
The Spirit said, "Write," but you had planned
Some different work and you thought
It mattered little; you did not know
'Twould have saved a soul from sin and woe,
You were out of touch with your Lord.

Only a song, yes, only a song.
That the Spirit said, "Sing tonight-
Thy voice is thy Master's by purchase right?
But you thought, "Mid this motley throng
I care not to sing of the "City of Gold.
And the heart that your words might have reached grew cold,
You were out of touch with your Lord.

Only a day, yes, only a day!
But, oh can you guess, my friend,
Where the influence reaches, and where it will end
Of the hours that you frittered away?
The Master's command is "Abide in Me,"
And fruitless and vain will your service be
If out of touch with your Lord."

Jean H. Watson

Dad's Retirement

One month before my dad's retirement from Laclede Gas Company, he was diagnosed with lung cancer. He was a chain smoker. His single cell carcinoma cancer was directly linked to his cigarette smoking. My mom never smoked, and neither did any of his three daughters. Watching my dad's constant, horrible cough scared us. My dad was addicted to the nicotine and couldn't quit. Dad always said he would never go through chemotherapy after watching what my mom went through, but changed his mind to endure chemo. Following his diagnosis, he lived for another 11 months. Dad retired from a successful career as the Senior Vice President of Labor and Industrial Relations negotiating the contracts for over 1,000 employees. That was a perfect job for my dad who never seemed to get emotional on the outside. My dad always felt he had to be the provider; whether he was happy or not he stuck with his job. I think he lived in fear of being like his father.

His retirement parties after 41 years at his job marked a proud time for my dad. Even so, we all knew my dad's days were numbered. At one of my dad's parties, one of his closest friends suggested to me that before my dad died we should go over to his house to get all the family pictures marked so we could learn all the family history since we didn't have any other relatives. I didn't have the heart to tell this friend that we weren't allowed in my dad's house. Obviously, my dad was embarrassed about the situation with his wife if he couldn't even tell his best friends.

Now that I have been able to get to know my dad in a way that I never did when he was alive, I think that he saved all of his family memorabilia he was so proud of, to help erase the pain of growing up in a life of poverty as a child.

Even as my dad's cancer became progressively worse, his wife did not allow us to visit him at his house. He was too sick to come to our houses or go out to a restaurant – the only places we were allowed to see him. We occasionally talked to him on the phone. Unbeknownst to us, dad was taken to the hospital via ambulance early in the morning of February 12th of 1993 because he had had multiple seizures. Not until that evening did we find out that our dad had died. His wife called us to tell us only after he was gone. I was upset that I never received a phone call at any time during that day. I would have dropped everything to go out to the hospital and say goodbye to my dad. I did not have that opportunity. His wife told me she would have an open casket at the funeral so we could see him one last time. Maybe that was her idea of a consolation, but not in my mind. At the funeral home, I couldn't even look at my dad in the casket. I stood in a corner at a distance, glancing at my dad. I realized that he did not even resemble himself with his jaws wired shut and chemicals pumping him up so that he looked puffy. That was not how I wanted to remember my dad.

Following my dad's passing, my sisters and I thought all of the family memories had died with him. It was a real sense of loss for his three girls in so many ways. Many years later when we discovered all of the boxes of family genealogy treasures, my sisters and I wondered if dad had a motive in keeping them from us. Perhaps he did not tell us about them on purpose because he wanted us to discover them on our own. On the other hand, maybe he never found the time to share the family genealogy treasures with us. No matter what the reason, I am grateful the old papers were saved.

We knew our dad loved us even if it was difficult for him to show us. I carried on with my life after becoming an "orphan" in my thirties. I had two beautiful children to fill my life with joys and challenges. I learned that I needed to enjoy life to the fullest because you never know what is around the corner.

CHAPTER EIGHT

FROM GENEALOGY TO GENETICS

As I finished writing, transcribing, and researching my family genealogy, I thought my story had ended. Ironically, it was just beginning in a serious way. It felt gratifying and humbling to learn about my grandparents' and parents' lives through all of their triumphs and tragedies. I spent the last decade looking at family pictures, yearbooks, charts, diaries, letters, and tangible objects that cultivated so much meaning to me. While noticing many visible resemblances of eye and hair color, and athleticism, I also related to the many similar personality traits that helped me learn about why I became the person I am today. Little did I know how incredibly relevant and valuable my family's genes were; they were going to save my life.

There were many soldiers in my family, each fighting their own battles since their feet landed on America's soil at Plymouth Rock in 1620. Most soldiers are forever changed by their experiences. After the battle, if they live to see the end, they all have to make peace with their varied experiences whether inside their mind or with their body. We fight for what we believe in whether in the trenches of the battlefield or in a hospital room. For some soldiers it is too difficult to talk about their experiences; they are best left tucked away in a compartment in their mind that remains untouched.

For me, it was cathartic to learn how my family members dealt with their own battles to give me strength for my own.

When I was diagnosed with Acute Myeloid Leukemia (AML) in 2012, I realized from what the doctors told me that my genes were going to play a major role in my future health. The family pictures I treasured were only the beginning of my genealogic journey. I learned that I would need my family's genes to fight to keep me alive. I had given so much thought and study to my grandfather's experience in World War I; now I would be fighting a war of my own.

Unlike World War I, the war against leukemia blood cancer takes place on a battlefield that is mostly silent and invisible. The weapons used to fight the disease do not include guns, cannons, tanks or bombs. Instead, the armaments are needles, transfusions, chemotherapy, drugs, stem cells, and genetics.

Historians agree that the assassination of Archduke Franz Ferdinand touched off World War I, but no doctor or scientist can pinpoint the reasons that incite leukemia. While there are a variety of risk factors, it is a rare disease without a lot of specific answers for the questions about what causes this war. No one voluntarily enlists or is drafted to participate in this battle. It doesn't begin with land disputes, nationalism, power, or money. We cannot negotiate with leukemia to reach an Armistice agreement to end the battle.

Leukemia patients do not have an official uniform to wear, only a hospital gown. Upon discharge, leukemia patients are not awarded with official documents or medals like those the Doughboys received. There are, however, scars to represent courage in battle; you can find them where the "intravenous line" was removed and the challenges of a new quality of life in many ways.

AML leukemia begins inside the bone marrow where abnormal white blood cells, called myeloid cells, grow rapidly and "interfere with normal mature blood cells, including red cells, white cells, and platelets." (www.mayoclinic.com) "Cancer occurs when changes in a person's DNA cause a certain type of cell to grow unchecked." (www.genome.wustl.edu) Only a microscope can see the disease and determine the treatment for the leukemia battle.

The research into my genealogy began as an emotional journey, but became a scientific one. I needed to go to a completely new genetic level not visible to the naked eye. The parts of my body that would provide the answers to my future were my blood, bone marrow, and DNA. I felt like I had become a science experiment beyond my level of comprehension. Maybe it was better that I was somewhat oblivious to the complicated process so I had less to worry about.

As a lay person in the scientific field of medicine, I was thrust into the surreal, confusing, and overwhelming battle for my life. After watching my mother battle the same disease with massive amounts of chemotherapy I did not know there was another treatment method available today. I soon would learn the rudimentary facts of how my genes would become a part of my treatment.

Little did I know that my genetic story would come full circle as I was learning more about what was going on inside my body that I had no control over, couldn't see, and knew little about. My studies of our family genealogy lead me to an immersion into a whole new realm of genetics, and ultimately a stem cell transplant from my sister, Alice, with younger cells, even though both sisters were perfect matches. I am grateful that my parents and grandparents left me posthumous genealogical gifts. Down the road, all of my time and effort studying our family genealogy would become something far deeper and more meaningful to me. Of the three grandchildren, I was the one who took the most interest in the family genealogy: coincidentally I ended up being the one who needed our genes to survive.

I feel that I have a purposeful life that enables me to spread the word about genetics, research, and how important family is in so many ways. I never thought in my wildest dreams that I would be writing these words today about my own illness. My wish is that it provides hope and purpose for others.

The Black Eye

My first clue something was wrong inside me was the huge black eye I was sporting, as if I had lost a fight of some sort. When the doctor called me on September 21, 2012; it was surreal. She gently told me I had leukemia, AML, the same type my mother died from in 1975. And, I had to see the oncologist in the next hour. I knew this was serious. How could this be? What would my battle be like? I had felt tired the last few months and did not know I was about to begin the biggest fight of my life – for my own life. My will to live was stronger than I can put into words. Still, I had absolutely no idea what was ahead of me.

In 2014, the American Cancer Society estimated there were 18,860 new cases of AML. It is a relatively rare form of cancer, accounting for less than three percent of new cancer cases. (www.americancancer.org) The fact that AML is not as common as many other cancers made it even more difficult for me to comprehend that I was diagnosed with the same cancer as my mom.

Growing up, I never lived in fear of getting leukemia myself because my doctor told me that my mom's leukemia was probably caused by a virus. I dismissed it as very bad luck. I was also told leukemia was not genetic but now I really began to wonder. My mom was diagnosed with the same blood disease 41 years before.

Of all three daughters, I am the one that resembled my mom the most. When I was little and we took walks around the neighborhood, her legs were so long that I had to take two or three steps for every one of hers. I have her same long arms and legs, even though she was six inches taller than me. We loved to eat together, especially macaroons from our favorite bakery. We could finish off a dozen in the car on the way home. My mom never seemed to get old; she was so tall and thin that she looked very young. One day when she came home from the eye doctor with reading glasses. I cried and cried, asking her not to wear them because they made her look old. My mom was different than a lot of other moms - so youthful and glamorous. Was I going to go down the same path because I looked like her? My mom was 38 when she was diagnosed with AML; I was 55 years old. Did I get leukemia because I caught the same virus? Was it bad luck again? Or was there a genetic explanation? I certainly learned from her example how to be strong, positive, and to take care of myself.

Then all of my research into my family history gave me hope in an unexpected way. I felt my family was pulling for me, even posthumously. I gained strength from working through adversity, something that really helped my outlook. When I felt pain, I thought my mom was feeling it too in her own way. I knew she was always there for me, and it gave me hope. However, my mom lost her war, and I did not want to repeat that tragic ending, especially for my children's sake.

Coming from a background where both of my parents died of cancer, I did everything in my power throughout my life to stay healthy and to see my kids grow up, graduate from high school and college, and start their careers. I did not want history repeating itself. I ate well, worked out, lived a spiritual life, and took great care of myself so that my dreams would come true. In fact when I told people I got sick the first thing almost everyone said was "Of all people, not you. You just swam in the Senior Olympics." Ironically, I got sick three months after Tyler, my youngest, graduated from college. Was my time limit up? My wish was fulfilled, so was that all I got? I wanted more. This was not enough. I wanted to be here for the little and big things for my kids for many more years to come, for my sake and theirs too. I was not going to succumb to this illness.

Preston, Tyler, Mom, and Lauren (2012)

When I checked into the hospital in St. Louis, I gave the doctors my medical history and told them I swam competitively in the Senior Olympics winning two gold medals. By the time the third or fourth doctor came in my hospital room, the story had evolved that I ran marathons! Never could I claim that feat.

After lots of tests, I began my first round of intense chemotherapy immediately, requiring a thirty day stay in the hospital. By the time I finished, I went into remission. During this time, the doctors learned through genetic testing that I had a type of AML (FLT3) that could not stay in remission. I had to make the huge decision whether or not to have a bone marrow transplant while I was in remission - a difficult decision to make because of all the risks and side effects involved with the transplant. However, the longer you are on chemotherapy the more difficult it is to keep you in remission. You can only have a transplant if you are in remission so this was my window of opportunity. While I mulled over this decision, I felt that my mom was with me guiding me in the right direction. Thinking about what she went through year after year of chemotherapy and in and out of remission; I decided that she probably had the same type of AML as I did. I did not want to go through four years of chemotherapy to finish with a fatal result, as she did. A stem cell transplant (SCT) was not available for my mom in 1971. Even if a SCT would have been available, my mom did not have any biological siblings as possible matches, since she was adopted. Tragically, I benefitted from her horrible experience and decided to take the risk to proceed with the transplant, with my mom's heavenly guidance. I hoped for many more years with my family once I recovered. I knew the transplant would possibly be as tough as my mom's four years of chemotherapy; I just dreamed of a positive end result.

Time was of the essence. I wanted to be aggressive and move forward as quickly as possible. The doctors and the social worker talked over all of the risks with me, making me extremely anxious. Not knowing anyone personally that had experienced this, I was completely afraid of the unknown.

After my sisters went through testing to see if they would be matches for my transplant, we waited and waited for the genetic results. Luckily, both sisters were perfect allogenic matches for my transplant. Unbelievable! Since Alice's cells were almost nine years younger than Jean's, the doctors considered Alice's cells healthier for a transplant. So, Alice was going to give me the gift of life! My adorable little sister who I loved so dearly that I almost raised as my own after my mom died, was giving back to me in a way no one would ever dream possible. Alice was only eleven years old when mom died so I took over all the mom jobs for Alice after Jean left for college: doctor appointments, clothes shopping, haircuts, and playdates with friends. When I would pick Alice up at school in my Galaxie 500, she would hide on the floor in the back seat so her friends wouldn't see her because she thought my car was so ugly! Alice and I had a special bond that was now even more meaningful. Who knew Alice would give something back to me that no one else could? Once again, the Rainey genes were so powerful.

Many patients are less fortunate than I was finding a genetic match for their transplant. Family members are the best option, if possible. Patients who need to get stem cell donations from non-family members account for more than half of patients who need stem cell transplants. It is very easy for possible donors to "bank" their genetic information. A simple swab on the inside of their mouth is all that is needed to possibly be a match for a patient in need some day in the future – and possibly save a life. Donors for patients in St. Louis are often from Germany because St. Louis has a lot of German immigrants. The stem cells are flown from Germany on dry ice! If my sisters weren't matches, I might have ended up with a German donor since my grandmother and the Viets' family came to America from Germany. Luckily, I did not have to depend on the "bank" or central registry of unrelated donors, termed MUD (match unrelated donor). I really needed my family, friends, network, and prayers to help me through this. Luckily, my family genes were a key to my success. I couldn't do it alone.

While at home for about fifteen days between the chemotherapy and stem cell transplant, I had an out-of-body experience. I was lying in bed half-awake before I got up to start my daily routine of taking pills, drinking fluids, and watching funny television shows. This particular morning during the last moments of quiet time, I was praying for a successful stem cell transplant. I started to feel something lifting out of my body. Although my body didn't physically lift off my bed, I felt a heavy weight leave my body. It was as if something was flushed out of my body, then released above me. While it seemed like it lasted for several minutes, it could have been several seconds. I wasn't going to interrupt what was going on so I stayed in my bed. I was completely awake when it was over. I came out into the kitchen to tell my sister Jean about it. Neither of us knew what happened, but it was not a dream. It was real. Something that I needed to get rid of left my body that day.

On November 29, 2012, I had a stem cell transplant from my little sister, Alice. The best way I can explain how my transplant felt is like an extremely exaggerated form of morning sickness similar to that during pregnancy. It felt as if someone else was taking over my body. Through the transplant, my blood type changed to Alice's, making us even closer genetically. As I sat in the hospital for another 30 days, I had a lot of time to reflect, experiencing the roller coaster ride of the ups and downs of my treatment. My white cell blood count was taken down to almost zero, which meant my counts would have to climb back up before I could go home. During this precarious time when my immunity was so low that I could not fight off any infection, I relied on the expertise of my doctors. I was in a very good place and felt lucky to live in St. Louis where there is such a highly respected hospital that is world renowned for stem cell transplants. Horrible as it was to be sharing the same disease with my mom, I knew she was with me pulling for me. I felt her strength everyday as she was my guardian angel watching out for me. She didn't have her biological mother to be her guardian angel – she never knew who she was because her adoption was sealed. That must have been hard for my mom, but she never complained. I remember listening to cassette tapes about the power of positive thinking with my mom. I sat on the couch when she was in her hospital bed. It influences me to this day. When times get tough, I would try to remember the grace she had when dealing with the same disease.

I had a lot of free time in my hospital bed to daydream about my future during those long and grueling 60 days in the hospital. As I looked out my hospital window at the beautiful Forest Park, I dreamed a lot about all the many reasons I knew it wasn't my time to leave this planet yet. I knew I had a purpose and wanted to live to tell my story about how genetics and genealogy saved my life.

I envisioned walking my daughter down the aisle in seven months at her wedding in Forest Park, something my mother never experienced with any of her daughters. I was determined to accomplish my goal. I could not let that happen to my daughter the way it had happened to me.

I dreamed about supporting my son, Tyler as he began his career, also something my mom was never able to do for us. Tyler was always interested in the field of medicine, specifically genomics and treatments of highly unmet medical needs. Following college, he was teaching 6th grade Science and Math in the "Teach for America" program when he received word that I was sick. He came home often and immersed himself into the details of my treatment, specifically in genomics, his interest. It is ironic that seeing me experience a stem cell transplant firsthand piqued my son's innate interest in genetics. Tyler has continued with a career in the biotechnology and biopharmaceuticals industry. As difficult as it was for Tyler to watch his mom sink into the depths of my illness,

I am proud of how he helped me remain positive as we all continued to learn from the daily science experiment also known as his mother.

As part of my family legacy, I wanted to help others too and pay it forward. I participated in many research studies to make sure that other AML patients benefit from my experience by banking my blood and bone marrow. It is my hope that my participation in all of the studies will benefit many patients in the future. During my battles against AML, I was constantly reminded of the gifts my mother gave me to fight the same illness she battled so many years ago. My mom's spirit and resilience made her the most unique woman I ever would know. I hoped I could be as strong as she was. I knew that I wanted to do everything I could to pay it forward, just as my mom did for me.

As I lay in my hospital bed, I also dreamed about finishing my book. Following this experience, I had more to add when I got home. I wanted to spread the word about how common people can live uncommon lives and deal with uncommon challenges and give hope to others. I took my relationship with my grandmother as a sign. A sign of something far deeper than getting to know the small details about what kind of food my grandma ate or which songs she song. The words she wrote in her Ivy Oration speech at her Mount Holyoke graduation in 1919 were ever present in my mind: "We plant with tender care the ivy, in the hope that it will grow sturdily, and will increase in luxuriant beauty as the years pass by. The ivy, reaching ever upward, should symbolize the hopes we have in ourselves; for hope lies just where there is growth and development. In the spirit of reconstruction, in the desire for up building and uplifting, may we adapt our happy idealism to a world that is not scorning the practical application of idealism to all vital problems of the day." I believed getting to know my grandmother when I needed her most in my life was a sign that I was meant to discover her vision of hope. I never look at an ivy plant the same any more. At a time in my life when I was feeling disconnected from our family because of our tragic losses, I found my grandmother's optimism as a sign of our Rainey family strength, connecting me to my family even more. Of all three of her granddaughters, due to my active nature, I was probably the least likely to have spent the time transcribing grandma's diaries; however, serendipitously, I was the one who needed a sign from her the most.

Taking my mind into private places where I could dream about positive events in my future helped me endure pain, worry, and uncertainties. As an athlete I knew what it took to push myself farther than I thought humanly possible. This was the toughest race I ever swam or ran in my life.

I also learned from my parents and grandparents to always have compassion for other people. There are always people who are not as fortunate as we are and need help. I will donate a portion of proceeds from the sales of this book to help blood disease research and stem cell matches. In 2013, 2014, and 2015 my team for The Leukemia & Lymphoma Society "Light the Night Walk" raised a total of over $10,000. I am very proud of my team.

Post Transplant

My life is now measured by the number of days or years since my transplant on November 29, 2012, coincidentally also my daughter Lauren's birthday. So, we share a birthday! When I was in the hospital, the nurses posted a chart on the wall with the number of days since my transplant as well as my blood count levels. In order to be able to go home, my counts had to reach certain levels. Each day after the nurses drew my blood out of my port in the morning, we waited anxiously for the results in the afternoon. The nurses posted my progression on the chart. As we watched the counts slowly rise, I hoped to be able to go home to spend Christmas with both of my children.

The invisible battle continued inside me. Alice's transplanted stem cells regarded my body, the host, as foreign. Alice's transplanted cells attack my host cells, causing a complication known as graft versus host disease (GVHD). Since this is common after a transplant, I took medicine to decrease the effects of GVHD. There can be no clear winner in this battle. I needed Alice's healthy cells but couldn't have them attack me - a delicate balancing act.

After the transplant, I had to stay sequestered in my house for 100 days due to my compromised immune system. I was on more pills than I can even remember – anti- everything; anti-viral, anti-fungal, anti-bacterial, anti-GVHD, and more. I didn't feel well enough to go anywhere so it didn't matter. I needed caregivers around the clock. They organized my pills each week in one of those plastic containers with 21 compartments. Fortunately my family and friends were there for me when I needed them. It was six months before I could drive a car or go to the grocery store or church.

I continued to improve every day. Following all of the doctor's instructions, I took all of my medications, drank tons of fluids, and tried to increase my endurance by walking every day. I found many services that helped me in my recovery: yoga, physical therapy, massages, exercise, nutrition, mindfulness, keeping my mind active, work, support, a sense of humor, therapy, lots of rest, religion and spirituality, being your own advocate, a positive attitude, and a good hairdresser when you start to have unpredictable hair again! It is amazing that my undergraduate college degree in Food and Nutrition, Dietetics, which stemmed from my interest in trying to help my mom get healthier, would now be invaluable to me in my own recovery. My diet post-transplant was very sensitive and I had to learn how to adapt many recipes to deal with my delicate digestive tract. I would experiment with different recipes to see what would work and what would not. I found that cooking fruits and vegetables helped rather than eating them raw. And, I found ways to get my nutrition in new ways.

I still have inconveniences due to the GVHD but am learning how to manage them better each day. I will never have the same immune system as I had before. I am compromised when it comes to childhood vaccines such as measles, mumps, rubella, DPT, and chicken pox. Thank goodness I was not a preschool teacher or pediatric nurse! I probably would have to find a new career!

At seven months post-transplant, the day of the big wedding was about to arrive. I had been increasing the lengths of my walks each day so that I was strong enough to be a part of the wedding ceremony. I was not at all happy that I did not have much hair or look the way I would have liked to look as the mother of the bride at my only daughter's wedding but I was determined to be strong enough to walk my daughter down the aisle. I figured my daughter would be so beautiful that no one would be looking at me any way. At least I was going to be there. I fought the battle of my life to be able to be a part of her ceremony. It would be an honor and joy to share one of the biggest days of my daughter's life with her. I was determined to walk down the aisle; my short hair was my medal of honor.

June 22, 2013

"Mom I am really nervous" Lauren said just before the doors of the church at Graham Chapel at Washington University were about to open and the wedding song began to play. As I held Lauren tightly I said, "Take deep breaths." I could feel her shaking as we walked down the aisle. Lauren never likes to be the center of attention, but I knew she would be fine once she stood at the altar beside her husband.

My daughter was the most beautiful bride I had ever seen and I was the luckiest mother to be able to walk her down the aisle. It was her day and I was so grateful that I was able to be there. I was truly given a "second chance" at life through my stem cell transplant. I have been able to be a part of events that my mother never was able to.

I looked out at the church guests in the pews and was overcome by a sense of gratitude and comfort. So many people who meant so much to us were there to support our family at this momentous occasion. I never knew a wedding could mean so much. My dreams are coming true!

Still it was a bittersweet moment for me. It was particularly meaningful that my daughter was getting married on the campus where my mom graduated in 1954, yet I could not help but think about how my mom succumbed to her AML before she saw any of her daughters get married. I would have given anything to have my mom be a part of my life.

I found this poem in my grandmother's diaries about a man on his way to a wedding ceremony who is stopped by a mariner, who had returned from a long sea voyage. The mariner begins to narrate his story. What is written below is a small part of the longest major poem by the English poet Samuel Taylor Coleridge, an English author, born in 1772 in Devonshire, England. This poem "signaled a shift to modern poetry and the beginning of the British Romantic literature." (www.wikipedia.org) "Kirk" means church in the Church of Scotland as distinct from the Church of England or from the Episcopal Church in Scotland." (ibid)

"Ancient Mariner" (Verse VII)

"O sweeter than the marriage-feast,
'Tis sweeter far to me,
To walk together to the kirk
With a goodly company!-

To walk together to the kirk,
And all together pray,
While each to his great Father bends,
Old men, and babes, and loving friends
And youths and maidens gay!

Farewell, farewell! But this I tell
To thee, thou Wedding-Guest!
He prayeth well, who loveth well
Both man and bird and beast."

Samuel Taylor Coleridge

Heroes

The following year, I took my son to the World War I Museum in Kansas City, Missouri. The two of us shared a unique experience. As we entered the museum we walked over the glass bridge atop a field of 9,000 poppies, each one representing 1,000 deaths in World War I. (Poppies symbolize World War I because they figure in the poem, *In Flanders Field*, by John McCrae.) As we experienced this beautiful but sad sight, we knew this was part of our heritage.

In the museum, we saw an authentic WWI ambulance that never made it across the pond to serve. Next to it we saw a glass case containing a stretcher, and a portable operating table. Looking at these artifacts brought tears to my eyes as they made the experiences of war become real to me. Seeing pictures and reading letters is different from seeing the actual equipment the soldiers used - the experience came alive for me. I thought of how many injured soldiers placed their faith in my grandfather as he carried them on stretchers, loaded them into his ambulance, as he rushed them to a field station for first aid or surgery. Many soldiers trusted my grandfather to drive them safely to a hospital to get them the help they needed to survive. I cannot imagine the horrors Howard saw on the stretchers – the smell of blood, screams of pain, and sense of urgency. I think the war stayed in my grandfather's mind the rest of his life. My grandfather, Howard, made a difference in the war. We are proud of him for his service and thank him for sharing his life with us. For all of my grandfather's shortcomings, he was the right man to be an ambulance driver. Athletic and calm, he was a hero.

Despite all of Marian's hardships, if she were alive today and I were able to ask her how she thought her life turned out, I am sure she would say she was blessed with a wonderful life and that all her dreams came true. My family was full of heroes.

Nevertheless, of all Marian's dreams that she wrote about in her diaries, there is one dream that I know did not come true: to write a book. Back in 1915, Marian took a walk on the mountain in E. Granby with her Grandfather Clark. She wrote so beautifully: "In the late afternoon, I went up onto the mountain with Grandpa after the cows. We picked black eyed Susan's and wild roses while we were up there. The view was wonderful. Grandpa is the finest old man. I would like to put him in a book. There are so many fine people I should like to put in a book, but I know I never can. No! That sounds discouraged. I would rather say that I fear that I never can. And, yet perhaps – how I should love to write, just write down things as I see them. But I am only seventeen now."

So, here it is. Over one hundred years later, I am fulfilling Marian's last dream. I wrote this book as my gift to Marian for all that she gave to me and for everyone whose life she touched. The grandmother I never knew well helped me dig deep to fight my illness and to face my fears. Marian was my hero. She helped give me hope. Here is my gift to all of you: never lose hope no matter how difficult life seems.

N.B. (Nota Bene): At one of my recent appointments, my doctor told me that all my blood work looked great. Each year post-transplant marks a positive milestone, and I look forward to many more. It is so nice to know, I am one of the lucky ones. I have lost several friends in the last three years who did not experience successful transplants and passed away before it was their time. My heart aches for their families.

I know this is going to sound strange but if I got leukemia at the same age as my mom at 38 instead of 55, I probably wouldn't be here today. Seventeen years ago, they did not have the procedures they do now and 17 years from now, these procedures will no doubt look primitive. My doctor and I chatted for a while about all of the advances every year in research. She has been at BJC for over a decade and cannot believe the amazing changes every year thanks to research. She was telling me unbelievable stories – controlling other types of leukemia (not AML) with a daily pill in the future, like taking insulin for diabetes.

I feel lucky that I got the AML now instead of in 1995 because so many advances have been made. I also feel very lucky that I live in St. Louis and have such a great hospital and great doctors so close to my home. I am so grateful every day!

When I take a walk around my neighborhood at night and look up into the sky and see the beautiful stars, moon, and tree shadows, it brings me such peace and joy that I am able to experience the beauty of nature. I was in a wheelchair periodically the first three weeks I was home from the hospital and walked with a cane for support. I remember when I took my first walk to the mailbox and out to get the newspaper; it was quite an accomplishment. Looking back, I have come so far and I only hope to progress further and become stronger each day. I am truly blessed that I am here to laugh until I cry with my family and friends. As I experience each milestone with my children it is very bittersweet for me because I never was able to experience many of those milestones with my own mom. Until I realized what she missed, and what I could have missed, I did not know how sorrowful I was for my mom's losses. Any child that has lost a parent at a young age knows the empty moments that we all have when we wish the one we miss so much is not there to be with us. I cannot undo what was done, I can only move forward and "take heart with the new day and begin again" as so aptly written in the poem below. My wounds need to be yesterday's wounds.

Thanks to everyone for your unbelievable help every step of the way during my journey. Keep the hope alive that research is going to be able to help so many more people in ways we can't even imagine. Our family is our gift; our genes can give us life and hope.

The following poem written by Sarah Chauncey Woolsey, under the pen name of Susan Coolidge, was one of hope for the future every day. The author worked as a nurse during the American Civil War, and then began to write. She never married and resided in Newport, Rhode Island until her death in 1905.

This is my favorite poem of all the poems that my grandparents saved because it speaks about hope for new beginnings every day for everyone.

"New Every Morning"

Every day is a fresh beginning.
Every morn is the world made new;
You who are weary of sorrow and sinning,
Here is a beautiful hope for you, –
A hope for me and a hope for you.

All the past things are past and over,
The tasks are done and the tears are shed;
Yesterday's errors let yesterday cover;
Yesterday's wounds, which smarted and bled,
Are healed with the healing which night has shed.

Yesterday is a part of forever,
Bound up in a sheath, which God holds tight,
With glad days, and sad days, and bad days, which never
Shall visit us more with their bloom and their blight,
Their fullness of sunshine or sorrowful night.

Let them go since we cannot re-live them,
Cannot undo or cannot atone;
God in his mercy receive, forgive them!
Only the new days are our own;
To-day is ours, and to-day alone.

Here are the skies all burnished brightly,
Here is the spent earth all re-born:
Here are the tired limbs springing lightly
To face the sun and share with the morn
In the chrism of dew and the cool of the dawn.

Every day is a fresh beginning;
Listen, my soul, to the glad refrain,
And, spite of old sorrows and older sinning,
And puzzles forecasted and possibly pain,
Take heart with the day, and begin again.

By Sarah Chauncey Woolsey
(Coolidge)

The End

CAST OF CHARACTERS

The cast of characters includes her family, many friends at Central High School (C.H.S.), Mount Holyoke College friends, Hudson, New York family, and close family friends. Their nicknames are in quotations.

Chapter One:

Marian's Family:
- Mother, Gertrude Clark Viets
- Father, Samuel D. Viets
- Uncle Daniel Clark "Umpa" and wife Theo
- Uncle Charles Clark and his wife Fern
- Uncle James Viets, and his daughter, Buela
- Grandma Myra Smith Clark and Grandpa Benjamin (B.P.) Clark
- Aunt Mame

Marians Friends:
- Richard "Dick" (B.) Burdett, CHS Class President
- James "Jimmy" Doherty
- Florence Fisk
- Helen Francis
- Margaret Gantt
- Margaret Kemater (engaged to Roger Laurence), and sister, Elizabeth
- Marjorie "Joe" Lane
- Malcolm Law
- Marjorie "Spot" Lyman
- Edna "Max" Maxfield
- Dorothy "Dot" Pease
- Beatrice Putney
- Jack Sawhill, and sister, Marjorie
- Priscilla "Pris" Spaulding
- Louise "Squeeze" Talbot (engaged to Larrie)
- Elizabeth "Bid" Trask
- Ruth "Mit" Woodin (engaged to Jimmy) and Dorothy "Dot" Woodin (engaged to Paul)
- Barbara White

Family Friends:
- The Bemis Family - Marian Bemis married Frank Schlessinger, 10.24.1914
- The Coe Family
- The Ellis Family — Carlos, Margaret, Sherman, Elizabeth (deceased)
- The Kemater Family
- Ruth Kenyon, Gertrude's friend
- The McKinnion Family, Marian shared birthday celebrations with their son, Donald

Chapter Two:

Howard Eugene Rainey's Family:
    Father, S. Mitchell Rainey
    Mother, Ida Miles Rainey
    Uncle Eugene Miles
    Uncle Howard Miles
    Aunt Mary "Maude" Rainey
    Grandfather, S. Rossman Rainey
    Grandmother, Helen Cornelia Macy Rainey

Pawling Preparatory School friends"
    Phil Carter
    Herbert Grabau
    Jack Lummis

Chapter Three:

Mount Holyoke College:

Doris Campbell	Windsor, Connecticut
Emma "Pop" Frazier	East Lynn, Massachusetts
Hilda "Hild" Jones	Newtonville, Massachusetts
Dorothy "Dot" Hall	Erie, Pennsylvania
Freda Harris	Skowhegan, Maine
Elizabeth "Canary" McNarey	Freeport, Illinois
Florence "Shep" Sheppard	Passaic, New Jersey
George Sheppard, Florence's brother	Passaic, New Jersey

Chapter Six:

"Old Reliables", boarders at Mrs. Lyons:
    Sonny, Mount Holyoke class of 1918, teacher at Hudson High School
    Miss Anderson, "Grandma"
    Ruth S.
    Katherine Ferris, teacher at Hudson High School, Wellesley graduate
    Margaret Talmage, teacher at Hudson High School, Wellesley graduate

Miss Dowsland, teacher at Hudson High School
Miss MacMaster, principal of a grammar school
Mrs. Lyons, boarding house landlord
Mrs. Sheldon, boarding house cook
Mr. Williams, (C.S.W.) Hudson High School superintendent
Mr. Knapp, Hudson High School principal

BIBLIOGRAPHY

Abbott, Lyman. *The Outlook*. 1893.
American Field Service Bulletin.
American Expeditionary Forces. *The Stars and the Stripes*. 2.8.1918 to 6.13.1919. Newspaper.
Amherst College. *Jeff Newspaper*. n.d.
Amherst College *Olio Yearbook*. 1945.
Amherst Student. 7 June 1958.
Angell, Sir Ralph Norman. *The Great Illusion*. 1909. Pamphlet.
Antin, Mary. *The Promised Land*. Boston and New York: The Riverside Press, 1911.
Archer, E. Margaret Du P. *Sorrow*. Westminister Gazette. n.d. Poem.
Ashford, Daisy. *The Young Visiters*. 1919. Novella.
Atlantic Monthly Magazine.

Barrie, J. M. *The New Word*. Play. 1915.
Barrymore, John. *Raffles: The Amatures Cracksman. The Honor of his House. The Man From Home* By Booth Tarkington and Harry Leon Wilson. Director Cecil B. DeMille. Performance Charles Richman. Jesse L. Lasky, Feature Play Company, Inc. Paramount Pictures Corporation, 1914.
Ben Blair. Director: William Desmond Taylor. Performance: Dustin Farnum. 1916.
Bingham, Elizabeth F. *The Christmas Ship*. 1914.
Breltigam, Gerald B. *In the Trenches*. Kansas City Star. n.d.
Brooke, Rupert. 1914 and Other Poems. Complete Press, West Norwood, London, England. 1915. *The Soldier; The Dead*. Poems.
Burroughs, John. *City Life versus Literature. Waiting*. 1862.
Byron, Alfred. *I Didn't Raise My Son to be a Soldier*. 1915.

Campbell, Joseph. *The Old Woman*. n.d. Poem.
Carroll, Harry. *Smother Me With Kisses*. New York. 1914.
Clarke, Dr. Edward. *Sex in Education, or, A fair chance for the girls*. 1873.
Coleridge, Samuel Taylor. *Ancient Mariner*. 1798. Poem.
Collins, Gail. *400 Years of Dolls, Drudges, Helpmates, and Heroines*. William Morrow, imprint of Harper Collins, 2003. Excerpts from pp.81, 128, 152, 153, 162, 182 (550 words) from AMERICA'S WOMEN by GAIL COLLINS. Copyright © 2003 BY GAIL COLLINS. Reprinted by permission of Harper Collins Publishers.
Columbian Republican. Columbia County, New York. Newspaper.
Conde, Bertha. *Glimpses into the Student Movement of Other Lands*. n.d.
Coolidge, Susan. *A Few More Verses. New Every Morning*. Poem. Boston: Little, Brown and Company, 1907.
Curtis, George William. *Prue and I*. Harper and Brother Publishing. 1899.

Daily Star. Hudson, New York. Newspaper.
Davis, Fannie Sterns. *The Hermit on the Dunes. Myself and I*. New York: Macmillan Company. 1918.
Dawson, Coningsby. *The Glory of the Trenches*. 1917
Department of Education National Center for Educational Statistics. n.d.
Dickens, Charles. *Little Dorrit*. 1855-1857.
The Pickwick Papers. New York: Charles Scribners Sons. 1901.
Dobson, Austin. *Daisy's Valentine*. The Graphic. 1874. Poem.
Dorman, Marjorie. Smith Alumnae Quarterly. March, 1915.

Edmonds, Anne Carey. *A Memory Book Mount Holyoke College 1837-1987*. Mount Holyoke College. 1988.
Eliot, George. *Felix Holt, The Radical*. Boston: De Wolfe, Fiske, & Company. 1868.

Farmer, Fannie Merrittt. *The Boston Cooking-School Cook Book*. Boston: Little, Brown & Company. 1896.
Fawcett, John. *Blest Be the Tie that Binds*. 1782. Poem.
Field, Katie. *Sphere*. n.d. Poem.
Foley, James W. *The Way of a Boy*. Youths Companion. 1917. Poem.

Fone, Byrne. *Historic Hudson An Architectural Portrait*. Delmar, New York: Black Dome Press. 2005.
Frost, Jack. *I Didn't Raise my Ford to be a Jitney*. 1915. Poem.
Frost, Robert. *North of Boston*. New York: Henry Holt & Co. 1915.

Garison, Theodosia. *Youth*. Everybody's Magazine. 1910.
Goodenough, Arthur. *The World Gone By*. 1914. Springfield Republican Newspaper. Poem.
Gorney, Jay. *Brother Can you Spare a Dime?* 1930.
Greely, Horace. *The Book of World Classics Restricted to Prose Volume X America II*. 1909.

Harper's Bazaar Magazine.
Harrison, Henry Sydnor. *Queed*. Boston and New York: The Riverside Press Cambridge. 1911.
Hayden, Alma Pendexter. *The Little Refugee*. *Under the Harvest Moon*. Poems.Rochester, New York.n.d.
Hearts of the World. Director: D.W. Griffith. Performance: Lillian Gish. 1918.
Hemingway, Enerst. *Farewell to Arms*. 1929.
History of the American Army Ambulance Service. n.d.
Holland, Josiah Gilbert. *Bittersweet*. New York: C. Scribner's Sons. 1858. Poem: *Persons*.
Holmes, Oliver Wendell. *The Autocrat of the Breakfast-Table*. poem:*The Chambered Nautilus*. Boston: James R. Osgood and
    Company, 1873.
How Could You Jean? Director: William Desmond Taylor. Performance: Mary Pickford. 1918. Silent Film.
Howells, William Dean. *The Mouse Trap and other Farces*. 1889.*The Register*. 1911.Performance.
Hudson Daily Star Newspaper. Hudson, New York, n.d.
Hudson High School Blue and Gold Yearbook. 1961

Ibsen, Henrik. *A Doll's House*. 1879.
Irving, Minna. *I Wish I Were Rich*. Frank Leslie's Illustrated Newspaper 1914.

J. Wrigley, Publisher of Songs, Ballads and Toy Books. *I Want to be A Soldier*. New York. n.d.
Jordan, Adelaide S. *Bridal Chimes*. 1912. Poem.

Kilmer, Alfred Joyce. *Literature in the Making by some of its Maker*. *Main Street and Other Poems*. New York. 1917. *In Memory
    of Rupert Brooke*. n.d.; *Our Honored Dead*.*The Peacemaker*. Poetry Magazine. 1918. *Trees and Other poems*. 1914.
Kipling, Rudyard. *Gunga Din*. 1892. Poem.
Kringle, George. *With the Child*. Christian Advocate. 1914. Poem.

Lady Windemere's Fan. By Oscar Wilde. St. James Theatre, London. 1892.
Lagerlof, Selma. *The Christmas Rose*. New York, NY: Holiday House Inc. 1900.
Leukemia Lymphoma Society (LLS), "Light the Night Walk"
Lewis, Judd Mortimer. *The Baby Who Romped with Dad*. New York: Robert J. Shores, 1917. Poem.
Library of Congress American Memory.
LLamadra Yearbook. Mount Holyoke. 1919.
Longfellow, Henry Wadsworth. *The Complete Personal Works of Henry Wadsworth Longfellow*. *The Footsteps of Angels*. London:
    John Dicks.1868. Poem.
Lowell, James Russell. *The Writings of James Russell Lowell*. *Under the Old Elm Tree*.Volume 10. 1890. Poem.
Lyon, Mary. Mount Holyoke College. Quotation. 1837

MacCathmhaoil, Seosamh (Joseph Campbell). *The Old Woman*. n.d.
Masefield, John. *The Story of a Round-House and Other Poems*. New York: The MacMillan Company, 1915.;
    Truth. 1915. Poem; *The Word*. 1915. Poem.
Masters, Edgar Lee. *Spoon River Anthology*.*Silence*. St. Louis: Reedy's Mirror. 1915.
Mason, A. E. W. *Green Stockings*. 1916. Performance.
McRae, John. *In Flanders Fields*. 1915. Poem.
Mickey. Director: F. Richard Jones. Performance: Mabel Normand. 1917.
Milton, John. *Il Penseroso*. Boston and Chicago: Allyn and Bacon, 1901. Poem.
Morley, Christopher. *The Man Worth Knowing*. Our Dumb Animals. June 1914 Volume 49. Poem.

Mount Holyoke College. *Into the World of Mount Holyoke.* 1921.
Mount Holyoke Class Book of 1919. The Ninth Wave.
Mount Holyoke College. *Letters from the Class of 1919.* 1937
Musings, Monday. *Comme Ci Comme Ca in Old Artois.* n.d. Poem.

Noyes, Alfred. *On the Western Front. The New Morning Poems.* New York: Frederick Stokes, 1918. poem.

Oppenheim, James. *Bread and Roses.* The American Magazine. 1911. Poem.
Owen, Wilfred. *Dulce et Decorum est. Poems by Wilfred Owen. Preface* to *Poems by Wilfred Owen.* 1915.

Parry, Martin L. *A Way of Life The Story of John Burroughs School 1923-1973.*
Perkins, Frank H. *Handbook of Old Burial Hill Plymouth, Massachusetts.* Plymouth, MASS: A. S. Burbank, 1902.
Pidgin, Charles Felton. *Quincy Adams Sawyer and Mason's Corner Folks A Picture of New England Home Life.* Boston: C.M. Clark Publishing Company, 1904.
Pierpont, John. *The Old Buying-Ground.* Perkins, Frank H. *Handbook of Old Burial Hill Plymouth, MASS*: A.S. Durbank, 1902. Poem.

Raffles the Amateur Cracksman. 1917. Performance.
Railroad Telegrapher. *Growing Old.* Poem.
Ready Money. Director: Oscar Apfel. 1914. Comedy/Drama.
Republican, Springfield. 13 October 1918. Newspaper.
Rice, Henry Grantland. *The Empty Stocking.* 1914. Poem.
Rickard, Mrs. Victor and James. *The Story of the Munsters.* London New York Toronto: Hodder and Stoughton, 1915.
Riley, James Whitcomb. *Child-Rhymes. A Life Lesson: There Little Girl Don't Cry.* 1890. Poem.
Rittenberg, Sidney S. *Albert of Belgium.* Richmond Times Dispatch. n.d. Poem.
Robbins, L.H. *Young Imagination.* Youth's Companion. n.d. Poem.
Ryley, Madeleine Lucette. *An American Citizen: An Original Comedy in Four Acts.* New York: Samuel French, 1895. Performance.

Schneiderman, Rose. *Rose Schneiderman's April 2, 1911 Speech.* Jewish Women's Association.
Shelley, Percy Bysshe. *The Indian Serenade.* Poem. 1822.
Seeger, Alan. *I Have a Rendezvous with Death.* Poem. 1910.
Shepley, Carol Ferring. *St. Louis An Illustrated Timeline.* St. Louis, MO: Reedy Press. 2014.
Springman, Mary Jane. *East Granby the evolution of a Connecticut town.* Canaan: Phoenix Publishing, 1983.
Statistics, Department of Education National Center for Education. "High School and College Graduates." 1899-2010.
Stevenson, Robert Louis. *The Works Of Robert Louis Stevenson Volume Fourteen. To Will H. Low.* London: Chatto and Windus. n.d.
Streeter, Edward. *Dere Mabel.* Frederick A. Stokes. 1918.

Taft, William Howard. Service with Fighting Men: An account of the Work of the American YMCA in WWI. Association Press. 1922.
Tarkington, Booth. *Penrod.* Bloomington: Indiana University Press, 1915. *The Turmoil.* Harper. 1915.
Taylor, Bishop Jeremy. *Marriage.* 1633. Quote in letter. *The Imperfect Grace of our Friendship.* 1657.
Teasdale, Sara. *Love Songs. Sorrow.* New York: MacMilan Co. 1917. *The Answering Voice: One Hundred Love Lyrics by Women.* Boston: Houghton, 1917.
Telegrapher, Railroad. *Growing.* July 1910. Poem.
The Blue Bird. Director: Maurice Tourneur. Performance: Tula Belle. 1918. black and white, six reels.
The Cheat. Director: Cecil B. DeMille. Producer: Cecil B. DeMille. 1915. Performance: Fannie Ward. 1915.
The Chocolate Soldier. By George Bernard Shaw. Avenue Theatre, New York. 21 April 1894. Operetta: Arms and Man.
The Dawn of a Tomorrow. Director: James Kirkwood. Performance: Mary Pickford. Producer: Daniel Frohman. Paramount Pictures, 1915.
The Guest of Honor. By Arthur William Hodge. n.d.
The Judge. *The Christmas Prayer.* 1912.

Thoreau, Henry David. *The Wisdom of Thoreau*. Boston: Ticknor & Fields, 1854. *Thoreau as Spritual Guide*. Boston: Skinner House Books, n.d.
Tompkins, Vincent. *American Decades: 1910-1919*. Detroit, Michigan: Gale Research, 1996.
Tosti, Francesco Paolo. Song: *Goodbye*. 1881

United States Draft Record. June 5, 1917.
US Department of State Office of the Historian. n.d.

Van Dyke, Henry. Poems: *America for Me*. 1909; *Ancestral Dwellings*.1909; *Who Follow The Flag* 1918; *Spirit of The Everlasting Boy*. 1910; *America's Welcome Home from Poems of American Patriotism*..n.d.; *The Way*. n.d;. *Four Things*; *Love and Light*. n.d.;. *Lover's Envy*. n.d.;. *Recontre*. n.d. *Preface The Story of the Other Wise Man*. New York: Harper and Brothers, 1895
Vermude. *To My Wife*. Christian Register. Volume 97. 9.19.1918. *Little You'd Care What I Laid*. Poem.
Viets, Francis Hubbard. *Genealogy of the Viets Family*. Hartford: Hartford Press: The Case, Lockwood & Brainard Company, 1902.
Viets, Samuel D. *Newgate Of Connecticut and other Antiquities of America*. Meriden: The Meriden Gravure Co., 1895.

Warner, Frances Lester and Elizabeth Crane Porter, Editors. *A Mount Holyoke Book of Prose and Verse*. Cambridge: Riverside Press, 1912.
Watson, Jean H. *Out of Touch*. Lutheran Women's Work International Good Templar. 1 January 1907. Poem.
Wattles, William. *Little Town of Amherst*. 1915. Poem.
Wells, Amos Russell. *Cape Cod*. Christian Endeavor. 1921. Poem.
Wells, H. G. *Research Magnificent*. Classic Publishing. 1915.; *Mr. Britling Sees it Through*. Read Books Ltd. 1916.
Westminster Gazette. London, England
Wharton, Edith. *The Marne A Tale of the War*. Macmillan. 1918.
Williams, William Carlos. *Sicilian Emigrant Song*. 1913. Poem
Willmott, H. P. *World War I*. New York: Dorling Kidersley Limited, 2003.
"Reproduced from *World War I* by H.P. Willmott with permission from DK, a division of Penguin Random House LLC. Copyright © 2003 Dorling Kindersley Limited"
Wilson, V.B. *Poems of American Patriotism. Ticonderoga Carillion*. 1882. Poem
Wilson, Woodrow; *America's Purpose in the War;* April 2, 1917
Woolsey, Sarah Chauncey see also Susan Coolidge

wikipedia.org/wiki/Great_Depression_in_the_United_States. n.d.
www.americancancer.org. n.d.
www.amherst.edu
www.answers.com. n.d.
www.answers.com/topics/hearts-of-the-world. n.d.
www.amherst.edu. n.d.
www.Armenian-genocide.org. n.d.
www.commandposts.com. n.d.
www.dar.org
www.economichistory.net
www.encyclopedia.com. n.d.
www.english.emory.edu. n.d.
www.famouspoetsandpoems.com. n.d.
www.fort-ticonderoga.org/history. n.d.
www.genome.wustl.edu
www.google.com. n.d.
www.great-depression-facts.com. n.d
www.harpers.org. n.d.
www.historichudson.org. n.d.
www.history.amedd.army.mil. n.d.
www.history.com. n.d.